Inventing
Motherhood

By the Same Author

A–Z of Babies
A Child is Born (with Ronald Sweering)
The Intelligent Person's Guide to Modern Medicine
Cicely: The Story of a Doctor
Mothers: Their Power and Influence
The Morbid Streak
Why Women Fail

Ann Dally

Inventing Motherhood

The Consequences of an Ideal

SCHOCKEN BOOKS • NEW YORK

First American edition published by Schocken Books 1983
10 9 8 7 6 5 4 3 2   83 84 85 86
Published by agreement with Burnett Books Ltd., London
Copyright © 1982 by Ann Dally

Manufactured in the United States of America
ISBN 0–8052–3830–1

for my sons
Simon, Mark, John and Adam

Table of Contents

7

Preface and Acknowledgments

I have written this book because for many years I have been conscious of an impending crisis of motherhood in the western world, and this crisis is now upon us. It has developed because of profound changes in society and the effects of these changes on mothers and on women contemplating motherhood have been neither understood nor appreciated. During the twentieth century, for the first time in history, the majority of women have had, increasingly, to bring up their children virtually alone. Their husbands are away at work all day and hardly see the children except at weekends. They have no domestic help. There is little or no community life or life on the street. They are likely to have little or no everyday contact with their own families. Coming from small families themselves they have probably had little previous contact with young children or experience in caring for them. If they are lucky they have homes of their own fitted with modern labour-saving machines, but very likely there is nowhere for the children to explore or play safely or build up a social life of their own. The outside world is no longer safe for children on their own and it no longer provides support for their mothers. Mothers have no respite in the early years except, for some, the presence of a husband at night and during weekends (not always helpful), and perhaps a play group for a few hours a week.

What is particularly fascinating is the way in which society in general and mothers in particular have reacted to these changes. In line with what so-called 'experts' have told them they have accepted these changes as though they were not changes at all but rather as though they were part of the discovery that children need the continuous and exclusive presence of their mothers and that anything which separates mother and child is destructive and psychologically damaging to the child. This has been a most convenient philosophy in a world which is dangerous and unsuitable for children on their own and in which the cheapest form of social existence is to make no provision for them – spend no money on the everyday lives of mothers and children. By insisting that the only psychological essential is to keep mother and child together, the individual needs of both can be conveniently ignored.

No one, so far as I know, has yet chronicled the changes that brought this about. Few books even look at them historically. In our century child care has been regarded not as a social process with a historical perspective but as a scientific or pseudoscientific subject based on the idea that we are discovering what is best for the child. Yet it is fascinating to see how the theories of child care that have developed over the last fifty years match the social situation and so justify and idealize it. And women have accepted it unprotestingly if not always willingly. When large numbers of mothers have never before the mid-twentieth century been shut up alone with their small children for most of their working hours, suddenly it appeared that this was the ideal, the norm, essential for the healthy psychological development of the child and a demonstration of feminine normality in the mother. As far as I know no one has pointed out that this segregation of mothers and children is a new phenomenon, that there is no scientific evidence to justify it on psychological grounds and that if one wanted to look for evidence one might even come up with the suspicion that the era of unbroken and exclusive maternal care has produced the most neurotic, disjointed, alienated and drug-addicted generation ever known.

Theories justifying the isolation of mothers and children have been so powerful in recent years that they have driven women to submit and have drawn on aspects of women's minds and feelings that make them wish to submit. They have assisted professionals to be powerful and governments to leave things be and not invest money in the next generation. Recently two women consulted me because they were unable to live in peace with their pre-school children and as a result felt depressed, inadequate and hopeless. They were typical of hundreds whom I have seen over the years. One feature in their stories struck me as particularly relevant. Both were being criticized by their own mothers or mothers-in-law who insisted, 'If you can't look after your own children, you shouldn't have had them.' Although these comments increased the despair of both young mothers, further questioning revealed that these critical older women had raised their own families with considerable assistance from others. One had always had a nanny and the other had been much helped by neighbours in a working class street with her own mother just round the corner. The differences in circumstances were immeasurable, yet both generations of mothers had so accepted the current theories of what a mother ought to do that none of them spotted the discrepancies.

The modern feminist movement has shown us clearly how the attitudes of the oppressor enter the minds of the oppressed so that women become the means of their own oppression. Nowhere is this seen more clearly than in mothers of the twentieth century.

This book has been written largely from ideas developed over thirty years of bringing up my own six children and working professionally with women and their children. Thousands of women have told me of their experiences in bringing up children and many more men, women and children have told me of their experiences with their own mothers. During these years of professional and personal life I have seen enormous changes in women and their children and I have become aware of other changes that are still beneath the surface. There are problems both obvious and as yet largely unrecognized which will surely erupt in the near future. The book attempts to outline the most urgent problems and to suggest what might be done to avert them and to improve the situation. I am particularly interested in the ways in which the women's movement could incorporate these ideas and through this not only achieve a better deal for women and children than exists at present but also touch the hearts and interests of many more women and men than it has so far.

As background reading to this book I have read or reread much social and feminist history. This has been enjoyable. Before studying medicine and psychiatry I took a degree in Modern History. It has given me much pleasure to return to this interest of my earlier life and to discover much of what has been done and published since I was an undergraduate, in particular the work by historians of the 'new social history' who are unearthing the ways in which ordinary people lived in the past and what they thought and felt. Their books have been of great assistance to me in filling in the background to my own ideas and experience. I have also read with great interest much modern feminist literature. (I do, however, deplore the habit of many feminist writers of writing books without indices. Some do

11

not even provide a table of contents or give titles to their chapters. Inevitably this reduces the impact of their message.)

I have written this book very much as it has come to me. I am aware that it could have been written in a dozen different ways. It could, for instance, have been a social history of motherhood, including a social history of childbirth. An appraisal of attitudes to motherhood in general and childbirth in particular is mucĥ needed but would be an enormous extension of this book. It is, however, written with strong consciousness of the way in which up to the mid-eighteenth century medicine took little interest in women and children and childbirth, maladies of pregnancy and children's illnesses were held to be the responsibility of 'old wives'. Or it could have been a literary journey through the ages – taking in Sarah Gamp, Mrs. Grundy, the great novelists of the nineteenth century down to Martha Quest and Margaret Drabble. But fascinating as it would be to make that journey, I have not made it here. I have tended to concentrate on the psychological more than on the social aspects of modern mothering, since herein, I believe, lies my most original contribution. Much has been written elsewhere about the social aspects, mostly based on 'normal' mothers. It has become customary to discuss in general terms what is known as 'the ordinary devoted mother and her child' and to separate the 'abnormal' mothers into different categories and regard them as 'problems'. One of the contentions of this book is that conditions in western society today make it extremely difficult to be a 'good mother' and the way our society is organized is creating enormous problems for women and their children. Rutter has pointed out[1] that the concept of 'maternal deprivation' has been useful to our understanding of some of the serious consequences of bad care in early life. But the different kinds of 'bad' care need to be delineated and their effects assessed, together with the reasons why children are so different in the way they respond.

The book is divided into two parts. Part One is an attempt to give some historical explanation for the crisis that has arisen though it makes no attempt to be a comprehensive history of motherhood. Rather I have sifted through social history to find some reasonable explanation for our current fashions in motherhood. I have concentrated on those social historians and feminist writers whose work I came across and whom I have found most illuminating, and on those child care 'experts' and psychologists whom I believe to be or to have been the most influential. The work of Elizabeth Badinter, whose book *The Myth of Motherhood* was published as this work was going to press, is unfortunately not included. Part Two looks at the actual consequences of the idealization of motherhood, consequences which have led to an unprecedented crisis for women and their children.

I have had certain problems of terminology. Words and phrases such as 'traditional', 'modern', 'western society', 'hybrid family' and 'good mothering' require careful definition if they are to have any meaning. They are all defined somewhere in the book but one cannot keep repeating the definitions. I have also had problems over words denoting sexual differentiation. The word 'mother' is essentially female but those who do the mothering are sometimes male. 'Motherliness' is a quality, or group of qualities, that is by no means confined to the female sex and often not found in mothers. Another problem has been whether and when to use 'he' or 'she' when I am referring to someone of either sex. This has been particularly difficult in writing about children. 'He or she' is clumsy. 'It' is too impersonal. In desperation I acquired the pamphlet *Non-Sexist Code of Practice for Book Publishing*, prepared by the Women in the Publishing Industry Group, but I found that this avoids the issue by failing even to mention it. On the whole therefore, I have used 'she' when referring to a mother and 'he' when referring to her child. This is purely for the sake of clarity.

I have dedicated the book to my sons, partly because my last book was dedicated to my daughters (and mothers like to be fair to all their children) and partly because I believe that much of what this book proposes will only come about when men take an interest in the subject and achieve some understanding of it.

The book has been written in my spare time from practising as a psychiatrist. Therefore I should like to thank first and foremost my family for having tolerated my many hours of seclusion and withdrawal and my failure to do those things which would otherwise have been done. I thank my children for giving me so much practical experience of motherhood and of the difficulties of working while bringing up a family. I thank my husband for so patiently tolerating my long hours of wrting, often at night or during unsociable hours (hours when I would otherwise have been sociable), for the many meals and the countless cups of coffee that he has provided during these months, and even more for his endless good temper and encouragement.

I thank John and Janet Marqusee who first commissioned the book and obtained for me a number of books that I could not otherwise have read. I thank Farrell Burnett for publishing and editing it, and Hilary Arnold for her friendly help, particularly in arranging for me to meet a number of active feminists who came to my house on several occasions to discuss their feelings about motherhood and the problems they encountered. I thank my daughter Emma for her interest and her practical help in obtaining books and other literature in both London and New York. I thank my secretary Anne Lingham who, despite managing a busy psychiatric practice, has typed and retyped most of the manuscript and made a number of helpful criticisms: also Maria Ellis, who did some of the typing and Sally Paine, who provided a quotation.

Lastly I should like to thank my patients, who have taught me so much and without whom I would never have learned enough to write this book.

I should like to acknowledge my debt to the following for their kind permission to quote extracts from books mentioned:

Jonathan Cape Ltd. and Alfred A. Knopf, Inc.: *Centuries of Childhood* by Philippe Ariès, translated by Robert Baldick. Copyright © 1960, 1962.

George Weidenfeld & Nicolson Ltd.: *Family, Sex and Marriage in England 1500–1800* by Lawrence Stone. Copyright © 1977.

Souvenir Press and Psychohistory Press: *The History of Childhood,* edited by Lloyd de Mause. Copyright © 1974.

Jonathan Cape Ltd. and Random House, Inc.: *The Second Sex* by Simone de Beauvoir, translated H. M. Parshley. Copyright © 1949, 1952.

Routledge & Kegan Paul, Ltd. and Humanities Press, Inc.: *Women's Two Roles* by Alva Myrdal and Viola Klein. Copyright © 1968.

Laurence Pollinger Ltd. and W. W. Norton & Co., Inc.: *The Feminine Mystique* by Betty Friedan. Copyright © 1963.

Granada Publishing Ltd: *Controversial Issues in Child Development* by P. Pilling and M. K. Pringle. Copyright © 1978.

Introduction

The word 'mother' is one of the oldest in the language. But the word 'motherhood' is relatively new. The *Oxford English Dictionary* contains no reference to it earlier than 1597, and then seems to refer merely to the fact of being a mother. Only in the Victorian era did the word emerge as a concept rather than a mere statement of fact. Phrases emerged such as 'the warm sun of motherhood' (1869) and 'true motherhood' (1875). There have always been mothers but motherhood was invented. Each subsequent age and society has defined it in its own terms and imposed its own restrictions and expectations on mothers. Thus motherhood has not always seemed or been the same.

The idea of motherhood grew with idealization. And, during the Victorian era, the idealization of the mother strengthened the idealization of the wife and woman. In our own times there has been less idealization of women and wives but idealization of the mother has reached unprecedented proportions. The result is that we now face a crisis of motherhood.

Many crises face the western world. Some, such as those of energy, inflation and unemployment, having come suddenly, if predictably, are now recognized and widely discussed. Others are creeping up on us just as certainly but are not yet fully recognized. Of these, one of the most important is the crisis of motherhood. This concerns directly most women and all children and thus, indirectly, everyone. We ignore it at our peril. It is already with us, but its full importance and implications are as yet largely unrecognized.

Motherhood has become full of uncertainty and paradox, fraught with dilemmas at all stages, arousing passion and anxiety, creating illusion and also being altered by it. It has thus become particularly

17

liable to disillusion which is often catastrophic. Motherhood is often used by the state for political purposes and by mothers themselves as an escape from the threatening modern world which they feel they cannot face and to whose rapid change they cannot adapt. On the one hand the importance of mothers is emphasized. On the other hand little is done to help them and they are used shamelessly by governments, local authorities, schools and male chauvinists as public and private conveniences and cheap sources of labour. When things go wrong with children and young people, as so often happens in our complex and difficult society, mothers are blamed, usually for having gone out to work and neglected their children or for having stayed at home and overprotected them. Mothers bear the burden not only as child-rearers but also as scapegoats. Their rôle is becoming increasingly uncertain and untenable. The needs of young children are increasingly at variance with the organization and way of life of our society, and this gap is filled partly by idealizing the mother and partly by denigrating and humiliating her. The situation is frozen by making it extremely difficult for her to see the situation realistically and so she is unable to do anything about it.

Many people, not all of them mothers and not all of them women, have become caught up in these dilemmas. Some are aware of it, others are aware only of the unease, dissatisfaction, depression or physical symptoms that result from this situation. It is not surprising that many young women today are wondering whether they wish to be mothers at all. At present we are confronted with an epidemic of depression in women, most of them mothers. Many convert their depression into physical symptoms and are often treated by their doctors as though the cause of their troubles was ulcers, colitis or hormonal imbalance. Many make suicidal gestures as acts of despair or as desperate bids for attention – now the commonest cause of emergency admission to hospital.

Yet for huge numbers of women, including many of those who are distressed and disturbed, bearing and rearing children is the most satisfying experience of their lives and it continues to be so despite the paradoxes and difficulties. For some it may be the only satisfying experience they have ever known and these mothers tend to run into difficulties when the active phase of mothering is over, especially if they have made no preparation for the second half of their adult lives.

This book concerns all mothers, not only those who at present are actively engaged in bringing up children but also those whose active life as mothers is finished and who now have to face the outside world. There is also another kind of mother whom I have very much in mind; the future or potential mother. Since becoming a mother is no longer automatic and can be controlled, it now involves choice. Many young women contemplate this decision with awe and uncertainty. The prospect of becoming a mother seems a tremendous step, a total change in life style, a fearful responsibility, an impossible expense, a frightening emotional commitment. I hope that reading this book will help them to take this decision realistically or, better still, will help them to find that there is no real decision.

In order to cope with this crisis in motherhood we have to examine the illusions that surround it. Only then are we in a position to know whether we can embrace it, cope with it realistically, and make something good out of it, or whether we have turned it into an institution that can only be tolerated by creating illusions with which to support it. But first we have to understand motherhood as an institution in our society and how it came to be that way.

It has always been regarded as important to have children. 'Give me children or else I die,' cried Rachel as long ago as Genesis, and St. Augustine wrote 'Give me other mothers and I will give you another world.' But attitudes to these mothers and children and the reasons why they were regarded as important have varied from time to time and from place to place. In some cultures only boys are desired, as many as possible, and girls are regarded as undesirable. Elsewhere huge families of children are thought to be normal. In the western world today a couple who wanted as many boys as possible and no girls would be regarded as abnormal and those who produce twelve or twenty children are thought to be irresponsible and incapable of giving each child sufficient attention.

Today we put great emphasis on the individual child, so much so that it is widely believed that we should only produce a child if we have a reasonable prospect of giving it the prolonged and intensive loving care that we believe it needs. This attitude is now so strong that large numbers of people, probably the majority in Protestant countries, believe that killing an unborn child is desirable if its likely circumstances after birth are inauspicious. But more money and care than ever before is now lavished on unborn babies who are thought to be perfect and wanted. There is a strong feeling that each individual child is of great importance and everything possible

19

should be done for its welfare. During the last twenty years a whole new science of the foetus has grown up with its own research centres and its own specialists. Concomitant with this is the widespread expectation of young mothers that their babies shall be normal and even a demand that this be so. Failure to produce a living, normal child is often followed not only by self-recrimination but also often by blame laid on the doctors. In former days this failure was much commoner and was likely to be regarded as an act of God.

It might seem that motherhood has changed less than other institutions in our society. Mothers have always borne children and been responsible for their care. They continue to do what they have always done and what is in their biological nature to do. Yet motherhood has changed as much as any other institution in our society and more than many. One need go no further back than one generation to find enormous, immeasurable differences, and the further one looks back, the more one sees that it has changed. Until one gains some understanding of those changes it is impossible to have a good insight into modern motherhood or its problems.

Raising children is nowadays frequently thought of as both difficult and mysterious. It is difficult because mothers know that they will have to devote most of themselves, and their time and energy to it for many years, and that however diligently they do this they will be blamed for whatever goes wrong. It is mysterious partly because few people have practical experience of family life with young children before they have their own, partly because conditions and ideas are changing so rapidly that the future of children seems uncertain, and partly because society tends to idealize the experience of motherhood which means that the darker side is not readily or openly discussed. The situation facing a potential young mother today is not unlike that of the young Victorian bride described in that apotheosis of Victorian marriage, *The Angel in the House.*

Every thought
Pure as a bride's blush when she says
'I will' unto she knows not what.[1]

The young mother today, like the nineteenth century bride, has little means of knowing what she is really in for. But added to this, she has the new problems of our time. Most people in the last century had no doubt that family life was best or that raising children was a duty to God. Now we are not so sure about the family, the children or God. We are uncertain about what kind of a world we are raising our children into and about how best to prepare them for it. Do we, for instance, deliberately prepare them for uncertainty and change? Or try to ignore outside uncertainty and provide security within the family? Or we ignore the question altogether and bring them up according to how we feel or according to some abstract theory about what is 'best' for children? Our ancestors did not have to decide these questions. Parents can and do fail because of insufficient thought and attention to these matters, or because of inappropriate answers.

No one before has had to raise children in a world that changes so rapidly. In that other era of change, following the Industrial Revolution, our ancestors responded by tightening the rules of family life and idealizing wives, which made it difficult for women to protest or even to see what there might be to protest about. We have responded to more recent and more rapid change by widening the rules of family life, and idealizing mothers. We therefore include and acknowledge very different kinds of family, such as the single parent family and the hybrid family (which usually results from divorce and remarriage) both of which have increased enormously in our time. But the idealization of mothers makes it difficult to see what is happening and still more difficult to alter it or even to see what might be altered. Idealization, as we shall see, is a means, albeit inadequate, of tolerating an intolerable situation without having to face up to it or to recognize it for what it is. But idealization leads to vicious circles, for it prevents understanding and insight.

As an institution motherhood today is a mixture of old trends and new trends, tradition, reaction and misunderstanding. We cannot begin to understand it unless we know something of what went before. Old trends need to be followed back. New trends can be traced back into the past and often then acquire new meaning and depth. The future emerges from the past and thus helps us to understand and come to terms with the present.

PART ONE

Changing Motherhood

CHAPTER ONE

Confidence in
Survival

Most of us assume that our children will survive. So confident are we about this that few of us even question it. Yet we can have little understanding of families and child-rearing today unless we realize how new this assumption is, and understand something of the extent to which our ideas and our practice are now based on it.

The development of confidence in the survival of children has been a basic change not only for parents but for society as a whole all over the western world. This confidence has come rapidly, extensively and recently. Nearly everything that is said, written or thought about children now takes it for granted that children will survive. Confidence in the survival of ourselves and our children is the basis of modern parenthood and is essential to virtually all our ideas about it. Whatever else we may think, hope and fear, we expect to have children if and when we want them and we expect those children to be born healthy and to grow up and, like ourselves, to lead a long life. If our lives do not conform to this pattern we are likely to feel that there is something wrong with us or that life has cheated us. If we cannot have children or if they are damaged or unhealthy or die or lose their parents or do not 'develop their potential', these matters are to us problems or tragedies.

Yet only in recent years has such confidence been possible. Our ancestors, even our near ancestors in the last century, were accustomed to losing a high proportion of their children, sometimes most of them. Exact figures are impossible to find,[1] but even the official figures show that in England and Wales in 1885–74, out of every hundred infants registered alive, some 14 to 16 died in their first year of life. In some areas and in some groups the death rate was much higher. In a typical enquiry in 1872, it was found that 62 mothers who went out to work had borne 185 children of whom 127

(68.6%) had died under the age of 5 years. 110 mothers who did not go out to work had borne 544 children of whom 248 (45.5%) had died before they were five years old.[2]

The development of confidence in our children's healthy survival is now so much the foundation on which the ideas and customs of the western world are built that we tend to take it for granted. This lack of awareness has important implications for the modern tendency to idealize motherhood and also for our understanding of it. For if we are to reach some understanding of ourselves, our families and the various aspects of modern motherhood it is essential to look at this new confidence carefully, examine its origins, nature and significance, and have some idea of how different it is from former times and other societies in which it did not and does not prevail.

Throughout history until recent times motherhood was always close to death. A high proportion of babies always died, and in certain times and places *most* babies died. If they did survive infancy they were likely to die as children, adolescents or young adults. At any time one might lose the new baby, or an epidemic might carry off two or three of one's older children within a few days or weeks. Improved nutrition and social conditions together with increasing knowledge of and control over health, disease and death has been one of the most spectacular aspects of post-industrial technical advance and social change.

Never before in history have people been so healthy or lived for so long. In these days of healthy security it is difficult to imagine the time when one in three adults died of infection, many thousands died of starvation or malnutrition and only a minority of babies born lived to adult life. But anyone who thinks seriously about these things is bound to be impressed by the profound change that this trend from disease to health, from death to life, has brought to the mothering of young children. The situation was even worse for mothers and children than for the rest of the population because the incidence of sickness and death among them was even higher. Two centuries ago, of every four babies born alive, only one was likely to be alive on its first birthday, as gravestones in any eighteenth century churchyard remind us. Moreover, these figures exclude stillbirths, which were almost never recorded, and also exclude many infants who lived for a few days or more, for it was often more convenient and cheaper to take a small corpse to the undertaker and say that it had died at birth. Ecclesiastical lawyers and theologians

26

took the view that 'a child before he is baptized is not a child of God but a child of the Devil.'[3] Charles Dickens once asked the Rector of a parish in a large English town: 'What do they do with the infants of the mothers who work in the mill?'. 'Oh' replied the cleric, 'they bring them to me and I take care of them in the churchyard!'[4]

Because exact figures are impossible to obtain, small studies are particularly valuable. A doctor's records in one probably fairly typical time and place showed that no less than one third of all infants died within fourteen days of birth and many more, unspecified, during the first year. The death rate between the ages of one and five was a further eighteen per cent,[5] and the death rate throughout the rest of youth was also very high. Thus large numbers of those who survived the hazardous first months of life died in childhood. This was just as true in royal and aristocratic families as among peasants. To mention just a few, Queen Anne of England had fifteen pregnancies: all except one of her children were born dead or died during infancy. The survivor, William, Duke of Gloucester, died at the age of 11. Because of all these deaths there was no direct heir to the throne and the succession passed to George, elector of Hanover. Another royal, the Duc d'Orléans ('Monsieur'), brother of Louis XIV and ancestor of every Roman Catholic royal family, had eleven legitimate children of whom seven died in infancy or were born dead. These were not exceptional cases. Although mortality in infants and young children seems to have been somewhat lower in colonial America than in Europe, the situation was basically the same. Examples can be seen everywhere, such as in the early colonial families of Sewall and Mather. Samuel Sewall and Cotton Mather each had fourteen children. One of Sewall's was stillborn, several died as infants and several more as young adults. Seven Mather babies died soon after birth, one died at two years and of the six who survived to adult life, five died in their twenties. Of these twenty-eight children, only three outlived their fathers.[6]

Although infant mortality has fallen fairly steadily for the past two hundred years it was still high during the early part of the present century. Only since World War I and still more since World War II have parents been able to have reasonable confidence that all their children would survive. Stillbirths and neonatal deaths, of course, occur, but in industrialized countries in only about eight to twenty per thousand births. Children die, notably from accidents,

27

cancer and inherited disease, but these deaths are even rarer. After the first month of life death has become extremely rare.

What was it like to be a mother with the possibility that at least half one's children would fail to survive birth or infancy or would die during childhood? What was it like to be a mother whose apparently healthy child suddenly sickens and dies? We cannot be sure, even though both these situations occasionally occur today. Today children occasionally die, and there still are a few individual mothers, such as those whose children suffer from inherited diseases, who have to face the problem. For these mothers it is a personal tragedy, but it is different from what it would have been in former times because it is rare and unexpected. The very fact that such mothers are few means that, although many of their feelings may be the same, their situation is different from that in the past, when it was the likely lot of every mother. In the past, mothers who lost children were unlikely to feel isolated in the way they do today. It happened around them all the time and to nearly everyone they knew. When things, however sad or tragic, are the same for everyone, they are different for all. Society supported bereaved families in what was likely to be regarded more as a sad little happening than as a deep family tragedy. They would have been less likely to blame themselves, as they might today, and they were less likely to feel that they had failed. Moreover, other people would not condemn them, as they might today, believing it to be irresponsible to bring sickly children into the world. Losing one's children by death was regarded as a normal hazard of life and hence it was important to have many children so that at least some might survive. This led to a resigned, even a detached attitude to the deaths of children epitomized by Montaigne: 'I have lost two or three children at nurse, not without regret but without grief.'

In the 1770s, Mrs. Thrale, devoted mother of many children, was extremely upset when one of her older children died but showed no grief over the deaths of infants. She took an instant dislike to one baby since 'she is so very poor a creature I can scarce bear to look on her.' Later, when another newborn baby died, she commented, 'One cannot grieve after her much, and I have just now other things to think of.'[7] It is difficult to imagine a modern mother saying such a thing. Philippe Ariès, who has made an extensive study of iconography in his search for evidence, points out that there were no portraits of individual children during the Middle Ages, and no children's tombs until the sixteenth century. Even then children appeared not on their own but on their parents' tombs. No one thought of keeping a picture of a dead child. The general feeling was, and for a long time remained, writes Ariès, 'that one had several children in order to keep just a few.' In the Basque country it was long the custom to bury children who died without baptism in the house, on the threshold or in the garden.[8] And sometimes the deaths of children were positively encouraged or hoped for. Ariès quotes the seventeenth century *Le Caquet de l'accouchée* in which a neighbour, standing at the bedside of a woman who has just given birth, the mother of five 'little brats' calmed her fears with these words: 'Before they are old enough to bother you, you will have lost half of them or perhaps all of them.' In Bavaria 'people are generally pleased with the quick death of children and say "they're well provided for".'[9] Lebrun writes of eighteenth century Angevin peasants, 'The death of a small child, provided it had been baptized, is considered in the religious plane as a deliverance, for the infant has had the grace of acceding directly to paradise without knowing the bitterness of this life . . . On the human plane infant death is almost a banal accident, which a subsequent birth will recuperate.'[10]

Thus one big difference between today and the past is in the nature of realistic and unrealistic expectations. In the past mothers hoped that their children would survive but it was unrealistic to expect them to do so. A young woman embarking on motherhood knew that she was likely to lose several children, especially babies. Nowadays for most women it is realistic to expect that every child will survive and grow up. Many women today have fears that they will lose their children or hidden suspicions that they are incapable of producing normal, healthy children, but these, though understandable, are usually neurotic projections of personal anxieties, or manifestations of the problems of personal identity that are so characteristic of our time.

Another result that one would expect if every mother was in danger of losing her children and knew no other state of affairs is that she would not and could not have the strong individual feelings about each child that are customary today, when each child is regarded as unique from the moment it is born or even before. Only with the new confidence is it possible to regard each new life as unique, valuable, personal and permanent for the rest of one's life. In the past a woman who became pregnant was extremely unlikely to feel this way. People are likely to invest less time and love on something or somebody whose existence is likely to be transitory and there is a good deal of evidence to show that this was so, quite apart from the evidence of the easy acceptance of death. It was, for instance, long the custom to give the same name to several children in the hope that at least one John or William or Richard would live to carry on the family name. In the medieval period the same name was often given to two living children. Later, from the sixteenth to the eighteenth centuries, it was more the practice to give a newborn child the name of one who had recently died. This practice was brought to England from colonial New England. When John Wesley was born in 1703 both his names, John Benjamin, were those of elder brothers who had died three and four years before.[11] But the older practice lingered on, as Edward Gibbon tells us. After his birth in 1737 'so feeble was my constitution, so precarious my life, that in the baptism of my brothers, my father's prudence successively repeated my Christian name of Edward, that, in the case of the departure of the eldest son, this patronymic appellation might still be perpetuated in the family.'[12] One wonders what effect this custom had on family relationships. Such practices would be inconceivable today and would be regarded as both an insult to the memory of the dead child and a monstrous imposition on the living, a threat to its unique existence and personality.

Another way in which our ancestors indicated that their attitude to the individuality of children was different from ours was their frequent failure to record their births. Parish Registers of Birth were introduced in England in 1538 but long after that the records were inexact.[13] It was not possible to ascertain a person's age precisely until after the Registration of Births Act of 1836, and even after that in by no means every case. Judges decided people's ages, simply by looking at them or by consulting relatives. When in 1620, E. Chamberlayne first published *Reflections on the Present State of England* he wrote so that 'the whole state of England might be seen at once.' Out of its 516 pages he devotes less than four to a section 'Concerning Children in England' and then dealt exclusively with the legal rights of children in the holding and disposing of property.

Lack of confidence in survival applied not only to children but also to their mothers; and to a lesser extent, their fathers. Health and death in young mothers have also changed profoundly. Stone[14] cites evidence that throughout the Early Modern period nearly one

30

in ten of all children under three and one in five of all children living at home had lost at least one parent. Until recent times death was frequent at all ages and killing diseases such as tuberculosis, diphtheria and typhoid were rampant. Epidemics of cholera were frequent in the nineteenth century. The last big outbreak, in 1887, is said to have killed 250,000 people in Europe and 50,000 in America,[15] and in 1892 a million people are said to have died from the disease in Russia.[16] Yet amidst all this, one of the greatest hazards that women had to face was childbirth. At times and in certain places it killed as many as fifteen or even twenty mothers out of every hundred and was particularly likely to occur in maternity hospitals expressly designed for their protection. In the seventeenth century John Donne referred to the womb as the 'house of death'.

'Death in childbirth' as a fact and a concept was once widespread everywhere, but few people now come into contact with it in the western world. Few have much idea of what it entails and most doctors never encounter it. Yet until the 1930s every woman embarking on pregnancy knew that her life was in danger. Death in childbirth was so common that it shaped royal dynasties and influenced the course of history. For instance, it killed three Tudor queens, Elizabeth of York, wife of Henry VII and mother of Henry VIII; Jane Seymour, third wife of Henry VIII, following the birth of the future Edward VI; and Catherine Parr, his sixth wife, who died in childbirth after Henry's death, when she was married to Thomas Seymour.

'Death in childbirth' covers a number of different conditions. The best known is probably puerperal or 'childbed' fever. This is an infection, most commonly associated with the organism *haemolytic streptococcus*, but sometimes with other organisms such as those which cause gas gangrene in war wounds. The infection usually occurs during delivery but only manifests itself some days later, leading to septicaemia with fever and a high mortality rate. Death usually occurred 8–12 days after the baby was born. The disease was known to the ancients, including Hippocrates, but became particularly common after the development of dirty, crowded towns, especially where charitable organizations established hospitals where the poor might give birth! Between the years 1652 and 1862 there were two hundred so-called epidemics of the disease. In 1660 it killed two thirds of the women confined in the Hôtel Dieu in

31

Paris. In 1773 it killed more than a tenth of the population of lying-in hospitals in Europe. It was reported that in Lombardy for more than a year no woman survived childbirth.[17] Though commonest in hospitals it was also found elsewhere, for example in America, where there were few hospitals. Jane Seymour caught it in Greenwich Palace. Mary Wollstonecraft, one of the first pioneers of English feminism, caught it and died of it after a home confinement. The description of her suffering is typical of what women went through.

Puerperal fever is much commoner after deliveries that have been complicated and in which there has been some operative interference. So it was with Mary Wollstonecraft. She was full of good spirits when she went into labour with the future Mary Shelley, wife of the poet and author of *Frankenstein*. Her experience during her previous confinement had been so good that she planned to present the new baby to her husband herself as soon as it was born and to get up for dinner next day.[18] This was to give a pioneering example to other women, whose custom was to stay in their rooms for a whole month after delivery. She hired Mrs. Blenkinsop, the chief midwife from the Westminster Lying-In hospital. The labour was slower and more painful than is usual with a second child, but after eighteen hours the baby was born. Now came the first serious difficulty. The placenta, which is usually born a few minutes after the baby, did not arrive. Moreover, it had separated partially which meant that the womb could not expel it. The partial separation caused bleeding and, because the retained placenta kept the womb distended, the bleeding was likely to continue dangerously until the placenta was removed. Nowadays a retained placenta is usually removed in sterile conditions under anaesthetic and lost blood is replaced by transfusion. In 1797, without anaesthetics or blood transfusion, and without knowledge of the source or nature of infection, a retained placenta was extremely dangerous. Mrs. Blenkinsop sent for Dr. Poignard, the chief obstetrician at the Westminster Lying-In. Mary was already half-conscious from loss of blood and could easily have died from this alone. When Dr. Poignard arrived he did the only thing which could save her life, though it could also easily kill her. He put his hand arm right up into the womb and extracted the placenta in pieces with his fingers, working through the night till dawn. Without an anaesthetic, Mary could easily have died from shock but in fact she survived this second danger to her life and later slept. When she woke she was much better and for two days everything seemed to be fine. Then she began to feel ill and had an attack of shivering so bad that the bed shook. This was a typical 'rigor', a common start of puerperal fever. Late that evening she had another rigor in the presence of her husband who described it: 'every muscle of her body trembled, the teeth chattered, and the bed shook under her. This continued probably for five minutes. She told me, after it was over, that it had been a struggle between life and death, and that she had been more than once, in the course of it, at the point of expiring.' Mary tried to fight back but she was exsanguinated from the bleeding and exhausted. There was no treatment for the infection. The disease developed relentlessly during the next few days until she was clearly dying. She lingered on for yet a few more days.

Ironically, Mary Wollstonecraft died of puerperal fever at a time when the incidence seems to have been remarkably low. No national figures exist before the Act of 1837, but at the City of London Lying-In Hospital in the year 1797 only one mother died in 402 deliveries, an incidence of 2.4 per thousand deliveries. Over the next 80 years the figure fluctuated from 2 to as many as 14 deaths per thousand births. Although the cause of puerperal fever was discovered in the ninteenth century and ways of preventing it were known, it continued to be common far into the twentieth century and killed many healthy women until the 1930s.

Eclampsia was another common killer. This is a disease which only occurs in pregnancy, usually develops slowly and, if not detected and prevented, proceeds to severe fits and often rapid and dramatic death. It is fairly common (perhaps three to four per thousand births) where preganancy is left to nature but almost wholly preventable with good antenatal care. Its marked decline with medical effort was shown dramatically in Sydney, Australia. At the Women's Hospital, Crown Street, between 1936 and 1948 the incidence among booked cases was one in 400. In 1948 it was decided to attack this high incidence by the simple measures of meticulous observation of blood pressure and control of weight gain. After this was organized there was only one case of eclampsia in approximately 15,000 booked cases. Nowadays eclampsia still occurs in the western world, but it is almost always in women whose antenatal care has been poor or non-existent.

Obstructed labour was another common cause of death and old

33

textbooks of obstetrics are fully of heroic measures to deal with a situation that had gone too far to save the life of the child and often, especially in the days before anaesthetics, of the mother. Every obstetrician carried destructive instruments designed to kill and crush or decapitate the foetus in the hope of saving the mother's life. The operation or craniotomy is much older than the procedures which eventually replaced it, forceps and Caesarian section. Decapitation seems barbarous to us and to modern obstetricians. It is virtually never performed today in the western world but it is perhaps salutary to note that as late as the present century a new device was invented for performing it – the Blond-Heidler thimble, which, placed on the thumb, carries a fine wire-saw round the neck of the child.

Another constant hazard in childbirth is, and remains, haemorrhage, particularly post-partum haemorrhage, usually from a retained placenta. Even in a 'normal' birth, it can strike suddenly and dangerously despite every precaution and the most skilled care during pregnancy and labour. It is one of the main reasons why many obstetricians say that no delivery is 'normal' until it is finished and believe that all births should take place in hospital.

One serious condition attacks women early in pregnancy. This is *hyperemesis gravidarum* which is an exaggeration of the common 'morning sickness'. The expectant mother, usually of a nervous disposition, vomits so much that if she is treated inadequately or not at all she may lose her life. This seems to be what happened to Charlotte Brontë. Although her death during pregnancy is often attributed to tuberculosis, in fact Mrs. Gaskell's description of her last illness supplemented by Charlotte's own letters, is a classical description of *hyperemesis gravidarum*.[19] In November 1854, just over three months after her return from a honeymoon in Ireland, Charlotte developed a cold, which lingered, but does not seem to have been serious. In the new year (1855) 'she was attacked by new sensations of perpetual nausea, and ever-recurring faintness.'[20] Charlotte wrote in January 19th to her friend Ellen Nussey. 'My health has been really very good since my return from Ireland till about ten days ago, when the stomach seemed quite suddenly to lose its tone – indigestion and continual faint sickness have been my portion ever since.' She seems to associate this with her pregnancy for she continues 'Don't conjecture – dear Nell – for it is too soon yet though I certainly never before felt as I have done lately.' Her husband called in Dr. MacTurk from Bradford, who 'assigned a natural cause for her miserable indisposition.'[21] Martha the maid 'tenderly waited on her mistress, and from time to time tried to cheer her with the thought of the baby that was coming. "I dare say I shall be glad sometime," she would say: "but I am so ill – so weary – ." Then she took to her bed, too weak to sit up.' Some time in February she wrote to Amelia Taylor: 'Let me speak the plain truth – my sufferings are very great – my nights indescribable – sickness with scarce a reprieve – I strain until what I vomit is mixed with blood.' Mrs. Gaskell tells us: 'About the third week in March there was a change; a low wandering delirium came on: and in it she begged constantly for food and even for stimulants. She swallowed eagerly now; but it was too late.' On March 31st she died.

Hyperemesis gravidarum still occurs. But no one would leave a sufferer to vomit her life away in her own home. A few days in hospital with suitable diet, drugs, fluid replacement and perhaps some psychotherapy are usually all that is required. Probably never again will it be possible to follow so closely the natural, untreated course of the illness.[22]

Death in childbirth was often precipitated or hastened by ignorance, impotence, neglect, interference or a mixture of these according to the knowledge and custom of the time. Throughout the history of obstetrics there has been conflict between those who believed in leaving everything to Nature and those who believed in interfering whenever any delay or abnormality became apparent. Today this conflict is as strong as ever, though the criteria have changed. A period in which leaving matters to Nature was very much in vogue was the early nineteenth century. This idea and also the belief in 'meddlesome midwifery' can both be studied in the story of the labour of Princess Charlotte in November 1817. The hour-to-hour notes of Sir Richard Croft, Bart., Accoucheur-in-Chief have enabled us to follow the progress of labour in some detail. Thirty-eight years before Charlotte Brontë's death her namesake the Princess Charlotte, daughter of the Prince Regent, died in childbirth. Her death and the circumstances that surrounded it are of interest for several reasons. First, it created a crisis in the succession to the throne of England; second, it was a turning point in the history of midwifery; third it can be seen as part of a conflict that continues in the present time and is of particular interest to feminists: the conflict in the management of childbirth between control and interference by a male obstetrician and leaving it to nature.

Princess Charlotte was the only child of her estranged parents, the Prince Regent, later George IV, and Queen Caroline. King George III had had fifteen children. He was now 79 years old, sick, and likely to die soon. His heir was already 55 years old and estranged from his wife. Charlotte was the king's only legitimate grandchild. If no new heirs were born the crown would pass to the Duke of Brunswick, aged 13, and mentally weak. Charlotte's death meant that the dissolute pleasure-loving princes were urged to attend to the important matters of royal marriage and producing an heir. The Duke of Cambridge won the race with a son. But two months later the Duchess of Kent, wife of his older brother, gave birth to a daughter. This child, in the aftermath of her cousin's tragic death, was destined to become Queen Victoria.

The story of the Princess Charlotte's labour has been ably told by Sir Eardley Holland, and named 'a triple obstetric tragedy' because not only did the mother and child both die as a result of it but also the obstetrician.[23] Sir Richard Croft, the obstetrician who conducted the labour, became severely depressed amid all the criticism and shot himself three months later. Only during the reign of George III had midwifery become respectable, and as it became respectable it also became ultra-conservative. Smellie, a brilliant man-midwife and careful operator who invented a number of techniques that are still used today had retired in 1760. There followed a period in which forceps were used so freely that William Hunter, who became England's most prominent man-midwife, is said to have told his class that it was 'a thousand pities that it was ever invented.' When Hunter died the next leading society obstetrician was Thomas Denman, an exponent of the non-intervention school. Denman trained Richard Croft according to the principles he had laid down in his *Introduction to the Practice of Midwifery*, first published in 1788, which went into many editions. In his conduct of Princess Charlotte's labour Croft followed Denman's precepts, which meant that, despite the length of the labour and the complications that arose, he did nothing and left it all to nature.

Charlotte's labour started with the breaking of the waters at 7 p.m. on Monday, 3 November, 1817. Her contractions were irregular and the first stage of labour lasted for twenty-six hours. There is nothing unusual in this, but Croft bled her and refused to allow her food or drink. The second stage of labour began. This is the stage during which the child is actually born. In modern practice it is allowed to last no longer than an hour and often less because of the risks to child and mother. Charlotte's second stage lasted for twenty-four hours, including five to six hours when the head was actually pressing on the perineum and any but the most ultra-conservative practitioner would have lifted the baby out with forceps. At 9 p.m. on November 5, Charlotte, exhausted after this immense labour, gave birth to a 9 lb. stillborn boy. We can find the reason for this long delay in Denman's book. He tells us the 'cessation of pains, which is the consequence of long continued fruitless action, and of great debility is to be considered the only justification for the use of the forceps.' He also formulated what came to be known as 'Denman's Law', 'that the head of the child shall have rested for six hours as low as the perineum before the forceps are applied, though the pains should have ceased during that time.' Even by the most conservative obstetrician today, this would be regarded as malpractice.

This delay was disastrous for Charlotte. Her baby was dead and she was exhausted. Twenty minutes later, as is liable to happen after a long hard labour, she had a post-partum haemorrhage. Croft removed the placenta manually as Poignard had done twenty years before on Mary Wollstonecraft. Although the Princess seemed to be reasonably well afterwards, shortly before midnight she was sick and complained of noises in her head. She was given camphorated mixture and was sick again. After a cup of tea she slept for half an hour, then woke irritable and restless. She was given 20 drops of laudanum in wine and water and she told Baron Stockmar, her husband's secretary, that the doctors had made her tipsy. At 12.45 a.m. on November 6 she complained of uneasiness in the chest and difficulty in breathing. Her pulse was rapid, feeble and irregular. She became increasingly restless and at 2.30 a.m. she died. At the post-mortem 'about a pound of blood' was found in the uterus. This probably contributed to her death but Croft had ignored or not bothered to find it. Denman's book advised *against* releasing accumulated blood from the uterus after delivery.

Baron Stockmar, himself a trained physician, who was in the next room during the labour commented, 'It is impossible to resist the conviction that the Princess was sacrificed to professional theories.' The public thought so too. There was widespread hostility to Croft until he killed himself, and a change in the customary practice of midwifery to a greater willingness to interfere when things do not go well.

Princess Charlotte's labour was better documented than most but probably was not in other ways atypical of complicated labours at the time. But many of the mothers who died were different in one respect. Charlotte had no children. Since childbirth becomes more dangerous with each birth after the third, many of these mothers left large numbers of children behind them.

No accurate figures are available for deaths in childbirth in England and Wales before 1838. We do know, however, that from that date, in spite of improvements in knowledge during the nineteenth and early twentieth century, and in spite of improvements in general health in overall mortality and in infant mortality, the maternal death rate remained almost stationery for nearly 100 years (1838–1935). Some of the causes of this are to be found in the attitudes of men to women and the lack of time, energy and technology devoted to the health of expectant mothers. Only when special attention was paid to the problem of death in childbirth did the situation improve. After women won the vote pioneer suffragettes together with men and women of strong social conscience turned their attention to such problems and one of these problems was maternal mortality. As a result institutions were founded, including the Royal College of Obstetrics and Gynaecologists and the National Birthday Trust Fund, which aimed to increase knowledge by research and to raise standards of practice. The maternal death rate has been falling ever since. In England and Wales in 1855–64 the maternal mortality rate was 4.7 per thousand live births. In 1925–34 it was 4.3. In 1945–50 it was 1.2 and in 1979 it was down to .12, now expressed as 1.2 per 10,000 live births. When we give birth today provided we look after ourselves and follow expert advice, we can be confident of survival.

Today almost no woman who follows the advice of her doctors is in danger of dying during childbirth. Women who, in spite of modern medicine, are still in genuine danger, usually suffer from severe disease, perhaps of the heart or kidneys, but they are so rare that when one of them survives a hazardous birth, she is liable to make headlines in the newspapers. The essence of safe childbirth for all women is good health and food, good antenatal care and good obstetric care during delivery. This is one of the great scientific truths of our time. The aids are careful observation and record-keeping, frequent monitoring and preventive action, antibiotics and other drugs, blood or its derivatives for transfusion, and the skilful performance of Caesarian sections and other obstetric procedures when necessary. Only recently have we discovered that, even though many healthy babies can be born 'naturally', without medical care, huge numbers of babies and many mothers die if all is left to nature. Antenatal care did not exist at the beginning of the twentieth century, apart from general advice about such matters as diet and exercise. In Boston in 1901 the Instructive Nursing Association began to pay antenatal visits to some of the women in the out-patient department of the Boston Lying-in Hospital. In 1909 Mrs. William Lowell Putnam of the Infant Social Service Department of the Women's Municipal League of Boston organized intensive pre-natal care of patients registered for confinement at the Boston Lying-In Hospital. In May 1911 the pregnancy clinic of the hospital was opened for out-patients. A similar clinic had already been started the year before in Adelaide, Australia, followed in 1912 by one in Sydney, Australia and, in 1915, in Edinburgh, Scotland. In 1919 the Maternity and Child Welfare Act provided for advice, treatment and social assistance of pregnant women in Great Biritain. Nowadays all western countries and many others provide compre-hensive antenatal care and it is known that the mortality among the babies of those who attend early in pregnancy is only half that of those who do not attend before the sixteenth week.

The wheel has turned again. No sooner has the lesson been learned than there are pressures to forget it. This time it is the women who clamour that childbirth is natural and should be left to nature. In the generation that followed the first mothers whose childbirth was safe there is disquiet concerning 'inhuman' obstetrics and 'patriarchal' obstetricians. Childbirth has been made so safe that we tend to forget that it is potentially dangerous. We are also aware that this safety has been achieved at considerable emotional cost. Childbirth is now a highly technological process and many mothers experience the 'factory belt' system and the clinical and scientific atmosphere that accompanies it as dehumanizing. For some years there have been movements for 'natural' childbirth and for home deliveries. This has created one of the new dilemmas of motherhood. It is virtually impossible to be or to feel 'natural' as a patient in a modern obstetric ward, and although some wards make efforts to satisfy their patients' feelings, these efforts must, by the very nature of the situation, be rudimentary and unsatisfactory. There can be enormous emotional satisfaction in giving birth in one's own home with just a midwife in attendance I can testify to this personally as two of my own babies were born in this manner. But the scientific evidence is strong. Nature tends to be wasteful of life and however healthy the mother and however normal the pregnancy, things are liable to go wrong, often very fast. If things go wrong, the safest place for both mother and child to be in is a well-equipped obstetric unit. A delivery can only be described as normal when it is finished and the baby is alive. My own homeborn babies were perfect, but one of the changes that has taken place in my own adult life is the realization of these dangers. Given the opportunity I would not again risk my children's lives in this way. However, I can sympathize with the current argument that modern obstetric methods also create complications that would not occur in the patient's home.

So much death as existed until recent times meant that large numbers of children grew up motherless, and often fatherless too. The word *orphan* has almost gone out of our language but was all too common until recent times. Lawrence Stone has told the story:

> In pre-modern times only a minority of adolescent children had two living parents. Of those marrying for the first time in Brittany and Anjou in the late eighteenth century, on the average in their middle twenties, one in five were orphans and two in three had lost one parent. Among the sixteenth and seventeenth century English aristocracy, one in three children had lost one parent by the age of fourteen, and the proportion of English apprentices (who normally entered service at fourteen) who were fatherless was thirty-four percent at Bristol, twenty per cent in the London Stationers' Company and twenty-five per cent in the London Fishmongers' and Bakers' Companies. These figures are on the high side, since appreticeship was a common way of looking after orphans, but they are nonetheless very striking. More typical are the records of first marriages in Manchester in the 1650s, where over half the brides and almost half of the grooms had lost their fathers. In 1696 one-third of all the children in Bristol were orphans.

One only has to look at biographies of famous people to see that this state of affairs was common in all sections of society. Illingworth has collected some of them. Descartes, Rousseau, Froebel, Paderewski and Mary Shelley all lost their mothers in their first year of life. Those who lost their mothers at the age of two included Nero, Tolstoy and Anne Brontë, at three, Isaac Newton, Pascal and Ronald Knox; at five, Dante, Lavoisier and Charlotte Brontë; at six, Michelangelo, Mahommed and William Cowper; at seven, Robespierre and Hume; and at eight, Wordsworth, Voltaire, Charles Darwin, Joseph Conrad, Ivan the Terrible and Ernest Bevin. Today it is rare for a child to have no living mother. If he is separated from her it is more likely to be because she has abandoned or deserted him or cannot cope with him, or is physically or, more often, mentally ill. We have few orphans but there are large numbers of children in care, and their numbers are tending to increase.

We hear a great deal today about 'broken homes' by which we usually mean a family in which the parents are divorced or separated. Since there was virtually no divorce between the middle ages and the late nineteenth century and very little until the middle of the present century, it is sometimes assumed that before our more permissive age, families were more intact than in our time. This was not the case. They were broken by death, probably at least as often as they are now broken by divorce. It was rare for a couple to marry and raise all their children together, and even if they managed this they probably did not have long to live after they were grown. Aging grandparents were rare. Of course, the deaths of so many young adults meant that there were large numbers of remarriages, just as there are today, though for different reasons. Not only orphans but also wicked stepmothers feature largely in Victorian children's books and fairy tales. Cinderella, Hansel & Gretel and the Babes in the Wood are just a few of those who suffered from their fathers' second wives. It is interesting to note that in these stories it is nearly always the children's mother who has died, sometimes both parents, but rarely the father alone. In real life it was common for a man to have several wives in succession, each of them dying, often in childbirth, and each leaving behind a family of small children. But of course it was not always the mother who died. Sir Ralph Verney died in 1543 leaving nine young children. Their mother subsequently remarried four times and, we are told 'had other matters on her hands than the care of her first husband's children.' A later member of the same family, Sir Francis Verney, lost his own mother when he was five years old and was brought up by his father, who had frequently to be away attending to his business. The children were left in the care of their father's third wife, Mary. We are told that Francis 'seems never to have been under any control either from affection or education.'[25] Thus widespread loss of parents, their remarriages, and difficult relationships with step-parents are not new in our time though the causes differ.

Death at home was accompanied by rituals and patterns of behaviour in which the children participated and had a special role to play. They were accustomed to losing playmates and brothers and sisters. Sometimes they were aware that they or their parents were not long for this world. When his wife Emily was seriously ill with consumption in 1861, the poet Coventry Patmore wrote to his schoolboy son: 'Remember that you are not likely to have your poor Mama long so you should make the best of the time you have left to please her . . . Although your learning well is important, there are other things much more important . . . to be *pure* (you know what I mean). If you are not pure . . . you will not see your dear Mama any more when she is gone.'[26] Another child, the seven year old son of Benjamin Haydon the painter, was not unusual when, on the death of his sister, he remarked that his turn would come next. He duly died the following year.[27] Nearly all modern western children grow to adult life without thinking of the possibility that they might die young, and often also without losing a single friend or close relative. Some even think that death is something that happens by violence on the television screen. The taboo about death which has developed in our society often creates a powerful and sinister 'conspiracy of silence' between parents and children.

Along with control of survival has come control of conception. In the past, no matter at which period or place one looks, and still in parts of the world, there was no sure method, apart from total abstinence, of preventing the arrival of children. True, fertility has varied from time to time and from place to place according to such influences as nutrition and social customs, for example, variations in age at marriage. There have always been women who have attempted to prevent pregnancy by various means, some of them surer than others but all of them uncertain. There have also been periods when whole groups of people have produced small families as a result of deliberate choice. An example is the Victorian middle classes from the 1870s onwards.[28] But only in our own time have the

Pill, other contraceptive devices, and abortion made it possible for an individual woman to choose with certainty whether or not to have a baby as and when she pleases. Choice is now absent only in those whose religion forbids contraception and those who wish to become mothers but turn out to be infertile. There are of course those who do not exercise their choice for any of a number of reasons including ignorance, personal motives, medical advice and fecklessness. There are also those who cannot choose because they have been brought up and trained not to choose.

The fact that any woman can choose, at least in theory, whether or not she becomes a mother has profound effect on women, on men, on families and on parenthood itself. First there is the common idea that one should only have children if one is able to care for them properly, physically, economically and emotionally, according to today's high standards. For most people this means getting married, acquiring what is regarded as adequate material possessions, and, at the time chosen, producing a small family, usually two children, and devoting to them a tremendous amount of time, emotion and money over many years in order to give them what one believes is the best chance of a good life. The wherewithal to organize things like this has had a profound effect on family life. Without it many of our ideas about families, children and mother-hood would inevitably be different. It also raises new questions and creates new dilemmas. For instance, questions are now being asked about whether motherhood is any longer a woman's chief *raison-d'être*. The belief that woman's chief role in life is motherhood has existed through the ages and persists today but is now seriously questioned, probably for the first time. Many women resent the years they would have to give to motherhood or regret that they had children before they felt they had a choice. Many reject convention-al family patterns and either choose to have children without mar-riage or not to have them at all. Today if a woman is unmarried with a family, or if she decides never to have children, she will find com-munities and social circles where such attitudes are wholly accept-able. Moreover, fertility is now regarded as a world problem, and, for the first time in history, having babies is, in some circles, regard-ed as antisocial and irresponsible. At the same time the belief that one should only have children if one can provide them with the love, care and material needs that are needed for optimum development also creates dilemmas.

CHAPTER TWO

Has Mother Love Changed?

In the days of high infant mortality rates parents accepted the deaths of babies and children in a way they do not today, but did they lack love for them? This question has been much debated by historians in recent years. Many believe that parents lacked love for individual children, particularly infants, largely because it is a normal human reaction not to become attached to what one is likely to lose. Ariès writes of parents' 'indifference' which was a direct inevitable consequence of the demography of the period.[1] Stone refers to 'indifference to the deaths of infants or young children, resignation before the deaths of adolescents and young adults, and sheer egocentric panic in the face of epidemics.'[2] He does however describe the Reverend Richard Napier, a 'popular psychological practitioner' in the early seventeenth century who 'treated a number of women who were mentally disturbed by the death of their infant children.' It may well be that these were cases of what we would now call puerperal psychosis. Some parents tended to blame themselves for the deaths of their children. When Ralph Josselin's ten-day old son died in 1648 he regarded it as a punishment imposed on him by God for his excessive fondness for playing chess.[3] When the infant son of Mary, Countess of Warwick, fell ill, 'my conscience told me it was for my backsliding.' The boy recovered but died of smallpox at the age of twenty, whereupon his mother recorded her reaction thus: 'I could with all the willingness in the world have died either for him or with him, if God had only seen it fit.' She 'was constantly fixed in the belief that this affliction came from a merciful Father, and therefore would do me good.' It was 'that sad but just chastisement of me'. In Massachusetts, when Cotton Mather's daughter fell into the fire and burned herself badly her father wrote: 'Alas, for my sins the just God throws my child into the fire.'[4] But when the Puritan

Simon D'Ewes' fourth and last son died at the age of two he took it not as a sign of God's displeasure but rather as a test of his faith.[5] There were also direct warnings to limit emotional commitment. In the eighteenth century Richard Baxter tells his readers to 'prepare for the loss of children and friends. It is your unpreparedness that maketh it seem insupportable.'[6] Of course, some parents did find the deaths of their children insupportable, at least for a while. In the eighteenth century an English visitor to America heard of her daughter's death at home in England. For a week or so she lamented in her diary that she could not go on. Esther Burr, wife of the president of Princeton College, also described real anxiety when her son Aaron died.[7]

There seems to be no doubt that mothers in the past reacted differently towards their children from mothers today. But there were many reasons for this, and only one of them was the children's poor expectations of life. Other factors included the nature of family life and its economic basis, the prevalence of traditional Christian views and outlook, and current ideas about children. One historian, Edward Shorter, goes so far as to say that mothers in the past did not care about their children and that this led to the high death rate rather than the other way round.[8] He is of the opinion that children died in large numbers because mothers lacked maternal love. The high death rate among children, he writes 'came about as a result of circumstances over which the parents had considerable influence: infant diet, age at weaning, cleanliness of bed linen, and the general hygienic circumstances that surrounded the child – to say nothing of less tangible factors in mothering, such as picking up the infant, talking and singing to it, giving it the feeling of being loved in a secure little universe. Now by the late eighteenth century, parents knew, at least in a sort of abstract way, that letting new-born children stew in their own excrement or feeding them pap from the second month onwards were harmful practices. For the network of medical personnel in Europe had by this time extended sufficiently to put interested mothers within earshot of sensible advice. The point is that these mothers did not *care*, and that is why their children vanished in the ghastly slaughter of the innocents that was traditional child-rearing.'[9]

This seems rather a harsh judgment: In order to understand the reactions of those parents in the past, whose experience and reactions were so different from our own, it is important to realise that longstanding customs that are part of a way of life do not die just because a few people know that they are harmful, or even because most people know they are harmful. And this is not because people do not care about the harmful results when they occur. The impetus of social custom easily overrides knowledge and common sense. There are many examples of this in our own society. For instance, young men have not stopped riding motor cycles, and often do not even ride them carefully, though they know that the death rate of young men on motor cycles is high. There has been little reduction in smoking since people have known that it is likely to kill them – indeed in some sections of the community, particularly the young, the consumption of cigarettes has actually increased. This does not mean that people do not *care* whether they die or not. They just cannot believe that it will really happen to them and meanwhile they carry on as they and their friends have always done. It is significant that one section of the community that has reduced its cigarette consumption is the medical profession. Doctors know more about the subject than most other people and are trained to take notice of new knowledge. It does not mean that doctors care more about their lives than other people. No one, so far as I know, has studied infant mortality among doctors' children in the eighteenth century. The results of such a survey might well show that the new knowledge was being put into practice there with good effect, long before it spread throughout the community. It is impossible to make reliable judgments about the feelings of those in the past or from a totally different culture, or to think that because of their reactions the expectations of their society were different, that they were somehow inferior to us. As Peter Laslett has written in his book with the brilliant title *The World We Have Lost*: 'The emotional pattern of that society has vanished for ever.'[10]

Until a few years ago historians had written little about the history of childhood and family life. 'Serious history' writes one who has tried to remedy the defect, 'has long been considered a record of public not private events. Historians have ... generally ignored what is going on in the homes around the playground.'[11] Previously what had been written about the history of childhood was mostly what one might call 'peripheral' or popular history, dealing with practical details such as dress, toys and games, rather than with ideas and influences. One important reason is the lack of sources. People do not on the whole keep records of what they consider to be unimportant. Laslett doubts whether we shall ever know much more than we do already about children in the world we have lost.[12] Yet children were present in 'a good 70 per cent of all households. . . . In the pre-industrial world there were children everywhere; playing in the village street and fields when they were very small, hanging round the farmyards and getting in the way, until they had grown enough to be given child-sized jobs to do; thronging the churches, for ever clinging to the skirts of women in the house and wherever they went and above all crowding round the cottage fires.' Yet 'these crowds and crowds of little children are strangely absent from the written record. . . . There is something mysterious about the silence of all those multitudes of babes in arms, toddlers and adolescents in the statements men made at the time about their own experience.'[13]

Knowledge of what ordinary families were like in the past has only begun to emerge in the 1960s and 70s with the 'new social history', which gives us information about unknown, ordinary people in the past, people who left no written record. The raw material for this knowledge came from historians patiently going through parish registers all over Europe and North America, slowly compiling genealogies of everyone living in a village and putting records such as court lists and tax lists onto magnetic tape for computer analysis. This kind of history is still only at its early stages but already much information has emerged which gives a very different picture of ordinary families in various times and places from the court gossip, diaries and chronicles of the rich and educated which is what has been predominantly available in the past.

During the past twenty years a number of important books have been published about childhood and family relationships in former times. They form a sound beginning to a subject about which our knowledge will doubtless increase and our ideas change. They also form an important background to the subject of motherhood and modern women. I shall therefore give a brief account of those recent history books that I have found most helpful, emphasizing those aspects of them which have most bearing on the problems and dilemmas of modern motherhood. All these books have been written during the last quarter century and are therefore cast, as they are bound to be read, in the framework of our modern (though not exclusively) beliefs that children need loving care, that early childhood experience has a profound influence on the adult personality, and that children are not born with vices that must be eradicated and controlled, but with personalities that need to be developed by good mothering and child care and by happy family life. I propose to discuss these books separately, partly because they are very different and scarcely overlap and partly because each one makes in its own way a special contribution to modern motherhood and can be discussed in a way that contributes to the theme of this book.

Recent books based on the 'new social history' were preceded, and in a way the stage was set, by an important book, *The Image of Childhood* by Peter Coveney, first published in 1957 (as *Poor Monkey*) and later revised. It is a study of childhood as it has been presented in literature written for adults in, for the most part, the nineteenth and early twentieth centuries. The author was impressed at the enormous growth in the number of books about children in English literature since the end of the eighteenth century. Before then the child did not exist as an important and continous theme in English literature. Apart from Elizabethan lyrics and later minor complimentary verse addressed to young 'children of quality' the child is scarcely mentioned. Yet, beginning with Blake's *The Chimney Sweeper* and Wordsworth's *Ode on Intimations of Immortality from Recollections of Early Childhood*, he becomes the object of considerable literary interest. Coveney believes that this change was the result of changes in society. At the end of the eighteenth century began a spiritual crisis as the world moved into the era of revolutions, both political and industrial. From that time European intellectuals began to become deeply concerned with

the maintenance of individual integrity within the search for the security of universal order. Society has been increasingly inimical to art and the influence of writers on public affairs has declined. In this context of isolation, alienation, doubt and intellectual conflict, the child became attractive as a literary theme. The child could symbolize the artist's dissatisfaction with the increasing harshness of society. It could symbolize imagination and Sensibility in an increasingly utilitarian world. It could symbolize Nature in a society riddled with forces that were actively re-naturing humanity. The child could also symbolize the conflict between Innocence and Experience, through whom could be expressed difficulties of adjustment, and feelings of insecurity, isolation, fear, bewilderment, vulnerability and potential vulnerability.

For some authors the child became a means of escape and withdrawal from a difficult world into a world of fantasy and nostalgia for childhood. An extreme example of this is Peter Pan. In others the child became an important symbol for the subjective investigation of the Self. Blake, Wordsworth, Dickens and Mark Twain all used childhood in this way. Later, the scientific investigation of the infant and child consciousness became important. Freud contributed greatly to this already-existing interest, and increased awareness of the child and objective appreciation of the importance of the childhood experiences to the development of the adult personality. Thus through writing of childhood there were those who wanted to go back to the beginning to begin again and others who wanted just to go back.

Another extremely influential, though much criticized, book is *Centuries of Childhood* by Philippe Ariès. Ariès is a demographic historian who, 'struck by the original characteristics of the modern family, felt the need to go back into the more distant past to discover the limits of this originality.' He emphasizes the difficulty of distinguishing clearly the characteristics of our living present, except by means of the differences which separate them from the related but never identical aspects of the past. The book is about the development of the idea of childhood, and, because children are essentially part of families, he examines the growth of the idea of the family. He points out that it is possible to regard the family as a biological rather than a historical phenomenon, which 'partakes of the immobility of the species' because it has always existed. Since the beginning of the human race, people have built homes and begotten children 'and it can be argued that within the great family types, monogamous and polygamous, historical differences are of little importance in comparison with the huge mass of what remains unchanged.'[15] On the other hand 'the great demographic revolution in the West, from the eighteenth to the twentieth century, has revealed to us considerable possibilities of change in structures hitherto believed to be invariable because they were biological.' He attacks the idea that the family constituted the ancient basis of our society and that, starting in the eighteenth century, the progress of liberal individualism had shaken and weakened it. The history of the family in the nineteenth and twentieth century has often been portrayed as one of decadence: the frequency of divorces and the weakening of paternal and maternal authority have often been seen as signs of its decline. But Ariès believes that, on the contrary, 'the family occupied a tremendous place in our industrial societies, and that it had perhaps never before exercised so much influence over the human condition. . . . The idea of the family appeared to be one of the great forces of our time.'[16] He goes on to examine evidence, including iconographical evidence, that the idea of family, like the idea of childhood, is relatively new.

In the medieval world, says Ariès, there was no place for childhood. Until the beginning of modern times, and for a long time after that in the lower classes, children were mixed with adults not long after they were weaned and immediately 'went straight into the great community of men, sharing in the work and play of their companies, old and young alike.' Collective life dominated society and 'carried along in a torrent all ages and classes, leaving nobody any time for solitude and privacy. The family ensured the transmission of life, property and names, but it did not penetrate very far into human sensibility.' Medieval society was not concerned with education. Only when it was gradually revived was it recognized that the child required preparation for life, 'a sort of quarantine before he was allowed to join the adults.' As a result the family, instead of being simply an institution which transmitted name and property acquired 'a moral and spiritual function, it moulded bodies and souls. The care expended on children inspired new feelings, a new emotional attitude . . . the modern concept of the family.' The family organized itself around the child 'and raised a wall of private life between the family and society.' People lost 'the old sociability' and family 'satisfied a desire for privacy and also a craving for identity: the members of the family were united by feeling, habit and their way of life. They shrank from the promiscuity imposed by the old sociability.' The change was originally a middle class phenomenon. When the middle class 'could no longer bear the pressure of the multitude or the contact of the lower classes,' it seceded. The quest for privacy and comfort further emphasized the contrast between the material ways of life of the lower and middle classes. 'The old society concentrated the maximum number of ways of life into the minimum of space and accepted, if it did not impose, the bizarre juxtaposition of the most widely different classes. The new society, on the contrary, provided each way of life with a confined space in which it was understood that the dominant features should be respected, and that each person had to resemble a conventional model, an ideal type, and never depart from it under pain of excommunication.' Ariès believes that the concept of family is a manifestation of intolerance towards variety and an insistence on uniformity.

Ariès has been much criticized for 'idealizing' children's lives in the old world, when they were free to mix with all classes and ages, for regarding childhood as 'invented', resulting in a tyrannical concept of the family 'which destroyed friendship and sociability and deprived children of freedom.'[17] Nevertheless his theory of the increasing restrictiveness of the family in modern times has important implications for the understanding of motherhood today.

Another influential book has been Peter Laslett's *The World We Have Lost*, published in 1965 and widely discussed and quoted. It is not a history of the family, or of childhood or of ideas about them, though it contains much information about these subjects. The words 'mother' and 'motherhood' do not appear in the index but the author gives us a fascinating picture of a world whose 'fundamental characteristic' was 'the scene of labour, which was universally supposed to be the home.'[18] The basis of the modern world is the separation of the private life of the worker and the work itself. 'Time was when the whole of life went forward in the family, in a circle of loved, familiar faces, known and fondled objects, all to human size. That time has gone for ever. It makes us very different from our ancestors.'[19]

How did these changes come about and what did they mean in terms of family life?

Two important books, published in 1975 and 1978, respectively, discuss family changes more directly. Edward Shorter's *The Making of the Modern Family* aims to be a general history of the average family in Western society and the New World, based on the 'new social history'. Lawrence Stone's magnificent and monumental *The Family, Sex and Marriage 1500–1800* was published three years later. Stone attempts to chart and document, to analyse and explain, some massive shifts in world views and value systems that occurred in England over three hundred years. He attempts to understand 'these vast and elusive cultural changes' by studying the way in which they expressed themselves in the ways members of the family related to each other, in terms of legal arrangements, structure, custom, power, affect and sex. The main stress of the book is on 'how individuals thought about, treated and used each other, and how they regarded themselves in relation to God and to various levels of social organizations, from the nuclear family to the state.' Studying the family is the means of obtaining a view of 'this wider landscape of cultural change.' Both Shorter's and Stone's books cover much the same ground in different ways and both throw much light on what we are trying to understand here, modern motherhood, because they give us an indication of how it has emerged in the way it has.

At the end of the Middle Ages, the beginning of the modern world, the usual pattern of family life, both in town and country, was very different from what it became later and also very different from many popular ideas about 'traditional' families. By 'family' is meant members of the same kin living under one roof. Shorter defined the term 'traditional' in a useful way as 'a *kind* of attitude that coincides closely with a certain *period* of time.' This attitude is characterized by permeability to outside influences and its members' sense of loyalty to their ancestors and kin. Hence Stone has called this type of family the 'Open Lineage family' and in his view it prevailed in Europe from the mid-fifteenth century until the mid-seventeenth century. The main ties were not between husband and wife and parents and children as they later became but to the wider group, village, community, as kin whether ancestors, living relatives or future generations. Its basis was economic: the protection and management of property and lineage and the means of transmitting property and lineage from generation to generation. It was a unit for production and reproduction rather than for emotional satisfaction – as Shorter puts it, being together at the dinner table was not important. Being part of the community was essential for economic survival. It was regarded as essential to conserve and increase property and to prepare coming generations to do what past ones had done. Happiness was regarded as something that could only be anticipated in the next world, not in this. Sex was regarded as a sinful necessity. Individual desires were not considered important and were subordinated to the interests of the group. Theologians advised that even affection should be prudently limited by the prospect of the early death of the subject. Spontaneity and individual variation were not encouraged. There was no privacy for anyone and no desire for privacy, even though the neighbours were continually watching. Stone writes: 'The gigantic flood of denunications of domestic moral transgressions that poured annually into the arch-deacons' courts between about 1475 (when good record-keeping began) and 1640 show that little went on in the home that was not noticed or reported by the neighbours.'[20] Marriages were arranged according to the advice of the group, either tying together two kinship groups or as an economic necessity for partnership and division of labour in the shops or in the fields. Essentially, it was based on material considerations. The emotional ties between husband and wife were hardly closer than those with neighbours, relatives or 'friends' – the group of influential advisors who usually included the senior members of the kin. Children, if they survived, did not stay long with their parents. They were sent away early to other households as servants or apprencitces. Infants were not con-sidered important, as their mothers had too much else to do to spend much time with them, particularly as the chances were they would not survive anyway. They were often left alone for hours on end while their mothers worked. Since adults tended to die young there were few old people and three-generation families were relatively uncommon. There was virtually no divorce, but because of the high death rate in young adults (those who had managed to survive child-hood were as likely to die in their twenties as they are in their sixties today), marriages lasted, on average, for a shorter time than in the mid-twentieth century, only about twelve to seventeen years. Then another spouse was taken, and often another family was introduced and yet another produced. Stone remarks, 'Indeed, it looks very much as if modern divorce is little more than a functional substitute for death.' He reckons that in the pre-modern families perhaps a quarter of all families were of this hybrid nature.

This open, unemotional, authoritarian and materialistic type of family gradually changed. Loyalties declined towards kin and com-munity and increased towards Church or sect. The nuclear family became more closed off, and its boundaries more defined. Patriachy, which had always been strong, was increased and was ac-tively encouraged by state and Church. These trends increased until the eighteenth century, greatly reinforced by the rise of puritanism. Domesticity and privacy increased, while ties with the outside world continued to weaken and the family unit became more and more of a shelter against them. Ideas about the value of the individual grew. Each member of the family became important in his own right rather than just a member of the kinship. Individual self-development and personal happiness became important. In America these trends were always more advanced than in Europe and the idea of the 'traditional' family crossed the Atlantic already mixed with the new ideas. During the eighteenth century these trends had reached an advanced stage of development. There was now in many families much greater freedom for children and equality between spouses; companionate marriages were common. In the Declaration of Independence of 1776 Thomas Jefferson substituted 'Life, Liberty and the Pursuit of Happiness' for the previous 'Life, Liberty and Property' as the three inalienable rights of men which it was the duty of the state to foster and preserve.

In this atmosphere much greater attention was paid to children. The farming out of babies to wet nurses, a source of much infant death, became unfashionable. In 1789 Lady Craven reported, 'You will find in every station of life mothers of families who would shrink with horror at the thought of putting a child for them to nurse.'[21] Particularly in the upper classes there was a shift to the 'permissive' upbringing of children to a degree not seen again until the middle of the twentieth century. Education often now took place at home and teaching methods became less authoritarian and brutal. As early as the late seventeenth century the Quaker William Penn advised parents to 'love them with wisdom, correct them with affection, never strike in passion, and suit the correction to their ages as well as the fault.'[22] In 1798 mothers were told that 'the first object in the education of a child should be to acquire its affection, and the second to obtain its confidence.... The most likely thing to expand a youthful mind ... is praise.'[23] The idea of Original Sin became less strong and it was felt that children should be allowed to do what they want as much as possible. There is a story that when the young Charles James Fox announced that he intended to smash a watch, his father Lord Holland said, 'Well, if you must, I suppose you must.' In 1782 Mary Butt (later Mrs Sherwood) visited a house where the son was lying in front of the fire. When told by his mother to get up and greet the visitor he replied, 'I won't.' Later Mary wrote 'I have lived to see this single specimen multiplied beyond calculation.'

It is doubtful whether this permissive form of family life reached far down the social scale and it seems to have been confined to

England and New England. During the same period there was an enormous and increasing scale of mercenary wet nursing among the labouring and artisan classes of urban France.[24] And in England during the next stage in the evolution of the family there was a strong revival of moral reform, paternal authority and sexual repression. The status of women declined and the ideal of womanhood became one of passivity and total submissiveness to husbands. The attitude to children became more intrusive and discipline more rigid. The open expression of emotion again became unfashionable and was condemned. Prudery became an obsession and girls were taught to assume that they were frail and sickly.

Nevertheless the standard of living was rising even for the proletariat. There was better nutrition, better housing, and a little money left over. Infant mortality was declining. Contraception was spreading. Even though methods were again repressive, concern for children was growing at all levels of society.

CHAPTER THREE

Projection, Reversal and Attack

A more direct attempt to trace the evolution of certain aspects of parent–child relationships as a factor in history can be found in *The History of Childhood*, edited by Lloyd de Mause, an influential book that was first published in 1974. The editor is both a professional historian and a committed Freudian. He applies Freudian ideas to the history of childhood with the fervour and certainty that many modern writers have brought to the subject of childrearing. The result is sometimes bizarre, but also interesting, informative and challenging. In these days when we see so clearly, particularly in relation to women, that Freud was a product of his time and that many of his views and theories, far from being universal truths, have meaning in the context of middle class Vienna in the nineteenth century, and when we have seen that psychoanalysts are no more successful in rearing their children than anyone else, it is disconcerting to find Freudian ideas applied so rigorously to other ages and societies. Nevertheless, the book is stimulating and, apart from the information it gives, provides excellent material for trying to test the validity of some of these psychoanalytical ideas which have tended to become received truths in our own time.

The History of Childhood is a collection of essays. The editor himself contributes the first and most far-reaching chapter. 'The history of childhood,' he writes, 'is a nightmare from which we have only recently begun to awaken. The further back in history one goes, the lower the level of child care, the more likely children are to be killed, abandoned, beaten, terrorized, and sexually abused.' He believes that the earliest periods of history were dominated by the 'Infanticidal Mode' of childrearing, in which parents 'routinely resolved their anxieties about taking care of their children by killing them.' This affected those who survived so that there was 'widespread sodomization of the child.' This is a curious idea.

From the fourth to the thirteenth century A.D. the 'Abandonment Mode' predominated. Parents began to accept the child as having a soul, so the only way they could escape the dangers of their own projections was by abandoning the child to the wet nurse, to the monastery or nunnery, to foster families, to the homes of other nobles as servants or hostages, or by severe emotional abandonment at home. De Mause suggests that symbols of this mode might be Griselda, who willingly abandoned her children to prove that she loved her husband, or the many pictures of the Virgin Mary rigidly holding the infant Jesus. At this time, 'the child was still full of evil and needed always to be beaten.'

De Mause describes how, since about 1250 childrearing has been gradually improving. The 'Abandonment Mode' was succeeded by the 'Ambivalent Mode' (1300–1600), when the child, when it was allowed to enter into the parents' emotional life, was still a container for dangerous projections, so that it was the parents' task to mould it into shape. During this period, parents displayed strong conflicting feelings of love and hate for their children, who were seen as 'soft wax, plaster or clay to be beaten into shape.' This period shows an increase in the number of child instruction manuals, the expansion of the cults of Mary and the infant Jesus and the proliferation in art of the 'close-mother' image.

In the eighteenth century, according to de Mause, the 'Intrusive Mode' predominated. He sees it as a period in which there was a tremendous reduction in projection and the virtual disappearance of reversal. The child was now much less threatening to the parents so that 'true empathy' was possible, infant care improved, infant mortality declined and paediatrics came into being.

The nineteenth and early twentieth centuries produced the 'Socialization Mode' in which the raising of a child became less a process of conquering its will than of training it, guiding it into proper paths, teaching it to conform and socializing it. Finally, de Mause produces his own favourite, called the 'Helping Mode', which he thinks began in the mid-twentieth century.

In his idea of progressive improvement, de Mause is thus immediately at variance with Ariès, whose view of traditional childhood he criticizes with some contempt for a misleading lack of psychoanalytic insight. De Mause attempts to assess how much of childhood history can be recaptured from the evidence that remains to us and suggests that the central force for change in history is neither technology nor economics, but the 'psychogenic' changes in personality occurring because of successive generations of parent–child interactions. He presents a number of hypotheses which form what he calls the 'psychogenic theory of history'. The first of these is that the evolution of parent–child relations constitutes an independent source of historical change. The origin of this evolution lies in 'the ability of successive generations of parents to regress to the psychic age of their children and work through the anxieties of that age in a better manner the second time they encounter them than they did during their own childhood.' He compares the process to psychoanalysis, 'which also involves regression and a second chance to face childhood anxieties.' He postulates that this 'generational pressure' for psychic change is independent of social and technological change, arising spontaneously in the adult's need to regress and in the child's need for relationship.

He believes that in each age the main source of child-rearing practices is the reduction of adult anxiety which occurs as approaches between adults and children become closer and closer. Obversely, he suggests that the further back one goes in history, the less effective parents are in meeting the developing needs of the child. He suggests that this would indicate that 'if today in America there are less than a million abused children, there would be a point back in history where most children were what we would now consider abused.' He also suggests that because psychic structure must always be passed from generation to generation through the narrow funnel of childhood, a society's child-rearing practices are not just one item in a list of cultural traits. They are the very condition for the transmission and development of all other cultural elements, and place definite limits on what can be achieved in all other spheres of history. Specific childhood experiences must occur to sustain specific cultural traits, and once these experiences no longer occur the trait disappears.

De Mause points out that such an ambitious evolutionary psychological theory cannot really be tested in a single book and so his immediate goal is to reconstruct from what evidence remains what it felt like to be a child and a parent in the past. He believes that most of what had previously been written badly distorts the facts of childhood in the periods they cover. Biographers tend to idealize childhood or fail to give useful information about the subjects' earliest years. Historical sociologists tend to produce theories explaining changes in childhood without examining actual families. Literary historians write about fiction as though it were life. Social historians tend to be deficient in psychological understanding and assessment.

His analysis, though limited, is relevant to the subject of this book for several reasons. First, it makes a serious attempt to apply psychological principles to the past in a way that can be helpful in understanding the problems of our own time. Second, it shows the way toward constructing a scientific history of human nature such as John Stuart Mill envisaged as 'a theory of the causes which determine the type of character belonging to a people or an age.' Third, it shows that motherhood and attitudes to children *have* changed. Its value is limited by its naïveté, through which, paradoxically, de Mause contributes to the idealization of motherhood. De Mause's simple belief that childrearing has been getting better and better over the years – supported by demonstrations of the obvious ways in which it has – leads him to ignore the ways in which it has not. He does not discuss the ways in which the increasing complication and sophistication of society lead to increasingly complicated and subtle ways of failing with children, which are often more damaging than the direct abuse he so much condemns. He does not discuss the revolutions that have taken place in sexual customs and in the position and expectation of women or the profound importance these are having on motherhood in our time. He does not look at motherhood from the point of view of the mother, which is actually just as important for the child and for society as a whole as it is to look at it 'empathetically' from the point of view of the child alone. He presents an already old-fashioned view of how children should be brought up, which seems to him to be the apex of the progress of mankind that has gone on through the ages: the parent should act towards the child in the way that a therapist acts toward a patient. It does not seem to occur to him that this is a sophisticated way not of becoming closer to a child but of distancing from him and thereby avoiding the pains of parenthood, using the very mental mechanisms which he condemns in the past. He describes their cruder, physical manifestations which were certainly commoner and acceptable in the past, but fails to notice that they live on in subtle disguises.

De Mause believes that in studying childhood over many generations 'it is most important to concentrate on those moments which most affect the psyche of the next generation; primarily this means what happens when an adult is face to face with a child who needs something.' The adult has, he believes, three major reactions available. First, he can use the child as a vehicle for projection of the contents of his own unconscious (projective reaction). He points out that this was common in the past and lies behind the concept of original sin. He quotes Richard Allestree in 1676: 'The newborn babe is full of the stains and pollutions of sin, which it inherits from our first parents through our loins.'[1] Baptism used to include actual exorcism of the Devil, and the belief that the child who cried at his christening was letting out the Devil survived long after exorcism was finally omitted from baptismal services. Children who cried excessively were thought to be changelings. Methods by which adults tried to control their own fears which they projected onto their children included frightening the child with ghosts, witches and devils who would get them if they misbehaved. A common practice was to take children to public executions or to view rotting corpses on gibbets.

De Mause writes as though projective reactions of parents are things of the past, but this is not so. True, parents today do not take their children to view rotting corpses and only the unsophisticated frighten them with threats of bogeymen or even policemen. But projection is also part of normal life and essential to successful child-rearing. Pride in one's children, their existence, characters, talents and achievements are projections of oneself and lead one to invest part of oneself in the children and devote time and energy to them. As a result, children gain feelings of personal enrichment. Life for them has a purpose. Without projections from parents the child tends to feel lost and purposeless. It is interesting that Freud seems to have believed that this kind of projection was the essence of parenthood: 'If we look at the attitude of affectionate parents towards their children we have to recognize that it is a revival and reproduction of their own narcissism. . . .' and again: 'Parental love, which is so moving and at bottom so childish, is *nothing but* the parents' narcissism born again.'[2] [emphasis mine]. Projections from parent to child still abound, for instance regarding the child in fantasy as a bad parent or as an instrument for acting out the parent's own unconscious antisocial desires. De Mause, despite his devotion to psychoanalytic theory, ignores these. Certainly projection is the basis of parenthood in a traditional society or in one whose changes are slow and scarcely noticeable. In the old world it was not necessary to go beyond it, and what was projected was by no means all bad. As de Mause writes, 'Projective care is . . . sufficient to raise children to adulthood.'[3] In an unchanging society people belong and know where they belong, but nowadays in a society that changes more rapidly than ever before and which is very different from Freud's, we know that children still need projections from their parents. Over most of the Third World projection still tends to be the customary pattern in childrearing, and it is not only concerned with evil projections and unpleasant thoughts. In the West, it is still important but something more is needed. Without a suitable social structure to support it, it can no longer predominate successfully. The result is that in highly projective families the mother herself is often, usually unconsciously, the terrifying creature who will punish if her projections are not appeased. Compliance, or trying to meet the expectations of others, usually the mother, and usually also unconsciously, is one of the biggest psychological problems of the western world today and it is doubtful whether it has diminished as de Mause suggests, though it has become less crude and less physical.

The second major reaction which de Mause believes a parent has available when a child is in need is the reversal reaction, in which the parent uses the child as a substitute for an adult figure important in his or her own childhood. It tends to be expressed in terms of what the child can give the parent and not what the parent can give the child. An example is seen in Euripides' Medea. Before she kills her children she complains that she won't have anyone to look after her in her old age. A common modern version is the woman, often a young, unmarried girl, who deliberately has a baby because she wants to have someone who will love her. Once born, the child represents the mother's own parent either positively or negatively, in a manner unsuitable to the child's actual age.

De Mause points out that the reversal reaction, in which the child is supposed to care for and provide for the parent was very common in the past and can begin long before the child is born in the powerful desire for children. The child is often dressed in the style of clothes similar to that worn by the parent's mother, at least a generation out of date. The parent's mother is thus reborn in the child. Ariès points out[4] that the first children's costume was the costume which everybody wore about a century before, and which now

61

became a style of dressing only for children.

A common idea in antiquity was that a grandparent is actually reborn in the baby, and various languages show similarity in the words for both (*baba, babuschka*). The breasts of infants were often kissed and sucked by adults and milk sometimes produced by the breasts of newborn babies due to circulating maternal hormones squeezed out by nurses. In our own time George du Maurier wrote of his newborn daughter: 'The Nurse brings her to me every morning that I may lick it with the "basting tongue". I enjoy the operation so much that I shall persevere till it reaches the age of discretion.'[5] 'One receives the impression,' writes de Mause, 'that the perfect child would be one who literally breast-feeds the parent.'[6]

According to de Mause, reversal reactions in parents virtually disappeared during the eighteenth century, though he admits that they are still found today in some parents who batter their children.[7] These parents expect the child to love them and when it cries they take this to mean that it doesn't. In fact, reversal reactions are still extremely common, much commoner than battering parents, though nowadays they are not usually so concrete as they seem to have been in the past. Most parents like and appreciate a caring attitude on the part of their children and this seems to stimulate and be part of normal mothering. Children who totally fail to respond in this way, for example, autistic children, are hard to love. Then, quite common are mothers whom we would now call immature, who expect their children to love them, pamper them, pander to their moods and generally look after them. Women who are lonely and under stress tend to use their children as parent-figures and confidants. In wartime, many children suffer anxiety from feelings of responsibility towards their mothers during their fathers' absence, and this is often increased by the father who tells the child to 'look after Mummy while I'm away.'

As children get older, and more of an age to care for their parents, reversal reactions tend to become more obvious. A big problem nowadays, as I shall discuss later in this book, is the devoted mother whose children grow up and leave home. Reversal reactions on the part of these mothers are particularly common and some will go to almost any lengths, such as perpetual drunkenness or serious illness, in attempts to persuade their grown children to stay at home and look after them.

As with projection, reversal reactions have become more subtle.

But they still exist and are widespread partly within the normal variation of individuals and partly in abnormal mother–child relationships which are damaging to the child and often to the mother as well.

De Mause tells us that projective and reversal reactions often occurred simultaneously in parents in the past, producing an effect which he calls the 'double image' where the child was seen as both full of the adult's projected desires, hostilities and sexual thoughts and at the same time as a mother or father figure. That is *both* bad *and* loving. He admits, however, that 'the further back in history one goes the more 'concretization' or reification one finds of these projective and reversal reactions, producing progressively more bizarre attitudes towards children. As he says, 'The child is loved and hated, rewarded and punished, bad and loving, all at once.' Again, he suggests that it is a reaction typical of parents in the past, not the present. Yet conflicting reactions are extremely common today but they tend to be subtler and are not usually acted out in a manner that is so overtly physical. We shall see some of them in the second part of this book.

When we come to questions of parents showing hostility toward their children, abandoning them and attacking them we find the same picture. The further back into the past we go the more overt and crude are the customs. The modern era is characterized by increasing subtlety of approach, by fewer physical manifestations of feelings and by an increase in theories about what to do and what not to do, but there are not necessarily fewer hostile feelings, fewer attacks or less powerful attempts to control.

In antiquity (for example, Sparta), and among primitive peoples infanticide and child abandonment were always common and its forms variable. Children were exposed on hillsides, flung into rivers and dung heaps, sacrificed on altars or even eaten.

It was only during the so-called Dark Ages and early Middle Ages that attitudes gradually changed. After AD 442 the finding of abandoned children was supposed to be announced in church and gradually asylums were founded for abandoned infants. In England infanticide was long regarded as a lesser crime than homicide. It was left to the Church, rather than the secular courts, and punishments were limited to shame – exposure in public or public whipping.[8] During the sixteenth and seventeenth centuries infanticide became a much more serious offence punishable with death because it deprived the infant of baptism. As a result it became almost totally confined to unmarried mothers. In 1527 a priest wrote that 'the latrines resounded with the cries of children who have been plunged into them.'

As late as the early eighteenth century in Anjou, priests were instructed to warn their congregations in a sermon every three months of the mortal sin of killing an infant before baptism. In America the practice of abandoning newborn children where they were likely to be found was almost non-existent,[9] but in Europe increasing numbers of children were left in the streets. During the 1730s, Captain Thomas Coram, on frequent walks from the docks into London, was so distressed by the sight of babies thrown out into dunghills that in 1741 he founded the famous Foundling Hospital 'to prevent the frequent murders of poor miserable children at their birth, and to suppress the inhuman custom of exposing newborn infants to perish in the streets, and to take in children dropped in church yards or on the streets, or left at night at the doors of church wardens or Overseers of the Poor.' But during and after the Industrial Revolution there was increasing employment for teenage children and many left home to earn their livings independently. This meant a great increase in illegitimacy and it was mostly illegitimate children who were abandoned. In the 1890s dead babies were still a common sight in the streets of London.

Today infanticide and casual abandonment have become, in comparison with former times, extremely rare. Not only do all the moral and legal forces of our society militate against it but it is no longer the easiest method of controlling the number of children.

Institutionalized abandonment is another traditional method by which parents have exercised their hostile feelings against their children. The most extreme form was the sale of children or using them as political hostages or as security from debts. In medieval times it was customary to give young children as hostages to guarantee an agreement and to make them suffer for their parents' transgressions. When Eustace de Breteuil, husband of a natural daughter of Henry I, put out the eyes of the son of one of his vassals, the king allowed the angry father to mutilate in the same way Eustace's daughter whom Henry held as hostage. Francis I, when taken prisoner by Charles V, exchanged his young sons for his own freedom, then promptly broke the bargain so that they were thrown in jail.[10] Many Anglo-Saxons and Scandinavians sent their children to other families to be reared and returned to the parents when they were seventeen years old. Up to about the eighteenth century most children of wealthy parents were sent away to a wet-nurse for their earliest years, returned home to the care of servants, and, at age seven, were sent away to service, apprenticeship or school. De Mause emphasizes that 'besides institutionalized abandonment practices, the informal abandonment of young children to other people by their parents occurred quite often right up to the nineteenth century.[11] Augustus Hare's mother was probably not unusual when she said, 'Yes, certainly, the baby shall be sent as soon as it is weaned; and, if anyone else would like one, would you kindly recollect that we have others.'[12] Among the English the practice of sending young children away from home persisted longer than in other countries, at least in well-to-do families. The public school system still flourishes and most of these are boarding schools which the boy attends from the age of twelve or thirteen. The entrance examinations for these schools are difficult and competitive and cannot usually be taken from a state school. So if boys are to reach the right standard at the right age they often have to be sent away to a suitable 'preparatory school', also boarding, from the age of eight. Recently an upper class mother, influenced by modern views on child care and filled with longing to keep her children at home said to me, 'I hate to let them go, but I really have to because I know that if I don't, they'll never get on in life.' This practice has however declined considerably in England since World War II and many parents, even if dedicated to the public school system, now find schools that their children can attend daily, at least during the 'preparatory' years.

In the past children whom parents decided to keep and raise were often attacked, mutilated or treated roughly. Renaissance parents would 'burn in the neck with a hot iron, or else drop a burning wax candle' on newborn babies to prevent 'falling sickness'. Throwing a swaddled child was sometimes practised. One little French child died in this way: 'One of the gentlemen-in-waiting and the nurse who was taking care of him amused themselves by tossing him back and forth across the sill of an open window. . . . Sometimes they would pretend not to catch him . . . the little Comte de Marle fell and hit a stone step below.' Doctors denounced the customary violent rocking of infants 'which puts the babe into a dazed condition, in order that he may not trouble those that have the care of him.'[13]

William Brehan in his *Advice to Mothers*, published in 1804, warns against cradles because of the common 'ill-tempered nurse, who, instead of soothing the accidental uneasiness or indisposition to sleep of her baby, when laid down to rest, is often worked up to the highest pitch of rage: and, in the excess of her folly and brutality, endeavours, by hand, harsh threats, and the impetuous rattle of the cradle to drown the infant's cries, and to force him to slumber.'

During the nineteenth century it was still common to dip children in cold water to tender them up or to make them atone for their sins. De Mause quotes one example in which a 'large, long tub stood in the kitchen court, the ice on the top of which often had to be broken before our horrid plunge into it.... How I screamed, begged, prayed, entreated to be saved.... Nearly senseless I have been taken to the housekeeper's room....'[14]

Another form of attack in children which was common in the past is sexual attack. The facts are difficult to obtain because, as de Mause points out, most libraries are Victorian in attitude and most books relevant to sex in history are locked up and are not available even to historians. But there is still much evidence that the sexual abuse of children was much commoner in the past than in the present. De Mause believes that the habit which has developed during the last two hundred years of punishing children severely for their sexual desires was the product of 'a late psychogenic stage' in which the adult tended to restrict his own sexual fantasies through restraining the child rather than acting them out on him. Pederasty was common in ancient Greece and Rome. Boy brothels flourished and children were sometimes sold into concubinage. Plutarch said the reason why freeborn Roman boys wore a gold ball round their necks when they were very young was so men could tell which boys it was not proper to use sexually when they found a group in the nude. Suetonius condemned the Roman Emperor Tiberius because he 'taught children of the most tender years, whom he called his *little fishes*, to play between his legs while he was in his bath. Those which had not yet been weaned, but were strong and hearty, he set at fellatio....'[15] But the favourite sexual use of children was anal intercourse, especially with boys who had been castrated for the purpose.

The sexual innocence of children was a Christian concept and the long campaign against the sexual use of children had Christian origins as did the later customs which began in the eighteenth century of punishing the child for touching its own genitals. The myth developed, and was widely propagated by doctors, that masturbation would cause insanity, epilepsy, blindness and death. This gave a new excuse for attacks on children. This reached its height during the nineteenth century, when it was quite common for both doctors and parents to threaten to cut off the child's genitals, and restraint devices were common. Circumcision became widespread and clitoridectomy and infibulation were sometimes used as a punishment for masturbation in girls. It is interesting to note that by 1897 Freud decided that most of his patients' reports of early sexual seductions were fantasy, yet he was not at all concerned, in the history of his famous subject, Judge Schreber, with the fact that this man's father was a paediatrician famous for his use of devices of torture.

Again, we can pick out these examples from a world that was in many ways much more crude than our own. Today we attach much importance to the physical care and sexual protection of infants and young children and this has improved to a marked degree. But, in recent years we have discovered, to the astonishment of some, that the battering of infants by their parents is actually increasing in our society. The psychological battering of children in this so-called enlightened age is probably much greater but is more difficult to detect or to measure. We know that hostile feelings of mothers towards their children and fantasies of attack are extremely common.[16] Although overt attack is undoubtedly less frequent, we cannot say that hostile feelings have diminished. We can only say that, like projective and reversal reactions, they have become less obvious.

When we come to de Mause's 'Helping Mode', the triumph of the late twentieth century, we meet a theory which is likely to be both familiar and depressing to those who work professionally with parents and children. The 'Helping Mode' seems to consist largely of the parents behaving rather like full-time joint psychotherapists to their children. The helping mode 'involves the proposition that the child knows better than the parent what it needs at each stage of its life, and fully involves both parents in the child's life as they work to empathize with and fulfil its expanding and particular needs.' Parents make no attempt at all to impose discipline or to form habits. Children are neither struck nor scolded. Parents devote 'an enormous amount of time, energy and discussion' to helping a young child to reach its daily goals which means continually responding to it, playing with it, tolerating its regressions, being its servant rather than the other way around, interpreting its emotional conflicts and providing the objects specific to its evolving interests.[17] Few parents, he tells us, have yet consistently attempted this kind of child care and he cites (among others) A. S. Neill, headmaster of the progressive school Summerhill which started between the wars and whose ideas have not proliferated, and his own son who has apparently been brought up by this method.

Before accepting this one needs to realize that these ideas have been around for much longer than de Mause believes. He says they began in the mid-twentieth century but in fact they were strong in Britain and the United States in the 20s and 30s and have since declined. One needs to speculate on why the progressive school movement, so popular with British parents, particularly intellectual parents, between the wars and popularized not only by Neill but also by Bertrand and Dora Russell, no longer thrives. One needs to know why it is that these ideas are no longer so popular as they were before although they produce, according to de Mause, children who are 'gentle, sincere, never depressed, never imitative or group-oriented, strong-willed and unintimidated by authority.'

The theory behind the 'Helping Mode' is based on the principles of applied psychoanalysis, and many people who were once its devotees have discovered that it tends to produce children who have severe difficulties in adult life in making their own way. The children may have the characteristics mentioned by de Mause but they tend to have others too, for the theories on which they have been raised abound in denial, which, like the projection and reversal already discussed, has profound consequences in growing children. It is an extremely cerebral process, denying the passions of family life by 'interpreting' them in an intellectual way, and the children are left without boundaries, without common sense, and often with an extraordinary inability to cope with the world. Here is one example.

A married couple thought that they knew all the answers to child-rearing. The mother, a woman of strong personality, had been a social worker in a children's therapy clinic. The father, who was rather weak, was a psychotherapist. They decided that at no stage should their two children be frustrated because they believed that the child knows better than the parents what it needs. Both parents were very involved in their children's lives and spent a great deal of time playing with them and helping them to develop their interests. Frustration and difficulty were dealt with by interpreting the children's conflicts as they saw them. 'Discipline' and 'good habits' were positively avoided. They never hit the children and made every effort not to frustrate them or to impose any boundaries on them. They spent a great deal of time discussing the children's emotional life.

What was striking about these parents was that they were as full of projection and reversal reactions as any old-fashioned parents who beat their children and felt no guilt or who left them to fall in the fire and then felt that God had punished them for their sins. The difference was that they did it in the modern way. Like parents in the past they denied to themselves that they were doing anything but what was right. What was clear to the observer was that these children as they grew up had no boundaries in their lives and were always pushing to try to find them. The daughter, to her parents' alarm, married a foreign revolutionary and went with him to his own country where they both eventually received long jail sentences for preparing explosive devices. The son dropped out of school without a single qualification. (He was an intelligent boy but the frustration involved in working for examinations was beyond his capacity to tolerate.) He worked in a series of jobs, mostly organized through contacts of his parents, but was invariably sacked after a few weeks, mostly for trying his bosses' patience to the limit or for doing things on his own initiative to an absurd degree. I thought of this family when I read de Mause's theory of how the old projections and reversals which parents exercised in former times have given way to what he calls the 'Helping Mode' and believes that it is the ultimate in 'progress'. Both these young people could be described as 'gentle, sincere, never depressed, never imitative or group-oriented, strong-willed, and unintimidated by authority' but they would be described by most people as 'quite impossible' and both are making messes of their lives.

To sum up then, there seems no doubt that physical brutality in all its forms has declined immensely and is probably less now than ever before. But this does not mean that we have made progress in other ways or that we now have a particularly effective way to deal with the feelings and the conditions that engender hostile attacks on children. We also have many other problems not faced by our ancestors. Modern childrearing probably involves just as many projection and reversal reactions as did childrearing in the past, but because they are based on modern circumstances and modern theories we tend to accept them without question; it is as difficult for us to see them as it was for our ancestors who were imbued with the spirits of kinship, community, or religious fervour. We must now concentrate on these modern trends if we are to understand motherhood and modern women.

CHAPTER FOUR

Fashions in Child Care

We have seen that until modern times babies were taken much less seriously than they are now and through most of history children were regarded as small adults. When special interest was taken in the very young, the overwhelming problem was how to keep them alive. This is a strong motive behind all writing about child care right into our own century. The first major writer on child care who seemed to take it for granted that the child would survive was Dr. Spock in the middle of our own century. True, the Victorians added strong moral overtones to their advice, but basically it was a question of survival. It is not surprising that the earliest writers on child care, like most of the influential ones ever since, were doctors. Each age projects its own problems into its advice on child care.

The first person whom we know to have written on child care was Hippocrates. None of his works deal specifically with children (this may be because what we have is incomplete), but he did leave us one treatise dealing with a particular period of childhood, which he called 'On Dentition'.[1] It is interesting that the obsession with teeth and belief that teething is a cause of the problems of infants lasted right down the ages and can still be found today. Hippocrates at least showed awareness that children are different from adults and that infants need special care.

Aristotle was interested in the resemblance between children and parents. He was probably the first to study the physiology of the normal infant, and he made observations such as 'All children directly they are born have their eyes bluish, but afterwards these change to the sort they are destined to remain.'[2] He also noticed the differences between the proportions of the body in the infant and the older child and asserted that they were a factor in determining the date at which a child walks.[3] It was 450 years before another

71

physician, Celsus, wrote his *De Medicina*, in about A.D. 55. He was the first author to state categorically that 'children require to be treated entirely differently from adults.'[4] The first known treatise which deals specifically with children was written by Soranus (A.D. 98–138). He thought about infant care in a detailed way and like all ancient writers, in terms of symptoms.

The first book in child care to be translated into English and printed for practical use was Roesslin's *Rosegarten*, first published about 1512 and printed in London in 1540. It contains sections on 'Howe the infant newly borne must be handled nouryshed and looked to,' 'Of the nourse and her mylke and howe longe the child shold soucke,' and 'Agaynst fearefull and terrible dreames.'

The first work on diseases of children ever written in the English language was the *Boke of Children* by Thomas Phaer, probably first published in 1544. It devotes much space to the quality of the breast milk, another obsession that lasted until our own times, doubtless because of the high infant mortality, the custom of putting children out to wet-nurses, and the difficulties of choosing these. Phaer was not unaware of emotional disturbance, and, like so many right into our own times, advised physical treatment for it.

There were many popular books published on the subject during the next three centuries, many and and they mostly deal with physical health and disease. One of the most important was published in 1748 by the Committee of the Foundling Hospital, London. It was called 'An Essay upon Nursing and the Management of Children from their Birth to Three Years of Age', and was written in a pioneering spirit by William Cadogan. He was concerned with the excessively high death rate of infants which he believed was partly due to ignorance and customs handed down from generation to generation. If anyone wants proof of the faulty character of the present mode of managing children, he says, 'let him look over the Bills of Mortality, there he may observe that almost half the number of those that fill up the Black List are under five Years of Age.' Some of Cadogan's advice would still be relevant today:

> The first great Mistake is that they think a new-born Infant cannot be kept too warm: from this Prejudice they load it and bind it with Flannels, Wrappers, Swathes, Stays, etc. commonly called Cloaths, which all together are almost equal to its own Weight, laying aside all those swathes, bandages, stays

and contrivances, that are most ridiculously used to close and keep the Head in its Place and support the Body, as if Nature, exact Nature, had produced her chief Work, a human Creature, so carelessly unfinished as to want those idle Aids to make it perfect. Shoes and Stockings are very needless Incumbrances, besides that they keep the Legs wet and nasty if they are not chang'd every Hour.[5]

Cadogan insisted that the baby should be put to the mother's breast soon after birth and that nothing else be given first. He advised plenty of light, and also cow's milk, (though he specifically says it should not be boiled and also advises feeding infants with 'Good Bread'). He recommends that the sucking child should be fed 'Twice a day and not oftener' but that 'as to the Quantity at each Time, its Appetite must be the Measure of that.' The child is to be 'kept clean and sweet, tumbled and toss'd about a good deal, and carried out every Day in all Weathers.' (There were of course no perambulators or baby carriages until the early nineteenth century.) He inveighs against the practice of sending children out to nurse: 'I am quite at a loss to account for the general Practice of sending Infants out of Doors to be suckled or dry-nursed by another Woman, who has not so much Understanding, nor can have so much Affection for it as the Parents: and how it comes to pass that People of good Sense and easy Circumstances will not give themselves the Pains to watch over the Health and Welfare of their children: but are so careless as to give them up to the Common Methods, without considering how near it is to an equal Chance that they are destroyed by them. The ancient Custom of exposing them to wild Beasts or drowning them would certainly be a much quicker and more humane way of despatching them.'[6]

The book attracted much attention. It went through at least ten editions in England over twenty-five years. William Cadogan became a famous and popular physician and was several times Censor of the Royal College of Physician and Harveian Orator.

By the end of the eighteenth century the value of child life was appreciated much more than earlier. Even the lay press – the *Spectator*, the *London Magazine* and the *Tatler* – all urged improvements in the care of infants. The widespread desertion of infants was becoming a matter of public concern. Attitudes were becoming gentler towards children. In general, moral control became the hallmark of childrearing. The emphasis was often on psychic, rather than physical, control. Glenn Davis (1976) has surveyed thirty years of popular nineteenth century American magazines including *The Mother's Magazine and Family Circle*, *The Child at Home*, *The Mother's Journal* and *Family Visitant* and finds 'a fairly homogeneous ideological definition of the maternal role', which evolved only slightly over thirty years.[7] In 1833 the charter of the association that was to begin publishing *The Mother's Magazine* announced that one reason for its formation was to show 'the best method of regulating the temper and disposition of children' and communicate to mothers 'the full importance and responsibility of their tasks'. Davis writes, 'As the stage of childhood was elevated in correspondence with the emergence of intensive socialization through psychic control, so the position of the mother was defined as the chief molder of the child.' Though the father remained absolute sovereign in the household and the final and often the only vote concerning the management of worldly affairs, it was the mother who was now entrusted with 'the monumental test of intimate socialization.' He quotes typical passages from these magazines to show how they are 'filled with a concern for tying the child to the mother as tautly as possible.' These include: 'The destiny of a nation is shaped by its character: and that character, the aggregate character of all its individual citizens, will ever be found to be molded chiefly by maternal hands' and 'As the first impressions on the mind of a child are the most permanent, so are they also exceedingly important.' The mind of a child may be likened to 'a piece of . . . paper, the surface of which, being free from every strain, as far as actual transgressions is concerned, may be made to receive whatever impressions we see fit to stamp on it.'

But meanwhile, alongside these gentle thoughts, something more unpleasant was going on. This was a growing obsession with control, morality and sex that runs right through the nineteenth century and into the twentieth. Much of this obsession centred on masturbation, which was widely thought to be an immoral act that caused insanity. This idea can be traced back over centuries. As early as 1715 a book was published anonymously called *Onania or the Heinous Sin of self-pollution, and all its frightful consequences (in both sexes)*: 'This abominal sort of impurity is that unnatural practice by which persons of either sex may defile their own bodies without the assistance of others, whilst yielding to filthy imaginations.' The author describes 'licentious masturbators' in terrifying terms: 'we shall find them with meagre jaws, pale looks, with feeble Hams and legs without calves, their Generative faculties ... destroyed.... A jest to others and a torment to themselves.' This book became a bestseller throughout Europe and was translated into several languages. By 1830 it had reached its fifteenth edition and it continued to sell widely and be reprinted for many years.[8] It was rewritten by Tissot in 1758 under the title *Onanism: or a treatise upon the disorder produced by masturbation*, in which he 'raised masturbation to the position of a colossal body.'[9] He claimed that sexual excesses of all kinds, but especially masturbation, were liable to cause widespread physical and mental disorders, particularly of the nervous system. During the early years of the nineteenth century the belief that masturbation caused physical disease declined with the increased belief that it was a major cause of insanity.[10] Benjamin Rush, Professor of Medicine at Philadelphia, who wrote the first American textbook of psychiatry (1812) warned that masturbation commonly caused insanity. In 1848 Dr. Samuel Howe wrote 'One would fair be spared the sickening task of dealing with this disgusting subject; but as he who would exterminate the wild beasts that ravish his fields just not fear to enter their dark and noisome dens, and drag them out of their lair – so he who would rid humanity of a pest must not shrink from dragging it out from its hiding-places, to perish in the light of day.'

At this time there was much concern about an increase in the number of lunatics, which led to the building of large public asylums to contain them. It is doubtful whether there was a real increase or whether it was only apparent, due to the increase in the population, better counting methods, better diagnosis, greater awareness of their presence, perhaps influenced by the madness of George III. But true or untrue, doctors attributed the increase in madness to masturbation, and after the middle of the nineteenth century childrearing became inextricably linked in the minds of many with strong and essential measures which it was felt must be taken against masturbation and potential insanity. Childrearing advice became more aggressive. David[11] attributes this to the new parents who were reacting against their own upbringing in the age of psychic control.

It was into this atmosphere that a sinister figure appeared in the middle of the century. He has been described as 'the first guru of the

nursery'.[12] His name was Dr. Daniel Gottlieb Moritz Schreber
(1808–61). His influence on childrearing was profound. Dr. I. M.
Politzer wrote of him in 1862, 'Every age produces its man who
expresses its spirit as if with the power of Providence . . . the generation of our century demanded and created a man like Schreber.'[13]
He was widely renowned as a great pedagogue. Freud said that his
work 'exerted a lasting influence on his contemporaries.' His books
went through many editions and translations in many languages
which, wrote Politzer, were 'the most glowing testimonial that his
doctrines and methods have been adapted by most people.' He was
read widely not only in his native Germany but also in France,
England and America. His system and theories have been linked
with Nazism. A friend of mine who was brought up in Hamburg in
the 1920s and 30s told me that her upbringing was 'definitely Schre-
berian'.

Schreber's book which deals most with the upbringing of children was his *Kallipädie*, whose title when translated reads *Education
towards Beauty by Natural and Balanced Furtherance of Normal Body
Growth* (1858). Other titles include *The Characteristics of the Child's
Organism* (1852), *The Harmful Body-Positions and Habits of Children, Including a Statement of Counteracting Measures* (1853), *The
Systematically Planned Sharpening of the Sense Organs*, (1859) and
*The Friend of the Family as Pedagogue and Guide to Family Happi-
ness, National Health, and Cultivation of Human Beings: For Fathers
and Mothers of the German Nation*.

Schreber believed in the supremacy of the father:

> When the man can support his opinions by reason of demon-
> strable truth, no wife with common sense and good will will
> want to oppose his decisive voice.[14]
> If one wants a planned upbringing based on principles to
> flourish, the father above anyone else must hold the reins of
> upbringing in his hands. . . . The main responsibility for the
> whole result of upbringing always belongs to the father. . . .'[15]

Schreber believed that for the sake of health, moral, mental and
physical, harsh disciplines were needed, starting with cold baths for
babies and constant discomfort.

> The noble seeds of human nature sprout upwards in their
> purity almost on their own if the ignoble ones, the weeds, are

sought out and destroyed in time. This must be done ruthlessly
and vigorously. It is a dangerous error to believe that flaws in a
child's character will disappear by themselves. The blunt
edges may disappear, but the root remains, shows itself in
poisoned impulses, and has a damaging effect on the noble tree
of life. A child's misbehaviour will become in the adult a
serious fault in character and opens the way to vice and base-
ness.[16]

He thought it 'especially important and crucial for the whole of life
with regard to character ... to form a protective wall against the
unhealthy predominance of the emotional side against that feeble
sensitiveness – the disease of our age, which must be recognized as
the usual reason for the increasing frequency of depression, mental
illness, and suicide.'[17]

He believed that parents should start to follow the 'law of habitua-
tion' when the child is about five months old:

> *Suppress everything* in the child, keep everything away from
> him that he should not make his own, and guide him persever-
> ingly towards everything to which he should habituate
> himself.
>
> If we habituate the child to the Good and Right we prepare
> him to do the Good and the Right later with consciousness and
> out of free will.... The habit is only a necessary precondition
> to make possible and facilitate the proper aim of *self-
> determination* of free will.... If one lets the wrongly directed
> habits take root, the child is easily put in danger; even if he
> later recognizes the Better he will not have the power any more
> to suppress the wrongly directed habit....[18]

Still referring to infants under one year he writes:

> Our entire effect on the direction of the child's will at this
> time will consist in accustoming it to absolute obedience,
> which has been in great part prepared for already by the appli-
> cations of the principle laid down previously.... The thought
> should never even occur to the child that his will could be in
> control, rather should the habit of subordinating his will to the
> will of his parents or teachers be immutably implanted in
> him.... There is then joined to the feeling of law a feeling of
> impossibility of struggling against the law; a child's obedience,

the basic condition for all further education, is thus solidly founded for the time to come.[19]

and he continues 'Now, the ways and means of developing and consolidating moral will power and character do not need to be sought... The most generally necessary condition for the attainment of this goal is the *unconditional obedience* of the child.'[20]

Schatzman has commented: 'He sees a child trained to obey parents unconditionally as "nobly independent" and likely would have induced a child to see himself similarly. While teaching a child to do what parents wish, he teaches him to think he does what he, the child, wishes and makes it hard for the child to see he is still doing what his parents wish, which might be what the child would *not* wish, were he able to think clearly. Dr. Schreber seems unaware he is misrepresenting submission as freedom: he appears to see submission *as* freedom.'[21]

Schreber had strong views about deportment:
... One must see to it that children always sit straight and evensided on both buttocks at once ... leaning neither to the right nor left side.... As soon as they start to lean back ... or bend their backs, the time has come to exchange at least for a few minutes the seated position for the absolutely still, supine one. If this is not done ... the backbones will be deformed...[22]

He invented shoulder bands to hold back the shoulders, 'straightholders' to force children to sit straight, belts to tie children down in bed to make sure they lay flat while asleep, and a head-holder with chin clamp which was firmly strapped and pulled the child's hair if he did not hold his head straight.

Not unexpectedly Schreber has plenty to say about sexual matters. He refers to nocturnal emissions as 'pollutions' which are associated with 'nervous overstrain' of 'over-tense nerves'. He suggests an extraordinary series of exercises (paradoxically, most of them highly masturbatory) to be done from four to one hundred times a day and if these do not work he suggests a complicated ritual of baths, enemas and washing the sexual organs with cold water. He forbids masturbation, as Schatzman says 'sometimes without saying what he forbids, why he forbids it, why he does not say what he forbids, or that there is something he does not say....' Schreber leaves no doubt, however, of his views on youthful sexuality:

One must strictly see to it that children rise immediately after awakening in the morning, that they never stay lying awake or half asleep. . . . That is because with this is mostly connected the temptation of thoughts into an unchaste direction. The secret sexual strayings of boys as well as girls, well known to doctors, teaches us that we must keep keenly aware of this point already many years before the development of puberty. For this very reason . . . sleeping in unheated rooms is absolutely to be preferred from now on if this is already not the case.

Schreber was anxious that his system should have enduring effects. He dedicated his *Kallipädie* 'to the salvation of future generations.' He urged governments to 'take in hand "children's training" in a much more serious way than has happened before'.[24] He impressed Freud, who wrote of him:

(He) was no insignificant person . . . (his) memory is kept green to this day by the numerous Schreber Associations which flourish especially in Saxony . . . His activities in favour of promoting the harmonious upbringing of the young, of securing co-ordination between education in the home and in the school, of introducing physical culture and manual work with a view to raising the standards of health – all this exerted a lasting influence upon his contemporaries. His great reputation as the founder of therapeutic gymnastics in Germany is still shown by the wide circulation of his *Ärztliche Zimmergymnastik* (Medical Indoor Gymnastics) in medical circles and the numerous editions through which it has passed.[25]

The Schreber Associations mentioned by Freud continued to flourish. According to one source in 1958 there were over two million members in Germany.[26]

The Freud connection is of special interest for several reasons. First, Freudian ideas have had a considerable influence on theories of bringing up children, yet Freud himself clearly saw no flaws in the Schreber system. Second, both Schreber's sons went mad, and one of them, Daniel Paul, was analyzed vicariously by Freud and is the subject of a famous paper by him. Freud does not seem to have considered a possible connection between the methods of the father and the madness of the son. This connection is the subject of Morton Schatzman's fascinating book, *Soul Murder: Persecution in the Family.*

Meanwhile the speciality of paediatrics was growing and it was from this field that subsequent advances in child care came. We must remember that paediatricians in the nineteenth century were particularly concerned, as they are now, with keeping children alive and physically healthy. Abraham Jacobi (1830–1919), the first professor of paediatrics at New York Medical College, was one of the first to recommend the boiling of milk used for infant feeding.[27] The next 'guru of the nursery' was Luther Emmett Holt (1855–1924). His book *The Care and Feeding of Children* was published in New York and London in 1894, went through many editions, and was enormously popular and influential. Older American mothers will remember it well. Significantly, the subtitle of the book was 'A catechism for the use of Mothers and Children's Nurses.' 'Reading Holt's book is like journeying back into the elegant world of tea dances at the Ritz, summers at Newport, Gatsby-like champagne parties on the lawns at Easthampton. Baby, with his or her petticoats and "fine flannels", was not brought into the fun, like today's infant on mother's hip at midnight parties, but kept in the higher reaches of the mansion with nurse in charge.'[28] Holt advised a simple, boring diet for children until the age of three (gruel, cereal, hominy grits, milk, no sugar). He was obsessed with cleanliness. Much of the book was concerned with the details of dealing with teats and bottles and getting rid of germs. This advice was very much needed at the time but he carried it rather far. He advises against kissing babies because of the dangers of transmitting 'tuberculosis, diphtheria, syphilis and many other grave diseases'. This may sound rather ridiculous today but was probably sensible advice in the days when those diseases were rampant and babies often died of them. He still carried the feeling of the time about masturbation, which he describes as 'the most injurious of all the baby habits', although he did suggest it be stopped not by punishment but by rewards.

American mothers, at least the affluent ones, followed Holt. For the English, the guru at this time was Frederick Truby King, three years younger than Holt, and not so obviously directed in his work towards the rich mother. Truby King was a New Zealander. His theories were worked out in a society where infantile diarrhoea alone

– caused by lack of hygiene – killed one baby in forty every year. He believed passionately that proper hygiene and raising babies in an environment as free from germs as possible was the most important aspect of caring for them. He proceeded to prove his point. Due to his teaching on infant hygiene, the death rate of infants from infantile diarrhoea in Dunedin dropped between 1907–22 to only one per thousand. He was deeply concerned about the children of the poor and most anxious to show what percentage of different foods a healthy baby needed, how long his mother could safely leave him and so on. He worked with livestock, decided how much protein their milk should contain and applied the same principles to babies. He found that even babies living in the very poorest circumstances flourished if their mothers had been taught the value of proper and regular feeding, regular weighing, hygienic techniques and fresh air. He believed so strongly in the importance of hygiene in saving babies' lives that he paid little attention to mother love. To him a loving mother was no good to her infant if she infected him with lethal diseases.

Truby King worked out a scheme of rigidly regular 4-hour feedings. No baby was to be fed until the clock struck, no matter how much he cried. Most particularly, they were not to be fed at night. They had to learn to sleep at the proper times and not be allowed to manipulate and dominate their mothers by their demands. Regularity of bowel movements were important and he advised pottraining from the age of two months, aided by enemas if the baby did not perform. He advised against much physical contact, particularly at bedtime, since he thought that babies were 'hypersensitive' due to the delicate structures of their brains and could easily become over-excited. Such 'spoiling' could have dire effects in later life. He wrote: 'Half the irritability and lack of moral control which spoil adult life originates in the first year of existence.'

It is interesting to speculate why a man whose main work had been on infants reared in poverty and ignorance became the nursery guru of the British middle classes. The short, but incomplete, answer must be that his ideas caught the spirit of the time. People wanted to know exactly what to do with babies. Mothers were beginning to realize that it was not necessary to lose so many babies and that they could be saved by adequate feeding and proper hygiene. The old fatalism based on the idea that infant death was the will of God was giving way to a new, more scientific attitude. Awareness of germs, a passion for cleanliness and a liking for scientific measurement were all gaining ground. Truby King turned motherhood into a 'craft' that could be learned and a baby into something that could be controlled. He became so popular that nearly all members of the British middle classes who were born between 1915 and 1950 were brought up by Truby King's methods. So powerful was he that mothers and nurses who did not adhere to his instructions felt guilty. The remnants of his teaching lasted in the teaching of doctors, nurses and health visitors even longer. When I was bringing up my babies in the 1950s it was an exceptional doctor or clinic nurse who did not try to insist on mothers applying the Truby King principles.

Nevertheless, there were other ideas abroad, though for a long time they penetrated little further than the *avant-garde*, the intellectuals and the Bohemians. In 1927 Sir James Spence in Newcastle-on-Tyne set up the first mother-and-baby unit. He believed that separation from the mother had deep psychological and physical effects on the child. In 1929 Susan Isaacs began to write about young children for *Nursery World* and during the next few years she published a number of books on the subject. She felt that there was a desperate need for children to be understood and she encouraged mothers and nannies to try to feel themselves into the situation of the children in their care and to try to help the child to attain the independence that he seeks.

In 1941 there was concern in America about the high rate of mortality among infants in hospitals and Dr. H. Bakwin and others realized that infants who were dying ostensibly of diarrhoea and 'wasting diseases' were actually dying from lack of cuddling. Untrained but motherly people were used in order to pick up and cuddle the babies. The babies stopped dying. René Spitz pointed out that once they survived physically it was clear how much they had been affected psychologically.[29] In England Dr. D. W. Winnicott, a paediatrician and psychoanalyst, gave wartime broadcasts to mothers emphasizing the importance of early relationships with infants. He talked about 'the care of the whole child, the whole child who is a human being with a constant need for love and imaginative understanding. The point is that you have done so much more than provide food, clothes and warmth'.[30] Anna Freud, working in a wartime nursery with small children who were separated from their parents, became convinced that young children needed to be cared for by their own mothers.

During and immediately after the war mothers were rebelling against the authoritarian rules of Truby King and his followers. Because of the disappearance of servants during and after World War II most mothers who would previously have had servants and who themselves had had nannies were bringing up their own infants. They could see and feel for themselves that the rigid schedules, the absence of cuddling, the fear of spoiling, were not good. Infantile infections were no longer a serious problem, as the powdered milk feeds and bottles were boiled and antibiotics quickly cured any infection that did occur.

Dr. Spock burst on a mothers' world that was tired of Emmett Holt and Truby King and he hit just the right note. 'Trust Yourself', he wrote. 'You know more than you think you do. . . . Don't be overawed by what the experts say. Don't be afraid to trust your own common sense. . . . We know for a fact that the natural loving care that kindly parents give their children is a hundred times more valuable than their knowing how to pin a diaper on just right or how to make a formula expertly. . . . What good mothers and fathers instinctively feel like doing for their babies is usually best. . . . Better to make a few mistakes from being natural than to do everything letter-perfect out of a feeling of worry.' Yet he does not idealize parenthood: 'The fact is that childrearing is a long, hard job and that parents are just as human as their children.' After all the dire warnings of previous generations, his attitude about such matters as masturbation is soothing. He describes it as a 'wholesome curiosity', and 'related to his feelings' . . . 'an urge . . . for reasons that are easy to understand'. The book is written in simple language pervaded by an air of confidence. Although Dr. Spock was trained not only as a paediatrician but also as a psychoanalyst, there is no psychoanalytical jargon in his book. It was exactly what mothers wanted. No wonder the book has sold over twenty-five million copies in thirty languages.

Spock has been criticized for ushering in the era of permissiveness leading to the 'Spock-marked' generation, full of drop-outs, junkies and neurotics. Yet his book is not really permissive. It contains plenty of definite advice about controlling children: 'Extra aggressiveness needs curbing. . . .' 'I don't think that you have to sit mute and just take it,' 'If the parent ... can firm up her discipline, she may ... be delighted to find that her child becomes not only better behaved but much happier,' and 'You can be both firm and friendly.'

Spock trained as a Freudian psychoanalyst but his books have never delved deeply into psychoanalytical theory and his influence has always been largely practical. The theoretical change in attitude has come via Dr. John Bowlby, a British Freudian psychoanalyst who is almost contemporary with Spock. He wrote no manual of child care. He didn't work with normal mothers or write about them, as did his influential colleague Anna Freud. He didn't communicate with mothers directly by writing or talking to them as did D. W. Winnicott in his famous wartime broadcasts addressed to 'the ordinary devoted mother'. He did some famous work on children in institutions and on monkeys. Yet more than anyone else in this half-century he has influenced mothers, professionals in child care, government agencies and governments themselves. He has had so much influence that many people who should know better seem to have forgotten that he did not actually write about normal mothers and children in normal situations. His ideas were transposed onto them.

To understand the reasons for this we shall have to go back to the changes that had been taking place in feelings and beliefs about children.

CHAPTER FIVE

Psychological Needs

One of the outstanding changes during the present century has been the recognition that the earliest years have a crucial influence on later personality and on the ability to cope with life. The first writer to record the profound influence of early experience in relation to motherhood was probably Wordsworth. In *The Prelude* he describes how the relationship with the mother conditions the way in which a child learns to perceive things and how this remains for ever in his mind.

The first writer to discuss the profound influence of the early years in a 'scientific' way and to apply it to problems and neuroses in later life was Freud. It is an aspect of his work that has been amply supported by later research in both human and animal infants; it has become so much part of our accepted knowledge that even those who believe most strongly in inherited influences do not doubt that it is true. Many changes of belief have occurred since the time of Freud and these have modified and are modifying informed opinion on the subject. One of these that has particular importance in child-rearing concerns psychological trauma. Freud believed in the importance of traumatic incidents in the formation of character. This has lingered on in popular belief, as though neurosis is 'caused' by some unfortunate and damaging incident in early life. Many people still think that the job of the psychiatrist is to 'find the cause and root it out'. But in fact we now realize that most so-called traumatic incidents that appear to be damaging in later life are actually manifestations or results of a continuous situation and often actually represent the moment when something became clear to us or when feelings that already existed unconsciously became conscious. Many people have the feeling that they were seriously affected in childhood by, for instance, a minor sexual assault, admission to hospital, getting lost in a crowd or other temporary separation from mother, or even by starting school. In fact such incidents probably only appear to be damaging because they became the focus of anxiety in those already sensitised. Those who are not previously sensitised to them do not experience these things as traumatic. For instance, the child who has absorbed from his mother a fear of sexual matters will appear to be much more 'traumatized' if a strange man fondles his genitals than a child who has not absorbed this fear. Similarly a child who has come to depend for his security on the continuous presence of his mother or who has had no opportunity to make relationships with strangers or has been actively prevented from doing so, will be much more affected by starting school, going into hospital or getting lost in a crowd.

It is of course true that sudden incidents that are overwhelming are likely to have a permanent effect on a child. Examples might be the death of a parent, a sudden uprooting and loss of everything familiar, or being raped. But the effects of even such extreme experiences vary considerably from individual to individual. They depend on what the child was like before and on the nature of the continual situations and influences in its life. Since, for most young children today 'continual situations' mean largely the personality and behaviour of their mothers, this has important implications for motherhood and modern women. As things are at present, much emphasis has been and is still placed on the importance of the mother's presence and the fact that she loves and cares for her child and little emphasis is placed on the importance of her personality and the nature of her love and caring. The reasons for this state of affairs are complex but largely discernible. They relate to the politics and economics of our time, to how public money is spent and taxes raised, to what people are paid and the way in which our society does or does not invest in its children. They relate also to the position of women and the idealization of motherhood that is characteristic of our century. More will be said of this later.

Few of us now believe that the Original Sin of children should dominate our ideas about them. We also do not believe that moral education should take precedence in the attentions we pay to children. We think more in terms of children's psychological needs, and to us the term 'need' no longer means violence, constraint and compulsion which is what it meant in earlier times. In relation to children we no longer even use the word in its general current meaning;

'a condition marked by the lack or want of some necessary thing'. We now tend to anticipate this state of affairs when we talk about children's needs and discuss them more as though they were in the same category as food, air, water, etc. without which the human being cannot survive. We do not wait until we are starving before considering our need for food; likewise, we try to do this with the children's psychological needs. This is partly because we do actually know a good deal more about the conditions under which infants and children flourish or wither. But it is also symptomatic of our particular way of looking at motherhood. We tend to think in terms of the ever-present all-providing mother who anticipates the needs of her infant, supported by an ever-present, all-providing state which is also engaged in the process of ministering to the needs of children in the light of modern belief and knowledge. This concept is what makes modern attitudes to children different in quality from those in the past, and comes from psychological theory and, in particular, from psychoanalysis, based originally on the work of Freud and developed by his followers, particularly Anna Freud, Melanie Klein and D. W. Winnicott.

We believe today, and there is considerable evidence to support it, that children need a sense of security and warm continuous relationships with adults, usually their own parents, if they are to develop well. They need to be protected from situations and problems with which they are too young to cope and to be introduced to changes in their lives gradually in ways that they can manage. There is however a good deal of argument about what is meant by 'a sense of security' and by 'warm continuous relationships'. For the past thirty years it has been widely and passionately believed that a child's 'sense of security' can only come from a warm, continuous relationship with one person and one person only, i.e. the mother or mother-substitute. This belief was first popularized in 1951 by Dr. John Bowlby in a monograph commissioned by the World Health Organization. He wrote:

What is believed to be essential for mental health is that the infant and young child should experience a warm, intimate and continuous relationship with his mother (or permanent mother-substitute) in which both find satisfaction and enjoyment. . . . A state of affairs in which the child does not have this relationship is termed 'maternal deprivation'.[1]

Partial deprivation brings in its train acute anxiety, excessive need for love, powerful feelings of revenge and, arising from these last, guilt and depression. . . . Complete deprivation . . . has even more far-reaching effects on character development and may entirely cripple the capacity to make relationships.

These ideas, and the report to which they were central, had a profound influence on the western world. They were further developed in his series of books *Attachment and Loss*. It is interesting that Bowlby's views were formed from the study of children in institutions who had no mothers or mother-figures at all. What he was actually studying was not maternal deprivation but institutionalization. Yet his views were widely interpreted to mean that it was essential that ordinary mothers everywhere should stay with their young children all the time. I have even known it to be seriously discussed whether it is 'psychologically safe' for a mother to leave an infant for an hour or two with his grandmother or with a neighbour, whether the 'trauma' of this 'separation' might damage its psychological development. But this was only an extreme form of ideas that were propagated everywhere – by doctors and social workers, psychologists and psychoanalysts, by official policy and by the media, particularly the women's magazines. The wide spread of ideas about the dangers of separating mother and child even for short periods, the way in which it was taken up in official circles and used for political and commercial convenience, and also the way in which it was supported by the mothers of the time themselves makes it one of the most interesting phenomena of the mid-twentieth century. We are now beginning to see, as we have seen all along (but only as voices crying in the wilderness), that this view of motherhood and of the needs of young children, when taken out of context and used for other purposes, can be just as false and just as misleading as the old ideas that children were individually unimportant and expendable or that the dominant problem with them was dealing with Original Sin or their moral development.

Yet it has been promoted strongly by state and society for over thirty years. There are a number of reasons for this. First, in Britain and to a smaller extent the United States after World War II, there was a great desire to restore families to 'normal'. Jobs were needed for men: women should not be encouraged to go to work. Collective child care was expensive and not to be encouraged. Middle class women, usually in the forefront of fashions in both theory and in practice, took up the ideas and applied the Bowlby theory to themselves. Many had had childhoods that had been overshadowed by mother-substitutes or nannies or else disrupted by war and they felt uncertain of their capacity to be good mothers. Bowlby and his followers *seemed* to be saying that all they had to do was stay with their children every minute of the day and everything would be all right. They fell for it in large numbers, supported by the women's press. Many saw the truth in Bowlby's theories. To many they were an enormous relief. They gave simple guidelines by which an undoubtedly important aspect of infant development could be understood by even dim mothers and professional workers and could be used simultaneously to allay the anxiety of mothers, to keep women tied to the home thus making things comfortable for men and avoiding competition, and to save government money that would otherwise undoubtedly have to be spent on children in view of the discovery of the importance of the early years. Today there is much talk in child care circles about 'bonding', the affective ties that develop between an infant and whoever cares for him. These bonds are known to be of profound importance in his development. As a result, some people behave as though bonding was the *only* aspect of childhood that matters. This narrow view deriving from Bowlby and still more from his followers has led not only to greater understanding of children but also to ignoring on a vast scale their other needs. These include the need for stimulation and opportunities for play, variety of experience and a stable, happy mother with the opportunity to be a mother in the way that best benefits her and her children. It also ignores the enormous variation in personality among mothers, many of whom are capable of being good mothers but not if they have to mother in this way. Put into practice it has also exposed vast numbers of infants to the exclusive care of women who are incapable of satisfying infant 'needs' in this way, but who happen to be their mothers. Exclusive care means that there is no escape and thus the child has no opportunity to rectify the situation or to find satisfactions that his own mother cannot supply. The fact that these matters have been ignored whereas the undoubted truth that young children need stable and continuous relationships with their mothers has been exploited to the full by state and society is one of the most important characteristics of motherhood in our time. This restricted view of the needs of young children is now being challenged but not before it has exerted a dominant influence on our pattern of motherhood.

Bowlby was describing deprivation of many things, yet chose to select the mother. The world chose to select this piece of writing and give it enormous importance, neglecting some of his other comments, such as 'In place of the broken home we need to put the concept of the disturbed parent-child relationship..... If the child's developing relationships with his mother and his father are used as the focal point, data of far greater precisions emerge, and much that is obscure in the origins of mental illness becomes clear,' and 'Parent-child relationships have many dimensions and there are many other ways in which they may become pathogenic. The commonest are (a) an unconsciously rejecting attitude underlying a loving one, (b) an excessive demand for love and reassurance on the part of the parent, and (c) a parent obtaining unconscious and vicarious satisfaction from the child's behaviour, despite conscious condemnation of it.'[2] However, public emphasis was all on 'separation'. Just as a whole generation of women felt guilty if they fed their babies outside Truby King's regular schedules, a whole generation of women now felt guilty if they had to leave their babies or felt unable to be good mothers for twenty-four hours a day. This kind of thinking dominated the generation following World War II and is still widespread today. It is fundamental to the subtle idealization/denigration of mothers which has accompanied increased public spending in other areas of life, such as health, education and unemployment. It has been a profoundly important influence on the women's movement and is a fundamental reason why, as we shall see, women's liberation has never come to terms with motherhood. It has led to many missed opportunities and has contributed to many of our present problems and dilemmas. It also reflects the attitudes of our society. We pay much lip service to the psychological needs of children, particularly in the restricted ways described, and very little to the needs of their mothers. Yet the truth is that an unsatisfied or unhappy mother cannot be at her best as a mother and this must reflect on her child. The bad effects of this ignoring of mothers' needs, following time-honoured methods of controlling women, including their idealization, is beginning to show in our society. We now know that many of the children of the 'Bowlby generation' are disastrous. We have epidemics of 'dropping out', and of suicidal gesture, wrist-slashing, anorexia nervosa, drug-taking, adolescent alcoholism and vandalism. Usually in the background of such cases is disturbance in the mother-child relationship. Middle-aged mothers, unable to cope with their children's adulthood, crowd every doctor's waiting room. Something has gone seriously wrong with motherhood in our time. In order to understand this more fully we must first explore the subject of idealization of mothers and the way in which this is related to the theories and influence of John Bowlby and others.

CHAPTER SIX

Idealization of the Mother

Perhaps better than anyone else, politicians understand the expediency of idealizing the mother. Here is a report of Richard Nixon's farewell speech on resigning the presidency:

> '... my mother,' at this point he sobbed violently, his tears somehow eluding the gravitational pull and remaining shining in his eyes – 'a saint. She will have no books written about her.'[1]

The thirty years following World War II, and in America the thirty years before that, could be described as the age of idealization of motherhood. One way in which this is shown is in the extent to which our society emphasizes the importance of the family, of mother love, mother-infant attachment and constant mother care, while at the same time making life increasingly difficult for mothers, doing little to help them beyond the physical health of babies and young children, and taking no steps to help mothers adapt to our fast changing world or to adapt that world to their needs and those of their children. Politicians of all parties make speeches about the sanctity of family life and the importance of families, but this is usually hot air which provides excuses for not spending money on mothers and children.

Idealization of parents is not new. Glenn Davis, in his *Childhood and History in America*, discusses a feature that was common in the nineteenth century. 'Idealization of the parents and a massive lack of self-worth demanding continual effort' was the basis of evangelical child-rearing. Davis' describes this as omnipresent, 'diffusing itself throughout mid to late nineteenth-century American life.' As an example he quotes a letter from one of Francis Wayland's sons to his brother. It was written just after their father's death in the middle of the nineteenth century.' Did you ever remark the resemblance between the character and that of Jesus of Nazareth? I speak with reverence. His unselfishness, his care of others, his courage for righteousness and justice, his sympathy for the suffering, his pity for the fallen, his prayerfulness.'[2] Much idealism was also directed specifically at the mother. Davis quotes The Rev. B. Stowe in 1850: 'A sign, a single sentence, a message received, a book loaned or given, and even a look, has, in thousands of instances, changed the entire character of a life, and placed a man where he never would have been, but for that single circumstance.' Another example, from *Mother's Assistant*, reads, 'Yes, mothers, in a certain sense, the destiny of a redeemed world is put into your hands,'[3] while *Mothers Magazine* in 1861 produced 'There is a special need that *maternal influence* – about, if not absolutely, the mightiest influence God has given to human being – should be sanctified, and all on the side of God. That influence lives while others die.'[4]

This form of idealization is full of fantasy with moral and religious overtones. It differs from the idealization of the mother that is characteristic of our time, which is not on the whole religious and not particularly moral, but has political overtones. One link between the two is the idealization of the mother which occurs in children who see little of her and whose day to day care is the responsibility of someone else. This subject is discussed by Jonathan Gathorne-Hardy in his book *The Rise and Fall of the British Nanny*.[5] He points out that children who are brought up by nannies tend to idealize their mothers, and, lacking the opportunity to make realistic assessments of her, they often carry this idealism over into adult life with marked effects on their sex lives and on their attitude to women in general. Before discussing this further we need to go into the nature, origins and effects of idealization.

Idealization can be described as a feeling of love towards something or somebody towards whom one actually has feelings of both love and hate. The hate is ignored and so kept from consciousness. The love is unrealistic because it is separated from the hate with which it is actually inextricably connected. Thus it becomes illusory, in that it is supported by distorted or falsified perception, which is used unconsciously to prevent the hate from becoming conscious. If it is pointed out that hate is actually present alongside the love, angry reactions are liable to be provoked. In his *Critical Dictionary*, Charles Rycroft points out that idealization in the sense of regarding some person as perfect and wonderful involves projection of parts of oneself as well as idealization. This means that one denies that one feels such and such but asserts that someone else does. 'Idealization differs from admiration in that (a) the idealizing person needs a perfect person to exist and ignores the existence of those attributes of the idealized person which do not fit the picture, and (b) it leads to dependence on and subserviance to the idealized person and not to emulation and imitation. Idealization is a defence against the consequences of recognising ambivalence and purchases freedom from guilt and depression at the cost of loss of self-esteen. Failure of the defence leads to disillusion and depression.'

In his interesting paper *On Idealization, Illusion and Catastrophic Disillusion*,[6] Rycroft indicates a number of important connections. (Since his paper was written for professional psychoanalysts and originally published in the International Journal of Psycho-Analysis, it uses psychoanalytical jargon. I have attempted to explain some of the points he makes in somewhat simpler form and language and hope that I have not thereby altered his meaning significantly.) The sequence of events goes something like this. The child loves the mother, invests much emotion in her, and needs her love. He also needs her to provide the stimuli enabling him to develop his love. If she fails to satisfy him or fails to provide the right stimuli, his love for her begins to wane. This is intolerable for him for without this love life is meaningless. So he withdraws his love and feeling away from her as a real person and directs it inwards, towards the image that he has of her in his mind. He splits this image into good and bad and directs his attention and his love only onto what is good, which he elaborates in his imagination. What is bad he ignores, denies or projects elsewhere. Thus he is in love with the 'idealized' image of his mother in his own mind rather than with his mother as a real person. And since the pattern of later loving relationships usually follows the first relationship with the mother, people who have developed in this way tend to repeat the pattern, idealizing those people, things, causes, or institutions that they care about in later life. This is the only way in which they can avoid the feelings of helplessness and hopelessness which arose at the original withdrawal of love from the real mother; and the only way they can avoid facing the hate mixed with the love which would have to be faced before they can again direct their feelings out towards a real person.

Since idealization is based on illusion, there is always the danger of disillusion, and this tends to happen in idealized relationships. The person one idealizes may not respond, in which case the disillusion comes from the lack of reciprocity. Or the person does respond, in which case of course he or she responds as a real person and not in a 'perfect' way, and this, to the person who idealizes, may be intolerable. So there is disillusion with anger, bitterness, emptiness and hopelessness.

One way of maintaining illusions is by making sure that the hate which has separated off from the idealized love is placed somewhere. For instance a man might keep his wife as an idealized image of perfection and go round trying to humiliate prostitutes or women with whom he works or attacking all ideas of freedom or choice for women in general. This is an important mental mechanism in male chauvinism, and is also the basis of Gathorne-Hardy's theory that the idealization of the mother by children brought up by nannies in Victorian nurseries led to the Victorian sexual underworld in which lower class girls were enjoyed sexually by upper class men who meanwhile kept their wives in comfort and purity, assuming that they had no sexual instinct. One still sees examples of this today.

Another way of dealing with the hate that is concealed in the process of idealization is by actually letting it out on the idealized person who is thus both idealized and injured at the same time. This method of idealization is important in the position of women today. A man may idealize his wife, regard her as perfect, set her on a pedestal, and express his hate towards her by controlling her – refusing to countenance the idea of her working or doing anything for herself, expecting her to be at his beck and call, insisting on rigid separation of labour, keeping careful watch on her movements, and perhaps actually degrading her and turning her into less of a person than she was before, a mere appendage to himself to be used for his convenience.

Conversely there is sometimes a kind of inverted idealism, which actually starts with the desire to use, control or humiliate. A kind of pseudo-idealism is set up as a compensation to the humiliated person or as a means of keeping the process going. This mechanism is illustrated in a story I heard on the radio about Mrs. Thatcher visiting an omnibus station. After being photographed repeatedly standing at the door of a bus she said 'Please stop photographing me or I'll begin to look like one of the clippies.' At this point, realizing what she had said, a practised sweet smile spread over her face and she added 'who of course are all doing a grand job of work.' Whether or not this story is true, most politicians are highly skilled at presenting idealized views of people whom they actually despise or wish to ignore or humiliate.

The idealization of motherhood as a social phenomenon in our time is a mixture of all these mechanisms. It can be regarded as part of the idealization of homemaking that took place in America after World War I and in Britain after World War II. During the war in Britain women without children under the age of fourteen were drafted. But at the end of the war the men came back. They wanted the jobs and they wanted wives to look after them at home. Many people felt that women needed controlling if homes were going to be run and men served in the style to which they were long accustomed. Women had to be put back in their place. One of the most effective ways of achieving this was to idealize that place.

At the end of World War II babies and young children had become a special problem, particularly in Europe. Many had lost their homes, their countries, their parents. At the same time the effect of good feeding had been amply demonstrated. Britain's wartime rationing schemes had brought a good if plain diet to large sections of the community who had never eaten healthily before. The result was an enormous improvement in child health and a drop in infant mortality. Yet at the same time there had been loss of support for the mother engaged in childrearing. Many of the cities had been bombed and much of the traditional community life of the working class had been destroyed. These were rebuilt as high-rise estates with no thought for the freedom or play of children or the community life of mothers. The whole middle class had lost its servants. Families who before the war would have had a nanny for the baby and a maid to open the door even if they found it hard to pay for the Sunday joint were now without domestic help or dependent only on the occasional services of a daily woman or foreign *au pair*. It was expensive for the government to run the day care centres that had been set up during the war to encourage mothers to work, so there were strong political pressures to save money and reduce unemployment by pushing women back into the home and finding moral justification for so doing. Consumer pressures added to this, for women do most of the shopping and the better a woman looks after her husband the more he is likely to earn, and the more time she has free the more likely it is that she will pass this free time in spending the money that she encourages her husband to earn. All these things were motives for deliberately increasing the idealization of mothers in an attempt to make them content with their lot. By being idealized, they could be controlled and, when necessary, denigrated.

What was new about this situation was the *official* idealization that now occurred. One might say that women had won enough freedom so that government action and pressures were now needed if they were to be kept down and segregated. The medium through which this official idealization was channelled, and also the medium through which it was accepted by the mothers, was the work of John Bowlby. The reason why it was chosen for support by official bodies is easy to see. It was catchy. It was convenient. It was cheap. It helped to solve a lot of problems that would otherwise be troublesome. The way in which Bowlby's work was tailored and directed towards governmental aims is interesting to analyze. The way in which his ideas have been kept going while excluding their obvious corollaries and implications is in itself an example of the idealization of motherhood. I shall endeavour to discuss the complex reasons why a whole generation of mothers embraced these ideas, if not without discomfort, then at least without serious questioning or protest.

It does not seem that Bowlby was deliberately commissioned by governments to find means of driving women back into the home, though this was the result. In April, 1948, the Social Commission of the United Nations decided to make a study of the needs of homeless children.[7] They were described as 'children who are orphaned or separated from their families for other reasons and need care in foster homes, institutions or other types of group care'. Few people can have thought that an investigation into such a subject would be central to a social revolution. When the specialized agencies interested in the matter were approached for their comments and suggestions, the World Health Organization offered to contribute a study of the mental health aspects of the problem. The offer was accepted. Bowlby was appointed to make the report. He was a doctor, a Freudian psychoanalyst, with a particular interest in mother-child relationships, and a member of the British upper class and heir to a baronetcy. I believe that all these facts are relevant to the report he produced, to its immense subsequent influence, and to the fact that only certain implications of the report were followed up while others were quietly dropped.

Since Bowlby's report, published in 1951, was concerned with children who were orphaned or separated from their families and living in institutions, it is not surprising that its conclusion was that 'an infant and young child should experience a warm, intimate and continuous relationship with its mother (or permanent mother-substitute) in which both find satisfaction and enjoyment.' In other words, almost any mother is better than no mother at all, and if one is thinking of war orphans, abandoned children, etc. this must be true. For such children mother love must seem to be the most important need without examining too closely the possible nature of that love. Bowlby therefore rejected the pursuit of the study of varieties of mother, how different mothers mother best, how some mothers are unsuitable to be mothers, and how disturbed relationships in a family are enormously important in the origins of mental illness. He mentions these things but tells us, 'These themes do not concern this report.'[8]

One would have thought that a logical consequence of Bowlby's report would have been to ensure that problems of variation in mothering would become extremely important once we were dealing with children who do have mothers. But these have never been popular themes. What happened was that certain aspects of Bowlby's report were taken out of context, blown up out of proportion and used to support the idealization of motherhood. As Rutter wrote, 'Bowlby's claim in 1951 that "mother-love in infancy and childhood is as important for mental health as are vitamins and protein for physical health" was probably correct, but unfortunately it led some people (mistakenly) to place an almost mystical importance on the mother and to regard love as the only important element in child rearing. This is a nonsense and it has always been a *mis*-interpretation of what was said in the 1951 report. Nevertheless, this view has come to be widespread among those involved in child care.'[9]

My suggestion here is that the reason why this exaggeration and *mis*-representation took place was to enhance the idealization of motherhood that was developing as a result of women's difficult social role at the time. The themes about good and bad mothers which Bowlby mentioned in passing were clearly of little concern to orphans but equally clearly they are very important when one considers children who do have mothers, as most children do. They are therefore central to consideration of motherhood, but to take those up at the time would not have increased the idealization of motherhood. On the contrary it would have damaged it by bringing disillusion into the illusion of mother love. So to perpetuate the ideal the idealizing process itself was used on the theory that supported it. Mother love was assumed to *be* as Bowlby said it *should be* and matters such as individual variation and unsatisfactory relationships were ignored until they could be ignored no longer and were then relegated to the doctor to treat as physical disease or eventually to the psychiatrist or the courts to treat as mental disturbance or deviance.

Bowlby himself has contributed to this process. Though he mentioned individual variation fleetingly, he then somehow managed to lose sight of it, both in the World Health Organization Report and in his later writings. He never discusses it in detail or emphasizes its importance. Sometimes he seems to forget it, even when he is writing about motherless children, and he describes what is really an idealized version of mother love as though it applied to normal family situations. For instance, Chapter 7 of the Report is called 'The Purpose of the Family'. He repeats his dictum that 'the infant and young child should experience a warm, intimate, and continuous relationship with his mother (or mother substitute), in which both find satisfaction and enjoyment.' He goes on to tell us that 'the child needs to feel he is an object of pleasure and pride to his mother; the mother needs to feel an expansion of her own personality in the personality of the child: each needs to feel closely identified with the other. . . . The provision of mothering cannot be considered in terms of hours per day but only in terms of the enjoyment of each other's company which mother and child obtain.' But he does not go on to discuss what happens when the relationship between the child and his mother is not warm and intimate, or when the child does not feel that he is an object of pleasure and pride and the mother does not feel an expansion of her own personality in the personality of her child. Instead he ignores all this and continues, 'such enjoyment and close indication of feeling is only possible for either party if the relationship is continuous. Much emphasis has already been laid on the necessity of continuity for the growth of the child's personality. It should be remembered too, that continuity is necessary for the growth of the mother. Just as the baby needs to feel that he belongs to his mother, the mother needs to feel that she belongs to her child and it is only when she has the satisfaction of this feeling that it is easy for her to devote herself to him.' The implication here seems to be that the remedy for difficulties is more continuity and he goes on to prescribe 'The provision of constant attention day and night, seven days a week and 365 in the year, is possible only for a woman who derives profound satisfaction from seeing her child grow from babyhood, through the many phases of childhood, to become an independent man or woman, and knows that it is her care which has made this possible.' There is nothing here about the woman who does not derive profound satisfaction from her children or who finds that her joy and satisfaction in them is considerably diminished by the constant attention that Bowlby insists is essential.

Paradoxically he continues 'It is for these reasons that the mother-love which a young child needs is so easily provided within the family and is so very very difficult to provide outside it.' This is the remark of an administrator, not of someone who knows about mother love and young children. It is really just another way of saying that if infants have mothers, it is much easier for the authorities to ignore them than if they do not have mothers and as long as you assume that all you need to do is to provide a mother then you don't have to spend any money. Bowlby says 'The services which mothers and father habitually render their children are so taken for granted that their magnitude is forgotten. In no other relationship do human beings place themselves so unreservedly and so continuously at the disposal of others. This holds true even of bad parents – a fact far too easily forgotten by their critics, especially critics who have never had the care of children of their own. It must never be forgotten that even the bad parent who neglects her child is nonetheless providing much for him. Except in the worst cases, she is giving him food and shelter, comforting him in distress, teaching him simple skills, and above all is providing him with that continuity of human care on which his sense of security rests. He may be ill-fed and ill-sheltered, he may be dirty and suffering from disease, he may be ill-treated, but, unless his parents have wholly rejected him, he is secure in the knowledge that there is *someone* to whom he is of value and who will strive, even though inadequately, to provide for him until such a time as he can fend for himself. It is against this background that the reason why children thrive better in bad homes than in good institutions and why children with bad parents are, apparently unreasonably, so attached to them, can be understood.'

Again Bowlby draws attention to 'the partial deprivation of living with a mother or parent mother substitute, including a relative, whose attitude towards him is unfavourable.' He admits that such cases are 'very numerous and of all degrees of severity from the child whose mother leaves him to scream for many hours because the baby books tell her to do so to infants whose mothers wholly reject them. The partial forms of maternal deprivation, due sometimes to ignorance but more often to unconscious hostility on the part of the mother deriving from experiences in her own childhood ... comprise a large fraction of all ... cases.' But he again dismisses it. 'This report has for its purpose the consideration of the grosser forms of deprivation,' he pronounces, 'And it is to the prevention of these that attention will be given.' Yet, having told us that the mother love which a child needs 'is so easily provided within the family', he now tells us that 'the great majority of cases of grosser forms of deprivation are the result of family failure.' The two statements seems to be contradictory until one realises that he is looking at it almost entirely from the administrative point of view.

So, although his words have undoubtedly been misrepresented and exaggerated, Bowlby's report was written as though it was calculated to increase the current idealization of mothers and to decrease the expense of young children to governments. But why was it so convincing to the parents themselves? There must be many answers to this. I shall only attempt to provide a few. First, Bowlby writes convincingly. Although in a way, particularly in his later books, he writes objectively, often about monkeys, nevertheless one can sense the passion. He has strong feelings about separating mothers and children and these feelings come through in his books. He feels that mothers should be there all the time, as he puts it 'constant attention day and night, seven days a week and 365 in the year'. This is to him much more important than how a mother feels about it, whether it suits her personality and ultimately her child, or what happens if she can't do it. I am convinced that the same kind of feelings were present in those who idealized Bowlby and who accepted his idealized version of mothers. Until the late 1940s almost no member of the British upper or middle class had experienced the continuous care of a mother 'seven days a week and 365 in the year'. Those who had had this experience would have had mothers who

101

were freaks and so would have had other problems. Yet, as we have seen, children brought up by nannies tend to idealize their mothers. They see her from afar and think how wonderful it would be if they could be looked after by her. The reality would always be very different from their expectations but because they have no opportunity to experience this they have difficulty in coming to terms with their real mothers. So the idealization lingers on.

Hence Winston Churchill:

> My mother always seemed to be a fairy princess: a radiant being possessed of limitless riches and power.... She shone for me like the evening star. I loved her dearly – but at a distance. My nurse was my confidante....[10]

Churchill's mother, a teenage socialite, would probably have been incapable of giving him continuous care even if it had been forced upon her. Many women from this class and much further down the social scale, when faced with the necessity of caring for their own children, as they mostly were after World War II, had mixed feelings of fear and excitement tied with remnants of their own childhood and the idealized views of mother which they had developed in the nursery. When governments and experts actually told a mother with such memories that continuous mother love was essential to mental health she tended to believe them, even though neither she nor anyone she knew had themselves experienced it. And when this was reinforced by statements such as Bowlby's that 'the mother-love which a young child needs is so easily provided within the family,'[11] it seemed the obvious thing to do. Once she was actually caught up in the business of childrearing as a 24 hours a day, seven days a week occupation, she was likely to deal with this by idealizing it still more. For by that time she had discovered that rearing children was not easy at all, that machines could only help with washing and cleaning, not with unrelenting exposure to babies and children, continual interruptions or the constant necessity for watchfulness and attention. The only thing for many mothers to do at that stage was to idealize it still further or else have a nervous breakdown. Virtually every mother's manual and magazine article of this period assumed that the baby in question was wanted, loved and had two loving and relatively well-off parents. It is interesting, however, that this period saw an enormous increase in illegitimacy, abortion, and baby-battering. Baby-battering or child-abuse was discovered in the late 1940s but very much kept under the carpet. Even in professional circles it was over a decade before the subject could be freely discussed because it went against the idealized picture of contemporary motherhood.

There was bound to be disillusion. Conditions of illusion always hold the seeds of potential disillusion. Now things are swinging the other way, against the idealized view of motherhood. Unfortunately this reaction often occurs without a serious attempt to understand it. Many of the most vociferous voices for change, for example in the women's liberation movement, have not even bothered to find out what motherhood is all about before they condemn and talk about it as a 'myth'. I believe that this period of disillusion is one that inevitably follows the period of idealization and that society has to live through it before it can take a deeper and more realistic look at the future of motherhood.

The illusion was bound to be shattered. Disillusion was bound to come. Simone de Beauvoir touched on it in *The Second Sex*. Betty Friedan detected it under the surface and called it 'the problem that has no name.' Adrienne Rich described how she became aware of it in her own life.

... The life of a Cambridge tenement backyard swarming with children, the repetitive cycles of laundry, the night-wakings, the interrupted moments of peace or of engagement with ideas, the ludicrous dinner parties at which young wives, some with advanced degrees, all seriously and intelligently dedicated to their children's welfare and their husbands' careers, attempted to reproduce the amenities of Brahmin Boston, amid French recipes and the pretense of effortlessness – above all, the ultimate lack of seriousness with which women were regarded in that world – all of this defied analysis at that time, but I *knew* I had to remake my own life. I did not then understand that we – the women of that academic community – as in so many middle-class communities of the period – were expected to fill both the part of the Victorian Lady of Leisure, the Angel in the House, and also of the Victorian cook, scullery maid, laundress, governess, and nurse. I only sensed that there were false distractions sucking at me, and I wanted desperately to strip my life down to what was essential.[12]

CHAPTER SEVEN

The Importance of Other People

One of the characteristics of modern motherhood is the way in which it has become separated from every other aspect of life and from the mother's own earlier and later lives.

In an earlier chapter 'Has Mother Love Changed?', we saw how in many ways members of families, parents and children are closer to each other than they were in former times. The bonds are personal and emotional rather than economic through community and wider family. We also saw how, as society became more complicated, special provision had to be made for children. In the pre-modern world children tended to be ignored as infants and, if they survived, were integrated into the adult world as soon as they were old enough to be of use. Most of them did not even go out to school, and father was likely to be at home all day. The custom among pre-industrial artisans, shop keepers, smallholders and unskilled labourers was for whole families to work together. Husband, wife and children tended to form a single economic unit in which the wife played a critical part. On a smallholding she managed the dairy, the poultry and the marketing of produce. She managed her husband's affairs when he was away. If he was a day-labourer, she worked with him in the fields. If it was a cottage industry she controlled the spinning, knitting and sewing. She might sell goods from door to door or set up an ale-house. In the towns she might manage the shop or help the craftman at his trade. In the early eighteenth century, Defoe observed that in the wool-manufacturing areas of the West Riding of Yorkshire, cloth was made in every house, 'women and children carding and spinning; all employed from the youngest to the oldest, scarce anything above four years old but its hands were sufficient for its own support.' Similar conditions developed in the early eighteenth century as the cotton industry developed round Manchester.[1] (Stone, p. 199).

Nowadays a child cannot be 'of use' in this sense. Modern society is complicated and sophisticated. People recognize that many years of separate preparation, in mid-adolescence or early adult life, are required before the young person is ready to spend his or her days alongside adults of all ages and play a useful and safe part in the working of society. The modern world of work has no place for children and is essentially apart from them. They are likely to come no nearer to participation in it than being taken to a child care centre where they will be looked after separately while their parents work, and, when older, doing a newspaper round. One cannot take them into the office or the factory. Before industrialization most people led agricultural lives. Relatively few are now so employed and even the farm, a traditional place where adults and children worked side-by-side and all but the youngest children could participate, has now become mechanized, complicated and dangerous, so that children are of much less help than formerly. They have to be kept away from adult work, and virtually their whole experience is of home and school. Because of the way our society is organized and because of the industrialization on which it is founded, we find it necessary to separate children from adults. And not only are children kept away from the world of work, but work has been taken away from home. Few parents earn their livings at home. Few fathers see much of their children except at weekends and mothers who wish or need to earn money mostly have to leave home and children in order to do it, or earn only a very small sum doing work at home. People no longer come daily to the home in order to work. Home is no longer a productive place. It is separate, private, and is supposed to be a place for leisure and repose, intimacy, and childrearing. Its work is in its maintenance, spending the money that has been earned elsewhere.

Children in our society are kept away not only from the world of work but also from many adult pleasures and leisure activities, particularly outside the family. Although there are places and activities which whole families can enjoy together, one cannot take young children to the cinema, Bingo hall, betting shop, pub or golf course. In a simpler, pre-industrial society pleasure as well as work tended to involve the whole community. Adults and children all participated. It was not necessary to separate the children along with those who mothered them. Adult pleasures were more childish than they are today and children's pleasures were more like those of adults.

Children played bowls, card games and games of chance for money. Young boys gambled with real soldiers rather than played with toy ones. Adults played games that today would be considered childish, such as leapfrog, bowling hoops and fighting with snowballs. Children also took part in seasonal activities which were important in the life of the whole community, such as folk dancing and dancing round the maypole. Adults who were less childish tried to make their children adult as quickly as possible and thus precocious education was encouraged. The history of the sixteenth to nineteenth centuries is full of precocious children, who included Queen Elizabeth I and Lady Jane Grey. Macaulay and John Stuart Mill both read Greek at the age of three. The future king Louis XIII of France, born in 1601, played the violin at seventeen months. At two he was 'taken to the king's apartment and dancing all sorts of dances to the music of a violin.' At five he watched with enthusiasm a farce about a comic husband and an unfaithful wife. Today a film on this theme would be forbidden to small children, even if they wished to see it. They are more likely to stay at home and view 'Watch with Mother' on television. The very title of this successful programme symbolizes a profound change in our society. Mothers and children stay at home and sit together.

What is not usually stressed, discussed or even realized is that the separation of children from the working world has meant the segregation of their mothers. People who are concerned with 'social problems' sometimes discuss this but I have found no book by a professional historian which discusses it in any detail or shows awareness of its implications, although many discuss the separation of childhood. This omission is, again, typical of society's attitude to its mothers, and to their own acceptance of it. What a child 'needs', or what society 'needs' for its children, are laid down and mothers are expected both to comply and to be fulfilled in so doing. Most people, including mothers, have internalized the situation so that they take it for granted, do not question it and are unaware of its implications.

Other trends have further increased the separation and isolation of motherhood in our time. The decline of community life and the increase in the sense of privacy have tended to shut each family into its four walls, which means, during the day, mothers with their children. Television has taken over from outside activities as the main source of amusement; again, mothers and children are shut away

106

with it. Although in some suburbs there is a good deal of friendship and neighbourly activity and young mothers meet others and help each other, in many areas there is little or no such contact. Small children have no opportunity of knowing adults (other than their parents) or even other children except perhaps a brother or sister.

The loss of contact with other people has been made particularly acute by the decline of servants. In these private and egalitarian days we tend to forget the importance of servants in the lives of all but the poorest children in England at least until World War II. In pre-modern times 'servants' included those who were engaged in the productive work of the household, apprentices, agricultural labourers and so on. In the seventeenth century a London bakery, as described by Laslett[2] was likely to consist of thirteen or fourteen people: the baker and his wife, four paid employees, two journeymen, two apprentices, two maidservants and three or four children of the house. In the 100 villages studied by Laslett, servants made up 13.4 per cent of the total population[3] and some of them were children of other families, often of similar social status. In those days the idea of service in another family was regarded as normal and respectable, and, in the pre-modern world there was much familiarity between 'family' and servants. They ate together, spent their days together and slept alongside each other. Ariès has pointed out that the servant was not paid, he was rewarded.[4] His master's relationship with him 'was not based on justice but on patronage and pity, the same feeling that people had for children.' As an example he gives Don Quixote's thoughts when he awakens and looks at the sleeping Sancho: 'Sleep, you have no worries. You have committed the responsibility for your person to my shoulders; it is a burden which nature and tradition have imposed on those who have servants. The valet sleeps while the master sits up, wondering how to *feed him, improve him, and do good to him*. Fear (of a bad harvest etc.) does not affect the servant, but only the master, who must support during sterility and famine he who served him during fertility and abundance.' This may be an extreme or idealized view but there is no doubt that there was considerable familiarity with servants which gradually disappeared in the modern world. Finding privacy became a problem. Rooms began to be organized for different purposes instead of everyone living and eating together in a house with beds all over the place. In 1725 Daniel Defoe complained that 'you are ... always at the mercy of every newcomer to divulge your family affairs, to inspect your private life, and treasure up the sayings of your family and friends. A very great confinement and much complained of in most families.'[5] Fifty years later Dr. Johnson wrote:

They first invade your table then your breast,
Explore your secrets with insidious art,
Watch the weak hour and ransack all the hearts,
Then soon your ill-paid confidence repay
Commence your lords, and govern or betray.[6]

But the servants remained, and so did the familiarity of children with them. This recollection of early nineteenth century childhood, quoted in de Mause, is not exceptional but typical of many:

The servants' hall and the maids' room provided the only keen enjoyment left to me. There I had complete liberty; I took the side of one party against another, discussed their business with my friends, and gave my opinion upon them, knew all their intimate affairs, and never dropped a word in the drawing room about the secrets of the servants' hall.[7]

During the nineteenth century there was a considerable increase in the number of living-in servants. They were not confined to the rich and even those who seemed to live near the bread line had them. Many biographies of the period testify that families who found it hard to pay for food and the basic necessities of life had servants. Readers of *Mansfield Park* will remember that the Price family, living in an impoverished and chaotic state in Portsmouth, kept two servants.

The existence of a child's world of adults who are not his parents and yet who care about him and are genuinely interested and involved with him has a profound effect on the way that child develops. For one thing it gives him the feeling that even though he loves his parents best, he does not totally depend on them. If they disappear for a while he can feel happy and secure for he knows that the world is friendly and supportive towards him. He also gains experience of different ways of reacting. He gets to know people with different personalities, feelings and interests. He learns much and enjoys much that he cannot get from his own parents. He is also less at the mercy of accidents and unforeseen events. If his mother suddenly disappears – perhaps she has an accident or has to go into hospital – he is much less likely to experience this as a traumatic event, a betrayal, and is less likely to feel damaged and betrayed when she returns, particularly if she brings a new baby with her. Finally he is less dependent on the personalities of his parents, particularly his mother. In these days when it is fashionable to insist that the basis of future mental health is the close, exclusive, early relationship between mother and child we tend to forget that many mothers are incapable of making or maintaining such a relationship or if they do, can only do it at great cost to themselves and so, also to their children. Or else they have abnormal personalities that warp the child for ever. The children of such mothers can be saved if they have other adults who are important in their lives, and often such a mother, relieved of some of the burden of mothering, is a better mother as a result.

An interesting phenomenon in the history of servants was the British nanny, who held sway over the nurseries of the upper and middle classes from about 1850 until World War II and even lingers on today. Jonathan Gathorne-Hardy has written an interesting book about it, *The Rise and Fall of the British Nanny*. The nanny was a highly specialized servant who, in her fully developed form, ruled over a nursery that was far removed from the rest of the house. Special meals were cooked and served there and she often had a number of nursery-maids under her. 'How was it,' asks Gathorne-Hardy, 'that hundreds of thousands of mothers, apparently normal, could simply abandon all loving and disciplining and company of their little children, sometimes from birth, to the absolute care of other women, total strangers, nearly always uneducated, about whose characters they must usually have had no real idea at all? It was a practice, as far as I know, unparalleled on such a vast scale in any other culture which had never existed.'[8]

Nannies, like mothers who do not have them, had despotic power over their charges which they used according to their temperament. Gathorne-Hardy's book contains examples of draconian nannies, sadistic nannies, eccentric nannies, loving and cuddly nannies. Clearly the best mother-nanny relationship was one in which the two women complemented each other, each making up for minor deficiencies in the other. Major deficiencies on either side were more difficult for the child to cope with but, even then, a good nanny could do a great deal towards helping the child of an inadequate mother to develop in a way that would not have been possible if the child had been left to the mother alone. Winston Churchill's mother, for instance, moved in political circles and was always on the go. It is inconceivable that she could have devoted herself exclusively, totally and successfully to a small child. Little Winston found his security in his Nanny and they loved each other dearly until she died. One wonders what would have happened to Churchill had he had a cruel nanny or frequent change of nannies, or had been left exclusively to the care of his mother.

The old system of sharing mothering with paid helpers in the home lives on till the present day in a section of society that is seldom studied because it is small, scattered and can defend itself against the onslaughts of researchers. This is the upper class.

The ideas and standards regarded as normal mothering in most books on child care and in scientific works are class-determined. Most studies of motherhood have been carried out on animals, primitive people and the working and lower middle.classes. Many people who write these books, do these studies or apply them professionally or unprofessionally to real life write as though they live in a middle class world whose standards they tend to impose, albeit unwittingly, on those whom they think do not yet live up to them.

Anyone who tries to study or to write about families and mothering knows how difficult it is to see beyond the concepts of the standard middle class family, Mum, Dad and usually two kids, a boy and a girl. This is the image that is always thrust before us as the ideal or even as the existing situation. Yet only 7% of Americans live in such a family. All the same, mothers and children who do not live in such a family, or who live in it unhappily, are apt to feel deprived.

The accepted norms have also been influenced by psychoanalysis, which stems from nineteenth century Jewish Vienna and has been perpetuated in this country largely by immigrants from Central Europe. The psychoanalytic study of mothering has also had some distinguished American and British contributors. It is interesting to note that one of the best known of these, John Bowlby; doyen of modern British mothering and official attitudes to it, has never apparently regarded the traditional upbringing of his class as suitable for inclusion in his studies. As far as I know, none of his writings so far discuss nursery life, nannies, boarding schools, or any of the other features that make traditional British upper class mothering so different from the kind he writes about.

Yet for several reasons the way in which the British upper class traditionally raises its children is of special interest in the study of mothering. The system shows how a stable method of personality development is perpetuated in a manner which has long suited the society which embraces it, maintains it, strengthens it and furthers its aims. It also occurs in America, but to a smaller extent. In the South it was developed with the aid of slaves but since the Civil War has been largely confined to the very rich. Important reasons for this are that the roots of modern American childrearing lie in the colonial tradition and that servants have never been as widely available in America as in Britain. This difference was particularly marked between the two world wars. During the years when Mom was becoming powerful in America, her middle class counterpart in Britain was still following the traditions of former times.

Historically, the British upper class system of childrearing is important. The rise and fall of Britain's power in the world during the past two hundred years has been, if not due to it, at least closely connected with it, and is important in understanding the Establishment even today. Almost every member of the upper and upper middle classes whose memory goes back before the 1939 war was brought up more or less in this fashion. Moreover, although many upper class parents today choose to care for their own children or for financial reasons are compelled to do so, the traditional system is still chosen by many of those in public life, those with power and those who can afford it, even when they themselves do not come from this background. It is of special interest for a number of reasons. First, because of the political influence it has had and still has. Second, because it was at its height at the time when the early feminists fought to make a better world for women and their children. So efficient was it that these feminists failed to see its temporary nature or the consequences of its collapse. Its faults were realized long before its advantages. Third, it is of interest because although the system as part of a class system has diminished and become modified, it is by no means dying, and it is even undergoing a recandescence in a different form among many intellectual or *avant-garde* mothers, especially in the new women's movements. Last, it gives some insight into those qualities of motherliness which are so important and which, according to the thesis of this book, need to be spread much more widely through the community if we are to overcome the present, severe problems of motherhood.

Traditionally the system pays little regard to the principle of the supreme importance of the individual, but provided an individual fits into it moderately well, it offers support, breadth of vision and opportunity such as is found nowhere else in our society, together with a tolerance of deviance and eccentricity that is not found lower down the social scale except at the very bottom. It is a system of training for a role in life, to be part of the system. The training starts from birth and delegation of the mother's role is essential to it. It is a system of intermittent mothering, and for boys the early years are a serious preparation for leaving home at eight years old already adequately prepared for team spirit, playing the game, not letting the side down and already able to manage the stiff upper lip and equipped with the rudiments of good manners, good taste and good form. Girls leave home later, usually at eleven, and on the whole for them less emphasis is laid on team qualities and more on good manners and good taste. Education before the age of eight is usually provided by governesses or small local schools, either one-sex preparatory or mixed. At this age the mothering of both sexes is not dissimilar. After eight education is essentially in one-sex schools.

At its best the system turns out excellently integrated empire builders and their wives. It also produces its own problems and neuroses.

Perhaps I can best describe this system of rearing children by discussing certain aspects of my own upbringing and pointing out where I think it was not typical.

Mothers of this class tend to start young. In the 1920s, when it was beginning to be the custom for young women from professional and academic families to pass examinations and go to university, my mother, who came from a more conventional family, left Heathfield School (which still is a stronghold for young ladies of privileged background), attended finishing schools in Paris and Florence and was then presented at Court before 'doing the Season' as a debutante. By the age of twenty-one, never having travelled on a bus, boiled a kettle or even run a bath for herself, she was married, settled into a smart house in Kensington, giving dinner parties and awaiting my birth. Almost every detail of this history could happen today, though it would be much less common. There are still young women who are brought up like this, but it would now be a true picture of only a small section of a social class rather than of a whole social class.

Three months before my birth my mother advertised in *The Times* for a nanny who would 'take full charge' from the monthly nurse. Many young women in her position would have employed their own former nannies, but though hers was still in the family, my mother decided that she was too old. The nanny she chose stayed with us for twenty-three years, until the youngest member of the family was fifteen. During most of that time her wages were thirty shillings a week and she thought my parents were generous. We children lived with her in the nursery, where our meals were brought to us by the nursery maid. We saw more of our mother than many children in similar households because she enjoyed being with us and riding, swimming and playing with us. She used to join us for tea in the nursery and our father came up too when he arrived back from work. Nanny remained with us throughout World War II, during which time things changed. For the first time, and with considerable adjustments in the household, she 'lived as family' and turned her hand to activities such as housework and housekeeping. She consistently refused to cook and as the household shrank my mother learned to do this. Nanny left us after the war when my parents moved to a smaller house, but we continued to think of her as Nanny, kept contact with her and supported her financially until her death in the late 1970s. Had my parents not made this move, which was partly a concession to changing times, Nanny would undoubtedly have stayed, as did my mother's own nanny, in the family house. 'Old Nanny', as we called our mother's nanny, stayed with her employers until she died, living on the second floor of my grandparents' house. I never discovered exactly where her room was, in spite of spending most of our holidays in the house and more or less having the free run of it. Though definitely not a member of the family, she seemed to be above the servants in rank, though I noticed that sometimes she associated with the housekeeper, the butler and my grandmother's personal maid, who had also been in the house for more than thirty years. Old Nanny seemed to sew a great deal and talk a great deal, mostly about the earlier doings of 'Miss Gwen' and 'Miss Jean', as she called my mother and her sister. She used to come and look after us when our own nanny was on holiday (two weeks in the summer on the Isle of Wight in the company of a sister or another nanny). Old Nanny called me 'Miss Ann' and all our friends were 'Miss' or 'Master' too. Our own nanny called us by our plain Christian names and our mother, approving of this in rebellion against her own background, assured us that this was a sign that times were changing. Old Nanny was still alive in 1951 when I took my firstborn to meet his great-grandfather. She picked up the baby and addressed him as 'Master Simon'. I felt, correctly, that it would be the first and last time that he would be addressed in that manner.

Our nanny moved in when I was two weeks old, overlapping for two weeks with the 'monthly nurse'. I know nothing about this lady but such people still exist. They are usually trained nurses or midwives and are supposed to 'know all about young babies'. They move from 'case' to 'case' to start the baby off in its routine and training. According to modern theories of attachment and 'bonding', their function could have been designed specifically to prevent the formation of the close bond between mother and child which is the essence of the first stage of mothering. The monthly nurse helps to ensure that, whatever happened later, no close bond would form between mother and baby. As a result the system can form the child and the child perpetuate the system. If there is a monthly nurse a mother who feels 'broody' about her baby has a difficult time developing her intuitive and imaginative motherly interests. Breastfeeding is sometimes a desperate attempt to make contact with the baby in a world ruled by nurses and nannies. But this was not always easy. Breastfeeding was not fashionable at the time. Moreover, it was the age of Truby King, and the strict rule of the clock. Many a poor young mother who did breastfeed her baby was forced to sit up nodding and sleepy, with breasts aching and heavy, listening to a screaming baby, because the clock hadn't yet struck. Many of my mother's generation and class were only able to develop the feelings appropriate to the earliest stage of motherhood, and then of course only to a limited degree, with their grandchildren, since modern children are less likely to suffer from traditional forms of control and moulding.

Our nanny, unlike some of our numerous cousins' nannies, wasn't stiff or starchy or strict. Like many nannies, she came from a simple, rustic background and had left school at thirteen to become an under-nursemaid. Considering this, she was remarkably literate. She had had several posts before she came to us, and her former charges, especially 'Little Prudence' and 'my other Ann' played important parts in our imaginations. Nanny's father was a gardener and she was one of nine children. I knew a lot about each one of them and all their spouses, children and homes. Much of my childhood imagination was turned on 'my sister Florence in India', 'my sister Kath' who was always in difficulties, and 'my sister Betty' who was stone deaf (Nanny taught us deaf-and-dumb language so that we would be able to speak to her when we met her) and ran a chicken farm with her husband Fred, who was blind. I spent a lot of time thinking about them, and I believe that our experience of them, though mostly vicarious, helped us to develop imaginatively and to envisage other ways of life and attitudes to it that we could never have gained had we been in the exclusive care of my mother. It also gave my mother relief from our constant presence and enabled her to develop in ways which would have been impossible had she been totally bound by young children from the age of twenty-one to thirty-five.

Although she was relaxed and unconventional as nannies went, our nanny always wore white overalls and a stiff white belt. When we lived in London, she wore outdoor uniform as well, but when we moved to the country she discarded this. Presumably it helped to keep her end up among the other, rather posher, nannies in Kensington Gardens.

Nanny ruled the nurseries in a kindly way. She slept in the night nursery with the current youngest child until my mother decided that times had changed and after that she slept there alone and we all had our own rooms. She always came if we called out in the night and I remember an occasion when she was remarkably sympathetic towards me when I woke her at 3 a.m. suddenly in floods of noisy tears at the realization that I didn't own a tin drum. She promised to give me one for Christmas and went back to bed.

She was brought early morning tea, and all our meals, by the nursery maid. But unlike larger households, she did her job alone. We never had an under-nanny. On 'Nanny's day off', which was every Thursday afternoon and every other Sunday afternoon, we were looked after by our mother. I was made aware all through my childhood that we were a very 'advanced', informal family and that we saw much more of our parents than my mother had seen of hers, and though we might not be so rich, we were better off as we were. We spent a great deal of time riding with our mother and sometimes swimming or walking, and when we reached the age of seven we were allowed to eat Sunday lunch downstairs with the grown-ups. On Nanny's day out our mother would move upstairs, sometimes bringing our father too, and take over the nursery.

Even so, Nanny liked to keep up traditions and appearances. Sometimes we dressed up to go down to the drawing room for an hour after tea. Otherwise, except when we were playing in the garden or were out with our mother, we were mostly in the nursery with Nanny until we were old enough to want to read in our rooms. Nanny was full of typical nanny stories and aphorisms, though she quoted the more extreme with tongue in cheek. We had to eat bread and butter before cake, but sayings such as 'Jam yesterday, jam tomorrow but never jam today' were quoted to us as examples of how dreadful other nannies could be. 'In my young day...' she was fond of saying, and 'curiosity killed the cat'. But she didn't mind if we answered her with 'satisfaction brought it back.'

I always thought we were lucky to have Nanny. I knew a lot of nannies in my childhood and some of them made me thankful that they weren't ours. Even so, I sometimes wished that ours would go away, so that we could have our mother all to ourselves. On reflection I think that this was partly because I attended a day school where no one else had a nanny and I was teased for having one. I used to assure my friends that she was only there for the younger members of the family, and had nothing to do with me. Looking back on her, examining my own mixed feelings about her and remembering the characters and influence of other nannies on their charges helps me to understand the advantages and disadvantages of this system of upbringing to both mother and child. At its worst, the child has no chance to make a real bond with his mother and is left to the mercies of a paid servant, exposed to all the frustrations and distortions of her personality. At its best, the nanny is an extra mother figure and complements the mother, makes up for difficulties and distortions in the mother's personality and protects the children from these while allowing the mother freedom to develop as a person in ways other than unadulterated motherhood.

Mothers often seem to choose nannies who will care for their children in a manner similar to the way they themselves would do it if they did not wish or feel bound to follow the traditional pursuits of their class. Some choose warm and loving nannies, some choose cold and disciplined nannies, others erratic and fickle nannies and yet others choose sadistic and hostile nannies. Many mothers choose nannies to represent part of themselves, or to provide something lacking in themselves. A vague, unreliable mother is likely to choose a nanny like herself but she may choose a disciplinarian. Sometimes a mother may choose a cold or cruel nanny whom the child will not like because the nanny then represents no threat to the mother since there will be no competition. By allowing her unpleasant side to be vented on the child by the nanny, the mother can then be represented in the child's feelings as someone pure and perfect. Many mothers nowadays, particularly if they are highly educated, feel normally warm and loving towards their children as long as they can escape from them for part of the day to a life of their own which young children cannot possibly share. The most successful of such mothers choose nannies who are also warm and loving by nature and who also have the capacity for being so continuously, thus making up for a deficiency in the mother. Such a mother, if sufficiently secure and mature, will accept as part of the price of her own fulfilment the inevitable sharing of the children's affections. In practice, sharing of this kind seldom leads to serious rivalry or jealousy. I have also known mothers who are inadequate themselves, incapable of running a household or caring for children yet who have the talent or good luck to find a nanny who will be a nanny to them as well as to the children. I have known children saved from terrible insecurity and trauma by such nannies. The mother may be neurotic, alcoholic, or mentally ill, but nanny survives, runs the nursery as a safe haven for the children, and carries the burden of mother, children and household. Some nannies thrive on this situation and really come into their own, so much so that they may develop a vested interest in maintaining the mother's illness. If the mother improves to a point where she can take over some of her own functions and duties, nanny may start to give trouble or leave.

Certain difficulties and anxieties are specifically associated with traditional upper class mothering not only for the mother but for her children throughout their lives. First, as I mentioned before, the system makes it difficult or impossible to develop a full or adequate first stage of mothering. The mother whose baby is organized for her from birth has no opportunity to develop the particular kind of feelings that are characteristic of early mothering. Many mothers are unaware even of the possibility of doing so. They are likely to feel content to be relieved of the continuous burden and to be able to return to 'normal life' soon after the baby is born. They may feel scared of the baby, feeling that his care is something with which they could not possibly cope and which is better done by a 'professional'. This does not mean that a mother does not love her baby or that he is doomed. But it does mean that he will grow up without experiencing the earliest type of mothering and his personality will develop accordingly.

Nowadays many mothers, even if they intend to employ a nanny later, do not do so during the early months. They wish to do all the early care themselves and to devote themselves predominantly to this. They feel it is something that they can and want to do and can do better than anyone else. They eschew the traditional 'monthly nurse' and only when they feel that the baby is established do they seek substitute care.

The custom of sending boys to boarding school at the age of eight is an important part of traditional British upper class upbringing. It is not so universal as it used to be though there are still many such schools, tucked away in the country or by the sea. But nowadays, if a good day boys' preparatory school is available, or even a state primary school, some parents avail themselves of it. Many mothers are thankful to be spared the painful separation that not only tends to mould young English boys forever into the traditions of their class but is against modern theories of childrearing. But many continue in the old pattern, some through ignorance, some through positive belief in the benefits of the custom, or because of tradition, fear of stepping out of line, or because they are tired of having the boy at home.

The extra problems that the present state of society has brought to the traditional upper class mother include the difficulties of continuous care in paid substitute mothers. Nannies are more difficult to find, and on the whole not so long-lasting or so dedicated. They require more time off. It is not so easy to support them in their traditional role or to provide an array of helpers backed by a substantial kitchen staff. Except in the very richest families or those lucky enough to find a really good, lasting, traditional nanny, the upper class mother has to take a good deal more responsibility than formerly for the children's early mothering. Many thrive on this, especially if they have had good enough mothers and nannies themselves. They find childrearing satisfying and fulfilling and make a good job of it. It was these mothers who, to a considerable extent, were responsible for the social success of Bowlby's theories. Having been brought up by nannies themselves, they felt they wanted something better for their own children and they were convinced that rearing their own children was more worthwhile, more satisfying, and better for the children than being left to a surrogate while their mothers amused themselves. But many of these women are incapable of taking over in this way. Having known only nannies herself, today's upper class mother may be helpless on nanny's day off and incapable of providing her children with the emotional security and support needed by the children through frequent changes of nanny. I have seen young mothers who spend a whole week dreading nanny's day off and who pass the day sitting in the nursery weeping in the midst of chaos.

An upper class child whose mother cannot cope with the changes that have inevitably occurred in the traditional method of childrearing may well become deprived in the way that makes others criticize the whole system. Recently I saw a disturbed girl, twelve years old, whose mother was a socialite without motherliness. The child had had so many nannies that no one could count them – at least six in the first two years of her life, and many more later. No one seemed to have taken much trouble about finding them – they simply came from an agency, stayed for a few weeks or months, and departed. It was not surprising that the child suffered from nightmares, wet the bed, was markedly withdrawn and, despite a high IQ, seemed unable to learn.

In some ways upper class mothers have greater difficulty than others when they run into trouble. There are no recognized channels through which they can obtain help. Their private doctors are often the most helpful, especially if they have a feeling for and understanding of these problems. But if the doctor is unwilling or unable to provide the necessary help and support, they are often in a difficult situation. Using the social services is difficult for the upper class and can be disastrous. They are more likely themselves to be the magistrates, the Marriage Guidance Counsellors or the voluntary social workers than the clients of any of these, and reversal of traditional roles is difficult for both sides. They are unsuited to being on the receiving end. Some use the National Health Service and state education, but mostly only when it suits them. If they don't like what they get, they pay for these services privately. On the whole they do not communicate easily with social workers, who find them difficult to deal with or who do not accept the reality of their problems. A remarkable number of people seem unable to believe that it is possible to be rich and also unhappy and in need of help. Only exceptional social workers can understand these problems and help with them. The upper class often gets worse medical and social help than poorer people, and adjustment is often more difficult.

Traditional upper class mothering is most successful against a background of privilege. Though this still exists, it is no longer so protective. I have known a boy be bullied at Eton because he arrived with a title and a cockney accent and I have known another who went to a well-known school and found himself in difficulties because his was the only titled family. He was nicknamed scornfully 'The Hon John'. Another young man, the eldest son of a peer, was unable to pass the examinations necessary to enter the Cambridge college which his father and ancestors had attended. His father interpreted this as a personal humiliation. An aristocrat of great wealth and property, he forgot that he himself had never had to sit for a competitive entrance examination and that he had in fact left without taking a degree. As far as he was concerned it meant that his son was a failure. The boy became depressed and eventually committed suicide.

People who have experienced this system of upbringing successfully or at its best seem to withstand shock, change, war and all manner of assault and privation. Indeed it is probably one of the best training grounds not only for leadership but also for learning to cope with extreme situations. It is said that in prisoner-of-war and concentration camps members of the upper class tended to survive in better mental condition than most, along with Jehovah's Witnesses and working class communists. Successful products of upper class training are also adequate in human relations of the kind traditional to their class, so that 'happy marriages' and 'happy families' abound among them. But many are less fortunate. Many of those who are good leaders and good in war do not manage to make adequate relationships and cannot cope with the stresses and strains of modern everyday life.

There are certain problems particularly likely to be encountered by people who have grown up under the traditional British upper class system of mothering. First, if they have not experienced a good first stage, which few of them have, and are also not successfully part of the Establishment, they are more vulnerable to stress, more dependent on the system within which they are accustomed to live and less adaptable to adverse circumstances. Nowadays the traditional upper class and upper middle class world, although it is still with us, has to a large extent ceased to exist. It is still there for its more successful or wealthier members. It thrives in influential circles. It is still the standard in the upper reaches of public life. For instance, a diplomat's wife is still expected to attend cocktail parties rather than put her children to bed. But the system not only is often patently unable to support its weaker members, but also fails to give them the necessary equipment or experience that would enable them to fend for themselves. The peer's son who could not pass examinations is a case in point. Little attention had been paid to his education and even less to his mental state. When it became obvious that getting to Cambridge was beyond his capabilities, no alternatives were suggested though he was a sensitive boy who needed encouragement. Since he had a private income he was able to live, albeit unhappily, with no prospects. It is not surprising that he slid into disaster.

Other adults, particularly grandmothers, are also of vital importance in the lives of mothers and their children. Because of early marriage and childbearing and increasing longevity there are probably more active grandmothers than ever before and many of them play an important part in the lives of their grandchildren. Many provide those extra adults who can be so important both to young children and to their mothers, relieving both of the burden of exclusive and unrelieved contact with each other. On the other hand many grandmothers, being relatively young and active, are at work or have full lives of their own. They also often live far away. The changes of modern life have led to increased geographical distance between members of many families. Lucky indeed are modern families with a grandmother nearby who can play an important part in their lives.

The decline in the size of families and the decline of kinship, the close ties that people in many cultures maintain with more distant relatives, has meant not only that a young mother expecting her first child is likely to be relatively isolated from her own relations but also that she has probably had no previous experience of looking after babies or even of observing and learning about babies. Her only experience is of her own babyhood and the way she herself was handled. Though she will have a few conscious memories of this she will have absorbed it. In the way that she herself was mothered so is she likely to mother her own children, no matter how determined she may be to do otherwise. Her own experience has been absorbed rather than remembered and is less likely than in former times to be tempered by subsequent experience with younger brothers and sisters, nieces and nephews or neighbours' children. Because young mothers are likely to have little or no experience to modify their own experience of being mothered, ways of mothering tend to be polarized in our society. The good mother will tend to make her daughters into good mothers, and the not so good will similarly transmit her own ways and attitudes to future generations.

The segregation of motherhood from the rest of society is further increased by lack of facilities for children's play. There are now few communities with houses close together facing a street or countryside that is free from traffic or other dangers, where everyone knows everyone else and the children can play together in a common life of the street. Until recently this was much commoner than it is today in a world of motor cars, concrete jungles and high-rise flats. Even a generation ago, many more children were able to play safely not far from their mothers, who could supervise them from a distance and at the same time get on with their own work or chat with their neighbours, confident that even if they could not actually see or hear their children, they were secure and not far off. Today this is seldom possible and because young children are inevitably attached to the adults responsible for them, the gradual segregation of children from the world of adult work and leisure has inevitably meant the segregation of their mothers too. The increasing dangers of the world outside the home and the way in which architects of housing schemes since World War II have ignored the needs of children has increasingly kept young children, and their mothers, at home and alone together, away from the rest of the world. This segregation, like prospects of survival and psychological principles and the necessity of choice, is one of the bases of mothering today and one which makes it different from former times. Segregation has gone hand in hand with psychological theory and political and economic convenience.

One aspect of this segregation is that it greatly increases the mother's exposure to experts and her dependence upon them. Without previous experience and isolated from the rest of society she often has to turn to the doctors, nurses and social workers for information and advice, adding to this what she sees on television and by reading women's magazines. Experts of course can be valuable, but they tend to hand on the conventional wisdom of the day. Only a rare, exceptionally enlightened expert will be conscious of many of the problems discussed in this book, let alone be able to do anything about them. Moreover, learning through contact with experts increases, in its own way, the segregation of a process from the rest of life. It encourages a situation in which mothering is done by mental activity, conscious and striving, rather than by intuition and experience absorbed over many years. Mental activity is the way in which people overcome deficiencies in spontaneous activity and try to meet those needs which are otherwise not met. It also leads to a great deal of anxiety about whether one is 'doing the right thing' and to guilt when things go wrong.

So a modern parent, particularly a mother, feels she is taking on a huge responsibility when she has children. If she is versed in modern psychological teaching she may wonder whether she has the maturity and stamina to become a mother. She is probably aware that what she does will be crucial to the development of her child. She is likely to be less aware that what she *is* is even more crucial than what she *does*. She is probably anxious to get it right, as the experts tell her. She knows that children need her overwhelmingly during the early years. She knows that if she gets it wrong she can damage them irreparably. She is extremely anxious to succeed. If she is reasonably well educated and reads about the subject she is probably conscious of conflicts and disagreements among the experts and she knows that what experts say often conflict with her own feelings. She is likely to be confused and anxious. She is also likely to be alone with her child for much of the day and isolated from friends and relatives. She may feel, or have been told, that she must give up everything else for the sake of her children for unless they have the total devotion of their mothers during the early years, disaster is likely to follow. As Jessie Bernard has written:

> ... The two requirements we build into the role of mother – full time care of children and sole responsibility for them – seem, in brief, to be incompatible with one another, even mutually exclusive. In view of these findings it is sobering to note that in our society we seem to maximize this contradiction in the role.[9]

CHAPTER EIGHT

Feminism and Motherhood: Before the Vote

Feminism is the ideological unrest of women on the subject of sexual inequality or on a political issue. It is not possible to generalize about motherhood in relation to feminism any more than it is possible to generalize about the nature of motherhood itself. As we have seen, motherhood and the main problems and preoccupations associated with it have varied enormously in the western world over the last few centuries. Feminist movements have varied too and the part played in them by questions concerning motherhood has depended on the circumstances of the time and the situation.

Ideology grows from what are felt to be needs and deprivations. Given the situation of women in the past and what was known about the needs of children, it would be unlikely for anyone to have seen a conflict about motherhood. What the early feminists wanted was legal rights, opportunities for education and self-fulfilment, and acceptance by society as people in their own right. The problem was how to get society to accept these things as part of womanhood. It did not occur to early feminists that the raising of children would create problems. Childbirth itself might be a problem because it was so frequent and hazardous, but there was no problem about the care of the children once they were born. There were plenty of people willing to look after them and able to do so by the standards of the time. It would not have occurred to people that children needed special provision for play or stimulation, or that they needed the constant presence of their own mothers for several years from birth onwards. If they had time to play there was plenty of opportunity in both town and country and it is doubtful whether many children were ever looked after exclusively by their mothers until the present century. People might and did think that mothers should spend more time with them and many mothers wished to do so. But probably no one thought of *exclusive* care as a desirable objective.

Women first banded together to achieve political ends, not because of ideological principles but from sheer economic need. Before there was any trace of feminism women sometimes came together to lead food riots, usually with the connivance of their husbands. This was because women did the shopping and so were easily aware of rising food prices. They were also encouraged to take the lead by their husbands who knew that women would be handled more gently by the forces of law.[1] There was nothing ideological about these associations. But in the seventeenth century the rise of the companionate marriage brought awareness of inequality and of a need to share. Some women developed a desire for self-reliance, often supported by religious theory, and a feeling that patriarchy was, if not wrong, at least too strong. Ideas about motherhood seem to have played no direct part in the earliest and abortive movements, but they are there by implication because motherhood is part of family life. What these women's opponents found so threatening was the possibility of changes in family life.

One of the earliest movements that could be called feminist was a religious revivalist movement organized by Anne Hutchinson in Massachusetts in 1636–37. She believed that the individual conscience is the only test for law and obedience and that Grace is conferred equally by God on members of both sexes. Most of her followers were women and the movement was seen as a threat to the hierarchical system of the time in Church, state and family. Anne Hutchinson and her followers complained in public that 'men usurp over their wives and keep them in servile subjection.' They were opposed on the grounds that by luring away women from the family church, the movement was causing 'division between husband and wife', disturbing the conventional relationship between the sexes, demanding an equality between grown men and 'silly women laden with their lusts.' Anne was told 'you have rather been a husband then a wife, and a preacher than a hearer, and a magistrate than a subject.' As a result Anne was driven into exile, and her followers were excommunicated and punished. There was no immediate feminist reaction.[2]

A few years later much the same thing happened on a larger scale in England during the Civil War. Many radical sects arose based on the extreme interpretation of the doctrine of Grace, and women played a prominent part in these. In new churches women were allowed to vote, debate and even preach. Many left the old church without the consent of their husbands and some even left their husbands and chose new ones who shared their faith.[3] As in Massachusetts, their opponents felt that they were threatening traditional family life. In fact most of them were asking for liberty of conscience and religious belief rather than freedom from male domination.[4] Again, the movement did not unleash powerful underlying feminist feelings.

However soon afterwards came the first organized female movement and it came from the lower-middle and artisan class. Some four hundred women who were suffering financial hardship as a result of the decay in trade during the Civil War took political action independently of their male relatives. Early in 1642 they petitioned Parliament, demanding a change in public policy, but emphasizing that women were not 'seeking to equal ourselves with men, either in authority or wisdom,' admitting that their intervention 'may be thought strange and unbeseeming our sex.' In August 1643 they were back. Thousands of women mobbed Parliament and demanded peace. They were dispersed by guards. In 1649 masses of women again assembled at Westminster complaining of economic crisis and the imprisonment of the Leveller leaders. This time they were told that they were petitioning about matters above their heads, that Parliament had given an answer to their husbands, who legally represented them, and that they should 'go home and look after your own business and meddle with your housewifery.'[5] But this time the women were not put off. They insisted that they were not satisfied with the answers given to their husbands and they claimed an equal share with men in the right ordering of the Church and insisted 'we have an equal share and interest with men in the Commonwealth.' Lord Clarendon believed that this overthrew the principle of subordination and deference in the family. 'Children ask not the blessing of their parents. . . . The young women conversed without circumpection or modesty. . . . Parents had no manner of authority over their children, nor children any obedience or submission to their parents.' Again, the movement had no future, for there was no further activity after the Restoration.[6] It does show, however, that wives and mothers were able on occasion to challenge the traditional authority of husbands. As the political doctrine of the Divine Right of Kings was declining, so were flaws and weaknesses appearing in the divine right of men over women and children.

The English Revolution of 1688 inspired new clamour against patriarchy, particularly by a few feminists including Hannah Woolley, Aphra Behn, Mary Astell and Lady Chudleigh. The last wrote a bitter poem in 1703.

> Wife and servant are the same,
> But only differ in the name.
> When she the word 'obey' had said.
> And man by law supreme has made.
>
> Fierce as an Eastern prince he grows
> And all his innate vigor shows.
> Then but to look, to laugh, or speak
> Will the nuptial contract break.
> Like mutes she signs alone must make.
> And never any freedom take
> But still be governed by a nod
> And fear her husband as her God.[7]

But it was not until the later eighteenth century, in the period of revolutions in America and France, that a more extreme form of feminism emerged. By this time the hard life of the early pioneers in America, in which women played a prominent part, was over, and many women, as in England, were enjoying a life of leisure. But some were not enjoying it and were beginning to equate male domination with political tyranny. Hardship on the frontier had been shared equally and this may have encouraged the development of stronger minded women. It is interesting that one of the earliest truly feminist documents in American history, Abigail Adams' 'Remember the Ladies' letter to her husband, written shortly after the English occupation of Boston had been lifted, talks of the possibility of *rebellion*, a word that was very much in the air at the time.[8]

> I long to hear that you have declared an independancy – and by the way in the new Code of Laws which I suppose it will be necessary for you to make I desire you would Remember the Ladies, and be more generous and favourable to them than your ancestors. Do not put such unlimited power into the hands of the Husbands. Remember all Men would be tyrants if they could. If particular care and attention is not paid to the Ladies we are determined to foment a Rebellion, and will not hold ourselves bound by any Laws in which we have no voice, or Representation.

That your Sex are Naturally Tyrannical is a Truth so thoroughly established as to admit of no dispute, but such of you as wish to be happy willingly give up the harsh title of Master for the more tender and endearing one of Friend. Why then, not put it out of the power of the vicious and the Lawless to use us with cruelty and indignity with impunity. Men of Sense in all Ages abhor those customs which treat us only as the vassals of your Sex. Regard us then as Beings placed by providence under your protection and in immitation of the Supreme Being make use of that power only for our happiness.

Abigail Adams felt constricted in the way that modern mothers sometimes feel constricted, but her problem was not the limitations imposed by children but social pressures, lack of opportunity and male domination. Five years earlier she had written of her desire to satisfy her curiosity, travel and cease to live vicariously through her husband. 'From my Infancy I have always felt a great inclination to visit the Mother Country as tis call'd and had nature formed me of the other Sex, I should certainly have been a rover. . . .'

However Abigail got no encouragement from her husband. On April 14, 1776 he wrote to her: 'As to your extraordinary Code of Laws, I cannot but laugh. . . . Depend upon it. We know better than to repeal our Masculine systems.' However, he did think about it. Six weeks later he wrote to James Sullivan: 'But why exclude women?' and gives as his reason that they are too dependent on their husbands.

The history of feminism is often said to begin with Mary Wollstonecraft. In 1889 when Susan Anthony and Elizabeth Cady Stanton published their monumental first three volumes of the *History of Woman's Suffrage* they put Mary Wollstonecraft's name at the head of the list of earlier feminists to whom they dedicated the book. Ray Strachey, a later feminist, wrote that in Mary Wollstonecraft's great book, *A Vindication of the Rights of Women*, published in 1729 and inspired by thoughts of 'Liberty, Equality and Fraternity, the whole extent of the feminist ideal is set out, and the whole claim for equal human rights is made – and although at the time it was little noticed, it has remained the text of the movement ever since.'[9]

Mary Wollstonecraft considered motherhood and tried to

examine the part it played in the problems she was trying to analyze. She never discussed it as a burden and made no suggestion that child care be shared with fathers. 'The care of children in Their infancy', she states, 'is one of the grand duties annexed to the female character by nature.'[10] She makes no complaint about the burdens a wife and mother has to bear in the fulfilment of her maternal duties. Her argument is that she would carry them out more effectively if her education had fitted her for the task instead of concentrating on 'accomplishments'. Instead of 'a smattering of accomplishments' and 'libertine notions of body and mind', she would have preferred 'strength of body and mind'. Preparation for marriage makes 'mere animals' of women, unfit to care for children. She entreats men to assist women for it is in their own interest to 'snap our chains', for 'We should then love them with true affection, because we should learn to respect ourselves.'[11] Furthermore woman as 'a slave to every situation to prejudice' seldom exerts enlightened maternal affection', for she either neglects or indulges her children. Yet, in Wollstonecraft's view, 'the formation of the mind must be begun very early' with affection tempered by reason. 'To be a good mother – a woman must have sense, and that independence of mind which few possess who are taught to depend entirely on their husbands.' Only a woman of 'enlarged understanding' and her character made firm, by being allowed to govern her own conduct, will be able 'to manage her children properly.' This will lead the woman to suckle her own babies, develop 'filial duty' and not 'be content to transfer the charge to hirelings.'[12] Another passage follows about National Education using arguments that people use today in trying to get nursery schools established.[13]

There is a sad and ironical twist to Mary Wollstonecraft's concern about the upbringing of children. As we saw she died of puerperal fever ten days after the birth of her second daughter, Mary. Her elder (and illegitimate) daughter, Fanny, who was only three years old when her mother died, was brought up by her stepfather and committed suicide while still in her teens.

The movement for women's rights is often dated from the 1840 World's Anti-Slavery Convention in London. To the surprise and horror of Victorian Englishmen, some of the delegates from the abolitionist society of Massachusetts and Pennsylvania were women. There was a long and furious debate on the motion for admitting them in which opponents insisted that it would be better to dissolve the convention than to permit women to sit with men on an equal basis. Eventually the American women were informed that if they wanted to attend the meetings at all they would have to sit in silence behind a curtained enclosure. They were enraged at the absurdity of a World Convention proclaiming the black man's right to liberty, yet denying equal liberty to women. Among these women was Elizabeth Cady Stanton (1815–1902), who was to become one of the most prominent of nineteenth century feminists. At the time she was twenty-five years old and destined to be the mother of seven children. It was life with the first five of these children that seems to have goaded her to take further action. After four years in the stimulating environment of Boston she moved to Seneca Falls, then a dreary factory town, where her husband had taken a job. At this time she wrote:

> I now fully understood the practical difficulties most women had to contend with in the isolated household, and the impossibility of woman's best development if in contact, the chief part of her life, with servants and children. . . . The general discontent I felt with woman's portion as wife, mother, housekeeper, physician, and spiritual guide, the chaotic condition into which everything fell without her constant supervision, and the wearied, anxious look of the majority of women, impressed me with the strong feeling that some active measures should be taken to remedy the wrongs of society in general and of women in particular.[14]

Elizabeth remembered Emerson's remark, 'A healthy discontent is the first step to progress.' She took up reform activity. Other women followed, perhaps because it was difficult in those new cities to lead the life of a leisured lady for there was little social life. Pregnancy and the presence of small children did not satisfy them, nor deter them from seeking other interests. Presumably they had enough servants to do the housework and cooking and to care for the children, even if things were in a 'chaotic condition' when she was out. Elizabeth constantly complained about the unreliability of household servants and fell back on a dream of some 'co-operative housekeeping in a future time that might promise a more harmonious domestic life for women.' However, her attention did not remain on this idea. She organized the First Women's Rights Convention at Seneca Falls in July, 1848. This is usually taken to have been the beginning of the active feminist movement in America. But the *Declaration of Sentiments and Resolutions* issued by that convention[15] contained nothing specific about motherhood. Clearly, in the eyes of that group of early feminists it presented no problems, or at least none that would not be solved by what they were seeking. Nevertheless motherhood played an important part in most of their lives and it is worthwhile to examine this.

Most of the early feminists of the nineteenth century were married and most of them were mothers. Some saw motherhood as an important task, but few seem to have felt that it clashed with their fulfilment as people and as women. Probably typical of their attitude was that of Margaret Fuller (1810–1850):

> What a difference it makes to come home to a child!
> ... How it fills up all the gaps of life just in the way that is most consoling, most refreshing. Formerly I used to feel sad at that hour ... and I felt so lonely.... Seeing how full he is of life, how much he can afford to throw away, I feel the inexhaustibleness of nature, and console myself for my own incapacities.[16]

Clearly she had no problems about what happened to the children while she was out. The emphasis was much more on equality before the law and in education rather than equality in the type of work performed. Harriet Martineau (1802–1876), who never married, argued that women must be educated to be 'companions to men instead of playthings or servants'. John Stuart Mill (1806–1873), one of the few men who championed women's rights, believed implicitly in 'the equality of married persons before the law' and 'society between equals', but he did not question the different types of labour to be performed by those equals.

> When the support of the family depends, not on property, but on earnings, the common arrangement, by which the man earns the income and the wife superintends the domestic expenditure, seems to me in general the most suitable division of labour between the two persons. If, in addition to the physical suffering of bearing children, and the whole responsibility of their care and education in early years, the wife undertakes the careful and economical application of the husband's earnings to the general comfort of the family; she takes not only her

131

fair share, but usually the larger share, of the bodily and mental exertion required by their joint existence.[17]

Again the emphasis is on the importance of women who run households being educated.

In America the feminist movement developed largely through educated women who were bored and had time on their hands even though some of them, like Elizabeth Cady Stanton, had many children. They never complain of not being able to leave their children, only of the difficulties of 'supervising' the household. Elizabeth Cady Stanton eventually found the solution to her problems in what has doubtless been the solution of virtually every educated mother who wished to be active outside the home, right into our own times. Only recently has this solution become impossible except for the very rich and it is difficult even for them. In 1851, Elizabeth Cady Stanton found a competent housekeepr, Amy Willard, who fitted in with the family and could really substitute for Elizabeth. Alice S. Rossi comments on this: 'It is curious that it may be the help of a housekeeper and a friend that facilitates a woman's life work, while the closest analogy to Elizabeth's tribute one would find from the pen of a man is typically a tribute to his wife.'[18]

Elizabeth Cady Stanton's great friend and colleague Susan B. Anthony (1820–1906) was one of the few prominent feminists of the time who was not married. Sometimes she seems to have resented the time her colleagues spent with their children. The following letter from her gives us some indication of the situation. Susan is appealing to Elizabeth to help her in preparing a speech. 'There is so much to say and I am so without constructive power to put in symmetrical order. So, for the love of me and for the saving of the reputation of womanhood, I beg you, with one baby on your knee and another at your feet, and four boys whistling, buzzing, hallooing, "Ma, Ma," set yourself about the work. . . .'[19]

At this period Elizabeth Stanton, Antoinette Brown and Lucy Stone were all pregnant together. In the same letter Susan Anthony shows her resentment:

> Those of you who have the talent to do honor to poor womanhood, have all given yourself over to baby-making; and left poor brainless me to do battle alone. It is a shame. Such a body as I might be spared to rock cradles. But it is a crime for you and Lucy Stone and Antoinette Brown to be doing it.[20]

In reply Elizabeth urged Susan to let 'Lucy and Antoinette rest awhile in peace and quietness' since 'we cannot bring about a moral revolution in a day or year.'[21] But two years later, on hearing that Antoinette Brown had produced another baby, Susan wrote to her:

April 22, 1858.

Dear Nettie:

A note from Lucy last night tells me that you have another *daughter*. Well, so be it. I rejoice that you are past the trial hour.

Now Nettie, *not another baby* is my *peremptory command, two* will solve the problem whether a *woman can* be anything more than a *wife* and *mother* better than a half dozen or *ten even*.

I am provoked at Lucy, just to think that she will attempt to speak in a course with such intellects as Brady, Curtis, and Chapin, and then as her special preparation, take upon herself in addition to baby cares, quite too absorbing for careful close and continued intellectual effort – the entire work of her house. A woman who is and must of necessity continue for the present at least, the representative woman, has no right to dis-qualify herself for such a representative occasion. I do feel it is so foolish for her to put herself in the position of *maid of all work and baby tender. . . .*

Nettie, I don't really want to be a downright scolder, but I can't help looking after the married sheep of the flock a wee bit.[22]

But Elizabeth Stanton, mother of many children, wrote to Nettie in a different vein: 'How many times I have thought of you since reading your pleasant letter to Susan. I was so happy to hear that you had another daughter. In spite of all Susan's admonitions, I do hope you and Lucy will have all the children you desire. I would not have one less than seven, in spite of all the abuse that has been heaped upon me for such extravagance.'[23]

Yet in other ways Susan Anthony was not against babies. On September 29, 1857 she wrote to Elizabeth that reproduction was 'the highest and holiest function of the physical organism . . . to be a *Mother*, to be a *Father*, is the best and highest wish of any human being.'

In spite of Elizabeth Cady Stanton's excellent housekeeper she was very involved with her seven children and believed that only mothers could counteract the ignorance displayed and maltreatment given by nurses. In an engaging passage, she describes her own experiences.[24] She was one of the increasing number of parents who believed that the physical health of their children was their responsibility. She deplored the still prevalent attitude that children's illnesses were 'part of the eternal plan – that Providence had a kind of Pandora's box, from which he scattered these venerable diseases most liberally among those whom he especially loved.' She believed that nurses and other hired servants, including many doctors, were dangerous in their habits and advice. 'Besides the obstinacy of the nurses I had the ignorance of physicians to contend with,' and as a result of this her child was nearly crippled. After this, she tells us, she 'trusted neither men or books absolutely' but used her 'mother's instinct' and concludes: 'My advice to every mother is, above all other arts and sciences, study first what relates to babyhood, as there is no department of human action in which there is such lamentable ignorance.'

However, Elizabeth Cady Stanton's devotion to motherhood and her children seems to have been, to her, something quite apart from her work. Typically, in an industrial society, her children played no part in her work. Just as to a modern doctor, lawyer, political journalist, baker or factory worker, his children play no part in his work, however much he loves them, so it was with the early feminists. However much they were involved with their own children they did not find that the problems connected with them were relevant to that work. The important thing for them was for women to go out into the world and demand their rights and equality with men, presumably leaving their children at home with the servants. Motherhood and children were part of women's life, but were not singled out for special consideration.

In 1850, these early feminists wrote: 'The tyranny which degrades and crushes wives and mothers sits no longer lightly on the world's conscience.... The signs are encouraging: the time opportune. Come, then, to this Convention.'[25] Even more revealing is the Introduction to the classic six-volume *The History of Woman's Suffrage*.[26] This was written with mature hindsight with many years of experience.

The isolated household is responsible for a large share of woman's ignorance and degradation. A mind always in contact with children ... whose aspirations and ambitions rise no higher than the roof which shelters it, is necessary dwarfed in its proportions. ... Womanhood is the great fact in her life; wifehood and motherhood are but incidental relations.

This last idea, so succinctly expressed, could be taken as the motto of the feminist movement ever since. It is still expressed fervently today. Yet the fact that motherhood has in itself become a problem is partially because of this view. Motherhood was clearly an 'incidental relation' to Elizabeth Cady Stanton with her excellent housekeeper and to Susan B. Anthony, who was unmarried, but unfortunately this attitude has remained in the feminist movement into our own times. Few mothers today can regard motherhood as an 'incidental relation' yet many feminists have continued to treat it as such.

This attitude may be an important reason why early feminists seem to have neglected the subject of birth control. The Banks have made an extensive study of feminism and family planning in Victorian England.[27] They point out that since the rise of feminism coincided with the fall of the birth rate in England, it has often been argued that the relationship between the two was causal. In fact this was not the case. The emphasis of the early feminist movement was on equality betwen the sexes, and feminism did not necessarily entail the idea of birth control. The large family was not seen as a disability weighing more heavily on women than on men. Advocates of family planning tended to address their appeals equally to both sexes. Few feminists regarded the smaller family as providing opportunities for a wider emancipation of woman and hence as a means to equality. Arguments about the relationship between the sexes did not turn on this question at all but on the biological and social basis of inequality. After a diligent search the Banks came to the conclusion that the case for birth control was not put forward on any feminist platform during the crucial years when opinion may be said to have been forming on the issue. As far as they could find, family planning propaganda played no part in the demands of the feminist movement until the size of the average family was already falling substantially. They also came to the conclusion that the anti-feminists, while seeing many undesirable consequences in the efforts of the reformers, such as a retreat from marriage altogether on the part of single women with careers and the neglect of their homes on the part of married women who tried to combine both, at no time included birth control among them.

It is difficult to understand why there was no definite feminist policy on family limitation. The Banks point out that the answer to this question is made even more difficult to find because of the reticence of the period in sexual matters. But it is certainly evident that the early feminists did not regard motherhood as a problem because to them it was no problem. Anti-feminists might argue that emancipated women would neglect their children, for example an anonymous writer in *A Woman's View of Women's Rights:* 'A loveless home, a wearied, fretful husband and neglected children while she, the mother, rules and decides the fate of nations.'[28] Charles Dickens invented such a character in Mrs. Jellyby in *Bleak House*, who was always concerned about the welfare of the natives of Borioboola-Gha while neglecting her home and children. But feminists did not regard this as a problem because, like Elizabeth Cady Stanton, they thought they knew the solution. This was put concisely by Emily Davies in *The Higher Education of Women.*[29] While admitting that 'her own duties fall to the lot of almost every woman and nothing which tends to incapacitate the performance of them ought to be encouraged,' she goes on to say that professional life does not damage children.[30] 'An educated woman, of active, methodological habits, blessed with good servants, as good mistresses generally are, finds an hour a day amply sufficient for her housekeeping. Nothing is gained by spreading it over a longer time.' This is further developed by an anonymous writer in *The Victorian Magazine*, quoted by the Banks. 'A professional woman spending a short time a day in the superintendence of her nursery and enjoying the society of her children, would find it a means of rest and refreshment.'

Another reason why the feminist movement did not take up birth control as an issue may have been that, after the initial movement, organized largely by women who were themselves mothers it tended, particularly in England, to be concerned with the fate of single women. The Banks have calculated that between 1851 and 1871 there was an increase in single women aged fifteen and over from 2,765,000 to 3,228,700, an increase of 16.8 per cent in twenty years. At the same time the number of *surplus* single women rose from 72,500 to 125,200, an increase of 72.7 per cent in over twenty years. It is likely that the growth was greater among the more privileged and articulate levels of society than among the less. Mortality rates were lower, middle class men tended to emigrate but not middle class women, and there seems to have been increasing reluctance among men in the middle and upper classes to marry at all. And even the most progressive people were not concerned with the fate of the single mother and her child. The fact that the child suffered with the mother for what was regarded as her sin enlisted little public support.

Although most feminists confined themselves largely to the big objective – gaining the vote – here and there one can find evidence of a certain hostility to childbearing and to the care of young children. An example, quoted by the Banks, comes from Mrs. E. Lynne Lynton's 'The Modern Revolt' in *MacMillan's Magazine* in December, 1870: 'In the question of maternity lies the saddest part of the Modern Revolt. God alone knows what good is to come out of the strange reactions against the maternal instinct, which is so marked a social feature in America, and which is spreading here. Formerly children were desired by all women, and their coming considered a blessing rather than otherwise; now the proportion of wives who regard them as a curse is something appalling, and the annoyance or despair with practical expression in many cases, given to that annoyance as their number increases is simply bewildering to those who have cherished that instinct as it used to be cherished.' John Stuart Mill in *The Saturday Review*, in 1877, talked about the 'indifference if not aversion to maternity' produced by the Revolt of Women.

Towards the end of the century, to the middle class, moralistic element in the feminist movement, was added a radical element aware of the problems of an urban, industrial society. Their concern was as much for working class as for middle class women and many had first hand knowledge of it. For instance, Florence Kelley often went with her father on trips to the growing industrial areas, and was struck by the way in which the human element was ignored. She described her visits to factories and noted 'the utter unimportance of children compared with products in the minds of the people whom I was among.'[31] Feminists began to call themselves socialists. In 1910 August Bebel (1840–1913) published *Woman and Socialism* in which he argued that the reconstruction of society would have to precede true equality between the sexes. Bebel believed that in the new society women would be 'entirely independent, both socially and economically, and this would be achieved by the abolition of property.' 'So woman will be *free*, and the children she may have will not impair her freedom. They will only increase her pleasure in life. Nurses, teachers, women friends, the rising female generation, all these will stand by her when she is in need of assistance. . . .'[32]

Whatever we may think about women standing by each other, here at least is a recognition that children, whatever blessings they may bring, do impair freedom. This was something which the earlier feminists, with their hosts of servants, had never realized.

Another radical writer, Emma Goldman (1869–1940), had a vision that stretches to our own time. She foresaw, for instance, that even when they got the vote, women would not accomplish what men had failed to accomplish. She also foresaw what was to become one of the greatest difficulties in feminist progress: the apathy of women themselves.

> The right to vote, or equal civil rights, may be good demands, but to me emancipation begins neither at the polls nor in the courts. It begins in women's soul. History tells us that every oppressed class gained true liberation from its masters through its own efforts. It is necessary that woman learn that lesson, that she realize that her freedom will reach as far as her power to achieve her freedom reaches. . . . Indeed, if partial emancipation is to become a complete and true emancipation of woman, it will have to do away with the ridiculous notion that to be loved, to be sweetheart and mother, is synonymous with being a slave or subordinate.[33]

In searching through early feminist literature in order to try to understand attitudes to motherhood and the changing problems of motherhood, as well as useful prophecies that seem relevant in our time, no writer is more exciting to read than Charlotte Perkins Gilman (1860–1935). Chafe says 'she articulated more brilliantly than anyone else the point of view held by many of the founders of feminism.' It is interesting that she had an unhappy first marriage, and the unhappiness was made worse during pregnancy and after the birth of a daughter. Her depression lifted when she left her family but returned when she came home. She was treated by the new treatment, psychotherapy. Her therapist advised prolonged rest and complete withdrawal from intellectual activity. This prescription, Gilman later admitted, 'almost drove her to madness.'

Alice S. Rossi comments, 'It was beyond the ken of contemporary psychiatric theories that a problem might reside in restricted life choices and that Charlotte was chafing from, and their prescriptions exacerbated, this handicap. It does not seem to have been her intellectual efforts and interests, but an acceptance of marriage and maternity, uncongenial to her personality, that was at the root of Charlotte Gilman's problem.'[34]

The attitude of Charlotte Perkins Gilman towards motherhood, laid out in her book on child rearing, *Concerning Children*, which was published in 1900, argued forcibly that children needed greater freedom in order to acquire responsibility, self-reliance and self-discipline. Her major book, *Women and Economics*, was published in 1898. In it she argued that woman's human impulses to grow and to create were stifled because of sexual dependence. One result of this was that children were psychologically deprived because they were dominated by mothers who had never been allowed to grow to mental maturity. 'It would seem that the human maternal duties require the segregation of the entire energies of the mother to the service of the child during her entire adult life, so large a proportion of them that not enough remains to devote to the individual interests of the mother. . . . '[35] and, 'Human motherhood is more pathological than any other, more morbid, defective, irregular, diseased. Human childhood is similarly pathological.'[36] She writes that our system of motherhood 'brings perils upon both mother and child' and we should be ashamed of it. The more absolutely woman is segregated to sex-functions only, cut off from economic use and made wholly dependent on the sex-relation, the more pathological does her motherhood become.'

Charlotte Gilman believed passionately that economic independence would make better mothers.

Economic independence for women necessarily involves a change in the home and family relation. But, if that change is for the advantage of individual and race, we need not fear it. It does not involve a change in the marriage relation except in withdrawing the element of economic dependence, nor in the relation of mother to child save to improve it. But it does involve the exercise of human faculty in women, in social service and exchange rather than in domestic service solely. This will of course require the introduction of some other form of living than that which now obtains. It will render impossible the present method of feeding the world by means of millions of private servants, and bringing up children by the same hand . . .[37]

Gilman's solutions include some that are echoed in the writings of later feminists. She suggested that cities should open apartment houses for professional women and their families. These would contain no kitchens, but 'meals could be served to the families in their rooms or in a common dining-room, as preferred.' Cleaning would be organized by the manager and each block would contain 'a roof garden, day nursery and kindergarten, under well-trained professional nurses and teachers'. Gilman saw such an establishment as 'a permanent provision for the needs of women and children, of family privacy with collective advantage'. It would be 'offered on a business basis to prove a substantial business success.' In the suburbs the same purpose could be established by grouping adjacent houses, 'all kitchen-less and connected by covered ways with the eating house'. She believed that people would prefer the 'pure, clean houses' that would result, 'where no cleaning industry is carried on.' She forestalls the criticism that the arrangement would lead to loss of family unity by asserting: 'A family unity which is only bound together with a table-cloth is of questionable value.'[38] She is aware of the increasing importance attached to privacy, but clearly cannot conceive of a household without servants or hired labour and which is penetrated by no one except members of the family and friends. She tells us, 'The swift progress of professional sweepers, dusters and scrubbers . . . would be at least no more injurious to privacy than the present method.'[39]

Gilman also argues for the communal raising of babies, believing that the child is injured by a home which is 'the centre of a tangled heap of industries, low in their ungraded condition, and lower still because they are wholly personal.' Moreover, a baby would benefit, and grow up less shy if he spent certain hours a day among other babies, thereby learning that he is 'one of many'.[40] To this purpose Gilman envisages using the labour of those talented in the care of children and avoiding the disastrous effects of those mothers who, she asserts, simply are not capable of caring for babies successfully.[41] Furthermore, 'a mother will love her child as well, perhaps better, when she is not in hourly contact with it, when she goes from its life to her own life, and back from her own life to its life, with ever new delight and power.'[42] As today, however, there was little chance of Gilman's views being accepted.

The last of the important early feminist writers whose views are relevant to this book is Suzanne La Follette (b. 1893). She took a very different view from Charlotte Perkins Gilman, for she had a deep mistrust of state intervention, even in the interests of human welfare. Many of her views are gaining ground again today, particularly her consistent belief that it is only through full economic independence and personal autonomy that sex equality will be achieved.

> If responsibility for the upbringing of children is to continue to be vested in the family, then the rights of children will be secured only when parents are able to make a living for their families with so little difficulty that they may give their best thought and energy to the child's development and the problem of helping it to adjust itself to the complexities of the modern environment. Such a condition is not utopian, but quite possible of attainment, as I shall show later. But for the present, and for some time to come, marriage and parenthood will continue to make men and women virtual slaves of the economic order which they help to perpetuate....[43]

She is aware of the inherent dangers of leaving a child alone with its mother.

> Children are really as helpless as women have always been held to be; and in their case the reason is not merely supposition. Woman was supposed to be undeveloped man. The child *is* undeveloped man or woman; and because of its lack of development it needs protection. To place it in the absolute power of its parents as its natural protectors and assume that its interests will invariably be well guarded, would be as cruel as was the assumption that a woman rendered legally and economically helpless and delivered over to a husband or other male guardian, was sure of humane treatment. No human being, man, woman, or child, may safely be entrusted to the power of another; for no human being may safely be trusted with absolute power. It is fair, therefore, that in the case of those whose physical or mental immaturity renders them comparatively helpless, there should be a watchful third person who from the

141

vantage-point of a disinterested neutrality may detect and stop any infringement of their rights by their guardians, be they parents or other people. Here, then, is a legitimate office for the community; to arbitrate, in the interest of justice, between children and their guardians.[44]

Suzanne La Follette was also aware of the inherent dangers of community care and control. 'To institutionalize', she wrote, 'is to mechanize.' To take children from their parents 'would be dangerous so long as the work of educators continues to be as little respected and as poorly paid as it now is.' Moreover there is the further danger of 'the opportunity to corrupt young minds and turn out rubber-stamp patriots.' The best argument against such a system, she wrote, 'is that it would not work. If experience teaches anything, it is that what the community undertakes to do is usually done badly. Therefore the community should always be slow to interfere between parents and children.'[45]

At this point one might begin to think that the early feminists had achieved full understanding of the situation. Suzanne La Follett's book *Concerning Women* was published in 1926, eight years after the Nineteenth Amendment in the United States and the first (if limited) granting of suffrage to women in England. However, now that we can look back over the following sixty years we can see that although some of the objectives of the early feminists have been gained, many of the situations they describe are, in different ways, just as true today. The Victorian lady had become a woman. She wore different clothes and she could vote, but in many ways she was in the same situation. Feminism had always been weakest and had evoked the greatest opposition when it attacked, or tried to make changes in the family. The idea of privacy in the family had been increasing over many years and with the slow decline in the number of servants, first in America and then in Europe, this was increased, together with the isolation of the mother at home and public idealization of her situation.

CHAPTER NINE

Feminism and Motherhood: After the Vote

'An Englishman's home is his castle' was a popular Victorian saying. On both sides of the Atlantic there had long been considerable opposition to anything that seemed to threaten the family. By the end of the century the broad ideas of early feminists such as Elizabeth Cady Stanton and Susan Anthony had become submerged in the struggle for the vote, and there was little pressure to change the accepted differences in sex roles. Eileen Kraditor in her book *Ideas* has analyzed America's commitment to the idea that the family, not the individual, is the basic unit of society. Each home existed as a 'state in miniature', with one head, the husband, who alone represented it to the world outside. Anyone suggesting any change in that structure was felt to be threatening the whole basis of society. Suffragists linked themselves with progressivism and reform by social welfare legislation to improve the lot of the poor rather than to alter the structure of their own lives, and were careful to try to avoid arousing opposition by seeming to attack the family.

Moreover, women used their right to vote to a degree that was disappointing to those who had fought so hard for it: they voted neither in great numbers nor to further special female or feminist causes. Fairly typical was the New York election in 1920 when only about a third of women voters cast their ballot. And when women did vote they tended to vote in the same way as their husbands. Suffrage did not alter the structure of society nor the sexual division of labour. Moreover, feminism, having achieved its most tangible object, lost appeal. The League of Women Voters declined, the Women's Trade Union League abandoned politics entirely and chose to emphasize home economics and the distribution of electrical appliances. Carrie Chapman Catt, who had led the final struggle for the vote, turned her energies to the Committee in the Cause and

143

Cure of War and declared that women would never be liberated until war was abolished.[1] Jane Addams, another powerful leader, turned to the Women's International League for Peace and Freedom and other reformers concentrated on social welfare legislation. In England the situation was much the same. The younger generation of women, even those with feminist inclinations, had little interest in extending women's rights and tended to think that the battle was won. This is well described by Vera Brittain in *Testament of Youth*. Opportunities for careers were largely of interest to spinsters, of whom there were many, particularly in England, due to the enormous casualties of World War I. In the United States there was an increase of domesticity among the very groups likely to produce career women. Chafe has shown how, during the 1920s, an increasing number of female college students expressed a preference for marriage.[2] At the end of the nineteenth century, half the graduates of the best women's colleges had remained single and most of these entered the professions; the desire for a career was one of the most frequently cited reasons for having chosen a Vassar education. Of Vassar women in 1923, ninety per cent wanted to get married and most believed that marriage was the 'biggest of all careers'. At the same time the curriculum of women's education changed to include courses that would prepare women for the occupation of homemaking. Vassar offered a series of courses: Husband and Wife, Motherhood, The Family as an Economic Unit, designed to train students to be 'gracious and intelligent wives and mothers'. At the inauguration of one women's college president in 1925, the head of another college, in his address, said: 'One of the chief ends of a college for women is to fit them to become the makers of homes ... whatever else a woman may be, the highest purpose of her life always has been ... to strengthen and beautify and sanctify the home.'[3]

Chafe has made a study of the women's magazines of the period.[4] 'With increasing stridency,' he writes, 'women's magazines voiced the same theme, insisting that the role of mother and housewife represented the only path to feminine fulfilment. In the years immediately after the passage of the Nineteenth Amendment, occasional articles justified female independence and defended the right of women to work. By the late 1920s, however, the attitude of tolerant permissiveness had changed to one of outright condemnation. ... Women's magazines urged their readers to return to femininity and constructed an elaborate ideology in support of the home and marriage to facilitate the process.' One journal in 1929 urged that homemaking 'is today an adventure – an education in color, in mechanics, in chemistry.' Another said that homemaking 'exercises an even more profound influence on human destiny than the terrorism of war or the prosperity of peace.' Labour saving devices, it was said, increased the housewife's role by elevating her position in the world and giving her more time to develop socially and train her children. With fewer routine chores to perform a wife could devote herself to the more important job of creating happiness for her family. The *Ladies Home Journal* declared, 'The creation and fulfilment of a successful home is a bit of craftmanship that compares favourably with building a beautiful cathedral.' Liberated women, these magazines declared, had thrown away the essence of femininity without putting anything else in its place. A woman's career was to make a good marriage, to be 'deeply, fundamentally, wholly feminine'. Laura Cornell, dean of Temple University, wrote that women who demanded recognition for themselves were violating their own true nature because women required protection, and men needed to give it. Women such as Dorothy Thompson and Clare Callahan joined the chorus, though they themselves had made successful professional careers. To show how the magazines defended the boredom of housework and exploitations of husbands Chafe describes how they tried to make homemaking appear the most rewarding occupation of all. One article declared: 'Just as a rose comes to its fullest beauty in its own appropriate soil, so does a home woman come to her fairest blooming when her roots are stuck deep in the daily and hourly affairs of her own most dearly beloved.' A woman might resent at times 'the thoughtlessness and omissions of her husband' but once she accepted 'that big biologic fact that man was intended to be selfish' and woman self-sacrificing the way to fulfilment was clear. Only if a woman rejected her natural identity would she have cause to experience dissatisfaction and despair.

The Depression of the 1930s was also influential in diminishing feminist hopes of economic equality. It was widely believed that during a time of massive unemployment women should sacrifice personal ambitions and not compete with men who had families to support. The dean of Syracuse University urged women college graduates to enter volunteer work rather than accept a salary. A 'pin-money worker' was declared to be 'a menace to society and a selfish short-sighted creature who ought to be ashamed of herself.' Any woman capable of supporting herself without a job, the future U.S. Secretary of Labor declared, should devote herself to motherhood and the home.

This campaign for women to renounce education (except the purely feminine kind) and become perfect homemakers was much less marked in England during the 1920s and 1930s, and was held in ridicule there by those concerned with the higher education of women.

To compare with the previously mentioned Vassar figures I have analyzed figures from my own college records. From the time it was founded in 1879 Somerville College, Oxford, had the reputation of being the 'brainy' college. It would not have occurred to anyone there that its students should pursue courses specially designed for future housewives. Everyone pursued a standard academic course and took the same examinations as the students in the men's colleges. It is interesting to note that at the time when the Vassar girls were turning to homemaking, the Somervillians were going the other way. I have analyzed some of the information in the college register of 1969, the last available.[5] The results suggest a very different trend from those of Vassar. Of the seventy-six women who entered the college in 1902–04, thirty-two (42%) married before they were forty and of these twenty-four (31.5%) had children, an average of 2.46 each. Of the seventy-six women who entered the college in 1912–13 the marriage rate was slightly higher, 45%. But of the eighty-three women who entered the college in 1922–23, only twenty-eight (33%) married, of whom nineteen (22%) had children. Thereafter the rate of marriage increased steadily. Of the fifty-one women who entered in 1933, thirty-two (63%) married and of these sixteen (31.3%) had children, an average of 2.93 each.

This change was not based on the 'homemaking is glorious fulfilment' idea that was so widespread in the United States but rather more on the personal satisfaction of the many women who knew that they could now do what they wanted to do. For in Britain between the wars the women's rights movement had actually enabled an educated woman, if she could resist social pressures and had an accommodating husband, to combine an active family life with a career in a way that had not been possible before. This was much more difficult in America, and became much more difficult later in Britain. The reason was that there were still plenty of servants in Britain, and one did not need to be rich to employ them. To give just a few examples, Vera Brittain and Marghanita Laski were both mothers with careers. Dr. Edith Summerskill had a distinguished political career and a family. Barbara Hepworth, one of the best sculptors of this century, was the mother of triplets. Virginia Woolf, married but childless, made a distinguished literary career and probably would have done the same had she been a mother. Although she wrote passionately of the ways in which women had been made 'insignificant' in history, she was herself a liberated woman in the sense that she was able to do what she wanted. Her sister Vanessa Bell, who was a mother, became a distinguished painter. In medicine Dorothea Nasmyth became the first woman general practitioner in Oxford when her children were quite small. Dr. Sylvia Payne was in charge of a military hospital during World War I when her three sons were scarcely more than babies. After the war she took up the new specialty of psychoanalysis, and became one of its most distinguished practitioners and President of the British Psycho-Analytical Association. These are just a few. I talked to a number of these older women about their lives and was interested that none of them seemed to have found their dual role a strain. Their households ran smoothly: they did not have to hurry home in the evening to cook the evening meal or spend their lunch hours shopping for it; meals appeared on the table at whatever time they requested and they earned enough to pay for this; they were free of household chores. They were not pressured by psychological theory into feeling guilty if they were not with their children all day. No one talked of 'separation anxiety' or duties towards the under-fives. Like the other women of their class, many of whom spent the day in shopping or in social activity, they had nannies for their children. They saw their husbands and children for several hours a day, at least as much as their more conventional friends. They enjoyed being mothers and found satisfaction in marriage. Their children grew up to be normal and healthy. Most of them said that they were able to do these things largely because of a certain independence of mind and because they chose husbands who did not feel threatened by having professional wives. Given these two things, the rest was easy.

Even the most liberated women of this generation were conscious of how much things had improved for women, at least for women without serious financial problems, in their time. Not only did they have the vote but even during the Depression of the 1930s infant mortality continued to fall, childbirth became safer, and women's education continued to improve. If some paths were still blocked it seemed to them only a question of time before further progress would be made. There were so many new opportunities open to them that only the most imaginative, such as Virginia Woolf, seem to have been conscious or cared that there was a long way to go. In general there was a feeling that women had achieved so much that there was little more to achieve. Probably most of these liberated women between the wars envisaged, if they thought about it at all, that their daughters would grow up to have broadly similar lives to theirs, perhaps better, but not radically different. These daughters, who were my own generation, grew up wearing short skirts and with an indubitable right to vote when they were twenty-one. Many more of them than formerly were able to have a good education, as by this time there were many girls' schools with high academic standards and traditions of fifty years or more behind them. There were many more places in universities for women. There were State Scholarships and County Grants for those whose parents could not pay. The opportunities were there for those who wished to take them or whose family situation and traditions allowed it. But it was also an age when girls could still get away with virtually no education, with lying in bed on the first day of every period, and waiting for the right men to come along to support them for the rest of their lives. The vast majority of women, particularly married women, did not have freedom. Some lacked the qualifications. Some could not find suitable careers, since many were still barred to them. For instance, the civil service barred married women and until World War II it was extremely difficult for a married woman to get a teaching post. Some women could not resist social pressures, had husbands who disapproved of their wives having serious outside interests, or lacked the energy or desire. One of the facts that career women tend to ignore is that there are huge numbers of people who prefer leisure to paid work. They will do what they have to and no more and would not dream of working hard for its own sake or for their own self-development or fulfilment. Many women who had servants preferred to lie in bed late, play bridge or gossip with neighbours to spending their ample available time in purposeful or gainful activity. The same is true today of many women running their homes easily on their own aided by today's machines, gadgets and convenience foods. Housekeeping has been made easy and they like it that way. As long as their husbands are satisfied and their children well fed, they want it to stay that way. I am not suggesting that idleness is a female characteristic: doubtless many men would be idle too, given the opportunity, but social and financial pressures are against it, whereas they actually encourage women to be idle. Moreover, many women would not wish to do anything that might interfere with the convenience of husband or children. Many others positively enjoy the independence of being a housewife. Even when they have a great deal to do or find housework or child care boring, they like to do it in their own time and in their own way, without the feeling of being beholden to anyone. This feeling is strengthened by the fact that many of them, if they went out to work, would have to work strict hours, under supervision, and do exactly what the boss demanded and at his convenience. Homemaking can give a sense of freedom and autonomy that is found in few paid occupations.

There are also financial considerations. As tax laws are at present, a woman whose husband earns well gains little or nothing from working, unless her earning capacity is high. She will be highly taxed on what she earns, her housekeeping will become more expensive because she will have less time to do and make things for herself. She may need more expensive clothes and a car. If she needs domestic help to replace her at home, she will have to pay heavily for it and, in Britain, even someone to mind her children while she is earning has to be paid out of her taxed earnings. It is possible to have a job, earn good money and actually be out of pocket from it. True, some concessions have been made in recent years for working wives, but for the wife of the successful man, they are paltry. And many of these women are the very ones who, under other circumstances, would lead satisfying professional lives.

Last and, from the point of view of this book perhaps the most important, there are many women who, whatever their educational background and professional training, find that the most satisfying thing they have ever done is to devote themselves exclusively to their children, particularly in the early years. Those who were middle class, whose children were traditionally raised by servants and who had themselves been raised in this way, were the ones who so passionately embraced the new fashion and necessity to care for their children personally and totally. It was they who were the followers of the new psychological theories which justified and urged

149

this way of mothering. These women have been powerful since World War II. Their housework is done quickly and easily with the aid of the new electrical gadgets. Their husbands work away from home. All day and every day they devote themselves to their children who, at least until they go to school, are constantly in the presence of their mothers and often hardly meet anyone else except their fathers. In these mothers privacy and self-sufficiency have reached extremes but many of them enjoy it.

It is perhaps unfortunate from the point of view of problems facing mothers today that the achievement of votes for women coincided in the United States and, to a lesser extent in Britain, with this intense privatisation of motherhood and its subsequent idealization. For in this climate motherhood could never be raised in the way it might have been, and so opportunities were lost. For the state it was a cheap way out. It suited the government who could close down child care facilities and nursery schools without arousing significant opposition. It suited advertisers, too, to have an enormous market of homemakers each aiming to have a gleaming, shiny home full of gadgets and gleaming, shiny children.

This extreme privatisation of motherhood only caught on in Britain after World War II. During the war on both sides of the Atlantic there was official encouragement for women to work together with the establishment of day nurseries and day care centres for working mothers. After the war most of these closed down, and mothers who had enjoyed greater freedom to work and assistance in their working lives found that official help was now largely withdrawn, servants had virtually disappeared, and fitted kitchens and washing machines had become available. Thus the movement towards homemaking that had been so marked among college women in America after World War I swept Britain after World War II. It was dominated by the middle classes and it turned into a era in which motherhood was glorified and idealized. During the 1950s and 60s the birth rate rose, especially among the middle classes, and marriage became even more popular. This is reflected in the register of Somerville graduates. The desire to do something else as well also increased, despite the difficulties at that period of continuing a career with motherhood. Of my own class at Somerville College, Oxford sixty-eight women entered in 1943, fifty-three (78%) married under the age of forty and of these forty-one (60%) had had, by the time the information was collected, an average of

2.44 children each. These forty-one mothers include prominent women such as Margaret Thatcher, who pursued a parliamentary career with two children, and became Britain's first woman Prime Minister, and Nina Bawden, a successful novelist, who is the mother of three children. The same period within a few years at Somerville produced many other mothers who were successful in the world while raising children.

In spite of the existence of enormous and varied opportunities for those who looked for them, it was the leisure-loving women and the devoted mothers in western society just as much as men who were powerful in resisting ideas about equality for women and in perpetuating the idea that a woman should be a passive appendage to her husband and totally devoted to her children, so that if she has any activity outside the home, or personal activity inside it, it should only take place if it does not inconvenience her family in any way.

Much has been made of the complacency of the period, of the failure to press forward what had been gained and of the strong pressures to retain the idea that woman, whatever her political rights, is different from man. True, this idea was exaggerated and pushed to extremes by men fearing competition, by advertisers seeking markets, by women's magazines and by zealous devotees of Freud and, later, Bowlby. But in practice it was not usually as crude as that. The rationale among women who tried to understand what was happening was different, and less complacent than is often said. Because such trends are different in different times and places and among different women, it would require another book to attempt to analyse it fully here. But perhaps I can throw some light on it by giving examples from my own experience, how I and those I knew felt and how we viewed and coped with our experiences of motherhood in the 1950s and early 60s. We were probably fairly typical of the educated mothers in Britain at the time. In another era we would doubtless have been active in women's rights movements. Why then were we not?

These were women who were born between the wars. When they grew up many more of them married than in previous generations of educated women. Unlike the earlier generation there were few spinsters among them for far fewer men were killed during World War II than during the First. Bachelors had become uncommon. Fewer spinsters meant that there was more available work and employers, through sheer need in a world of full employment, relaxed their

views about employing married women and began to make concessions to them, for instance in part-time work, flexible hours, and,
occasionally, in the provision of facilities for child-minding.
Besides, this generation of women was now accustomed to the idea
of work and horizons beyond the home. They were aware of other
attractions, even though they wanted more than anything to be
married and to have children. There were many more of these well-
trained women than in previous generations and they wanted to
work, but not at the expense of marriage and motherhood. So the
idea grew up that the ideal was to be married and to have some
outside work as well, while arranging that husband and children did
not suffer in any way and probably not until the children were at
school. At the same time help in the home was becoming increasingly difficult to find. The modern western feeling that personal
service to others is demeaning was gaining ground. For some years
full employment gave new opportunities to those who might otherwise have gone into service, and by the time unemployment
increased again, personal service was held in such low esteem that
few would enter it.

Meanwhile ideas about motherhood were changing. The importance of the earliest years and of early relationships was beginning to
be understood. The ideas of Freud were spreading, though more
slowly and less widely in Britain than in America. In 1951 John
Bowlby announced to the world the devastating effects of prolonged
separation from their mothers on young children. His work was
done on children in institutions who were totally deprived of
mothering but his ideas were exaggerated and exploited by both
mothers and others. There was also considerable social pressure to
have children. The birth rate increased. Childless women felt guilty
and out of the main trend. Young mothers who felt that they needed
something more than the confines of home and the conversation of
young children mostly regarded this as an individual problem which
each woman had to solve in her own way, according to what was best
for her particular family. The Freudian view of women was fashionable. Even women with brains, education and drive tried to conform
to the idea that women should be passive, masochistic and supportive. Feminism was unfashionable. Women's Institutes flourished in
both Britain and the United States and promoted traditional arts
such as cake- and jam-making. Feminist organizations such as the
Fawcett Society were regarded as old-fashioned and failed to attract

the young women of the time. In 1936 Ray Strachey had written in the introduction to *Our Freedom and its Results*, 'Modern young women know amazingly little of what life was like before the war, and show a strong hostility to the word "feminism" and all which they imagine it to connote.' Sheila Rowbotham has commented, 'These young women had been taught to despise their own movement by a culture that was anti-feminist. But this was not the whole of it. They inherited a feminism which had lost its glory, and forgotten its power, and thus saw little that could capture their feelings.'[6]

Much of the feminism of the time, if one can call it feminism, became a question of trying to survive both as a wife and mother and as a woman and a person. Those educated women who knew that they could not give of their best to their husbands and children unless they were also fulfilled by exercising their minds, the skills which they had acquired and the professions for which they had been trained, devoted themselves totally to coping with the paradox in which they found themselves and solving the conflicts that arose as a result of it. They had little time to think about 'women's rights' or of how women were 'oppressed'. They assumed that they had to look after the husbands they had chosen to marry and to care for the children they had chosen to have. They regarded whatever else they did as their own business and there were far more opportunities available to them than there had ever been to their parents if only they could organize themselves sufficiently well. One might say that they were doing their best to take advantage of new opportunities in a world that they knew was not basically constructed for their needs.

Gradually the idea of work for mothers grew. Full employment meant that there was a need for women to work. The spinsters of the previous generation were retiring and it became difficult to find women to replace them. Efforts were made to lure trained women back into professions such as medicine and teaching and to train others. Training and retraining schemes were started, many of which made concessions to family commitments. Many part-time jobs were created and there was considerable pressure, never very successful, for more nursery schools. There were problems among mothers who found they lacked the confidence to go out into the world if they had stayed at home for years. The media were full of good advice to help them.

Since World War II two big, slow changes among women encouraged the rebirth of active feminism and a new awareness of inequalities between the sexes. One was the increase, on both sides of the Atlantic, of women who found it necessary to go out to work. The other was the gradual collapse of the idealized picture of the wife and mother.

There was little change in the numbers of married women who went out to work between 1910 and 1940 but since then there has been a considerable increase in working women married with children. In the United States twice as many women were at work in 1960 as in 1940 and 40% of all women over sixteen held a job.[7] The proportion of wives at work had doubled from 15% in 1940 to 30% in 1960. The number of single women in the labour force declined but the number of mothers employed increased from 1.5 million to 6.6 million, an increase of over 400% and 39% of women with children aged six to seventeen had jobs. By 1960 both the husband and wife worked in over 10 million homes – an increase of 333% over 1940 and mothers of children under eighteen comprised nearly a third of all women workers. Significantly, the greatest growth in the female labour force took place among well-educated wives. Before World War II married women workers came almost exclusively from the poorer sections of the community. By 1950 wives whose husbands earned $7,000 – 10,000 a year formed 7% of the female labour force in the United States. By 1960 this had risen to 25%. In 1973 the United States Census reported more than 6 million children under the age of six whose mothers worked full time outside the home. Chafe comments 'not only was the revolution in female employment continuing; it was also spearheaded by the same middle-class wives and mothers who allegedly had found new contentment in domesticity.'[8] He believes that the impetus was largely the new connotation of 'economic need', now including luxuries such as cars, recreation and restaurant meals. Personal satisfaction was also a powerful motive.

The trend was similar in Britain. In 1977 nearly nine million women worked outside their homes, an increase of more than a million since 1961, and the proportion of married women working increased dramatically, while the number of single women fell.[9] In a recent count 42% of married women were employed outside the home and married women composed 62% of the female workforce.[10] It has become clear that increasing numbers of families are dependent on the mothers' earnings.

Under such circumstances the idealized picture of the wife and mother in the home which had been supported for so long by governments, by advertisers, by husbands and by mothers themselves became less convincing and its disadvantages began to become more apparent. As long ago as 1942, Philip Wylie, in his *Generation of Vipers*, blamed 'momism' in America for much of the troubles of youth. The excessive adoration of the mother, said Wylie, symbolized a pathological emptiness in women's lives. With nothing else to occupy them, women preyed on their children, smothering them with affection and making them pathologically dependent so that they would remain at home. As a result they had developed an insatiable appetite for devouring their children and preventing them from developing into independent adults. Echoing this, Dr. Edward Strecker, a consultant psychiatrist to the Secretary of War, wrote about the alarmingly high rate of men rejected for the United States armed forces during World War II because of nervous disability – three million of them. Dr. Strecker blamed their mothers who had 'failed in the elementary mother function of weaning offspring emotionally as well as physically.' But these books and thoughts produced an anti-feminist backlash from such writers as Lundberg and Farnham.[11] It was not for over two decades, when the working mother was becoming both a necessity and a desire for so many that a new movement arose.

We have seen that motherhood was not experienced as a problem by the early feminists. They fought for the franchise and for equality before the law, and on the whole did not question the division of labour. Those who were mothers had plenty of servants and did not find child-rearing particularly irksome. They tended to emphasize the importance of education to women in the home rather than the importance of women outside the home. Once the vote was won or nearly won the emphasis of feminists was more on how to improve other people's maternity than on their own. For instance, Margaret Llewellyn Davies (1861–1944), who herself came from an upper middle class family, collected one hundred and sixty letters written by members of the Women's Co-operative Guild and, at the instigation of Virginia Woolf, published them in London in 1915 under the title *Maternity: Letters from Working Women*. The letters were a response to an appeal from Miss Davies for direct experiences of childbirth and childrearing which she wanted as evidence in the Guild's campaign against the Liberal government and local authorities, to improve maternal and infant care for poorer women. In his preface to the book, the Right Honourable Herbert Samuel, expressed the view of the more enlightened section of the community. 'The conclusion is clear that it is the duty of the community, so far as it can, to relieve mother-hood of its burdens, to spread the knowledge of mothercraft that is so often lacking, to make medical aid available when it is needed, to watch over the health of the infant. And since this is the duty of the community, it is also the duty of the State. The infant cannot, indeed, be saved by the State. It can only be saved by the mother. But the mother can be helped and can be taught by the State.' The letters came from wives of manual labourers but by no means from the poorest section of the community. Miss Davies wrote that the earnings of their husbands 'are certainly above, rather than below the level of their class,' yet their stories of pain and suffering, poverty, hardship, malnutrition and lack of knowledge are pitiful to read. So marked was the difference between these conditions and those of the middle class that the answer at the time seemed to be to close the gap. Miss Davies wrote: 'The roots of the evil lie in the con-ditions of life which our industrial system forces upon the wage-earners . . . The middle-class wife from the first moment is within reach of medical advice which can alleviate distressing illness and confinements and often prevent future ill health or death. During the months of pregnancy she is not called upon to work; she is well fed; she is able to take the necessary rest and exercise. At the time of the birth she will have the constant attendance of doctor and nurse and she will remain in bed until she is well enough to get up. For a woman of the middle class to be deprived of any one of these things would be considered an outrage. Now, a working class woman, is habitually deprived of them all. . . .'[12]

There was no suggestion at this time, or for another half century, that woman's role as mother might be questioned. It is often said that those years after the rote was won were dead years as regards feminism. Nevertheless the gradually increasing awareness of the plight of many women together with the formation during this period of certain ideas were the foundation of what later became the women's liberation movement. Virginia Woolf, in *A Room of One's Own*, published in 1929, wrote angrily of the patriarchy under which we live and pointed out that the overwhelming need for a woman's creativity was money and privacy (today we might add time, but then Virginia Woolf was not a mother and had servants to

attend to her). In 1935 Margaret Mead published *Sex and Tempera-*
ment in Three Primitive Societies in which she showed how the different roles played by the two sexes are determined by culture, not
nature.

Another book which had a great deal of influence was *Le Deux-*
ieme Sexe by Simone de Beauvoir. First published in France in 1949
and in America as *The Second Sex* in 1952, the book, though avo-
wedly non-feminist, represents a suitable transition between the old
feminism and the new. It is apolitical, is written to explain rather
than to reform, and captures the ambivalence of the era in a unique
way. As Alice Rossi writes: 'Its tone is caught by a quotation from
Kierkegaard which graced the introduction: "What a misfortune it
is to be a woman! And yet the greatest misfortune when one is a
woman is not to realize that it is one."'[13] De Beauvoir does,
however, bring home strongly the central theses of modern feminism, that we live in a patriarchal society, that as a result women have
had to take second place and that this is the result not of necessary
'feminine' characteristics but is of strong environmental forces of
education and social tradition.

'Enough ink has been spilled quarrelling over feminism,' says
Simone de Beauvoir in the introduction to her book. 'After all, is
there a problem? And if so, what is it?' I do not intend to summarize
the book here, but only to look at what the author has to say about
mothers and motherhood, since she clearly gave it much more
thought than have many modern feminists. Her first mention of
motherhood comes in a discussion on Christianity.[14] Paradoxically,
she points out, it was Christianity that first proclaimed the equality
of men and women before God. Yet the Church is part of a patriarchal civilization in which woman is an appendage to man and 'It is
through being his docile servant that she will be also a blessed saint.'
Thus arises 'the most highly perfected image of woman propitious
to man; the countenance of the Mother of Christ is framed in glory.'

De Beauvoir continues: 'It was as Mother that woman was fearsome, it is in maternity that she must be transfigured and
enslaved ... She will be glorified only in accepting the subordinate
role assigned to her. "I am the servant of the Lord." For the first
time in human history the mother kneels before her son; she freely
accepts her inferiority. This is the supreme masculine victory, con-
summated in the cult of the Virgin – it is the rehabilitation of the
woman through the accomplishment of her defect ... God alone is

king. Nature, originally inimical, is through grace rendered powerless to harm. Maternity as a natural phenomenon confers no power.
So there remains for woman, if she wishes to rise above her original
fault, only to bow to the will of God, which subordinates her to man.
And through this submission she can assume a new role in masculine mythology. Beaten down, trampled upon when she wished to
dominate and as long as she has not definitely abdicated, she could
be honoured as a vassal. She loses none of her primitive attributes,
but these are reversed in sign; from being of evil omen they become
of good omen; black magic turns to white. As servant, woman is en-
titled to the most splendid deification.' We have already seen the
practical aspects of this in Chapter Six.

In her long book of 741 pages, de Beauvoir allots only 41 pages to
the chapter called 'The Mother'. Of these nearly a quarter are used
to discuss abortion, which is perhaps not surprising since de Beauvoir never had a child but she did once have an abortion and signed a
public document admitting it. A further twelve pages are devoted to
pregnancy and childbirth and six more to the newborn. Only fourteen pages remain in which to discuss motherhood after the
newborn stage. Nevertheless in these few pages she has packed a
great deal of observation and comment on mothers both good and
bad and throws some light on those who are unsuitable to have total
power over their children. I have not read anything on the subject in
any later feminist literature so relevant to our time. The mother, she
says, 'is delighted to feel herself necessary; her existence is justified
by the wants she supplies, but what gives mother love its difficulty
and its grandeur is the fact that it implies no reciprocity. . . .' The
mother 'remains alone; she expects no return for what she gives, it is
for her to justify it herself. This generosity merits the laudation that
men never tire of conferring upon her; but the distortion begins
when the religion of Maternity proclaims that all mothers are
saintly. For while maternal devotion may be perfectly genuine, this,
in fact, is rarely the case. Maternity is usually a strange mixture of
narcissism, altruism, idle day-dreaming, sincerity, bad faith, devotion and cynicism.'

With great insight, de Beauvoir states that in our culture what
threatens the infant most is a discontented woman, sexually frigid or
unsatisfied, socially inferior to men, and with 'no independent grasp
on the world or on the future.'[15] She tries to compensate for her frustrations through her child. She coddles it but also tortures it,

taking vengeance on men, on the world, on herself. In the past this aspect of motherhood has been portrayed in the figure of the cruel stepmother who often punishes the children of a 'good' mother who is dead. In reality the 'badness' may be difficult to see because most women, being moral and decent, repress their unacceptable feelings. Nevertheless these feelings tend to come out momentarily in angry scenes and in general attitudes. Occasionally mothers are openly sadistic. Many are capricious, domineering, unpredictable or vain. Many expect too much gratitude or try to force the child to be what they want him to be rather than what he really is, thus harming the child and disappointing themselves and their lack of success increases their hostility.

De Beauvoir goes on to discuss masochistic devotion in which the mother makes herself a slave to compensate for her own emptiness and to punish herself for her unexpressed hostility.[16] 'Such a mother is morbidly anxious, not allowing her child out of her sight; she gives up all diversion, all personal life, thus assuming the role of victim; and she derives from these sacrifices the right to deny her child all independence. This renunciation on the mother's part is easily reconciled with a tyrannical will to domination ... The main excuse of the mother is that her child by no means provides that happy self-fulfilment which has been promised her since her own childhood; she blames him for the deception of which she has been the victim, and which he innocently exposes.'

Later she expresses the feelings that are apparent in much modern feminist literature: 'Most women simultaneously demand and detest their feminine condition; they live through it in a state of resentment.'[17] She also foresees some of the main psychological problems of our time when she discusses the 'dangerous falsity' of two currently accepted preconceptions.[18] The first is that motherhood is sufficient in all cases to crown a woman's life. In many cases it is not. Many mothers are unhappy, unsatisfied and bitter. Having a child is 'an enterprise to which one can validly devote oneself' but it is no panacea. It requires a 'woman who is well-balanced, healthy and aware of her responsibilities' and it is not an obligation imposed by nature but a freely willed obligation. She goes on to say that the second false preconception is that the child is sure of being happy in its mother's arms. Since there is no such thing as a 'natural' maternal love there can be no 'unnatural' mothers but for precisely this reason there can be bad mothers. One of the major truths of psychoanalysis is that the personalities of 'normal' parents may damage the children. 'In particular', says de Beauvoir, 'maternal sado-masochistic behaviour towards her children, and so on without end.'[19]

Later she identifies another big problem of our time: the way in which children tend to limit their mothers' horizons. Although modern humanity demands that women play a role in the economic, political and social life of our times and although the woman who enjoys the richest individual life has much to give her children and demands the least from them, society makes this difficult for women to achieve.

The Second Sex is an abstract and theoretical book. It contains few practical suggestions and is reforming only by implication. Nevertheless these few pages about the problems of motherhood antici-pated problems and situations that must be taken into account today but which are usually ignored. These include particularly the power of the segregated, isolated mother, the effect of her personality, and the paradox of her need to be 'well-balanced, healthy and aware'. They also include the difficulties of achieving this and motherhood too without 'dangerous falsity' under the present social system.

A more practical book, published a few years later and also im-portant in the transitional stage of feminism, was *Women's Two Roles: Home and Work* by Alva Myrdal and Viola Klein. At a time when more and more married women were going out to work, the idea gradually spread, largely from psychoanalysis, that the early years of life are of profound importance for the rest of life. New con-flicts, and new awareness of conflicts, began to be discerned. First published in 1956, this book arose from a suggestion made to Alva Myrdal by the International Federation of University Women for 'an international survey of the needs for social reforms if women are to be put into a position to reconcile family and professional life.' The book points out that the question of whether married women should be employed outside their homes had become the most topical issue concerning women. Women's role in society and the problem of 'women and work' had completely changed during the last decades. There was no longer doubt about what women could do. The question now was what *should* they do. Moreover it was no longer necessary for women to choose between one sphere and another. 'The best of both worlds is in their grasp, if only they can reach it.' But to make this a reality 'something in the nature of a mental revolt' would be needed. Society could be reorganized so that women could enjoy both family life and gainful employment, but 'a more clear thinking both about ends and means, and a courageous facing of facts' would be required before these two roles could be combined satisfactorily.

Myrdal and Klein's initial concern was with women's lost economic past and the 'recovery of women's lost territory' which, because it was lost, had to be restored by breaking 'completely new ground' by a 'long and painful process'. By this time the pioneer process was over. Countless comparative studies had been published testing the relative aptitudes and traits of men and women. They had proved that most women are as good as most men on most scores, that individuals of one sex always vary more between themselves than any averages for the sexes as a whole differ from each other; and that any measurable differences in average performance of one sex in a particular field are balanced by the differences in another. 'If men show a somewhat greater inclination towards one capacity, such as mechanics, women compensate by excelling in another, such as languages. If men more often excel in physical strength, women correspondingly excel in dexterity.'[20]

Women's capacity to achieve had been established in World War II and it was becoming accepted that in our highly complex and diversified economic structure there is a scope for all sorts of natural gifts. Physical strength was no longer essential for most jobs. Myrdal and Klein pointed out that the setting for participation in the processes of economic production was much more favourable for women at the time that they wrote than at any time since the beginning of the Industrial Revolution. Moreover, society had begun to accept the fact that women were in jobs to stay. They also pointed out that, due to increasing longevity and smaller families, 'modern mothers who make no plans outside the family for their future will not only play havoc with their own lives but will make nervous wrecks of their overprotected children and of their husbands.'[21]

Like Simone de Beauvoir, Myrdal and Klein accept the traditional role of mother without question. 'Since it is women's business not only to bear children but also to take the lion's share in their care and management,' they wrote unquestioningly, 'we shall have to study the effect of women's employment on both these functions.'[22] And they did not envisage any change: 'To combine a career with a family may be difficult at present; but it is clearly less so than it was thirty years ago, and it is likely to become easier as time goes on and technical efficiency increases.'[23]

Regarding the effect which the temporary regular separation from their mothers that some young children inevitably experience they point out that there was no evidence (as is still the case now) that this is harmful, and they point out what has been prominent in later feminist literature, namely that the studies done on this subject, e.g. those by John Bowlby, were on children who suffered total deprivation of maternal care, usually following some calamity and that in no way can these be compared with children who are separated from their mothers for only a few hours a day. They also make, but do not develop, the point that is discussed fully later in this book: that the all-important factor is the attitude and personality of the mother rather than the amount of time she spends with her children. 'The neurotic, neglectful or foolish mother is a menace to her children, probably no less if she devotes all her time to them than if she does not. On the other hand, the intelligent, sympathetic, loving mother may be able to give the child a sense of emotional security which is not disturbed by her regular, or even her irregular, absences.'[24] One might add here that the 'neurotic, neglectful or foolish mother' is likely to do *more* harm to her children if she is with them all the time than if she shares their care with others who are loving towards them and who can make up for her deficiencies. The same is true of mothers who have strong personal needs which cannot be satisfied in the constant presence of children, such as using their adult minds, exercising skills for which they have been trained, or even simply earning money. A contented part-time mother is better than a discontented, frustrated or inhibited full-time mother and, provided the substitute care is good, her children will do better. Myrdal and Klein, perhaps because of the atmosphere of the time, do not point this out, though it is implied in much of what they say. Cautiously they conclude that because impersonal care in institutions, or by changing servants or relatives, may reduce children's feeling of security and lead to undesirable results, mothers should, as far as possible, take care of their own children during the first years of their lives.[25] However they go on to quote Margaret Mead who pointed out the confusion that exists between the child's need for care by human beings and the 'specific biological situation of the continuing relationship of the child to its mother.' This had led to the insistence that a young child should never be separated from its mother or mother-surrogate, that all separation is damaging and that long separation inevitably causes irreversible damage. This, Margaret Mead said, was 'a new and subtle form of anti-feminism' by which men, while pretending to protect motherhood, were 'tying women more tightly to their child than has been thought necessary since the invention of bottle feeding and baby carriages.' (More tightly, one might add, than at any time in history.) Mead emphasized the absence of anthropological evidence to support these ideas and pointed out that on the contrary, cross cultural studies suggest that the child adjusts best in the care of warm, friendly people. She also pointed out that clinical and anthropological studies support the idea that strong attachments to single individuals in childhood tend to be followed by a limited number of intense, exclusive relationships in adult life. 'It may well be, of course, that limiting a child's contacts to his biological mother may be the most efficient way to produce a character suited to lifelong monogamous marriage, but if so then we should be clear that that is what we are doing. . . .'[26]

Twenty five years later we may look cynically at Mead's suggestion. This is because the era in which mothers were exhorted not to separate from their young children has been followed not by increased total monogamy but by the increasing fashion of serial monogamy. People are changing their partners at least once during adult life and often more frequently. In this connection it is interesting to note that the child brought up with the exclusive care of his mother has eventually to break that bond and change to another. Since adults tend to repeat the patterns of their childhood, it may be that the modern obsession with continuous and total relationship between mother and child has contributed to the rising divorce rate.

Myrdal and Klein continue by stating their own position. This is of course more scientific than anyone else's and, looking back on it some thirty-five years later, can be seen as a mixture of common sense and opinions and social pressures of the period. 'Even during the first months,' they say, 'short absences of the mother are not harmful to the child. The main thing is that all that is important to the child should be done by one particular person – a person ready to give and receive that love identification from which a child's understanding grows. Before the end of one year a second person can move within the horizon of the child, and very soon more people.

The demand for the round-the-clock presence of the mother is ready to be lessened. It ought to be relaxed in order that the child may go through the normal maturation process.'[27] Thus they accept the conventional wisdom of the time in a modified form but they also warn against the dangers of over-protection, which, they say, may 'cripple the psychological development of the child.'[28] Referring to children of school age, whose mothers are often criticized by teachers and others for going out to work, Myrdal and Klein state emphatically: 'There are no grounds for the belief that child neglect is the necessary result of the employment of mothers.'[29]

The authors make certain suggestions for changes of outlook needed by women. These are just as relevant today, a quarter of a century later. They include planning for a long and full life; developing a realistic attitude to work and career; great care in the choice of vocation; keeping up or improving vocational skill during years spent at home; and persuading men to regard homemaking as a partnership. These all run through modern feminist literature and will be discussed, along with their practical, social and governmental suggestions, in the second section of this book.

CHAPTER TEN

Women's Liberation

The new wave of feminism, which has lasted up to the present time, arose out of discontent with domesticity and the increasing need and desire of women to work outside the home. The first stirrings of the new movement occurred in the United States in 1963 with the publication of Betty Friedan's book *The Feminine Mystique* and, in 1965, in Britain when Hannah Gavron's *The Captive Wife* made its appearance.

The women's liberation movement has done much for women during the last two decades. It has produced new wisdom along with perceptive observations and analyses. By now it has probably influenced all women in the western world whether they like it or not and whether they know it or not. Yet in the area of motherhood the movement has been seriously deficient. The attitude of modern feminists towards motherhood and modern feminist writings about motherhood has on the whole been superficial, lacking in understanding and lacking in awareness of its own deficiencies in this most important area of life. I believe that this has led to a negative influence which has, unfortunately, been just as powerful in our time as the many positive influences that the movement has produced. It has done a disservice not only to mothers but to all women, and to society in general.

So how did this come about?

The modern feminist movement emerged and spread rapidly in the late 1960s. Its aim was 'liberation'. The best definition I have found of this is quoted by Bernard in *The Future of Marriage*.

Liberation: A Widening of Choices. Liberation means choice among alternatives, something which has consistently been denied women. Women have been conditioned to accept passive roles in which all major decisions are made by nature or

165

by men. The major choice in a woman's life is who her husband will be, and he then will determine all future choices. In any way, marriage can be seen as a way of avoiding the difficult and serious human choice of establishing an identity and purpose in life. To achieve liberation, each person must discover herself as an individual with significance in her own right. A woman cannot fulfil herself through her children or through her husband; she must do it alone. Identity comes openly through making choices and liberation is the process of obtaining ever wider choices for people.[1]

In a survey done in 1945, the Institute for Motivational Research, an American market research firm, found an increased desire for emancipation among American women, and advised its client – a women's magazine – to take steps to win these women back by glamorizing the work of the home.[2] It was probably this 'increased desire' in its negative form of unhappiness and dissatisfaction that crystallized in the mind of Betty Friedan as 'the problem that has no name', and led to the success of her book *The Feminine Mystique*. In the preface she wrote: 'Gradually, without seeing it clearly for quite a while, I came to realize that something is very wrong with the way American women are trying to live their lives today. I sensed it first as a question mark in my own life, as a wife and mother of three small children.' She goes on to write: 'The problem lay buried, unspoken, for many years in the minds of American women. It was a strange stirring, a sense of dissatisfaction, a yearning that women suffered in the middle of the twentieth century in the United States. Each suburban wife struggled with it alone. As she made the beds, shopped for groceries, matched slipcover material, ate peanut butter sandwiches with her children, chauffeured Cub Scouts and Brownies, lay beside her husband at night, she was afraid to ask even of herself the silent question: "Is this all?"'[3]

Betty Friedan began to look differently at the popularity in America of early marriage and large families. She began to see 'new dimensions to old problems' such as menstrual difficulties, promiscuity, frigidity, emotional breakdown and the passivity and immaturity of American men. She came to believe that the 'problem that has no name' was not a matter of loss of femininity and was not due to too much education or the demands of domesticity. It was a need for something more than husband, children and home.

Friedan defines 'the feminine mystique' thus:

The feminine mystique says that the highest value and the only commitment for women is the fulfilment of their own femininity. It says that the great mistake of Western culture, through most of its history, has been the undervaluation of this femininity. It says this femininity is so mysterious and intuitive and close to the creation and origin of life that man-made science may never be able to understand it. But however special and different, it is in no way inferior to the nature of man; it may even in certain respects be superior. The mistake, says the mystique, the root of women's troubles in the past is that women envied men, women tried to be like men, instead of accepting their own nature, which can find fulfilment only in sexual passivity, male domination, and nurturing maternal love.

In spite of deficiencies such as the lack of historical perspective, much of what Betty Friedan wrote in *The Feminine Mystique*, though far from modern feminism, is relevant nearly twenty years later. As any family doctor or psychiatrist could attest, there are many women today who feel exactly the same as those described by Friedan and who are just as unaware of the causes of their discontent. Most are still treated, and ask to be treated, by their husbands and advisers in exactly the same way. Significantly perhaps, Friedan's suggested solutions are the weakest part of the book. She could offer no alternative way of life or any solution apart from education. 'Education, and only education, has saved, and can continue to save, American women from the greater dangers of the feminine mystique.'[4] This may be part of the ultimate solution for society, and a preventive, but anyone who tries to deal professionally with the problems of women already caught in the trap knows that only a tiny minority can help themselves by furthering their education or taking courses. It is probably partly because solutions to the problems of those already afflicted are so difficult that the women's liberation movement has developed in ways far removed from the thoughts of Betty Friedan. My own view is that both the difficulty in finding solutions and the way in which feminism has actually developed are deeply bound up with questions connected with motherhood in ways which have not been fully acknowledged or discussed.

The new feminist movement which sprung up in the 1960s differed from the old in a number of important respects. It was not, for instance, an upper middle-class movement led by prosperous and well-connected ladies. Its initiators were intellectuals and academics who came from different parts of the world and not from the Establishment, though a common criticism is that it disregarded the plight of working class and minority women. The movement has had no real leaders in the way that past movements have done. It has deliberately avoided structuring itself in this way. Hence it has been profoundly influenced by books, and its 'leaders' have mostly been those who wrote the books. They were all young, and few of them were mothers. Few were old enough to be already caught up in the trap described by Betty Friedan. Rather, they saw it coming and wanted to prevent it. The fact that so few older women played an active part is, to my mind, another indication of the great difficulties women have in freeing themselves once they are set on a course of total immersion in homemaking and motherhood. Betty Friedan, who is often called 'the mother of modern feminism', had a family of her own. Much of what she describes as 'the problem that has no name' was discontent with motherhood. But, significantly, few of the other important books that led and influenced the movement were written by mothers. It is clear from reading these books that few of the authors had much idea of what motherhood involves and so their attempts to bring it into their theories and suggestions tend to be unsatisfactory and unconvincing. Because the subject has not been fully faced or explored, motherhood is an area in which questioning women's role has had least impact, and the area in which there is the greatest inequality. Meanwhile millions of mothers, conscious of the importance of both what the women's liberation movement is saying to them and of motherhood itself, are confused and nervous. They are aware that there is a basic conflict between motherhood and much of what the feminist movement is trying to achieve. To many it seems impossible to be a good mother in the context of feminism. Yet withdrawal from feminist ideas and practice seems a betrayal of themselves. They know that to betray themselves in this way will make them bad mothers. They are caught in a trap. So they doubt their ability to be good mothers, they direct much attention towards this and tend to feel guilty and depressed about it. At present many women find it impossible to be committed to both feminism and motherhood because the two have not been reconciled. I believe that this conflict is an important reason why many women who are influenced by feminism, have benefited from it, lead fairly liberated lives and believe much of what the movement stands for, insist on dissociating themselves from it, and make remarks like 'I'm not a women's libber but . . .'

The origins of the modern feminist movement, like previous feminist movements, lie not only in the tradition of feminism, earlier feminist movements and the discontent of women but also in other radical and revolutionary movements of the time. Earlier movements were linked with movements for the abolition of slavery and the improvement of social conditions. In the 60s the women's liberation movement grew from Black Power, Civil Rights, Ban-the-Bomb, resistance to the war in Vietnam, political conflict in the Third World, and movements against pollution of the environment. It has been strongly linked to revolutionary ideas and to Marxist theory, arguing that women are a people oppressed by men and by a male-dominated society. One of its cleverest aspects is its use of the theories of R. D. Laing, analysing society from the perspective of one's self. What is attractive to the women's movement in Laing's work is epitomized in the Introduction to *The Politics of Experience*: 'No one can begin to think, feel or act now except from the starting point of his or her own alienation. . . . Humanity is estranged from its authentic possibilities. . . . What is required is more than a passionate outcry of enraged humanity. . . . Our alienation goes to the roots. . . . We are born into a world where alienation awaits us. . . . Alienation as our present destiny is achieved only by outrageous violence perpetrated by human beings on human beings.'[5] Through this, in the words of Juliet Mitchell who has written what is probably the best account of the movement, 'women in the 1960s found the attitude of the oppressor within the minds of the oppressed. This, among many other factors, has led to the analysis offered by groups of radical feminists: the overthrow of male-dominated society (sexism) and the liberation of women is the primary revolution.'[6] Perhaps most important of all has been the growing realization and understanding of women's economic poverty and dependence.

Mitchell has pointed out that by 1970 there was some form of women's liberation movement in all but three of the liberal democratic countries of the advanced capitalist world.[7] The exceptions were Ireland, Switzerland and Austria. It is much more international than previous movements, which were chiefly Anglo-Saxon. Clearly there is something in it which appeals to women from many different places and backgrounds. The details of its origins are not relevant here but its concepts and to some extent its politics are.

Mitchell points out that most of the new feminist groups were revolutionary. Throughout the movement there is an acute consciousness that women are a severely oppressed section of the community. Their oppression is economic, but goes further than this into their mental and social debasement. 'Feminism unites women at the level of their total oppression – it is all-inclusive (of Black Power and "totalism"). Its politics match this: it is a total attack. The theory backs this: the first division of labour was the first formation of oppressor and oppressed – the first division of labour was between man and woman. The first domination must be given priority – it must be the first to go. This is poetic justice. . . .'[8]

Many modern feminists are also Marxists but radical feminism 'finds that the inadequacies within Marxian analyses of a comprehension of women's oppression, are due *not* to its chronic underdevelopment in this sphere (as Marxian women believe) but to the limitations of the theory itself.'[9] 'About the condition of women as an oppressed class [Marx and Engels] know next to nothing, recognizing it only where it overlaps with economics.'[10] Shulamith Firestone attempts 'to develop a materialist view of history based on sex itself.'[11] Not only is the general denigration of women regarded as an inevitable consequence of capitalism (little is said about its being also an apparently inevitable consequence of non-capitalism) but oppression of women is seen as *the* problem. In this, 'radical feminism would ingest Marxism.'[12] Firestone elaborates this theme by insisting that the elimination of sexual classes requires the revolt of women and the seizure of control of *reproduction* just as the elimination of economic classes requires the revolt of the proletariat and their seizure of the means of *production*. The aim must be, she says, not only elimination of privilege but also elimination of distinction itself, both class distinction and sexual distinction. 'Genital differences between human beings would no longer matter culturally.' She goes on to advocate artificial reproduction or at least its option. This would eliminate reproduction by one sex for the benefit of the both. The dependence of the child on the mother would be replaced by a curtailed dependence on a small group of others in general, and any remaining inferiority to adults in physical strength would be compensated for culturally.

'The division of labour would be ended by the elimination of labour altogether (through cybernetics). The tyranny of the biological family would be broken.' This is really saying that women can be freed only by the elimination of motherhood. Since this is far beyond the vision and desires of nearly all women (including most feminists) it can, on a more practical level, be taken as a statement that modern feminism is incompatible with modern motherhood. By proposing such an extreme solution – far more extreme than ideas of revolution – the problem is shelved so it is in fact a way of not examining or analysing motherhood in relation to modern women. This tendency runs through much modern feminist thinking, even though few are as extreme in their views or in their proposed solutions as Firestone and even though many pay lip service to the view that motherhood is central to the women's movement.

Juliet Mitchell points out that past socialist theory 'has failed to differentiate woman's condition into separate structures, which together form a complex – not a simple – unity. To do this will mean rejecting the idea that woman's condition can be deduced derivatively from the economy (Engels) or equated symbolically with society (Marx). Rather, it must be seen as a *specific* structure, which is a unity of different elements.'[13] She lists 'the key structures of woman's situation' as Production, Reproduction, Sexuality and the Socialization of Children. A modification of any one of them can be offset by reinforcement of another. For instance, women's freedom from production meant first increased emphasis on reproduction. This emphasis decreased as women had fewer babies so emphasis was then put on the socialization of children, which was equally binding. Attaining the right or even the obligation to work is not liberating unless attempts are also made to change sexuality and family life. She points out that women's absence from the critical sector of production historically has been caused not just by their assumed physical weakness in a context of coercion – but also by their role in reproduction. In a capitalist society work is 'an alienation of labour' because the product is confiscated by capital. But sometimes it can still be 'a real act of creation, purposive and responsible, even in conditions of the worst exploitation.' Maternity is often 'a caricature of this', 'a kind of sad mimicry of production'. The child is treated as if it were a product. Parenthood becomes a substitute for work, 'an object created by the mother' and 'a possession of the parents'. Thus the mother renounces her autonomy through reproduction and anything the child does is a threat to her. Mitchell adds, 'There are few more precarious ventures on which to base a life.'

Moreover, says Mitchell, the woman and her child are, both legally and economically, subject to the father. 'The social cult of maternity is matched by the real socio-economic powerlessness of the mother. The psychological and practical benefits men receive from this are obvious.' The situation will not improve as long as maternity remains 'a substitute for action and creativity' in women and the home remains 'an area of relaxation for men.'[14]

Regarding the socialization of children Mitchell writes, 'the qualitative importance of socialization during the early years of the child's life has acquired a much greater significance than in the past – while the quantitative amount of a mother's life spent either in gestation or child-rearing has greatly diminished. It follows that socialization cannot simply be elevated to the woman's new maternal vocation. Used as a mystique, it becomes an instrument of oppression.'[15]

Looking at child-rearing as one aspect in the quadrangle of forces (Production, Reproduction, Sexuality and Socialization of children), Mitchell points out that it is no use just changing one of them. She emphasizes the crucial importance of the early years in the development of the person and hints vaguely that major changes cannot be far off. There are contradictions in woman's position in production:

They are in the most advanced and the most backward economic sectors. Men are in *all* sectors, according to class. Women are crucial for the expansion of consumer-consciousness (e.g. their use as 'sexual objects' by the advertising industry), yet they are also a permanent source of the *cheapest* labour. . . . There is a contradiction between their position in production and an ideology that virtually excludes them from it. . . . This is the contradiction between their role in the family and their role in the labour force: the one denies the other. Then the family itself contains the contradictions of its ideology (which stabilizes it) and of its economic function (which changes it). Within the family, the reproduction and the socialization of children are made to balance each other, yet ever more precariously: contraception and the population explosion indicate the possibility, and need, for fewer births; psychology makes the period of early infancy crucial; the woman must spend the energy freed from child-birth in child-rearing. Yet with compulsory schooling, early maturing, for how long is a full-time mother really required? Probably just as long as she is denied the social possibilities (day-care, economic independence, etc) that would give her the option. . . .[16]

The idea that motherhood is an instrument of oppression and a burden from which women must be freed is found in most modern feminist literature. This is not surprising because bringing up children either alone, as do so many modern women, or without much active assistance from the father, as has always been the tradition, is, despite the joys and rewards, a tremendous burden and anyone who denies this is indulging in idealization. But in modern feminist literature, if the burden of motherhood is discussed at all, it is often in terms of sexism, male chauvinism, the sex war, hostility to men, and 'rights over our own bodies'. It is easier to find out what feminists think about abortion, the female orgasm, rape, sexist education and the rights of lesbians than to find out what they think about motherhood. For instance, in an otherwise comprehensive book Eleanor Flexner does not discuss the problems of motherhood or even mention it in the index.[17] Jean Baker Miller's book, *Psychoanalysis and Women*, contains virtually nothing about motherhood. In her book *Psychoanalysis and Feminism*, Juliet Mitchell italicizes the 'main references', but nothing remotely connected with motherhood is italicized. Bowlby and Winnicott, who have both had a profound influence on mothers, are only mentioned in passing, whereas there is a great deal about Laing and Reich who have had virtually no influence on mothers but a great deal on alienated people and revolutionaries. One can look through book after book in shelves marked 'feminism' in libraries and bookshops and find nothing beyond a few passing references. Sheila Rowbotham's useful bibliography, *Women's Liberation and Revolution*, contains a section on birth control and abortion and another on gay liberation but nothing about motherhood apart from a few references to publications on the subjects of day nurseries and childminding. Even a book called *Mother Was Not a Person* has no chapter on motherhood, though it

173

contains chapters on birth control, pregnancy, childbirth and abortion.[18] I recently analysed twenty issues of a popular feminist magazine. The only articles relevant to mothers was one called 'Deciding to Have a Baby', an article called 'Reproduction Rights', largely about babies for lesbians and the rights of mothers to control their own childbirth, and a series of four articles on collective child-care.

Another way in which the problems of motherhood are shelved is by trivializing the subject. Hence Germaine Greer: 'Bringing up children is not a real occupation because children come up just the same, brought or not.'[19] This must be one of the most untrue statements in the whole of modern feminist literature. But to be fair, not many go to such lengths, and elsewhere in the same book Greer herself has interesting and sensible things to say. This trivializing attitude runs through feminist literature, not only in the ideas it expresses and the impressions it gives but also in its terminology. Words like 'parenting' are flat and neutral. 'Caretaking', 'care-giving' and 'nurturing' are also emotionally shallow, suggesting farmyard life or the mechanical aspects of 'mothering'. Such words trivialize not only the whole concept of mothering but also those who participate in it.

Another method by which some feminists avoid facing the deeper problems of motherhood is by concentrating on its peripheral aspects, or on one particular aspect, such as abortion, collective day care or 'control of our bodies'. Mitchell lists the national campaigns of the early Women's Liberation Movement, which she says are 'aimed at all the major dimensions of women's oppression'.[20] In England these campaigns were for equal pay, equal work and equal opportunities; for free birth-control and abortion on demand; for a re-examination of the whole educational set-up and for after-school children's centres; for the provision of easily available, free pre-school crèches and nurseries. Particular groups attacked the ideological exploitation of women as 'sexual objects' by the media and industrial enterprises. In America and elsewhere there were much more extensive campaigns to reassess the role of women in history, to eliminate sexism from the law, press and school text books. True, she says, 'the promotion of birth-control involves investigating the attitudes of ... women.... The provision of nursery schools involves discussion and analysis of the mother-child relationship from the viewpoint of psychology – and of the mother concerned,' but in practice there is litle evidence of this in the literature produced by those campaigns. What does emerge loud and clear is a hostility to doctors in relation to women, particularly in roles concerned with motherhood, strong demands for collective child care and, often, a denigration of motherhood, hostility to the whole process of producing and rearing children and its relegation to the sphere of 'myth'.

A typical remark indicating the attitude of many feminists to doctors is: 'The whole process of childbirth today has been taken away from the women who actually bear the children into the clinical world of male obstetricians, and it is getting progressively harder for a normal healthy woman to experience normal healthy childbirth (though potentially 97 per cent of us could).'[21] Another typical example of hostile attitudes to doctors is as follows:

> Doctors are always enemies of women. They are an ultra-conservative group resisting any kind of social change. They consistently adopt an infuriating and patronizing attitude toward women. This is especially true of most obstetricians who elect to play the role of father and god to their patients, forcing women into the role of helpless, stupid, ridiculous little girls. The way we are treated by doctors is symptomatic of the conditioning we get in all aspects of our lives. Obstetricians are almost always men; we are therefore forced to give up all control of what happens to us and our bodies to a man who makes all the decisions for us. If a woman questions what is happening to her, her doctor will tell her not to worry, to depend on him, he'll take care of everything. He often tells her how painful it will be, but that she won't have to feel a thing because he'll sedate her. If she asks what drugs will be used on her, he insists that that decision must be made by him at the last minute.[22]

I am not saying that these remarks are not true. I have known many occasions in both professional and private life when they were true. But the point here is that remarks of this kind are much easier to find in feminist literature than are careful considerations of the wider problems of motherhood. (They are of course also easier to make.) And they also reveal another attitude that runs through much feminist literature: the idea that childbirth is an experience which women ought to have if they want it just as children are things that the women ought to have if they want them. The emphasis tends to be on 'my rights' and 'what I want to have'. It seems likely that these attitudes of 'haves' and 'rights' are fostered by the very nature and needs of the women's movement. There is seldom discussion of the needs of the children.

In contemporary feminist books one often finds childbirth described as though its chief function was to give the woman a valuable experience. Thus:

> Childbirth is (or may be) one aspect of a woman's entire life, beginning with her own expulsion from her mother's body, her own sensual suckling or holding by a woman, through her earliest sensations of clitoral eroticism and of the vulva as a source of pleasure, her growing sense of her own body and its strengths, her masturbation, her menses, her physical relationship to nature and to other human beings, her first and subsequent orgasmic experiences with another's body, her conception, pregnancy, to the moment of first holding her child. But that moment is still only a point in the process if we conceive it not according to patriarchal ideas of childbirth as a kind of reproduction but as part of female experience.[23]

Even those aspects of childbirth might legitimately be thought to belong to the child are turned into experience and sensation for the mother:

> Beyond birth comes nursing and the physical relationship with an infant, and these are enmeshed with sexuality. Mary Jane Sherfey has shown that during pregnancy the entire pelvic area increases in vascularity (the production of arteries and veins), increasing the capacity for sexual tension and greatly increasing the frequency and intensity of orgasm. Moreover, during pregnancy the system is flooded with hormones which not only induce the growth of new blood vessels but increase clitoral responsiveness and strengthen the muscles effective in orgasm. Thus a woman who has given birth has a biologically increased capacity for genital pleasure, unless her pelvic organs have been damaged obstetrically, as frequently happens.
>
> Many women experience orgasm for the first time after childbirth, or become erotically aroused while nursing. Frieda Fromm-Reichman, Niles Newton, Masters and Johnson, and

others have documented the erotic sensations experienced by some women in actually giving birth. Since there is a strong cultural force which attempts to desexualize women as mothers, the orgasmic sensations felt in childbirth or while suckling infants have probably till recently been denied even by the women feeling them, or have evoked feelings of guilt.[24]

The typical attitude is shown in the workshops program of the 'Congress to Unite Women – What Women Want' held in New York on November 22, 1969, which is reprinted in *Voices from Women's Liberation:*

10. REPRODUCTION AND ITS CONTROL. This group will discuss: the freedom to choose whether to bear children as a woman's basic human right, and as a prerequisite to the exercise of the other freedoms she may win; elimination of all laws and practices that compel women to bear children against their will (professional practices, public and private attitudes, and legal barriers limiting access to contraception and abortion), research in extrauterine gestation.[25]

Demands for free collective child care abound in feminist literature. An outside observer, coming into the subject for the first time, might be forgiven for thinking that feminists are against motherhood in general, preferring abortion on demand or cybernation; that children are something to which they have rights if they feel like it, particularly the right to produce them while retaining full control of the process as part of the right to control their own bodies, and rights over the father; and that once they are mothers they are interested chiefly in getting rid of the children for as often and as long as possible, preferably without having to pay anything. If one gets any impression at all of what feminists think their responsibility is towards children and about how children can best be raised, the overwhelming impression is that at all costs they must be raised in a manner that is free of the sexist stereoypes,which are the main limitation to development. It is a pity that these impressions come through so forcibly because they are probably not true for the majority of feminists and they obscure so much that is real, valuable and timely in modern feminism.

The first clause of the Southern Female Rights Union Program for Female Liberation reads as follows:

We demand free, non-compulsory, public childcare. The public schools must be extended to include all children from birth. Free and adequate care must be available on a fulltime (24 hours every day of the year) basis for infants and children of all ages, regardless of parents' income. All meals, medical and dental care, clothing, and equipment must be available for the children in the schools, so that no child is deprived by their parents' inadequate support. An equal number of females and males in all positions must staff the schools. Tracking and counseling, textbooks, games, equipment, and instruction must be free of sexual (and racial) discrimination at all levels of public education.[26]

The first topic listed to be considered by the 'Congress to Unite Women – What Women Want' in 1969 was 'More and better child care facilities are an absolutely urgent need, to make the liberation of women real. It is imperative we activate present laws in this area or find possibilities for political action, immediately. . . .'

Both these documents are reproduced in *Voices for Women's Liberation*, a collection of papers from the feminist movement both past and present. This book has many distinguished contributors and makes many important points. But it is paradigmatic of the present situation that the only section involving motherhood is called 'Families – Day Care'. Typically, one of the five papers in that section is called 'Producing Society's Babies' and another (though what it has to do with 'day care' is not made clear) is called 'The Abortion Problem'. In 440 pages there is almost nothing about motherhood. 'Society must begin to take responsibility for children,' states another article.[27] The 'Working Mothers Charter' produced by Mothers in Action and reproduced in 'Conditions of Illusion' states firmly: 'Adequate substitute care for babies and young children should be provided at all times necessary to enable the mother to work without undue worry.'[28] The cost of meeting these demands is seldom mentioned and neither are the important effects that this would have on children. The demand so often seems to be that day care, and sometimes day-and-night care, should be provided as though that was the end of the problems of motherhood.

Mary Kenny, calling herself a 'Woman's Liberation Revisionist', writes of her views in the days when she was a doctrinaire women's liberationist, 'As for children, it was only a matter of tidying up the problem. If the East Germans could supply every mother with a state crèche, so could we in the West. If the Chinese could solve this problem, what were we making the fuss about? The waste of women-hours being spent fiddling about at home on totally unproductive labour!'[29] '... I never really thought about children very seriously before I had them. Children were something that organized people dealt with in an organized way.'[30]

Ignoring and trivializing motherhood is a means of denying its problems and conflicts. If the feminine mystique was the 'problem that had no name' for unliberated women, one might say that motherhood is the problem that cannot be faced by modern feminists. Another way of avoiding it is by denigrating it. Running through the women's liberation movement has been a thread of hostility to mothers and babies. Lip service is paid to them but the effect is often the feeling that they are really rather a nuisance, obstruct the correct scheme of things and should be controlled and disposed of as quietly as possible. In the early days of women's liberation there were two concomitant and linked movements which joined suitably to spread this attitude. One was the movement to prevent world overpopulation and the other to protect the environment against pollution. In the early 70s car stickers appeared announcing 'Babies are Pollution' and 'World pollution is YOUR baby.' Earlier Simone de Beauvoir had written of the 'ordeal of pregnancy' (though, to her credit, she also writes a lot of good sense about mothering).[31] Mitchell writes of maternity as *possession*.[32] One writer discusses 'the negative role of "Mum"'.[33] Another writes 'The big push to have children, whether we are married or not, should be viewed as one of the strong links in the chain that enslaves us.'[34] Kate Millett writes that a woman is 'Simply by virtue of her anatomy ... prevented from being a human being.'[35] Some feminist writers are downright hostile to the whole business. Penelope Leach quotes an example from a widely-read women's liberation magazine which describes the full-time care of a baby or very young child as: 'Like spending all day, every day, in the exclusive company of an incontinent mental defective.'[36] Shulamith Firestone in her *Dialectic of Sex* describes pregnancy as 'barbaric ... shitting a pumpkin' and announces: 'Pregnancy is the temporary deformation of the body of the individual for the sake of the species.'[37] She equates labour in childbirth with labour by sweat of the brow. Her first demand for any alternative system she says 'must be: *The freeing of women from the tyranny of reproduction by every means possible. . . .'*[38] and later 'parental satisfaction is obtainable only through crippling the child.'[39] She ends her book with the following announcement: 'With the disappearance of motherhood, and the obstructing incest taboo, sexuality would be re-integrated, allowing love to flow unimpeded.'

Less aggressive but still clearly hostile to the usual concept of motherhood is another prominent feminist, Germaine Greer. In *The Female Eunuch*, she 'hit upon the plan' to buy a farmhouse in Italy, to be shared with friends with similar problems. Their children would be born there. Fathers and friends could visit. Mothers would come and go, leaving the house in the care of a local family. 'Being able to be with my child and his friends would be a privilege and a delight that I could work for.' If necessary the child need not even know that I was his womb-mother and I could have relationships with the other children as well. If my child expressed a wish to try London and New York or go to formal school somewhere, that could also be tried without committal.'[40] She continues, 'This little society would confer its own normality, and other contacts with civilization would be encouraged, but it may well be that such children would find it impossible to integrate with society and become dropouts or schizophrenics. As such they would not be very different from other children I have known. . . . I could not, physically, have a child any other way, except by accident and under protest in a hand-to-mouth sort of way in which case I could not accept any responsibility for the consequences. I should like to be able to think that I had done my best.'[41] She justifies herself thus: 'The point of an organic family is to release the children from the disadvantages of being the extensions of their parents so that they can belong primarily to themselves.'

Another form of hostility to motherhood that is displayed by modern feminist literature is in the frequent reference to and discussion of 'The Myth of Motherhood'. It is significant that it is always all-embracing – 'The Myth of Motherhood', never 'Myths about Motherhood'. It seems necessary to these writers to imply, even if they do not actually say, that the whole process, rather than certain aspects of it, is mere myth which can be discounted.

By the phrase 'The Myth of Motherhood' these writers really mean the idealization of motherhood which I have described. Lee Comer in her pamphlet *The Myth of Motherhood* attacks 'a central shibboleth of male domination', the idea that child rearing is, of necessity, the responsibility of women.[42] She criticizes women both in and outside the women's liberation movement for 'mouthing this radical idea' but being 'very reluctant to relinquish that supposedly special and dignified role of mother.' When a woman 'projects her ambitions and aspirations onto her children and her husband and when their achievements are embraced as her own, she is signing away her life.' True, but surely vicarious living is *one* of the myths of motherhood and one of its dangers. Inherently, it has nothing to do with motherhood. For women who choose to destroy themselves in this way motherhood is merely one path is socially acceptable. Central to the myth is 'this supposedly self-evident truth; a child needs its mother and, by implication, a mother needs her child.' True again, but there is all the difference in the world between total, neurotic and destructive dependence and mature dependence, that is, dependence related and suitable to the age of the child. Nothing is said of that. Much of the rest of the pamphlet consists of criticizing Bowlby and his followers, who are, as we saw, central to the idealized view of mothers in our society, but who have also taught us a great deal about children's needs. But Lee Comer is in danger of throwing the baby out with the bath water. 'The following quotation from the World Child Welfare Congress of 1958 exemplifies the attitude to child rearing which should be strenuously rejected: ". . . our most important task in regard to every child with whom we are concerned is to give him maternal and personal love . . . we must be there for them. In fact, if we are not the visible and tangible centre of their world and if we are not the stable hub of every change all our efforts are in vain."'

A more thoughtful writer might look at these words and think about exactly what is meant and could be meant by phrases such as 'maternal and personal love' and 'visible and tangible centre of their world.' But Ms Comer continues. 'Is it loving a child to make yourself the centre of its universe? And is it really love that compels parents to protect and defend the child against all the minor upsets it encounters outside the home in its own way? Most of what goes under the guise of good parental care is an elaborate rationalisation of gross possessiveness. It attempts to bind the child to the mother and provides a manipulative object whereby the parents rationalise their personal dissatisfactions. This is often consciously expressed by well-meaning parents who boast that they are giving their chil-

181

dren what they themselves lacked. What is understood as "loving" children is, in fact, using them.' This kind of writing misses the point. She is equating a certain type of bad mothering, such as is, for instance, described later in this book, with mother love in general. It is in fact the same error in reverse as that made by Bowlby, whom she criticises so vehemently. He tends to equate a particular form of good mothering with all mothers.

Ann Oakley, in her book *Housewife* (in other respects a valuable contribution to feminism), makes the same mistake. She devotes a whole chapter to 'The Myth of Motherhood' and again, she describes one popular myth *about* motherhood: 'The myth of motherhood contains three popular assertions. The first is the most influential: that children need mothers. The second is the obverse of this: that mothers need their children. The third assertion is a generalization which holds that motherhood represents the greatest achievement of a woman's life: the sole true means of self-realization. Women, in other words, need to be mothers. "Need" here is always vaguely specified, but usually means damage to mental or emotional health following on the denial of mothers to children, children to mothers, or motherhood to women.' If she described it as one common aberrant attitude to mothering her words would carry more weight. She goes on to attack the idea of maternal 'instinct'. This is another common shibboleth of modern feminism and certainly the idea of 'maternal instinct' has been abused in our society. Typically, Ms Oakley announces 'There is no such thing as maternal instinct. There is no biologically based drive which propels women into childbearing or forces them to become childrearers once the children are there.'[43] Unfortunately she makes no attempt to assess what people actually mean when they talk about or believe in 'maternal instinct', why they believe it and how these beliefs link with our society and with motherhood as it really is. Yet few people, when they refer to 'maternal instinct', are really talking about the biological definition. They are only talking about a feeling related to pregnancy, babies or children which they have or which they think they should have or which they think others have or should have. When people use the term they are not really thinking of the origins of that feeling, or whether it is biologically or socially determined. They only know, if they consider it thus far, that it springs from unconscious mental processes, and they do not usually consider it beyond that point. But many of the feminist critics take the standard biological definition (whose use is actually largely confined to scientists) and then criticize people or society for believing it, when all they are usually doing is to use the word loosely and inaccurately to express certain definite and strong feelings. It is clear that what they are really writing about is oppression and the oppressive aspects of motherhood, while avoiding the issue of motherhood itself.

One now begins to see why so many feminists extol the works of R. D. Laing – who, of all psychological theorists, has probably had the least impact on psychological theory and whose main contribution has been a popularized and excellent description, mostly based on the works of others, of the 'schizoid' personality and the feelings of many 'alienated' people in our time. Many professionals who work with people who suffer from serious mental illness mostly find his theories of little value in that field. He does, however, describe with vividness a certain type of mother and a certain type of family violence which is recognizable, though usually in the families of neurotics rather than the schizophrenics. Moreover, much of his writing can be interpreted as anti-mother, anti-family, anti-psychiatrist and anti-authority. But it is destructive to the feminist movement that so many feminist writers have attached themselves to his views and ignored others who could really teach them so much more. One of the reasons it is destructive is that much of it is so negative. It is negative because it latches onto one type of aberrant mothering and destructive family life and describes it as though this is what all mothers are like. Those who recognize it in themselves or in their own family backgrounds also come to believe that what he describes is universal, at least in a capitalist and sexist society. Juliet Mitchell in her book *Psychoanalysis and Feminism* discusses the reasons why Laing's theories became important in the radical politics of the 60s and 70s. She asks: 'Does it show us a way forward in understanding the oppression of women as it takes place within the family that is supposed to give them both their definition and their morale?'[44]

Recently, since some of the more vociferous of the women's liberationists have become mothers themselves, there has been a greater interest in motherhood and more awareness of its nature. But even now there is no attempt to bring motherhood fully into the arena. There is no attempt to show that motherhood can be women's great strength rather than their burden. Sometimes suggestions are

183

made that homemaking should be 'upgraded', by regarding the homemaker as employed, and so paid and protected.[45] But there has been no campaign to improve the quality of life of children, to alleviate their segregation, or even to point out the many ways in which our society seems to be designed to make life difficult for them. Only since the first draft of this book was written has there been a campaign to make the breastfeeding of infants desirable, acceptable or even easier. Plenty of feminist voices are raised against the display of breasts in order to sell cars or cigarettes, but few to make their biological purpose respectable. Motherhood has inspired no positive movements comparable to the 'Black is Beautiful' movement. No attempt has been made to identify true maternal devotion and to encourage it, or to study the varieties of motherhood that are needed in the modern world or the kinds that are likely to be needed in the future. Thirty years ago Simone de Beauvoir wrote: 'While maternal devotion may be perfectly genuine, this, in fact, is rarely the case. Maternity is usually a strange mixture of narcissism, altruism, idle day-dreaming, sincerity, bad faith, devotion and cynicism. The great danger which threatens the infant in our culture lives in the fear that the mother to whom it is confided in all its helplessness is almost always a discontented woman.'[46] And so it seems to have remained almost until the present day. On the whole the results of feminist efforts regarding motherhood have been largely to ensure that it stays that way, with hostility directed against it. But recently things have begun to change.

Most women, whether they call themselves feminists, and whether they are mothers, care deeply about motherhood, feel strongly about the children they have or may have, show responsible attitudes and wish to do the very best for them. This is an area in which I believe that feminism so far has failed them, but now many of the young feminists from the early days of the women's liberation movement have become mothers themselves and are beginning to look at things differently. They have found that they cannot learn what they want or find what they need from the liberationists themselves. The written attitudes of feminists about mothering was far from reality and from what most women felt they needed. It gave them no understanding of motherhood and indeed was often confusing. This has contributed to some of the greatest modern dilemmas of motherhood. A typical modern feminist statement was 'At the moment it is up to women to stop rocking the cradle and start

184

rocking the boat. We cannot any longer accept our passive role.'[47] Yet one of the most vital human roles is to rock the cradle. We might go further and serve future generations better if we regarded rocking the cradle as a privilege which should be done and shared only by those men and women who are wise enough, and developed enough and sane enough to be responsible for it.

So far the women's liberation movement has failed mothers. I am convinced that, although the movement has much to offer women, until it begins to think and write sensibly about mothers and motherhood it will continue to be a peripheral movement, shunned by most women, supported particularly by those who ignore or dislike motherhood and children and it will continue to be deserted by those of its supporters who discover that there is more to motherhood than they ever thought or dreamed.

PART TWO

The Crisis of Motherhood

CHAPTER ELEVEN

What Are Children For?

The many changes and influences discussed in Part One have combined to create an ambivalent muddle about motherhood today through which today's young women will have to find their own individual paths. Until recently nearly every woman wished to be a mother and most women became mothers. To most it was automatic, part of being grown up and doing what was expected in the world. Suddenly there are doubts. All is different. There seems much more to being a mother than was previously realized. There is more choice about it. Is it something she really wants?

A curious inconsistency has been running through most literature on child care and child rearing during the last thirty years. Anyone who has read much of it will recognize the theme. It goes something like this:

1. Babies and children need good mothering.
2. Mothers have a mothering instinct.
3. Some mothers are not good mothers. (This is usually only mentioned in passing and not followed up, but is clearly and strikingly uttered by psychiatrists who publish case histories).
4. Some mothers are not fit to be mothers.
5. The best person to look after a baby or small child is his mother.
6. Whatever goes wrong with a child is likely to be the mother's fault.
7. Some mothers turn their children into psychological cripples. (Again, uttered chiefly by psychiatrists).
8. A young child needs the exclusive care of his mother.

189

9. Even short or partial separation from the mother can be damaging to a young child.

The last two are losing ground, but slowly. They were particularly emphasized in the 50's and 60's and many still hold these views.

It is no wonder that many young women, now faced with the decision of whether or not to have a family, are awed and scared at the prospect. Everyone knows that influences acting on a child or, to put it in a more usual way, early experiences, have enormous effects in later life. Influences here means environment and 'experiences' means the way in which the child encounters that environment. Each child has its own hereditary make-up but it is the influence of the environment which determines how that inheritance develops. One of the wisest of writers on infancy, the late D. W. Winnicott, was fond of saying 'There is no such thing as a baby.' He meant that a baby cannot exist and develop alone, but only in relation to his environment, that is his mother.

Certain difficulties of terminology arise here. A mother can virtually be the environment to her baby, or she may be only part of it, or even none of it. At any one moment 'mother' may be the biological mother, or the adoptive foster, substitute or temporary mother. The 'mother' in this sense may be father, nurse, anyone else who cares for the child, or a variety of people, so 'she' may also mean 'he'. So when I write here of 'mother' I mean literally 'that which may be provided by a mother but may come from elsewhere'. By 'world' or 'outside world' I mean that part of the environment which cannot be the mother. The words 'environment' and 'influence' cover both.

The mother provides the environment for her baby and to a diminishing extent for the growing child. Some mothers provide a more total, powerful or longlasting environment than other mothers. Some, by design or from necessity, exclude other influences from the child. In so far as the mother is the environment or part of the environment the baby absorbs from her. He absorbs not only what she does but also what she is. The more completely she is his environment, the more he will absorb from her, the more powerful will be her influence and the less the effect of other influences.

The mother presents the outside world to her child. The more she is in control the more the outside world is filtered or adapted by her in presenting it to the child.

If the baby is to grow and develop well these inevitable functions have to be performed in ways that are suitable to the child: to promote his development, both physical and mental, and help him to realize his capabilities in ways suitable to his age and his heredity. These functions also have to be performed in ways suitable to the outside world in which he will live, for just as no baby exists without a mother so a child can only develop well in ways suited to the world he will have to live in. Of course, enormous variety exists, can be tolerated and indeed is *needed*, but basically that is true. Again there is a problem of terminology. In describing this complicated process I toyed with the idea of using Winnicott's excellent phrase 'the good enough mother' but he has made it his own in a special way and I do not wish either to steal it or to be bound by the particular way in which he saw it. I have therefore decided simply to use the word 'good'.

So the first requirements of a mother who is good in this sense are a sensitivity to her child's needs and the capacity to provide for them. She also needs an understanding of herself (which may be unconscious) in relation to the child's needs, so that she is aware of her own capacity and what she can and cannot do. Where she is lacking, she needs the ability to see that those needs are met elsewhere and through others. She may be able to provide a total good environment for her infant and to present the world to him in the way that is best for him, or she may not. The important thing is that she knows what she is, what she can do, and what is best for her child. The good mother knows how much of her child's environment she can and should provide, how to present the world to him, and how and when to delegate or relinquish functions. People (experts and advisers) who insist that the biological (or adoptive) mother is the best person to care for her child and that she should do this exclusively during the early years, rarely take all this into account.

Of all that the child absorbs from the good mother in so far as she is his environment, the most important are probably loving feelings that are not contingent. The word 'love' can scare those who associate it with romance or strange deep feelings that they wonder whether they can attain, so, to put it in another way, one might say that the child needs perpetual goodwill. This does not mean that the

191

mother does not at times hate the child or have angry or hostile feelings towards him. The important thing is that basically she is on his side and, no matter what he does or how he develops, she remains that way. Her love or goodwill does not depend on his being a credit to her or being what she wants him to be or achieving what she wants him to achieve. She also provides empathy, the capacity to feel in the way he feels while retaining her own identity. Without this she cannot have the sensitivity and flexibility that are also necessary. She gives continuity, reliability and a sense of confidence and optimism, which can only come from a mother who is satisfied with her personal life, that is her emotional life, her adult relationships, social life, exercise of skills, and participation in society. Later she needs a sense of, rather than a knowledge of, boundaries. The child will absorb these qualities, or the lack of them, and what he absorbs will be with him for the rest of his life.

The key to presenting the world to the child so that he can develop in the best possible way is not knowledge but sensitivity to the gradual intrusion of the outside world and what are appropriate experiences. The mother has to protect him from impingement by aspects of the outside world with which he cannot yet cope. Yet she has to present a true picture or experience. It is important not to deny reality, for this distorts the truth and leads to confusion. She has to be sensitive to what part of and how much of the true world she can present or allow him to explore. Of course, in so far as she herself is confused about the world outside she will confuse the child.

Through her goodwill and empathy the good mother can sensitively and actively adapt to the child's needs and to variations in both their feelings. She makes provision for his creative impulses and recognizes his personal idiosyncrasies, special needs and abilities. She has a realistic appreciation of what he is and what his talents are. She knows how to stimulate and she does this imaginatively. She is sensitive to distortions in his (and also her own) emotional development and can deal with them as they occur, taking suitable corrective action. She also has time and inclination for the job and the ability to delegate when necessary as well as an understanding of her own limitations without which she cannot know when or how to delegate. The good mother knows how to present the world at different ages and what is appropriate for each age. Finally, the good mother makes mistakes, lots of them. But she learns from them and does not allow these to shake her confidence or her basic goodwill towards her child.

All this may sound idealistic. But accepting that no mother can be a totally good mother and that all mothers make errors and have periods of being less good, it is a realistic guideline. Everyone fails to some extent. Theoretically, the variety of possible errors is infinite. So is the variety of mothers who are good enough.

Clearly, from this description of a good mother, failure lies in any or several of the following areas. First, what the mother is like as a person and what her feelings are about herself: she may be insensitive to children and incapable of empathy with them. She may identify with the child though without true empathy so that she foresees his feelings and needs before he knows them himself. She then does things for him that he could well do for himself and she thus deprives him of the experience of exploration and and the benefits of learning. She also confuses him because he finds it difficult to distinguish between what he wants and what his mother wants. So a mother of this sort can be intrusive and damaging. Winnicott describes mothers who 'begin to be so good at the technique of mothering that they do all the right things at the right moments, and then the infant who has begun to become separate from the mother has no means of gaining control of all the good things that are going on. In this way the mother, by being a seemingly good mother, does something worse than castrate the infant.'[1] Another area of potential failure as a mother is the mother's own problems and those aspects of her personality which others might see as problems. Is her basic attitude to life optimistic or pessimistic? Is she comfortable with her own body and its functions or is she inhibited or obsessed by them? Is she moody? Is she tense and anxious or assailed by fears? Is she at home in the present or always looking into the past or future? What kind of relationship does she have with her own parents and with her partner? What are her personal satisfactions apart from her partner and children? What is her view of love in general and of mother love in particular? Some have a romantic view of what love 'ought' to be and then have problems thinking that they do not feel it. Some think they feel normal love but on close examination one finds that their 'love' is really something else, such as control or reward for meeting their expectations. All these things will, in some form or other, be absorbed by her children.

Third, what does her child mean to her? What part of herself does it represent? A child can mean many different things to a mother, and a number of things to the same mother. Or different children can mean different things to her. A child can represent an achievement, or a project that must be done. It can be associated in her mind with something unpleasant that happened to her during pregnancy or during its birth – perhaps she was ill, or her partner had an affair, or she to give up a satisfying job. She will tend to project the feelings she has about this onto the child. She may regard the child as a possession, to be cherished and protected as such. It may be a projection of lost hopes or missed opportunities ('I want him to have everything that I never had myself'). It may have dynastic significance, an increase in family power – this was much more common in the past than now. More commonly now it may be an instrument of power, seen for instance, in the unmarried girl who has a baby in order to manipulate or spite her family or the woman who wants to triumph over her sisters. It may be seen as a protection, a defence against the outside world, an excuse to 'drop out', a means of building one's own little world to one's own liking. Many immature mothers expect their children, even babies, to mother them and some mothers equate their children, or a particular child, with one or other of their own parents, and not always lovingly. It may be a pastime, a toy with which to pass the time. Sometimes the child represents something which is basically threatening and which must be controlled at all cost, or some part of the mother which she cannot acknowledge in herself, and which is then projected onto the child. 'Something is wrong with my child' often really means 'something is wrong with me' – epitomized by the little boy quoted by Winnicott who said, 'Please, doctor, My mum says I've got tummy ache.'

Last, what is the mother's relationship with the outside world? Does she feel at ease with it or does she experience it as threatening, something which she must control as far as possible or from which she must be protected? Does she use her intellect to this end? Does she withdraw from the outside world to create her own? Is she aware of the fact that it is changing and does she experience this change as threatening? Is she narrow and unimaginative? Does she persistently deny what she cannot face? Does she have strong ideas that are impervious to reason? Does she actually have a false, even mad, view of the world?

194

These questions, are seldom easy to answer and many good mothers, if they are honest, will answer yes to some of them, for human beings are complicated and have many motives. What matters is the overall balance. It may take all sorts to make a world but the world would be better without some of the extremes.

At the beginning is birth, the child's first experience of the outside world. It is difficult to prove that the experiences of foetal life and birth are important and influential later on but there are many indications that this is so. It may turn out to be one of the tragedies of our age that at a time when the baby most needs a mother to present the outside world to him, she is usually obliged, under our present system, to deliver him to an outside world in the form of a clinical obstetric table under bright lights and the clatter of instruments, with receiving hands that may pull him, slap him, hold him upside down, enjoy his loud protests as evidence of his health, bathe him roughly, bind him tightly and leave him alone in a corner or in an incubator. Many mothers, and probably babies too, suffer under this regime, especially if they are deprived of early contact. It seems to be particularly difficult for mothers who are uncertain of their mothering capacities, who wish to develop them to the full and need all the support they can get to bring out their own capacities rather than having systems thrust upon them. Sheila Kitzinger, who has spent many years studying childbirth under different conditions and in different cultures writes: 'It may take a long time for a woman to love her child when the beginning of her relationship with it has been interfered with by outsiders.'[2]

During the early weeks the baby needs physical comfort and must be free from hunger, thirst and noise. He needs food presented quietly and without tension or anxiety. As the weeks go by he needs adaptation to his changing needs with quiet stimulation and eye-to-eye contact as well as cuddling. As he becomes mobile he needs increasing stimulation and the opportunity to explore, together with protection from the dangers inherent in this. Gradually he comes to need contact with other people, father, brothers and sisters, and other adults who care about him. Increasingly, the world that is presented needs to be realistic. A mad mother, or one who is able to present only a distorted view of the world, may still be a good mother during the first stage, but increasingly as the child grows she will create difficulties for him. Our modern industrial society presents new difficulties for mothers in their capacity as presenters of the world. Its rapid change and its uncertainty create problems for those who like to feel they know where they are and to have everything under control. It demands much more flexibility of character than does a settled world. It also creates problems for those who have difficulty with reality. A common example of this is seen in ideas about the social structure. Expecting children to follow in their parents' footsteps and to lead the life that their parents led is now unrealistic and presents a distorted view of the world. Yet many still do it. The changing world creates problems for those with strong prejudices which have often come down through the generations, for instance, prejudices about people of different race or of a sexist nature. A parent with strong prejudices against people of darker skins creates problems for her child at a modern multi-racial school. Parents with traditional ideas about 'women's rôle' may create much unhappiness in a daughter who wants to be a bio-chemist, or an airline pilot or a prime minister.

Lastly, there are special difficulties because the outside world has changed greatly during the last generation or two. Some parents use their children as a means of not recognizing or coming to terms with this. Only today I met a mother who will not allow her daughters aged 17 and 16 out on their own. She gave her reasons for this in the following order: they might meet a flasher and she doesn't want them to have to cope with that; they might meet undesirable men; they might make friends with boys and she thinks they are too young to have boyfriends; going out might interfere with their schoolwork.

Apart from this there is no doubt that in most places the world outside home is more dangerous and in many ways more restrictive for children than it used to be. The roads are too dangerous for them to play on yet few facilities are provided for them to play elsewhere. Sexual assaults on children have increased. Even farms, formerly almost perfect environments for children, are now hazardous places and, largely because of dangerous machinery, many farm children spent most of their early years indoors with their mothers.

Is there such a thing as maternal instinct? It is still widely though by no means universally believed that mother love is an 'instinct', inborn in all women or in most women which, if not apparent beforehand, will appear during pregnancy or soon after giving birth, thus making the mother the best person to care for her own child.

Yet for many woman today it is clearly not true. There must presumably at some stage in the development of the human race have been such an instinct, or the species would not have survived any more than it would have survived without a sex instinct. But to use that as an argument, as it often is used, about mothering in a complex post-industrial society is naive, political or an entrenched irrational belief. True, many women do develop strong feelings of involvement with young babies and these feelings may have instinctual origins, but many women do not. Most mothers become extremely attached to their children and try to do their best for them but, as we shall see, there are many reasons for this and to postulate that it is through 'maternal instinct' confuses the issue. So does the use of the word 'instinct' when what is really meant is 'unconscious', 'not fully understood' or even 'automatic'. Instinct is an inborn, inherited biological drive, whereas behaviour and feelings that are unconscious or 'automatic' are usually much influenced by experience and may be purely the result of this even if they are not experienced in this way or fully understood. Today one cannot convincingly say 'I want children because my maternal instincts drive me to have them.' One needs to understand the feelings that one has and to analyze them. This is particularly important now that the question of having or not having children has become a matter of personal choice.

Why choose to have children? Only recently has there been choice in the matter. Answers, if they came at all, might have been that children are sent from God, that they replenish the family and pass it on into the future. In some societies it might be said that children, particularly boys, give social status or increase the material wealth of the family. None of these answers is particularly relevant to us today. More recently the answer might be that an urge to become a mother is an 'instinct' or what women have always done. Women might say that children give life meaning and purpose, are 'part of life', ensure that one is like other people, provide security in one's old age, or even that a particular one was a 'mistake'. Not everyone would find them satisfactory because as reasons for positive choice they do not ring true. Social pressures provide powerful motives but are seldom voiced. Some women aim at motherhood because they feel it is necessary to self-fulfilment. Some find it an ambition or a necessary project. Some bear children to please (and occasionally to punish or spite) husbands or families, or because every one else is having them. Some have them in order to fill a void or to have someone to love because they feel they need to have a close relationship and either cannot achieve this in any other way or else feel that they must be in control of such a relationship. Such women tend to look on a male partner as merely a 'good begetter'.[3] There are also still many women in our society who choose to become mothers because they are influenced by the idealization of motherhood that has been widespread during this century. Some have them simply because they like children and enjoy family life, or envisage that they will enjoy it, or feel that they would like children to be part of their lives. This last, provided it is based on reality and not on an idealized picture of what children are like, is likely to be one of the most successful motives.

Motherliness is a complex quality and I propose to discuss it in some detail in this Part of the book because I believe it is one of the most valuable and undervalued talents to our society which, properly recognized, could have a profound influence on the condition of women today and on society in the future.

If we start with a baby, motherliness is warmth, caring in a sensitive way, together with a desire to protect and enhance the child and the capacity to do this. It means putting the other's interests first and knowing what these interests are without reading a book or being told (though experts may be of *some* help). It means constancy, the communication of security and optimism, and also patience, tolerance, the control of immediate feelings along with the recognition of negative and unpleasant feelings. It involves the capacity to delay satisfaction and the ability to think and feel in terms of the developing child. As the child grows older external reality becomes more important in motherliness, together with the capacity to balance it with the inner world of fantasy. It involves the ability to see another's point of view yet also to feel angry, to know when anger is felt and on appropriate occasions to be angry yet at the same time being forgiving towards a child who is understood in a realistic and not a projective way.

Most important in motherliness is a sense of boundaries and this deserves some space because it is usually ignored by those who write on these topics and because a sense of boundaries is often lacking when all other aspects of motherliness appear to be present. Some children from devoted and apparently excellent homes turn out disastrously because their mothers, or sometimes both parents, lack a sense of boundaries. By a sense of boundaries I mean an ability to discern the limits of a relationship with another or with society and to communicate this to the other. The wider the boundaries and the more unconscious the discernment of what they are, the more successful the relationship is likely to be. For then there is latitude and room for growth and experiment, but unconsciously (some would say instinctively, but I do not believe it is anything to do with instinct) each knows the limits when they are approached, threatened or transgressed. For there must be boundaries, however wide and hidden, and the mother who cannot recognize and protect them in herself and her child is courting disaster. The child who grows up lacking this sense tends to spend his life in seeking boundaries, and inevitably keeps reaching the point at which he collides with society.

No one can have a good sense of boundaries without a good sense of self and this in part of motherliness. A mother who lacks a sense of self will tend to merge with her child in a way that prevents both from developing. A motherly person needs a sense, not only of herself as a person, but also of her own abilities and how to develop them, her own needs and how to satisfy them and her own deficiencies and how to overcome them. This necessitates a considerable degree of personal development.

Lastly motherliness involves the ability to stimulate the child and to be stimulated by him. It also involves a certain amount of administrative ability, in frequent decision-making and problem-solving, knowing how to get the best out of a child and to balance the needs, hopes and expectations of different members of the family, and to do many different things at once while being aware of many others at the same time.

One cannot complete a verbal picture of motherliness without also describing what it is not. It is not destructive or self-destructive. It does not involve power struggles, possessiveness, strong controlling attitudes, ulterior motives or annihilation of self. It does not, or hardly at all, include projecting one's own bad feelings onto the child and believing that they come from him. It does not falsify experience or indulge in wishful thinking. Aggression and ambition are not part of motherliness, though they may be present in the mother. Motherliness is not self-enhancing or narcissistic, neither is it being a doormat and allowing motherhood to destroy the person who is the mother. Anxiety plays a certain part in motherliness and will be discussed later, but excessive or neurotic anxiety does not. The transmission of anxieties and phobias, often unconsciously, from mother to child is a frequent failure in mothering. Lastly true motherliness, being always suitable to the age and stage of development, contains a sense of what is and what is not appropriate. Good motherly feelings towards a very young child are different from those towards an older child or an adolescent.

A good mother has to be able to cope, in the early stages, with crying, non-verbal communication and lack of sleep. The crying will cease and opportunities for sleep will come but the need for non-verbal communication continues and is an important part of good mothering. At a later stage motherliness involves the capacity to deal with boredom, repetition, constant interruption, physical onslaught, destructiveness and demands. It also involves coping with and promoting endless curiosity while recognizing, understanding and preventing overreaction performed with a purpose that, unchecked, turns easily to deviousness. And all this often has to be carried out in a state of physical exhaustion. Motherliness requires stamina and is always loving even while hating.

This may seem to be an idealized picture of a good mother but it is not. Motherliness may be an ideal but mothers are infinitely variable. An awareness of themselves, and an understanding of their own difficulties and deficiencies in motherliness and the capacity to make up for them or to provide substitutes compensates for a great deal. It is those who lack this capacity and use their positions as mothers for their own neurotic purposes who are likely to run into trouble in their experiences as mothers.

Last, and perhaps most important, is the fact that motherliness is a human quality and by no means confined to women. The use of the phrase 'maternal instinct' is often used by those who wish to assert that only women should care for children or that the details of childrearing are beneath the dignity of men. In fact, many men have motherly qualities and many more could develop them if society and circumstances would permit it.

CHAPTER TWELVE

Conditions of Power

A mother's influence is greatest when there is no alternative and no escape. For the first time in history this has become the situation for the majority of mothers and children in western society. In the past there was usually relief for both mother and child in the form of other adults and other children. In the pre-industrial world, as we have seen, there were many more people around all day, including fathers, and often helpers in the work that went on at home. Families of all social classes were larger. In the late nineteenth century the average family contained about six children compared with about two today. For the middle class child there were always servants and in whom many found not only relief from unadulterated exposure to their own mothers but also enrichment through a variety of relationships. Servants also meant that mothers could escape from children. The poorer child and his mother had the life of the village or the street to provide alternatives. In both country and town there was physical space in which to move and explore which was neither as dangerous nor as regulated and tidy as are our traffic-ridden roads and our ordered parks or even our mechanized farms today.

Today mothers and children are confined together in small spaces. For many there is no alternative and no relief. Even if facilities exist, such as playgroups or mother and toddler clubs, they necessitate a special expedition which requires planning and preparation. Whole days may go by during which they see only each other and the mother may have no adult contact beyond the check-out girl at the supermarket. There may be no one else in her life who is interested in the baby and no one with whom she can discuss him. Yet he may be her only link with life apart from herself and, as well as the cause of her isolation, may be her only compensation for it.

The result is that today's mother probably has total power over

201

her child, and over no one or nothing else. He is exposed to the full impact of her personality, with all its quirks and difficulties. He may know no other adults, not even his father, well enough to be able to use relationships with them to help him overcome the over-whelming influence of his mother. For him there is likely to be no corrective, no escape and no freedom. For her there is unlimited power without accountability. Once she has a child she may have little or no opportunity to develop as an adult with other adults. She has to organize her anxieties and her emotional involvements round that child. With him she is dominant, but she loses contact with the outside world and so may lose her self-confidence about it. Even if she once held down a responsible job she may emerge from her period of retreat and total power unable to relinquish her power over her children which can become the strongest force in her life and the only thing that remains to motivate her. Even if she does wish to step outside she may find it difficult, because she becomes conscious that the world outside has been changing rapidly and she feels that there is now no place for her in it. Perhaps she fled to child-rearing as an escape from the outside world in the first place, in which case her problems will be even greater, as will those she imposes on her children.

Simon de Beauvoir saw this over thirty years ago, and it has become much worse since then. She wrote: 'There is an extravagant fraudulence in the easy reconciliation made between the common attitude of contempt for women and the respect shown for mothers. It is outrageously paradoxical to deny woman all activity in public affairs, to shut her out of masculine careers, to assert her incapacity in all fields of effort, and then to entrust to her the most delicate and most serious undertaking of all: the moulding of a human being.'[1] Adrienne Rich has written:

> Yet the helplessness of the child confers a certain narrow kind of power on the mother everywhere – a power she may not desire, but also often a power which may compensate to her for her powerlessness everywhere else. The power of the mother is, first of all, to give or withhold nourishment and warmth, to give or withhold survival itself. Nowhere else (except in rare and exceptional cases, e.g. an absolute ruler like Catherine de' Medici, or a woman guard in a concentration camp) does a woman posess such literal power over life and death. And it is

at this moment that her life is most closely bound to the child's, for better or worse, and when the child, for better or worse, is receiving its earliest impressions. . . .[2]

There are a number of questions we must ask. It is as important to be aware that these questions exist as it is to find the answers. If the mother is temperamentally unsuited to a cloistered life with small children, how does she survive? The answer is that if she survives, she does so at the expense of herself or her child, or both. Or she goes out to work, which brings other problems and dilemmas. If the mother is immature or incapable or neurotic or has a distorted personality, how does she develop? Of course she does not develop. She remains immature, neurotic or distorted. These things get worse. And what about her child? He will of course suffer from her difficulties and will himself be distorted and damaged by them. The less his opportunity of escape, and the less his contact with other adults, the more this is so. As things are today he is unlikely to find an escape or to be able to redress the balance. Mothers and children from families that are isolated from others often have serious difficulties. In my experience this is often particularly true of families who describe themselves as 'close' and pride themselves on being so. Being a 'close family' is often a means of building a little personal world as a defence against the outside world with virtually no connection with it. In this father often reinforces mother and finds there his own escape and his own compensations. The trouble is that the close personal world can only last for a few years while the children are growing up. Sooner or later the children have to go out into the outside world for which they are unprepared, armed only with what they have absorbed of their parents' personalities which may be insufficient or unhelpful in the outside world, making contact with it impossible. At the same time the mother also has to face either the outside world or else her own empty nest. She too may find both these impossible. This is an important reason why so many adolescents and so many mothers of grown children break down, often in the same family.

In this and the next two chapters I discuss various emotional difficulties I have encountered in my psychiatric practice with mothers and their children. Some of the problems I describe seem severe, but are only made so because of the effects of today's idealization of the mother.

The words mature and immature are easier to understand and more precise when used in a physical than in a psychological sense. But they are often bandied about in psychological jargon and are prominent in the vocabulary of many people who work in the psychiatric field. They are used loosely, with little thought as to their true meaning, and often when more appropriate contrasting words might be 'anxious' and 'calm', or 'dependent' and 'independent'. Bowlby has pointed out that using the words mature and immature in this sense is a misuse derived from an unproven theory about arrested development according to which adult personality structures described as immature are held to be a consequence of arrested development and to have remained in a state that is normal for childhood but is passed through during the course of healthy growing up.[3]

I propose to describe mothers as mature or immature according to the extent to which they think, feel and behave in a manner appropriate to adults or to children. Deviations from the normal behaviour of either are discussed elsewhere under appropriate headings. But first I shall make a short digression to explain the concepts.

In spite of their frequent conversational use, the words 'mature' and 'immature' are conspicuously lacking in books on psychiatry. I recently looked them up in large textbooks and found that only one of these even mentioned them and then only in relation to brainwaves altering with age. Nevertheless personally I find the concept useful when talking to patients and assessing family situations.

In biology maturation refers to that form of development which takes place due to innate potential aided only by those environmental conditions which are essential for the realization of that potential. The growing animal cannot do certain things until it has reached a certain maturity. Thus learning to walk is part of the process of maturation whereas learning a language is part of the process of learning. A three-month-old baby is not sufficiently mature to learn to walk or talk because his brain and body are not yet sufficiently developed. The process of acquiring a skill, either mental or physical, is learned, but there must be sufficient maturity for the learning to take place. Only then can experience lead to development. But without the necessary experience or opportunity, development is retarded. Similarly, anything which prevents someone from benefiting from experience will have the same result. Thus an immature mother – who thinks, feels or behaves more in the manner of a child than of an adult – either lacks the experience necessary for adult feelings and behaviour or else has some personal reason for not benefiting from it. This is usually a psychological need to avoid, deny or falsify experience so that no benefit accrues. There are many reasons why this happens.

By 'benefit' I mean a state which is achieved through the normal interaction of maturity and experience. Immature mothers are those who have in some way failed to reach that state. As a result they tend to be not so much in a stage of development that has been achieved as in one that has not been abandoned. This may be in matters of concept, feeling or activity, or in a mixture of these.

Mature conceptual thinking relevant to mothers particularly concerns the ability to regard other people as separate and with their own needs, and the ability to foresee the likely consequences of certain events or actions. The ability to regard people as separate is either the result of having been regarded as separate oneself or else is the result of exceptional mental powers resulting in one's own achievement of that state. For most people it is largely related to what happened with their own mothers. If the mother's mother continued to regard her as a part or as an extension of herself beyond the normal age, she is likely to have difficulty in regarding herself, and therefore her child, as separate. The achievement of separation on one's own requires special talents, such as perception, concentration and the capacity to endure anxiety and suffering. Anyone who can achieve it is likely to be adult in quality and personality.

Thus maturity is inextricably bound up with the capacity to be an adequate mother. The ability to foresee the likely consequences of certain events or actions is largely a measure of the capacity for observation and assessment. For instance, a child has to learn that running in the road without looking is likely to lead to an accident, that spending all one's money at once means that one will have none left, and that failure to do one's school work will be followed by failure in one's examinations. A mature person has an active sense of logical sequence.

A mature adult or a maturing child has active and realistic feelings of responsibility, and of right and wrong, and has also acquired the ability to delay satisfaction. In contrast to a child who, when he wants something, wants it immediately, the mature person knows and feels that there is a time and place for everything and is conscious of the advantages of waiting and working for desired objectives.

Mature concepts and feelings are revealed in behaviour. The ability to regard other people as separate is the basis of respect and consideration. The ability to foresee likely consequences is associated with making realistic decisions, seeing a way through complicated situations and conflicts, and dealing with several problems simultaneously. Stable feelings of responsibility and a sense of right and wrong add to these, whereas the capacity to delay satisfaction increases the powers of concentration and persistence and enables a task to be finished and to give satisfaction.

It can be seen that the attainment of separation, the ultimate achievement of mothering, is associated with the process of maturing. But being mature is by no means the equivalent of being a good or an adequate mother. Although a considerable degree of maturity is required, the price that has been paid for this may be high. If the mother has lost her spontaneity and imagination, the child will suffer, for although these qualities are characteristic of childhood, they are also necessary in adults. A mother who lacks spontaneity and imagination cannot be in touch with her child except in so far as his spontaneity and imagination have been eroded or erased. This is why immature mothers are sometimes more successful with their children than those who are mature.

Janie, aged 18, went to a teenage party, got drunk and became pregnant. She had no memory of the child's father and no means of supporting her baby but she knew she didn't want an abortion. She moved in with another man and lived from day to day. In a worldly sense she was feckless and irresponsible. She did not even bother to feed herself properly and she usually forgot to go to the antenatal clinic. Yet when her daughter was born she was healthy. Janie felt she knew immediately how to look after her. She understood her needs and the meaning of her occasional cries. She loved her daughter's company and she loved to watch her development. Since the baby was born Janie has never regretted getting pregnant or felt resentful of the baby. She has enjoyed her more than she has ever enjoyed anything, and is clearly a good mother.

But this kind of fecklessness often goes with inadequate mothering. Many teenagers do not make good mothers. They may be pleased with their babies but many lack a sense of what the baby needs. Thus they tend to be proud of their development rather than understanding what is really required.

Sally was rather like Janie in that she was unable to organize her life in any conventional manner. She only did what she wanted to do and she never did anything that bored her. Like Janie she kept her illegitimate child, largely, I think, because she thought he would bring her amusement and satisfaction. She lived in a fantasy world into which the crying baby intruded. Her temperament was changeable and she expected her child to accommodate himself to her moods. It didn't work. She got into more and more of a muddle with her baby, frequently became hysterical and eventually broke down. In the end she decided to have the baby adopted.

A common type of immature mother is the dependent mother. She is seldom seen as a single mother because she usually has a husband or other man on whom she can rely who usually enjoys caring for her. She can't budget or do accounts. She is confused and helpless when faced with a form to fill in. She finds it difficult to take even small decisions. If she needs to visit the doctor or her child's school teacher, her husband probably has to take time off from work in order to accompany her. He is usually pleased to be important to her, enjoys controlling the household and may seem to be almost proud of his wife's inadequacies.

Another form of dependent immature mother is even commoner, but the manifestations of immaturity and dependence are less obvious. This is the mother who conceals her immaturity and her dependence by devoting herself totally to her children. She often sails successfully through her children's childhood. But she tends to run into difficulties as they grow into adolescence.

Mrs. Barrett devoted her whole life to her family, and the organization of her children's lives depended totally on her. Her husband was away all week. The family lived far from public transport, shops and schools. Although Mrs. Barrett often complained about this her husband revealed that the house had been chosen at her insistence and rather against his will. It was clear that the isolation increased her power over the children, whom she ferried by car to and from school, parties, friends' houses, scouts and so on. She never accepted invitations or requests on her own behalf, giving the excuse that she was needed by her children. She refused to go anywhere alone with her husband. When the children grew up and tried to leave home she used every kind of excuse and emotional blackmail to keep them at home. When that failed she developed a severe depression for which she blamed her husband and children.

207

Mothers who display this kind of immaturity are common. They resist all forms of developing independence in their children. They often fail to teach them the rudiments of self-care because a child who cannot boil an egg or wash his clothes or even operate a machine in a launderette is less likely to be independent than one who has acquired these skills. They may even make it difficult for a child to settle down at school or do anything outside the house. They may, for instance, be so jealous of the child making relationships with anyone else that they instil in the child a deep mistrust of all teachers, of school work or discipline or of other children of their own age. This is often done subtly and insidiously. Such children may be regarded as disruptive by teachers and referred to child psychologists for treatment. Or they may be brought by the mother herself, who is happy to have the child 'treated' for something that is 'wrong' as long as no one has the temerity to suggest that what is wrong is the mother herself.

Immaturity is often associated with the excessive use of the psychological mechanism known as denial, which can be described as the falsification of experience for personal advantage. This advantage is often simply passive mental comfort. One falsifies what one perceives so that it accords with what would make one most comfortable to perceive. This involves failing to perceive what is inconvenient. In mothers this often goes with a tendency to identify with the child.

Clare was caught stealing at school. The evidence was incontrovertible. Her mother refused to believe it on the grounds that 'she is my daughter and I know that no daughter of mine could do such a thing.' She preferred to believe that the other children or even teachers had framed her daughter.

It is obvious that the extensive falsification of experience for personal reasons will delay maturation because if one falsifies an experience one cannot benefit from it. If one pretends to oneself that what has happened is different from what has actually happened then one is unlikely to foresee the likely outcome or to develop the ability to do this.

Psychological maturity is not normally completed with the attainment of adulthood. In the same way as the three psychological stages of mothering follow the physical stages, psychological maturation follows physical maturation in time and is extended beyond it, sometimes far beyond it. Some people continue to mature all their lives and into old age. With most people maturation slowly ceases sometime during adult life and is replaced by hardening. This involves a lack of flexibility, and a loss of spontaneity and imagination. If this happens in early adult life or before, the result is an obsessional, rigid, controlling person, incapable of further development.

The influence which the experience of having and raising children has on a mother's maturity can be considerable or negligible. For many people it is one of the greatest influences on their whole lives and the greatest of all influences in their adult lives. It is a strong maturing influence, a prolonged exercise in learning to see others as separate people and a training in learning to foresee the likely consequences of certain events or actions. It is also a training in responsibility, in delaying satisfaction, in making realistic decisions, in resolving conflicts and in the art of dealing with a number of different problems simultaneously. If all this can be achieved without loss of spontaneity, flexibility or imagination, then the experience of rearing children has truly had its best possible effect.

For a mother who is already mature enough to benefit from maternal experience, bearing and raising children is a reaffirmation of her own life and a reliving of her own experience. It offers opportunities to rectify what went wrong in her own upbringing. In passing through the stages of mothering, perhaps several times over with several children, the mother can redevelop herself and broaden, deepen and expand her personality, understanding and imagination.

Sometimes motherhood can be a considerable maturing experience to a mother who is rather immature. This is particularly true of those whose immaturity stems from lack of experience, through being very young, or having had a sheltered or an old-fashioned upbringing. But some immature mothers use their children as excuses or weapons in order not to mature. Suitably manipulated, the situation of having babies can be used as an effective excuse for not facing the world, for being the centre of attraction and for being cosseted. Growing children can enhance this, often taking over the role of minister and cosseter. Some immature mothers become dependent on their children almost in the way that normal children are dependent on their mothers.

Mrs G. hated her children to leave the house without her and at the slightest pretext she would keep them away from school. She sent them, singly, to do the shopping because she was afraid to leave the house. She always refused invitations on the grounds that she had to stay at home and look after the children.

Some children become almost like parents to their mothers, always lending sympathetic ears to troubles meanwhile concealing their own. This reversal of roles probably occurs normally when the mother is old and the daughter middle-aged but at a younger age this kind of mother-child relationship is developed at considerable cost to the child's developing personality.

Joyce was the only child of a famous actress and a successful business man. As long as she could remember she had had the feeling that she must support her mother emotionally and be responsible for her. She felt that she should never burden her mother with her own troubles but should always be ready to support and ease her mother's. Joyce found solace in solitary pursuits, particularly masturbation, which in her loneliness became more and more extreme. By the age of twenty she had developed a number of compulsive sexual perversions. At the age of twenty-five she married a man much older than herself but after a few months the compulsions returned. She felt terrified of his going away on business trips yet at the same time she longed for him to go. When he was away, and sometimes when he was not, she masturbated frequently, using any suitable object she could find, notably bottles and a running bath tap. She spent hours trying to arouse the dog and persuade him to have intercourse with her. The results of maternal traits are manifold and various. No one could have predicted precisely the influence that her mother's immaturity would have on Joyce.

Many women whose level of personal development is low are reasonably adequate in an environment which supports them. There are still pockets of traditional life where maturity is not necessary to become fully adult. Some husbands are adept at supporting and protecting an immature wife. Many immature women train their children, even quite young children, to support them and provide them with a protective environment. Their immaturity is only revealed directly if the marriage collapses or their children grow up and leave home. Indirectly it is often revealed in the difficulties or breakdowns of their children when they themselves come to face the adult world, or even the world of school.

Some of a mother's difficulties consist in sorting out the confusions of childhood. If the mother herself is confused, she compounds the difficulty. In the early stages mother is the reality and the world is to be explored. Gradually the child learns something of how reality works. He learns this through people who are important in his life, and this may be only his mother. The way in which he learns this will affect his relationship with reality for the rest of his life and this is immensely influenced by his mother. Some mothers cannot bear their young children to learn anything about the world except through themselves.

In learning about reality some confusion is unavoidable and probably desirable in normal development because of the differences in maturity and knowledge between mother and child. This normal confusion of childhood is of several types.

First there is exploratory confusion. Exploring the world is a basic drive which man possesses to a marked degree and which he shares with other animals. The baby begins to explore from the time of birth and soon he may find his exploration is confusingly frustrated. Even a new baby who is exploring his own fingers by sucking them may find them removed. Or the nipple that was there a moment ago has disappeared. The older he grows the more his exploration is likely to be frustrated. He is stopped from putting things into his mouth (dirt, faeces, knives, face powder), though at this age his mouth is the most sensitive organ of exploration. His mother allows him to explore a red cushion but not a red fire, and touch the family dog but not another dog. He may crawl or walk in the garden but not on the main road, drink from a cup but not from a chamber pot and so on. There is no end to the confusing frustrations that beset him as he sets out to explore the world.

Second is the confusion of love and hate. The baby has to come to understand that the mother who loves and cares and feeds and is there when needed is the same person as the mother who does not always produce what he wants on demand and who frustrates him in his desires. Not every child comes to terms with this.

Third is confusion of absence which comes from the child's difficulty in understanding that things go on when he is not present. Small children tend to believe that they are the centre of the universe, that they see and control everything and that they are responsible when things go wrong. As they grow up they gradually become aware that this is not so and this realization creates confusion and strong feelings. In psychoanalysis the situation is discussed in terms

211

of the child's awareness of curiosity about his parents' sexual intercourse and is known in jargon as 'primal scene fantasy'. Today there is less frustration and taboo about sex than there was in Freud's day and it is probably more practical to regard 'primal scene fantasy' as the child's reaction to the awareness of things that go on behind his back, over which he has no control and for which he is not responsible. His reaction to these things will become the basis of his sense of curiosity and desire to explore. His parents' confusions and difficulties about it will pass over to him.

Another kind of confusion is confusion of meanings. The meaning may concern what is concrete or what is abstract. Confusion of meaning about concrete things concerns such matters as what one may and may not put in one's mouth; who is part of one's personal life and who is not; what is and is not allowed for one's personal use; why one may run or shout or take off one's clothes or defecate in some places but not in others; and so on. A small child may search behind the television set for his favourite character, or even behind the mirror for himself. Another example of a small child caught in this kind of confusion was told me by a patient who took her family to a shop to choose bathroom fittings. In the middle of the transaction the two-year-old disappeared. She found him in the shop window, trousers down, sitting on a display lavatory pan watched by an amused crowd in the street outside. This little boy had learned that certain things are done in certain places, but the more subtle aspects of the situation still confused him.

Confusion of abstract meaning is sorted out by coming to understand the mode, or abstract level in which any specific communication is made, in other words what the person really means – fact or fantasy, serious or non-serious, joke or non-joke, ritual or spontaneous action. Most children become skilful at knowing exactly what is intended, but they all go through a stage of confusion. Is the animal character on the television real? Who does and who does not believe in Father Christmas? Did he *really* see a lion in the garden? Is that lady joking when she says she is going to eat me?

The last confusion is the confusion of rapport. Literally, it is a confusion due to non-rapport. Rapport between mother and child normally develops during babyhood. Another kind of rapport can develop later in childhood. The nature of this rapport, its deficiencies or its absence has a deep influence on the child's later development. It can never be total or perfect and sometimes it hardly develops at all. The child may grow up with considerable difficulty in assessing the mode of communication, even when he understands the words. The subtleties or even the more obvious manifestations of humour, irony, fantasy and so on may escape him entirely. In so far as this ability fails to develop the mother has usually not been sensitive to the child and does not give the child the sense of being in touch and as a result the child's normal confusion is increased. An example was Tony, a highly intelligent six-year-old, who seemed unable to learn the normal categories that make for peaceful family life such as where and when one eats, plays, sleeps, leaves the adults alone, makes a noise, and so on. He had violent 'primal scene' fantasies about his parents and told me that they were 'beating up' and 'bashing'. His mother complained that he attacked younger children, though his teachers denied this. He had, the mother told me, been 'born a screamer' and 'screamed for twenty hours a day until he was two and a half'. It was clear that there was little rapport in this mother-child couple and that this was an important source of Tony's confusion.

Gradually most children sort out their childhood confusion through increasing maturity and experience. Maturing is the process by which the innate potential unfolds. With an adequate environment this mostly happens automatically. For instance, the child's brain and mental processes develop to the stage at which he can understand why one can touch a red ball but not a red poker or run in the park but not on the highway. He comes to terms with the mother he loves and the mother he hates and he accepts her as one person who is not always amenable but is basically loving. He trusts her, and is likely to accept her as one person who is not always amenable but is basically loving. He trusts her, and is likely to accept what she is trying to teach him before he can work it out for himself. He comes to understand that things happen when he is not there and over which he has no control. He learns how to test reality with his senses, with his experience and with his judgment. He is no longer so confused about meaning. He knows what goes where and roughly why. He knows the difference between real and pretend, between actual people and characters seen on television. He knows most of the time who is or is not likely to be trustworthy and he can usually tell when people are joking and he begins to make jokes himself. He develops a wide repertoire of signals about the significance or mode of a communication and he learns how to use them himself. Sometimes he makes mistakes and is confused, but he learns from these experiences. His curiosity about the world and his desire to explore are as strong as ever and increasing in range and complexity. He is not unduly anxious about confusion which remains or which arises. He takes it in his stride.

Thus development of understanding and coming to terms with childhood confusion depends very considerably on the mother, on her relationship with herself and her feelings about herself, and her feelings about her child. Difficulties are likely to arise wherever her perception, understanding or relationship with her child is limited, distorted or dishonest. All mothers are to some extent limited, distorted or dishonest. Most are straight about most things most of the time. Most behave in a straightforward manner towards aims that are declared or clear. Such a mother genuinely tries to do her best for her child, regarding him as a vulnerable and loved person in his own right. She does not use him for her own undeclared and perhaps unconscious aims. If she is also mostly loving and patient by nature, has a wide range of emotional responses and the capacity to communicate in many different modes she will enrich his life and lessen the anxiety associated with sorting out confusion.

During this period of sorting out children go through a phase of believing that their parents know everything and that they know it better than anyone else. Mother is proved to be right on so many occasions and so impressively that the child may accept her information and judgment uncritically. One not uncommonly hears a small child say 'My Mummy says it, so it must be true.' Some people never get beyond this stage but most move to a more mature position in which the parents are still loved as parents but also viewed as human beings with human faults and weaknesses. They are gradually reassessed in the young person's mind and the final confusion caused by the uncritical acceptance and its disparity with the real world are overcome.

Of course for most children mother is by no means the only influence or guide amid these complexities, but she is always influential, and can be overwhelmingly so. Father may also be of considerable importance and so are brothers and sisters. It seems that some modes of communication can only be learned from peers and that children with several siblings, particularly older ones, have the advantage of being exposed to these modes from an early age rather than having to wait for the less certain and often more painful

experience of acquiring them at school. Recently I had an interesting discussion with a twelve-year-old on this subject. He told me
that he had never been teased at school because, as the youngest of
six children, he was wise to all the meanings, innuendoes, insults
and intentions that anyone at school had ever been able to produce.
He told me that in his opinion, failure to recognize these signals is
the most important reason why some children are teased. He had
found his own opportunities and experiences an immense advantage
and was sorry for others, particularly only children and eldest children who had little opportunity to acquire these skills before going
to school.

The child who has sorted out his confusions within the family or
at school usually emerges with a view of the world not unlike that of
most of the people round him, particularly his family. The normal
child eventually acquires a view of life which is partly his own and
partly a conglomeration of the views of his family, other adults
whom he knows and also to some extent his school and other aspects
of his environment. This is still true when he is in open rebellion
against his family. As he grows older, he gradually comes to terms
with this. If he is keen to understand himself and to discover the
truth he ends up with a view that is still much influenced by his
upbringing but is also his own original construct. In other words, he
now understands his mother and the other influences of his childhood. To be effective, this understanding is emotional as well as
intellectual. Such insight is often not reached until middle age.
Whether or not it is ever reached depends probably more than anything on the character, motivation and intelligence of the individual. Although most people can be seen as wholly products of
their environment and experiences, there are some who seem to defy
laws and probabilities and, by their own efforts, sort out the confusions in their lives and comes to terms with them. It is always easy to
find reasons why people have not overcome their confusion and
have not managed to establish themselves as adults. One has only to
go carefully into the history of anyone to find all sorts of difficult
problems. But it doesn't answer the question of why some people
succumb and others do not.

Childhood and often the rest of his life too can be viewed as a prolonged attempt to sort out confusions. This is a difficult task and the
difficulty is increased in so far as a mother is herself confusing. Most
mothers are confusing in some ways. Everyone has quirks and

idiosyncrasies, vulnerable spots that lie hidden, and strange, forbidden fantasies. Such things, even when unconscious, lead to confusion.

Though most mothers are confusing, some are abnormally so. Some are confused inside themselves so that their children have difficulty in finding fixed points. Some are at variance with the world outside, and may be virtually out of touch with reality. Some mothers are specifically confusing in relation to their children, usually because they have feelings about them, conscious or unconscious, which they can neither control nor condone. All these are what I call confusing mothers. Unlike most mothers they do not help a child through his developmental confusion. Instead they prolong it, or usually one aspect of it, so that either the child has to sort out the problem for himself usually with aid from other people, if they are available to him, or remains forever confused, maybe increasingly so. The more exclusively he is with his mother, the less likely he will be to sort it out.

A child may disbelieve or ignore a confusing mother and trust his own senses. For him this is the only path of true development and many reach it, if only by a devious route. But it may be too difficult to do this, at least during the early part of life. Instead a child, or an adult, may disbelieve or ignore his own perception, or fail to allow it to develop, and alter it to agree with his mother. Such a course distorts not only perception but also development and personality. This is pathological confusion. In minor degrees it is common and probably to some extent we all suffer from it from time to time. But if it arises in a major form it distorts the whole personality and way of life.

The normal confusion of childhood is strongly related to exploration. The stronger the exploratory drive, the greater is the awareness of confusion, and also the greater the overcoming of confusion. A weak exploratory drive is likely to be associated with less awareness of confusion but also with less sorting out of confusion. The most effective instrument for dealing with confusion satisfactorily is a strong curiosity that involves feelings as well as ideas. If children's curiosity is stifled, either directly or indirectly, confusion becomes less obvious but childhood confusions remain. There are thousands of ways of doing this. Conversely, excessive confusion leads to anxiety which is likely to stifle or damage curiosity. Many people suffer from some form of this vicious circle. There are two main ways of dealing with confusion. One is by seeking the truth and the other is by avoiding it. Most of us use both methods.

Pursuing the truth and trying to find out what really happened is the only permanently satisfactory way of overcoming confusion. This is often hard to do, especially in matters that are painful or which cause anxiety. It usually requires moral strength, an independent will and the opportunity to use it. It also involves the ability to tolerate confusion or ambiguity, for it is never possible to understand everything that we find confusing. And usually it necessitates contacts with different people with different points of view.

The process of seeking and finding truth is difficult to study. This is largely because we recognize it unconsciously and tend not to think about it. It is perhaps best seen in art. There are many differences between a great work of art and other productions but an important difference is that great art pursues truth wherever it leads whereas other productions usually do not, and may actively avoid it. To see this contrast in an extreme form we have only to compare *War and Peace* with a romantic novel, or the *Mona Lisa* with an advertisement. I say this about art rather than about science because on the whole science and scientific discovery excludes the emotions and so is a less authentic analogy. However, many of the most important and original scientific discoveries involve the emotions to a marked degree and involve the most painful conflicts.

Seeking the truth successfully always involves originality, even when the discovery has been made millions of years before. The baby has to discover for himself the reasons why it is unwise to touch the fire or run in the road, he has to come to terms by himself with the fact that things go on when he is not there and which he cannot control, and he has to learn for himself that the mother who does not understand, who frustrates and punishes is also the mother who loves and provides. For some people it means coming to terms with a reality that can be seriously depressing or even terrifying. For instance one may discover that mother and father are so limited or twisted that it is impossible to adopt their point of view and at the same time remain honest, or else that the parents didn't care at all, were only pretending, were subtly destructive or had positively hostile feelings. It is not surprising that many who set out to discover the truth are diverted, or scared off, while many scarcely start.

A diversion while still pursuing the truth can take a number of forms. For instance, curiosity may be limited to those matters in which confusion is tolerable while it does not extend to those which are not. This process is largely unconscious. There may even be an apparent excess of curiosity, but it shows in a form that is displaced from its true origins. For instance in a patient who wanted to give up business for archaeology, it was not difficult to see that his great interest in the historical past was a displaced form of interest in his own past and in what had gone wrong in his early life. Archaeology was safer and free from personal anxiety. This kind of diversion of mind is common in academics, scholars and scientists. The urge to understand what makes one tick or what happened to make one what one is is easily transformed into a general desire to understand how things work or how a particular thing such as the human body or a motor car works or what happened in history. Sometimes one finds extreme forms of this. There may be abounding curiosity, vigorous exploratory drive, but directed carefully away from painful topics. It may be confined to intellectual topics, self-justified by vigorous application of 'scientific' principles. In other words, the individual invents rules for his own explorations which give him some of the satisfactions of seeking truth without the pain and anxiety that is inevitably involved in uncovering personal truth.

Making rules for oneself can become a way of life and the search for truth can be abandoned to the rules. In such cases there is loss of spontaneity and curiosity, a reduction of available modes of communication, an increase in rigidity, and attention to irrelevant or unimportant detail. The personality suffers, exploration is forgotten and depression may be considerable but unpleasant truths are kept at bay.

Jonathan was a boy whose parents hadn't wanted him. Perhaps they would have wanted a child one day, but not then, when they were planning their social life and travels for the next two years. However, when it was clear that a baby was on the way they altered their plans and although they did this willingly, they were always aware of the good things in life that they had missed because of this unfortunate pregnancy. Although both parents were dutiful towards Jonathan, neither really cared about him. His mother was cold and controlling. His father was weak. At the age of ten Jonathan began to tyrannize over his parents and to control them by increasingly rigid rules of his own invention. The normal routines of life such as going to bed, getting up, eating meals and going to school became long, involved rituals often involving both parents, and lasting several hours. It took him so long to dress in the morning that it made him late for school and his father late for work. Eventually he became so bound up in his own rules and rituals that he could scarcely ever leave the house and neither could his mother.

Making obsessional rules is a way of trying to deal with confusion by reacting against it and trying to control the situation rather than by trying to overcome and understand it. Sometimes reaction against confusion is less structured and more aimless, violent or disorganized.

Bill's parents separated when he was three and divorced two years later. He and his sister lived with their mother and with a series of her boyfriends. Their father lived round the corner with a series of girlfriends. Both parents cared a good deal about their children and tried to cooperate in their interest, but they disagreed about how they should be brought up and each disapproved of the other's methods. The little girl developed severe asthma. But Bill, aged six, became a 'behaviour problem'. He bullied his sister and disturbed the household in every way that he could think of. He woke early and was noisy, he stole food and money, he refused to do as he was told, he was cruel to animals and other children, and he had a terrifying habit of playing with matches experimentally to see what caught fire and what didn't. One might say that in a way Bill was still searching for truth in his confusion or one might say that he was simply protesting at that confusion and at his own inability to understand it or come to terms with it.

Internal confusions and discrepancies generate external confusion which involves relationships in the outside world. There may be an emotional awareness or response to the world that is so limited or distorted that normal relationships are impossible. The children are left with as much disability in coping with the world outside as if they had been brought up to speak only a foreign language. They may for instance lack the general experience and knowledge that is characteristic of their generation. They may lack a sense of humour, be unable to tell whether someone is serious or not and unable to appreciate communications on any level other than the literal or able to communicate only in very few modes or even only a single mode. An example of this was a man of thirty-five who, because of his relationship with his mother, had no means of communicating with other people except by describing in detail every event which had recently occurred in his life, concentrating particularly on the minutiae of the functions and sensations of his own body. He did this regardless of the interest or response of those to whom he was talking. Such a severe lack of communication is unusual but minor degrees are common. For instance, most of us know people who should not be asked 'How are you?' because they answer literally and at considerable length. We all know people who talk boringly and inappropriately, regardless of what the other person thinks or feels. We all know people who misinterpret our communications, perhaps take offence where none was meant, are suspicious of what we say, fail to notice when we are joking or when we are serious and people who are confused at the normal variety and rapid change of modes of communication with which most of us conduct our daily intercourse. Most of us, if we are at all sensitive, unconsciously adapt ourselves to such people and do not have to work out what would be appropriate and inappropriate modes for communication with them. If a mother is limited in her range of experience or emotional response or if she suffers much anxiety about these, and her children have little close contact with other adults, she will pass on these limitations or anxieties to her children and if they overcome them it will be through other contacts or experiences, which she may also confuse or forbid.

The number of confused mothers may be increasing because it includes many of rigid personality who are adapted to the world they grew up in but who are unable to adapt to the rapidly changing world in which we live. Foreign and immigrant mothers of rigid personality have even more difficulty in adapting than do native-born mothers. Mothers who suffer from internal confusion include many with perceptual difficulties, often acquired from their own parents. Very often their own family was so limited in its range of modes of perceiving the world and of communicating that they have never been able to develop the wide range of responses necessary for comfortable social communication.

Although on the whole these problems of communication are overcome most effectively by straightforwardness and seeking actively to overcome the confusion, there is ironically a sense in which being too straightforward or too honest is disadvantageous. If a mother is too literal she limits the range of types of communication of which her children are capable. The children are at a disadvantage because a certain amount of simple deviousness that is neither confused nor malicious is an asset in social life and human relations. It forms the basis of tact and to be lacking in it is to be naive. White lies with their concealed but benevolent aims may be necessary for others' comfort. Good parents take trouble to see that children become skilful in this kind of deviousness with skill.

Another form of what we might call honest dishonesty is cultural phenomenon and is seen most commonly as a reaction to a child's misbehaviour. The mother threatens to fetch a policeman, give the child away to the gipsies, or take the little girl from next door to the treat instead. Such threats are on the whole a working class habit and often deplored by the middle class 'experts' in childrearing. I suspect however that this kind of overt lying is actually a traditional form of rather straightforward communication through which the child learns, as his mother learned from her mother before her, a particular method of communicating disapproval, not to be taken literally any more than a white lie. I also suspect that where it appears to have done harm is usually because there was more to the mother's communication than simple annoyance expressed in a traditional way. She was proabably using the 'honest lying' approach in order to unload real hostility and perhaps a secret wish to get rid of the child.

Confusion specific to the mother-child relationship springs from the strong feelings that mothers and children have for each other. This type of confusion is particularly likely to become pathological when it concerns feelings that are unacknowledged or unacceptable such as dependence, hostility, desire for control, and perverse sexuality. Sometimes the unacceptable feelings are in the mother and lead to confusion in her relationship with her child. Sometimes the unacceptable feelings concern the mother-child relationship directly. Many mothers with abnormal feelings have a good deal of understanding of their predicament and often struggle to be normal. Most have a strong desire to do their best for their children. But inevitably they are drawn into a kind of deviousness because they cannot be honest with their children about the way they feel.

Kathryn had been neglected in infancy and probably also physically ill-treated by her drug-addict mother. She felt she had a tenuous hold on life, suffered from a strong sense of futility, was frequently depressed, and had made several suicidal attempts. When her first baby was born she managed well for several months, breast-fed successfully and coped with the baby without too much difficulty both day and night. Even when the baby was difficult she was not excessively upset. But gradually she developed sadistic feelings about him and kept imagining herself burning him on the kitchen stove or with a red hot poker. She devised various tortures for him and thought of putting out his eyes. She noticed that these fantasies were particularly strong at times when the baby was well-behaved and easy to manage. She never did anything hurtful to him and continued to care for him lovingly and efficiently, though she was upset and frequently tearful about her hateful fantasy life and her fear that she might put it into practice.

Mary felt terrified that her son, aged six, might want to leave home. She was aware that she was dependent on him emotionally and found it hard to endure the hours when he was away at school. She was terrified that he would make friends of his own age and want to spend time with them. Yet all the time she knew that for his own sake he needed to be independent of her, with companions of his own age. Her life was a struggle between her feelings and what she felt was right.

Mrs Mackay did not get on well with her husband, who was often away from home. She was quite an attractive woman and thought that she had a number of male admirers who were anxious to visit her when her husband was away. I never knew whether this was true. She used to insist that her seven-year-old daughter slept in the double bed with her when she was alone, and told her that this was 'to keep the men away.' She used to play with the little girl sexually at intervals during the night. I formed the opinion that she had probably also done this with her son who was ten years older, though she denied this. Both children became neurotic and had breakdowns in early married life. The daughter, when she had children of her own, had violent sexual and sadistic fantasies about them on which she never acted. But when the house was empty and the children were at school she used to assault the dog, both hurtfully and sexually. She was deeply ashamed of this but felt it was the only way in which she could behave normally towards her children, of whom she was very fond.

Barbara felt unable to admit to her husband and children the fact that she had been born illegitimate. She was so ashamed of this that it coloured her whole life, which seemed to consist of a prolonged effort to keep the secret and to hide any evidence that might reveal it. This involved complicated plans and manipulations which neither her husband nor her children could understand and led to both marital discord and difficulty with the children. Both improved markedly when Barbara was helped by psychiatric treatment to feel less ashamed about her origins and to tell her husband about it.

Some people react against confusion by becoming devious. This is true of both mothers and children. Deviousness may be outward and directed towards the truth, or inward and directed away from it. For instance if exploration is forbidden it may be carried out secretly. This is not true deviousness. If a child (or adult) is afraid of the truth he may go to great lengths to conceal it not only from others but also from himself. If his mother does not love him or feel affection for him, somewhere in himself he will know this, but his conscious self may be unable to bear such knowledge. So he will vigorously and deviously reassure himself that he has approval, admiration and love and he does this by such methods as exaggerated behaviour, manipulating circumstances or by playing off one person against another. Deviousness becomes a means of avoiding confusion, but it means sacrificing honesty and search for truth. It is impossible to seek truth and avoid confusion at the same time. Restricted mothers and rigid mothers are confusing. But devious mothers are the most confusing of all.

CHAPTER THIRTEEN

Devious Mothers

A certain amount of simple deviousness is an asset in social life and human relations. It forms the basis of tact, provides that variety in modes of communication which is necessary for civilized behaviour and sophistication, and gives those who are inarticulate for cultural reasons a means of communicating with an acceptable and comprehensible subtlety which might otherwise be lacking. We have seen how some mothers develop a kind of straightforward deviousness that is directed either towards a richer or more emphatic variety of communication. In this chapter I propose to discuss true deviousness.

True deviousness is intended to avoid rather than to master confusing situations, and this means sacrificing honesty and search for truth. It is impossible to seek truth and avoid confusion at the same time. Deviousness develops initially as a result of confusion and is, for the child, the most confusing and often the most distressing of all maternal traits. For this reason some readers may find this chapter disturbing, especially since it is usually only in late adolescence or in adult life, often not till middle age, that people come to understand that their mothers were devious or had devious traits. Understanding this and coming to terms with it can be one of the biggest tasks which a maturing person ever has to face.

The devious mother is not straight. This may seem tautological but it needs stating because in the statement lies the paradox and confusion that is so hard for many people to face or understand. The aims of the devious mother are not what they appear to be. She may be self-centred and narcissistic, outgoing and manipulative, or overtly or covertly malevolent. Often she uses the child for her own purpose under another guise. She may to some extent be aware of what she is doing, but there is always a strong unconscious element

in her behaviour. Sometimes the deviousness is wholly unconscious.

Extensive deviousness in a mother affects a child's character profoundly. Devious people are often selfish, sly, dishonest, prying and
unreliable. They can show a staggering disregard for other people,
including their nearest and dearest. But they can also be imaginative, spontaneous, vivacious, warm and charming, sometimes so
much so that one has to be exceptionally perceptive to spot the
deviousness. They can also be lovable, at least on the surface. I
suspect that people fall for them, and fall in love with them, rather
more than with people who are straighter. This may seem strange
because devious people show this character trait, often to the point
of destructiveness, in human relationships, particularly close relationships, in marriage and within the family.

There are probably as many devious aims as there are devious
people. Some of these aims are commoner than others. Perhaps the
commonest aim is to provoke a response. To this end there is over-
reaction, both in word and deed, exaggeration, use of superlatives,
and all forms of dramatic behaviour and attention-seeking devices.
This often goes with a liking of and aptitude for dramatization,
which is frequently (though not invariably) a characteristic of
devious people. Similar exaggeration and dramatization is often
used for other devious aims, such as to make an impression, in
which case the exaggeration is often concentrated in the appearance,
or to make a point, in which case it is often pursued without regard
for truth. Closely related to these is the desire for the approval, admiration and love of others. This lies behind much devious behaviour. It may be pursued in the same dramatic, exaggerated way, or
much more subtly, by playing one person off against another or
simply by repeating things in a different tone of voice. The subtle
denigration of others not present, often for motives of envy or self-
support, forms a large part of much devious behaviour.

Closely related to much devious behaviour is the need for external
stimulation. One can often detect an emptiness in devious people.
Either they have no inner resources or else these resources are shut
away and are not available to them. To compensate they have to use
the external world, however unsuitable it may be. The result is often
excess, exaggeration, lack of balanced judgment, and mischief-
making.

Devious people have difficulty in experiencing real feelings. They make much of the superficial – hence, of course, the social success that they often achieve. The devious person is often charming and seems to make warm contact with others. You quickly feel that he is an old friend. The sense of personal rapport that we can feel with the devious character, if we have not spotted the deviousness, can be considerable and it may persist even after one has appreciated the true state of affairs.

The basis of this is a real need on the part of the devious person to keep up an illusion of human contact. It conceals a profound sense of inner insecurity and, usually, a low tolerance of frustration. A failure to elicit sympathetic responses from others often leads to low spirits, anger, temper tantrums or a display of devious behaviour aimed at avoiding unpleasant situations. Devious behaviour is often a form of repeating childhood patterns of behaviour. When a child cannot solve his problems he tends to repeat the unsuccessful type of behaviour, often over and over again, even throughout life. It is as though the personality knows no other response and for the sake of it will disregard reality.

Devious behaviour of mothers towards their children is usually based on unacceptable feelings or aims hidden under the guise of mother love or mixed with it. This is what is so confusing to a child. There may be suppressed anger, hostility, perversion, dislike of sex or society, sibling rivalry or a desire to control or to fail.

Common varieties of maternal deviousness include using a child as a weapon against husband or family, as an excuse for inertia, in an attempt to be the centre of attention, as the object of left-over feelings about parents or siblings, or as a substitute for parents. Sometimes devious behaviour is an attempt to mask depression and improves if the depression lifts.

Mrs. Oliver was the mother of three little girls, aged five, six and eight. 'We're all girls together,' she would say as she lined them up in formidable array against her husband. 'A mere man can't understand such things,' she was fond of saying contemptuously, or 'just like a man.' However, she found her husband useful when it came to housework, cooking or putting the children to bed. As soon as he arrived home in the evening she would fall into bed, as though overcome with exhaustion. 'You've no idea how tiring it is slaving away all day with the children,' she explained, omitting to mention that the children were at school all day and that she did virtually no housework or cooking. In fact at the time I saw her she spent most of her time chasing her general practitioner for whom she had developed a passion. She was fond of dressing her daughters in identical dresses which matched her own and tying their hair with ribbons which offset her own, usually rather startling, hairstyle. The four of them would call at the doctor's house and Mrs. Oliver would offer to do little jobs for him and to help him in his garden or practice. 'But the weeds are so terrible,' she explained when her husband protested. She had never been known to weed her own garden.

Shirley had felt insecure as long as she could remember. During her childhood she longed to have a mother who would cuddle her instead of her own mother who held her at arm's length both literally and metaphorically. During her adolescence she dreamed of a baby to cuddle, and during a brief, disastrous marriage she produced one. After her husband left her she felt lonely at night and would wake up her baby for company. She developed the idea that in order to keep her own sanity she must always keep him by her side. She dreaded his going to school. She taught him to comfort her when she cried and to feel guilty when things did not go her way. As she became more and more depressed and isolated, her obsession about her baby increased and seemed the only way to keep the depression at bay.

Much has been written about 'double bind' mothers who raise their children by an infinite series of impossible dilemmas. The child can only avoid guilt or loss of love or support from the mother, or a direct confrontation with her hostility, by denying the evidence of his senses. According to Bateson, Laing and other writers, this leads in extreme cases to schizophrenia in the child. There is some confusion here because of the different use of the word 'schizophrenia' in the US and Britain. It is a diagnosis made much more commonly and on a broader base in the US than in Britain, where stricter criteria are applied. This difference leads to confusion in the literature. British schizophrenics do not on the whole seem to have this kind of 'schizophrenogenic' mother. The confused and illogical behaviour and personality that tends to develop in the children of such mothers is more likely to be labelled hysterical. The pros and cons of these labels are not relevant here, but at times most of us use or are caught in double bind situations. Such a situation requires repeated experience in a relationship of two or more persons, one or more of whom is the 'aggressor', who is in a position of power over the 'victim' or 'victims'. The aggressor is usually the mother and the victim is usually her child, though this is not always so. The aggressor usually has contradictory feelings about the victim which she is anxious to conceal, usually from herself as well as from others. She usually wishes to achieve aims which she or society would think unworthy and so she makes them appear to be something else. She often tries to make out that what she is doing is for the good of the child.

Jenny's mother found that the presence of her energetic nine-year-old daughter made problems in her marriage and was a drag on her social life. She decided to send her to boarding school. At first Jenny was unwilling to go. Her mother promised not to send her away until she felt she wanted to go but then talked at length and persuasively about the joys of boarding school life. Eventually Jenny agreed, rather reluctantly and somewhat bewildered by the force of argument that was being aimed at her. When she overheard her mother saying to a friend, 'Jenny just can't wait to get to school. She's dying to go', she knew that something was wrong. She tried to put this into words but couldn't. She wept and said she didn't want to go to school but her mother then told her that it was now too late to change her mind and that she was certain to enjoy it when she got there. Later she discovered that her entry to the school had been arranged before her mother had ever mentioned the subject to her and that her apparent free choice in the matter was phoney. She was unhappy throughout her boarding years and deeply resentful of the trick she felt her mother had played on her. At the age of nineteen she was able to describe lucidly how her mother, with an adult's powers of argument, had persuaded her that it was all for her own good and had, in her view, taken advantage of her immaturity. In this case the double bind situation worked only partially. The nine-year-old Jenny knew that there was something devious and dishonest about what her mother was doing but she was too immature at the time to put it into words.

Many mothers today have the idea that it is wrong to tell a child what to do against its will but that it is right to argue the case until the child sees the logic of the situation. In my view this is false, and the mother who pits her adult wits against a child's in this way is likely to be far more damaging than the mother who merely insists. For a child cannot possibly be 'persuaded' in a logical way. All that happens is that the child absorbs the mother's feelings and is persuaded that they are his own. In other words, he denies his own feelings for the sake of retaining his mother's love, on which he has become dependent.

Johnny, though younger than Jenny, saw his problems more clearly. He was seven years old and illegitimate but had been told that his father was dead. He already doubted whether this was true. His mother complained constantly that Johnny tied her down, wouldn't let her hire a babysitter so that she could go out, never left her alone and so on. In fact she was emotionally dependent on Johnny and wanted him with her all the time he was not at school. One day a friend, accepting her complaints as true, invited Johnny to stay on a farm in the country the following weekend, leaving his mother to have peace and gaiety on her own. Johnny, an adventurous boy, was delighted and his mother accepted with apparent pleasure. However, two days later, when Johnny was expressing excitement in anticipation, his mother suddenly said, coldly and firmly, 'It's such a pity you can't go, Johnny, because Michael is coming to play on Saturday. Don't you remember?' Johnny became furious and shouted angrily at his mother, 'No he wasn't. I know you arranged that *after* I was invited just so I wouldn't be able to go. I thought you would do something like that.' Such clear perception of reality is unusual in so young a child, especially when being put into a double bind. Johnny's mother's intention, probaby largely unconscious, was that he should agree with her in her deception, thereby preserving her self-respect at the expense of his honesty or perception.

Probably much commoner are the reactions of the Lane children whose situation was a rather extreme example of a common problem. Mrs. Lane was jealous of the friendly relationship between her husband and children. She became increasingly hostile towards her husband and controlling in her attitude towards her three children. She did her best to turn them against their father. She stopped speaking to him, refused to cook meals for him or to wash his clothes. In the evenings she cooked for herself and the children and when he came home he would cook for himself from his own private food store. He took his clothes to the launderette while she used the washing machine that he had once bought for her. Sometimes he took the children out, and still got on well with them, but she disapproved of this and, with her considerable power of conveying strong emotion without saying a word, she made them feel so guilty that they refused to go. During the day, sometimes when the children were at home, she brought other men to the house and entertained them there. Eventually, in despair, when the children were aged twelve, fourteen and sixteen, Mr. Lane moved to a bedsitting room nearby and started divorce proceedings. The children all maintained that they loved him and wanted to see him, and since he had never quarrelled with them and had played a big part in their upbringing, it seems likely that this was true. But when he met them in the street at first they said they would like to visit him 'but it makes Mummy so cross.' Then they made excuses, 'I have to shop for Mummy,' 'We're going to visit friends,' 'I haven't got time.' Then he started receiving abusive letters from them, accusing him of 'being beastly to Mummy,' having 'refused to eat the food Mummy cooked' and 'walking out on Mummy and deserting her.' Then came a letter from his sixteen-year-old daughter accusing him of having 'stolen all our furniture'. The children now seemed to have forgotten the fact that they themselves had witnessed their mother's refusal to be a wife to her husband, and also his unhappy and unwilling retreat from an intolerable situation. They did not take into account the fact that his bed-sitting room was small and furnished by the landlord whereas they still had a whole house full of furniture. They concentrated only on the study lamp and bookcase that he had brought from home. If he tried to explain the truth to them, however gently, they accused him of telling lies, seeing things in a distorted way, bullying them or trying to rob them of their independence. Yet they still maintained that they would like to see their father 'if only he would see things as they are and stop bullying us.' In this disturbed family one can see all the elements of the double bind situation. The double bind was organized transparently by the mother using three child-victims, none of whom rebelled until much later. One can see how, by repeated experience, the double bind structure turns into an accustomed expectation.

Bateson, who first described the double bind structure in family relationships, insisted that in addition to the perpetrator (usually the mother), the victim (usually a child) and repeated experience of the situation, three negative injunctions are necessary, all of which are enforced by measures which are viewed by the victim as punishments or threats to survival. The second injunction conflicts with the first in a different mode of communication and the third prohibits escape. One can formulate the injunctions by which Mrs. Lane communicated to her children in the form of silent commandments

affecting perception, belief and action. Mrs Lane's three commandments for perception might go as follows:

1. Do not perceive reality or I shall punish you.
2. Do not perceive me as punishing.
3. If your perception differs from mine, I shall destroy you
   (i.e., withdraw my love from you).

Mrs. Lane's three commandments for belief might go like this:

1. If you do not believe what I wish you to believe I shall
   punish you.
2. You must believe that what you believe is the result of
   your own judgment and independence.
3. If you believe anything else, I shall destroy you (i.e., withdraw my love from you).

Her three commandments for action might be:

1. If you do not treat your father badly I shall punish you.
2. Do not believe that what you do is treating your father
   badly.
3. If you do anything else, I shall destroy you (i.e., withdraw
   my love from you).

A normal child, presented with conflicts such as those set up by
Mrs. Lane, reacts, as Johnny (p. 229) reacted, with rebellion. The
Lane children might have displayed anger with their mother at the
way she treated the father long before he left home. They could have
visited him at any time and normal children would have done this.
They could have refused to be drawn into their mother's vindictive
actions and accusations. But instead they gave way and were controlled by their mother, apparently able to see only with her eyes
while being unaware of what was happening. At least for the time
being, they felt that their security lay in conforming to her will.

However, some years later, as often happens in such cases, the
Lane story took a different turn. First the son rebelled, quarrelled
with his mother and went to live with his father. Within a year his
sisters followed. The mother, unable to change her devious ways,
became increasingly alienated from them and hostile to them. All
the children came to the conclusion that they would have to keep out
of her way, and so, in effect, she lost them.

So what are the differences between normal people and people
trapped in double binds?

The essence of the successful double bind is an intense relationship involving dependence. Without this the double bind is unlikely to work because the victim will escape. So a child is unlikely to submit to the assault unless his psyche is already damaged or distorted by an earlier emotional double bind situation in his life which might mean that the presence of any part of a double bind sequence provokes panic or disorientation. Another possiblity might be that he is too young or too stupid to think of methods of escape, and this is in itself a form of dependence.

The dependence that appears to be necessary to a double bind is something or someone basically unsatisfactory. A mother, or anyone else, who can successfully set up a double bind lacks the essential quality of motherliness, the caring for the other more than for oneself. Good mothers, who genuinely act for the welfare of their children, are incapable of setting up damaging double bind situations even if they would wish to do so. They may occasionally set up small ones, for no one is perfect. They may also set up binds which are devised for the purpose of escape and enlightenment.

Normal people are usually astonished at the degree of control acquired by double bind mothers over their offspring. But the truth is that the child of such a mother needs love as much as anyone else, and this is all he has. Unconsciously he knows that he does not have real love. He knows that there are conditions attached to what he needs, and he dares not risk losing it, so when confronted by the dilemma he retreats in panic and confusion, and then denies this by allowing himself to be manipulated. He feels that only by obeying his mother's commandments can he survive. He actually comes to see the mother's situation as 'real' and her perception or desire is his reality. Thus the Lane children came to see even the gentlest approach from their father as bullying and threatening. In such cases it is typical that the victims attack people who try to help them and accuse them of doing what in fact has already been done to them by another.

The younger the child the more difficult it is for him to escape and the more his dependence on his mother's inadequate love is real rather than imagined. The more other adults there are in children's lives, the less likely they are to be caught in the double bind trap.

The possiblility of escape also depends partly on intelligence and the ability to make use of it, as was shown in the case cited of Johnny, whose high intelligence undoubtedly helped him to see

232

what his mother was doing. But as a child grows older it becomes increasingly likely that intelligence will be separated from the double bind situation and often seems to be irrelevant to it. This is why submission to double binds in older children and adults usually involves loss of self-respect. This shows in many ways, including an inability to give a straight answer and an avoidance of areas of conflict. This was well illustrated in correspondence which Mr. Lane had with his daughter Sally. She was nearly eighteen years old at the time and her mother was pressing her strongly to have nothing to do with her father.

Dear Sally,

It would be nice to see you at the weekend. Perhaps we could go out somewhere for a meal? Please could you let me know what you would like to do?

> Love,
> Daddy.

The reply came two days later:

Dear Daddy,

I need £50 to go on a school trip to France (very educational!!!). Please would you send it to me.

> Love,
> Sally.

Dear Sally,

I should like to help you with your holiday if I possibly can. Perhaps you would come round and tell me about it. Are you free this weekend as I suggested?

> Love,
> Daddy.

There was no further communication for two weeks. Then:

Dear Daddy,

Sorry I couldn't make it at the weekend. We had to go and see friends and I was needed to do some cooking. Please could you send the £50 immediately.

> Love,
> Sally.

Dear Sally,

I told you that I would like to hear more about your trip to France. I haven't seen you for six months though I live just round the corner. Could you telephone me one evening so that we can arrange something?

Love,
Daddy.

The next letter shows the anxiety mounting and leading to irrelevant criticism.

Dear Daddy,

Surely it can't make much difference to your tax whether you send me the money now or later. Please could I have it immediately as I need it quickly.

Sally.

Dear Sally,

If you reread my letters you will see what I said. It has nothing to do with tax. I haven't seen you for a long time and I would like to hear about the trip you want me to pay for.

Love,
Daddy.

The next letter shows the fury of the victim of a double bind situation which is now itself threatened.

Daddy,

How can I cooperate with you when you bully me all the time? I am determined not to give up my independence however hard you try and force me.

Sally.

P.S. Please send the £50 immediately.

Years later, when Sally had rebelled against her mother and gone to live with her father, she was anxious to try to understand exactly what had happened. Typically, she remembered the above correspondence as one in which she had made a normal request to which her father had replied in vindictive and bullying terms and had refused to help her, invoking his tax problems as an excuse. So convinced was she that for a while she refused to see the correspondence (which her father had sensibly kept), which suggests that somewhere she knew the truth but was not yet ready to face it. But one day she asked to see it and for several days afterwards remained quiet and thoughtful. Later she told me that it had been a 'revelation'. She told me, 'I'm beginning to see how completely different everything was from the way I thought. It's like seeing a light at the end of a dark tunnel.'

One sees a variation on the double bind theme in what I call 'refusal' mothers. The mother exerts pressure on the child and this results in the child being unwilling or unable to do what, if left to himself, he would do easily and spontaneously. The child may refuse to eat normal food, go to school, visit friends, be nice to a younger brother or sister or, in older children, go out in the evenings or find companions of the opposite sex. There are many different types of 'refusal' from this cause. They include children who refuse to visit doctors, refuse to use lavatories away from home, refuse to go in trains, and refuse to talk to their fathers or even to play pleasantly with a brother or sister. Observation shows that the trouble nearly always arises in the mother.

In this common psychiatric condition, the mother uses the child for some purpose of her own, which she usually denies and which may or may not be easy for others to see. Her purpose is usually some unconscious form of wish-fulfilment. Sometimes the wish may be so blatant that it is difficult to believe that it is not conscious. For instance, she may be anxious when separated from the child (rather than the other way round) and so wants the child to stay at home. She may feel jealous or insecure about any relationship the child has other than with her. She may be afraid of the child growing up and so does what she can to keep the child immature. Or she may feel vindictive against the child's father or sibling and so unconsciously sets the child against him.

In cases of this type of 'refusal' the child usually believes that the feelings he has are his own and is either unable to explain them or else produces trivial or invented reasons to justify them. For instance, a child who has previously been successful and happy at school may suddenly refuse to go, saying that he doesn't like football or the maths master. Or a child with divorced parents may suddenly refuse to see one of them 'because he tell lies/isn't kind to me/

says horrid things about Mummy' or 'because I always feel sick when I come home.' Investigation or observation usually produces evidence that the statements are untrue or distorted and that the mother (or sometimes the father) has in some way 'worked on' the situation and brought about the present state of affairs.

Occasionally the same kind of situation can be created by an unusually controlled or powerful father, but mother is much more often the cause because she is the one who usually has most to do with the child. The mother usually insists, often vociferously, that she encourages the child to overcome the problem, and usually she really believes that she does. But again, close investigation or observation show that the 'efforts' she has made to help the child are minimal, that she has in fact had the opposite effect, and that this suits her purpose.

Among the methods by which the mother achieves this effect is subtle and unconscious distortion of the child's perception. To some extent all families induce in their members their own ways of perceiving, but in this particular situation the process is more extreme because powerful motives lead to extensive denial of reality.

The way in which the child's perception is distorted is through the mother's feelings transmitted to the child. Supposing a mother feels anxious about being alone (this is a common form of anxiety in mothers as their children grow older). The presence of the child means that she is not alone. She experiences this anxiety most strongly when the child leaves for school. She transmits this anxiety to the child, who then becomes anxious about going to school. But it is not regarded as acceptable in our society for a mother to admit that she feels anxious when alone or that she doesn't like the child going to school. It is also not acceptable for a child to admit that his mother feels anxious when she is alone or that she doesn't like him to go to school. So between them they reach a tacit, unconscious 'agreement' that the child feels anxious about school and they find those things at school which the child finds least congenial, for example, football or the maths master, and together they come to believe that these are the 'cause' of the trouble. Both really believe what they say.

Or take the case of a mother who feels hostile towards her husband or ex-husband, and perhaps towards all men. The Lane family described earlier in this chapter could be regarded as a case of 'father refusal' in this sense. The children absorbed the mother's feelings without being aware of it, refused to see their father and produced irrelevant excuses without apparently noticing any discrepancy. Any friendly approach to them from their father was regarded with suspicion. The smallest criticism or attempt to explain what was happening was perceived as a dangerous or unwarranted attack, which further enforced the feelings of hostility and 'proved' to them that what their mother said was true. Such children are likely to grow up unable to make satisfactory relationships. Often they either do not marry or if they do they become like their mother, basically hostile to their husbands or wives.

There are also 'divide and rule' mothers, who can't tolerate their children having friendly relationships with each other or with outside children. The mother's anxiety about the children's friendly play is transmitted to the children who 'refuse' to get on together and relieve the mother's anxiety by quarrelling. When one sees children who quarrel persistently with others, it is always worth trying to examine the situation from this point of view.

Sometimes children are able to perceive what their mother is doing. They may continue to love her but they have a hold on reality which enables them to remain detached from her. Such children often suffer a good deal. They may grow up with neurotic difficulties, they may be unhappy and are usually inevitably at loggerheads with their mothers during the actual process of sorting things out. But they grow up as whole people. This is one reason why the naughty, rebellious child is usually healthier than the quiet conformist. The rebellious child is aware that something is wrong and is trying to find a solution. His success will depend on his intelligence, his emotional strength, the degree to which his mother is controlling and confusing and the availability of other people, usually adults, to supply what is missing from his life and to act as fixed points from which he can get his bearings. For often the child is powerless. This is especially true when the mother is controlling or if she regards any attempt on the part of the child to form an independent or detached view as an intolerable threat to or attack on herself.

There are cases when an absent mother is usually better for the child than a mother who is active and present. For as long as the child remains with the mother, the situation persists. It may continue throughout the child's life. Some children miss virtually their whole schooling from this cause or they may become seriously ill from self-starvation, or settled into some permanent 'phobia' which can cripple their lives. Whatever the form the 'refusal' takes, if it is not overcome, the child tends to grow up restricted in personality, unable to withstand the normal stresses and strains of life and unable to make satisfactory relationships with the opposite sex. Such children frequently grow up to be 'part people' and often become long term patients of psychiatrists. They are also likely to become themselves the type of parent that made them what they are.

The only satisfactory solution to this type of 'refusal' problem when the child is unable to escape is to separate the child from the mother for long enough to be effective. They need to be treated or managed separately (though the mother often refuses to cooperate). If separation is achieved the problem then usually disappears rapidly, at least as long as the mother and child are separate, and especially if the child makes good relationships with other adults. Relatives and observers are often amazed at how easily it all resolves. If anyone becomes upset or breaks down it is the mother. Provided the separation is long enough and the mother's influence is not too malign, the child eventually develops his own personality sufficiently to deal with the problem on its own when he returns to the mother, and this is the aim of the long term treatment and supervision of the child. It is not usually possible to give much direct help to the mother although, in practice, her mental state sometimes improves as a result of improvement in the child. For the child separation is often a lifesaving measure, at least metaphorically, and sometimes even literally.

Such a solution is not easy to achieve. In extreme cases it is possible for a doctor to take the child into hospital, perhaps on some pretext that it 'needs investigation'. Unless there is a court order, which is rare on such an issue, it is often not possible to deal with the problem directly. Characteristically these mothers oppose psychiatric investigation or treatment or else they go along with it only as long as they feel sure that it will not reveal the truth.

Even when separation is possible to achieve, unless there is a real chance of the child developing normally, more harm than good may result. Inevitably, separation causes distress and disturbance in the child. If the child is not strong enough to cope with this, or if the mother is powerful enough to disrupt the child's achievement of independence, the result may be even worse than if the whole situation had been left alone. The child, instead of growing up as a conforming 'cipher' who is reasonably content, grows up as a disturbed, unhappy 'part-person' likely to work off his misery on whomever is at hand. In such a case the treatment by separation that was certainly essential for normal development has misfired and produced a disaster.

These are just a few of the tragedies that can result from maternal deviousness. Yet if understanding eventually emerges in the child or young person, he has been through an experience that will stand him in good stead all his life.

How far are such matters the mother's fault? The answer must be that they are her fault in the sense that they are due to her. Anyone looking at the situation might remark that it is 'all the mother's fault'. Yet she is nearly always unaware of what she does and she is genuinely trying to do her best for her child. She is likely to resist all help because this threatens her complicated system of defences. If one looks at the child one can easily imagine that the problem is the mother's fault, but if one examines the mother one becomes aware of the influences that made her what she is – perhaps she herself had a devious mother, perhaps she became devious as a reaction to an intolerable situation. She often has genuine love for her children underneath her deviousness but she is unable to make this effective. Because of the isolation which society imposes on her in bringing up her children she has, because of her own difficulties, been forced into this devious situation. She probably never had a chance to do anything else.

Mrs. Mills was transparently devious, not so much towards her three children directly as in avoiding doing things for them. She had a long history of illness and operations and boasted that since she married she had spent more time in hospital than outside. It was clear that most of her illnesses had been hysterical and most of her operations had been either unnecessary or performed in order to repair the damage done by a previous unnecessary operation. During one of these operations, she claimed, damage had been done to her right shoulder, which would not move. This had occurred just after the birth of twins and meant that she was virtually unable to care for them. In fact the only thing wrong with the shoulder was that she held it rigidly. She came from a wealthy aristocratic family and had never made a bed, bathed a child or cooked a meal. Occasionally she had to feed the children's dogs, which she found exhausted her. Once, she told me wide-eyed, she had had to break the ice with a hammer so that the horses could drink. This had obviously been a harrowing experience.

Mrs. Mills lay in hospital and tried to persuade the doctors and nurses to give her more treatment and more operations and more sympathy for her hard lot in life. A common reaction to such patients is to feel that they need a kick in the pants and that they should be made to look after themselves and work like anyone else. Mrs. Mills was inclined to provoke this reaction. But when one met her mother one could only feel immense pity. This lady was a foot taller than her daughter, noisy, strident, opinionated, dominating and lacking in any understanding, humour or compassion. She came to talk to the doctor in order literally to talk to the doctor. The doctor was unable to say anything to her. She organized her daughter in and out of hospital to suit her own arrangements and somehow it always seemed to be she who decided when Mrs. Mills was so ill that she needed to be admitted to hospital and when she was well enough to leave. It was clear that poor Mrs. Mills had never had a chance and had retreated into devious illness as an escape and a gesture of despair. One cannot help wondering what the *grandmother* was like, and her mother and grandmother before her.

It is not difficult to see, or at least to postulate, the origins of most devious behaviour and sometimes, in young children, one can actually observe its development. Take over-reaction, for instance, which is the simplest form of devious behaviour. The infant whose needs are not met easily and spontaneously may discover that if he increases his demands he will get the response that he needs. Since his parents are probably not very sensitive and cannot distinguish what is really important, he soon learns that if he makes enough fuss about something he will get what he is demanding, even if he makes his parents angry. Such difficult behaviour is likely to lead to conflict between the parents and the child soon learns to play one against the other, a typical devious behaviour pattern in later life. At the same time the lack of real rapport with the parents frustrate many aspects of normal development and leads to feelings of emptiness and often 'badness' which further increase the devious behaviour as a form of compensation. The stage is set for the development of a thoroughly devious character.

CHAPTER FOURTEEN

Restricted and Restricting Mothers

By restricted mothers I mean mothers whose personalities restrict their relationships with their children and the way in which they present the world to their children. These mothers include those who are obtuse, emotionally limited, rigid, prejudiced, and 'intellectually' ambitious. All types of restricted personality tend to be passed on to the children unless the children overcome them by their own efforts, and usually with the aid of other relationships.

First are obtuse mothers. These are mothers who either lack intelligence or who are unable or unwilling to use it, not in the narrow sense of Intelligence Quotient (indeed, many of them have high IQs), but rather common sense, perceptiveness, sensitivity, understanding and the capacity to learn from experience. Intelligence in this wider sense is the main instrument that helps one to grow up with a sense of identity, knowing who one is, what one wants, what one thinks is right and wrong, and with the courage to make these effective. Those with poor intellectual equipment have greater difficulty in developing this, as they also do in the childhood capacity for making up for deficiencies in the environment (or mother). But a high IQ is not necessarily an advantage. Although it goes with a capacity for abstract thinking, and an ability to grasp principles and make connections, it can militate against common sense, and can also be isolating and actually make difficulties.

Much apparent obtuseness comes from restricted modes of communication and an ineptness in using or recognizing them. For instance, people who have never played as children find it more difficult to play or to recognize the significance of others' play or its value in human communication than do those to whom play comes easily. The same goes for being teased, for appreciating *double-entendre*, for artistic appreciation. Other examples are a sense of humour and the form it takes and the capacity for that form of communication which makes rapport possible between adult and child, and particularly between mother and baby.

Some people are not so much stupid as caused to be stupid or used to being stupid. Some have never had the experience of responsibility or of making decisions. Some mothers have gone straight from parents who organize everything to husbands who organize everything. Such people lack the opportunity to mature and to learn from experience. Tracy came from a close-knit family where the parents took all the decisions. She married the boy next door who treated her like a precious doll and took all the decisions. But he became an airline pilot and was often away from home. This meant that Tracy had to take decisions, especially after the children were born. She felt incapable. She became depressed and weepy. She tried to persuade her husband to give up his job, but he refused. She became more depressed and took to drink. She neglected her children. By the time she was forty she was in a bad way. A necessary part of her treatment was trying to increase her self-confidence, to help her to be more independent and to encourage her to do things on her own. Although she has learned this to some extent, she will probably always have the feeling that she is worthless and incapable and that other people really ought to look after her.

A common type of restricted personality is caused by rigidity. By rigidity I mean a type of personality characterized by a tendency to persevere in a particular response or course of action, regardless of its appropriateness. Such people find it difficult to vary their responses. Rigidity is different from stability. In a constantly changing environment stability requires flexibility, the very opposite of rigidity. In our culture rigidity is often associated with lack of stability and a tendency to break down.

Some degree of rigidity, or slowness of adaptation of response, seems to be a natural and protective human phenomenon, but an extreme degree of rigid behaviour is usually seen either as a reaction to anxiety or as an excessively strong response to a stimulus. In the former case the person refuses to acknowledge that circumstances have changed and continues to cling rigidly to old responses, however inappropriate they may have become. An example of this was a mother who would not allow her sixteen-year-old son to go out in the evening or even during the day without permission and who was terrified that the boy would associate with those of a different social class. Neither she nor her husband could really believe that the world for young people was different from the one they had known, and they could not accept that their son had different needs from theirs.

A variation of rigid behaviour is seen in the person who is 'set in his ways'. Even if he is aware of changes, he himself cannot change.

Ruth, aged sixteen, became obsessed with the desire to be slimmer than all her classmates and her refusal of food led rapidly to open conflict with her parents, particularly with her mother, to whom preparing three substantial meals a day, which the family would then sit round a table and eat, was more or less a way of life. The mother was intelligent and able to see that constant harping on Ruth's refusal to eat only made matters worse. The mother was asked not to discuss food with Ruth or to try to force it on her. She was repeatedly told that she need not worry about the girl's weight or health because doctors were now in charge. But the mother was unable to refrain from mentioning the subject frequently. 'How can you say you love me when you don't eat?', 'I'm sure you shouldn't go away on holiday, you are too weak from all this starvation.' This mother needed help in understanding her own anxieties before she could relax and behave in a less rigid and repetitive manner. As soon as she became calmer, her daughter's condition improved.

Another type of rigid response is seen in those who are markedly prejudiced. A form of prejudice that psychiatrists often see is prejudice against psychiatrists. Donald, a young man of twenty-two, was seriously depressed and suicidal and I wished to discuss him with his parents. He lived at home and was keen for me to make contact with his parents. He told me that his mother was 'dead against psychiatrists', ashamed of his illness and convinced that if only he would pull himself together he would be all right. He knew that he could not pull himself together. In response to a letter from me stressing the seriousness of the situation both parents agreed to visit but they never came. Several appointments were made but each was cancelled by the mother because she was 'too busy cooking today,' or 'had to shop this afternoon' and, finally, 'because Christmas is only a month away.' In the end she persuaded Donald to stop coming to see me. Six months later he returned on his own accord because his depression had become worse. He was anxious that his mother should not know that he was again having treatment, which he continued to receive secretly. It was clear that as his mental condition deteriorated and as his mother became increasingly anxious about it, her prejudice against psychiatrists increased. One could only respect her beliefs, while questioning her motives, and at the same time to continue to do what seemed to be best for Donald, hoping that perhaps one day he would be able to come to terms with her over it. Rigid parents tend to produce rigid children. They request submission and obedience both overtly and covertly. They have the unconscious ability to impose their own standards and limited outlook on their children, often in a series of dichotomies such as good-bad, clean-dirty, masculine-feminine, order-disorder, dominance-submission. It seems that these parents make demands on their children for behaviour which can be neither understood nor achieved. The child can then only retain his parents' approval by learning what he is required to do without understanding it. Because it is not understood it cannot lead to personal values and so has to be supported by a rigid system of defences in which opposites are distinguishable and black and white are recognizable. Grey, or any other kind of ambiguity, is threatening because the standards that have been learned by rote do not allow for it.

In recent years a great deal of research, ably summed up by Leach, has shown that rigid, over-controlling parents produce children who are over-conforming, submissive to authority, extremely conventional and bound by rules in both attitudes and behaviour. Mothers with restricted personalities due to rigidity tend to be obsessional and controlling. The processes and results of extreme control will be discussed in the next chapter. Like the rigid person, the obsessional, who is usually rigid too, is afraid of feelings, and tends to concentrate on excessive detail in an attempt to control these feelings. Since children normally go through an obsessional stage, usually reaching its peak at the age of two or three, this interacts with the feelings and actions of an obsessional mother. Herein lie some of the failures and some of the successes of mothering.

Restricted and rigid mothering works best within a traditional system such as the upper class system described earlier. Mothers who limit their mothering to a set of internal rules need a system that will support those rules, otherwise the rules will be liable to collapse, especially in a changing world.

I include many intellectual mothers among those restricted in personality. Here I am discussing people who use their intellects to restrict their personalities and mothers who use intellectual processes as a substitute for feelings, particularly when attempting to understand or control their children.

Being an intellectual may mean having intellectual interests, or possessing good intellectual capacity. It may mean having an emotional involvement in ideas, or it may be a method of dealing with anxiety and with problems generally. It can be a mixture of any of these. Mothers who have intellectual interests or good intellectual capacity are not necessarily 'intellectual mothers' in the restricted sense, because they have the capacity to use their feelings as well as their intellect. Indeed many of these are extremely successful in mothering their babies, a process which is most successful when it is not intellectual. Mothers who have problems as 'intellectual mothers' are those who tend to deal with anxiety by intellectualization. Mothers of this kind who, if they are also low in maternal feelings and who feel that these need boosting by intellectual means, have severe problems. If they are extreme intellectualizers they inevitably lack intuitive maternal feelings because their constant intellectual activity prevents the development of authentic maternal feelings. These mothers are usually diligent and many of them are frequent attenders of general practitioners, paediatricians, clinics and social workers. They buy baby books and magazines galore, thrive on the whole idea of 'techniques' of baby and child care and are always searching for advice from outside rather than for their own feelings and intuition. They tend to fall for the current conventional wisdom in child care and if they manage to find and use their feelings at all, they do this by intellectual means which in turn tend to block the feelings. Common questions asked by such mothers are 'How do you think I ought to deal with this problem?' or even the more abstract 'How much should one *think* about mothering?' There is a tendency to overvalue thought in compensation for lack of feeling or failure to be in touch with feeling. Intellectualization is a powerful personality trait and, if it is troublesome, it is usually difficult (and also exhausting) for a psychiatrist to tackle successfully.

Many intellectual mothers are anxious about their children's mental development. They watch the baby closely for every milestone, compare his conceptual capacity with what the books say and with that of other children and do all they can to increase his vocabulary. Because they read the books intellectual mothers know that at present experts in child care insist that rigid toilet training is bad for a child so in this they tend to be rigidly permissive. But most experts at present are keen on, in the early stages, 'mother-child' bonding and later on language development. 'Make sure you form that vital initial bond with your newborn baby' insist the experts, and so the mother sits over her newborn baby trying to love him and trying to suppress the apathy, hostility or disgust which he really evokes in her. 'Bathe your child in language from the time he is born' is today's conventional wisdom. The intellectual mother tends to obey this with delight. She may take a pride in the size of her child's vocabulary or make sure that he learns a certain number of words each day. She has a programme of reading to him and keeps abreast with developments in children's literature. Feeling, rapport and spontaneity tend to be smothered by words.

Another form of restriction which influences mothering is ambition, which can show itself in more extreme forms of restrictive mothering. An ambitious parent is both restricted and restricting in ways not very different from the restrictiveness of intellectuality. A certain amount of ambition for a child can be a normal part of mothering, but in excess it is usually an attempt to gratify some hidden need on the part of the mother, who uses the child as an extension of herself. The case that comes most readily to my mind today concerns a father but I shall use it because it shows not only the effect of parental ambition but also the fact that fathers are also important and influential. Although I have asserted repeatedly that fathers can be as influential as mothers, can act as mothers and can be maternal, this important fact can easily be lost in a book that is essentially about mothers.

Mr Hews is an extremely neurotic and very able man of humble origins. He has managed, by the skilful use of psychiatrists and drugs, to avoid a total nervous breakdown and to become the successful managing director of a famous company. He has a teenage son, John, whom, he frankly admits, he regards as part of himself. It is essential to Mr. Hews' equilibrium, if not to his son's, that the boy shall be first in everything he attempts. This consists chiefly of school work and golf. When John came home, having been top in all school subjects except one, Mr. Hews was upset and conducted a prolonged and emotional inquiry into this failure. John is also a golf player and is ambitious in this. During tournaments, though Mr. Hews does not play himself, he stands near his son urging him on, shouting his advice and assuring him that 'winning' is the only thing that matters. He frankly admits that he is incapable of any other course of action and willingly and cheerfully pays psychiatric fees so that his son can be helped to understand and to deal with the situation. John, who is much more stable than his father, has been able to make good use of psychotherapy and copes with the situation with skill and understanding. But his father's ambition gives him many problems to overcome.

Many mothers are socially ambitious for their daughters. Such a mother was the wife of an ambassador who had recently been knighted. When they returned from abroad their daughter Meriel was seventeen. The mother was determined that Meriel should have social success. She made elaborate plans for her to 'come out' and 'do the season' and planned details of clothes, entertainment and social events. Meanwhile Meriel was still at boarding school and was terrified of growing up. Her intellect was highly developed but in every other way she was like a small child. She had plenty of experience of adult dinner parties but had scarcely met any boys of her own age. The idea of sex terrified her and so did the thought of 'doing the season'. She wanted to stay on at school and prepare to go to university.

Other types of limited and restricted mothers include those limited by poverty, lack of education, neurotic difficulties and also those whose maternal development is limited by their own neglect, but these are dealt with elsewhere.

Parents often have to impose physical restraint. Babies have to be pulled away from light sockets. Toddlers cannot be allowed to run in the road, play with fire and so on. But regardless of the amount of control that is necessary a mother may exert more because this is a measure of her personality.

Even more complicated is control that is necessary for the child to feel safe psychologically. Sometimes small children need to have their feelings controlled for them, often by physical restraint during a tantrum. If he is left to thrash about on his own a child may feel very insecure. An uncontrolled teenager who appears to resent his parents may actually be longing for them to force him to conform to their standards and their failure to do so can drive him to despair. In this way parents who are unable or unwilling to exert control can fail their children.

Failure to control is not the same as having no need to control. Some parents seem to gain their children's cooperation so that the

247

whole concept of control seems irrelevant. Provided this is authentic it is of course desirable. The parents are relaxed and spontaneous and so are the children, who are able to develop in their own way. Sometimes a family appears to be like this on the surface whereas underneath subtle controlling forces are operating. For instance, an adolescent may think he has decided for himself what he wants to do or be when in truth his parents have communicated to him their desire that he choose this and have passed on to him not only the motivation but also their desire that it should appear to be his own decision. Such a situation is often revealed by the breakdown or sudden rebellion of the child, usually to everyone's astonishment.

Failure to control children may be due to an inability to perceive what is necessary, to lack of rapport, to weakness in the parent or relative strength in the child, or to a combination of these. It can also be an unconscious intention on the part of the parent, who uses the child to act out her own unacceptable desires. Thus the presence of a noisy child prevents conversation, or a child who cannot be prevented from coming into the parents' bed may be being used as a means of avoiding sexual intercourse. A child who disrupts other people, damages property or attacks other children may actually be pleasing his mother in a way that neither would understand and which she would certainly repudiate. Yet in reality the child is not out of control. He is excessively controlled by his mother in an unconscious, subtle and devious way.

CHAPTER FIFTEEN

Anxiety, Depression, and Disturbance

Anxious mothers are the plague of all who work with them and their children. Anxiety in mothers seems to be one of the characteristics of our age. Yet it is abnormal for a mother not to be anxious. This paradox results from the falsity inherent in the idealization of motherhood that is so prevalent in western society today. Our society pushes the concept of 'natural', anxiety-free motherhood while at the same time creating anxious mothers.

A young mother put her baby daughter, aged six weeks, to sleep in her pram in the front garden. The mother heard her cry, thought it sounded a little louder than usual and was tempted to go and look. But then she scolded herself for being an anxious mother and decided to ignore it. But the baby was being attacked by a child who had come in from the street. She was rescued by a passer-by, who probably saved her life. Her face had been deeply scratched and her head had been beaten against the iron framework of the pram.

The mother of an undergraduate had a feeling that all was not well with her son. She wanted to go to Cambridge to visit him. Her husband dissuaded her on the grounds that she was being over-anxious. Next day the young man killed himself. Both these mothers felt anxiety and both failed to act on it because they were persuaded that they were over-anxious.

Recently I talked with a mother who couldn't bring herself to allow her son to cross the road on his own until he was fourteen years old. Is this an example of excessive anxiety or of a poor capacity to tolerate normal anxiety? Some people are unable to tolerate the normal anxieties that life inevitably brings, and whether it is because they feel them excessively or because they are unusually inept at dealing with them, the result is the same.

Anxiety is often defined as irrational fear but this is unsatisfactory

249

because we often equate 'irrational' with 'abnormal', and so anxiety, particularly in mothers, is often labelled abnormal. Yet all normal people at times feel anxiety that is neither abnormal nor irrational. It is not irrational to be anxious about an important examination or an interview for a job, though it is abnormal to have so much anxiety about these things that one's performance is ruined. Yet not to be anxious about them is abnormal and can be equally disastrous. Thus anxiety can be rational and rational anxiety can be normal or abnormal. Irrational anxiety can also be normal or even desirable. I prefer the *Oxford English Dictionary's* definition of anxiety as 'uneasiness or trouble of mind about some uncertain event.'

Few things are more uncertain than the outcome of motherhood and few bring more uneasiness and trouble of mind. I am not trying to say that motherhood is all trouble or even that it is a burden, but it is particularly liable to become so in those with serious anxiety problems. There are few aspects of life in which it is so important both to react to situations with the appropriate degree of anxiety and also to feel (as opposed to defend against) anxiety when it is there, and to be able to contain it when necessary. Of the many characteristics of motherliness this is one of the most important. Anyone who is contemplating becoming a mother, or who is having difficulty in being one, would do well to examine her own anxieties and the ways in which she deals with them.

A mother has to cope with three types of anxiety: her own internal anxiety, her anxiety about her child, and the child's anxiety. All these are interconnected and the last two are profoundly influenced by the first. How she deals with them depends on her personality, on the nature and strength of her personal anxieties and on the way in which she herself has learned to deal with them. It also depends on the stage which the relationship with her child has reached, what the child symbolizes to her and the relationship of his existence and character and the events of his life to her own anxieties. Last, it depends on the nature of the child.

There is a complex connection among anxiety, frustration, and tension. Frustration is the state of being balked, baffled or disappointed. It leads to aggression, anxiety and despair. Everyone experiences it. People vary enormously in their ability to tolerate it. Some accept it as necessary or inevitable. Others treat it as though it were something foreign to their lives and protest loudly, or try to get rid of it as quickly as possible. Others are unable to put up with it at all and they try to escape in a variety of ways. Tension is an internal state, partly measurable. For instance, the muscle in one's body is in a measurable, ever-changing state of tension. Probably everyone has an optimum level of tension, or an optimum rhythm of tension. Some people live successfully and even happily in a state of extreme tension. Some tolerate tension but suffer as a result. Others become anxious with more than a minimum of tension and so avoid it. Others become anxious if their level of tension falls below its optimum level and they deliberately seek to raise it.

At times all mothers, like anyone else, are likely to go through periods of considerable anxiety. These have their special effect on the mother-child relationship, depending on the nature of the crisis, on how the mother deals with it, and on everything that has gone before in both mother and child and between them. Such crises might concern both expected and unexpected events and include such matters as acute illness or death in the family, accidents, financial failure and other social catastrophes, life crisis, marriage crisis, intolerable family tension, and adolescent crisis.

Constructive ways of dealing with anxiety include enduring it, remaining conscious of it, coming to understand it and to master it, working hard, making things, doing something that uses talents whatever they may be and that is satisfying, and all forms of creative activity. People who react to anxiety in this way seldom attend psychiatrists because of problems related to anxiety. Motherhood is a powerful exercise in dealing with anxiety, but in some people it diminishes their normal resilience and capacity to deal constructively with anxiety.

Sandra was a talented painter and had always been able to find satisfaction and relief in this. But when she was twenty-eight the responsibilities of marriage and motherhood became too much for her and her anxiety was so great that she was unable to paint. Betty took to writing novels as a means of relief and relaxation while she was tied to the house and her two small children. She was successful and gained much satisfaction from it. Her two occupations balanced each other and each seemed to dissolve the anxieties and tensions of the other. But later, after a period of severe anxiety concerning one of her children, Betty became depressed and was unable to write until she had had treatment.

People whose normal methods of dealing with anxiety are destructive fare much worse. This can be seen most markedly in those who escape into alcoholism, drug addiction, self-starvation, hypo-chondriasis, promiscuity and suicidal attempts. Unfortunately all these are common in mothers and the effects can be disastrous for their children.

Josephine, after years of psychiatric treatment for depression, began to drink heavily. She would take no alcohol for several weeks at a time and keep none in the house, but if anything happened that caused her anxiety or frustration she immediately went out, bought a bottle of whisky and drank it. She had been divorced for some years and she lived alone with her ten-year-old daughter, Philippa. Philippa made an alliance with the family doctor and when her mother was drunk she tried to persuade her to go with her to the surgery. If the mother refused, then Philippa would telephone the doctor and he would come. Several times Philippa, knowing that her mother was out to buy drink, telephoned the doctor, who met Josephine at the door of the liquor shop and brought her home in his car.

Camilla, now aged twenty-five, had painful memories of her alco-holic mother, of how they would try to put each other to bed and fall asleep together on the bed. She remembered her mother vomiting over her and threatening her with a carving knife. Recently married and an abstemious drinker, she was frightened of the future and was particularly afraid that she might be unfit to be a mother and that she might lose control over her very tight emotions. She became ter-rified of leaving the house and found it difficult to cope with the hours when her husband was at work. Her children had to stay at home whenever they were not at school, for she felt she needed them for protection.

Those who are unable to tolerate even normal amounts of anxiety and frustration and are destructive in their ways of dealing with it tend to lose the will to live. This can take a variety of forms. Alice lay in bed all day while her husband was at work and her children at school. In this way she kept anxiety and tension at a minimum. When the children returned home Alice put on a dressing gown and sat in an armchair. Her children made the tea. When her husband returned home he did the housework. One day, while hoovering round her feet, he asked irritably when she was going to do some housework. She flew into a temper, swallowed a bottle of sleeping tablets and rushed out of the house.

Penelope was unable to tolerate normal anxiety. She had two children of five and seven and was estranged from her husband. She took little notice of the children and left them to get their own meals. Her love life was complicated and she could not cope with it. On seventeen occasions she had been admitted to hospital after taking overdoses of drugs. On a number of occasions she nearly died. After three years of living in this state of mind she improved sufficiently to lead a reasonably stable life, caring, with assistance, for her children and not taking overdoses. However, eventually she became disturbed again. It is typical of such people that even if the will to live and the capacity to enjoy life is restored, the next encounter with anxiety, or with a period of anxiety, tends to start the vicious spiral again.

Sometimes the vicious circle is complete. Queenie was a divorced lady with a tendency to alcoholism. She drank whenever she was upset. Her ex-husband was trying to gain custody of their one child on the grounds of her alcoholism. This upset her so much that she drank still more. At a crucial moment in the proceedings she travelled to her son's sports day. She was extremely anxious to give a good impression, in fact so anxious that she drank gin all the way in the train and arrived drunk.

There are also more complicated ways of dealing with anxiety. Eating disturbances, for instance, are common methods of easing anxiety. Some people starve themselves when anxious and though this keeps them fashionably slim it may reach unattractive extremes, impair health and even endanger life. Those who overeat for the same reasons keep up their physical strength but may become obese, which is destructive to health, social life and morale. Another doubtful though sometimes effective method is to 'lock up' anxieties. Although some people who do this seem able to endure anxiety well, they pay a price for this, and they may develop physical illnes or symptoms, limitation or distortion of character, or they may simply fail to mature.

Grania showed all these characteristics. She did not regard herself as an anxious person and probably her less perceptive friends would have agreed with her. She maintained an air of regal charm that was highly esteemed as a social asset on both private and public occasions. When she was well she enjoyed her role as the wife of a high-ranking service officer. She was pretty and dressed younger than her age (a common sign of emotional immaturity), and she enjoyed much admiration and social success. But she was plagued by almost constant physical illness which tended to be of the kind that is difficult to prove to be psychological in origin but which every doctor spots as being so, including surgeons who performed innumerable operations on her 'just in case we're wrong and there is an organic cause to her symptoms.' All Grania's anxieties were locked up in her illnesses. They were necessary to her psychological survival and too deeply entrenched in her personality and way of life to be amenable to any form of psychological treatment. In order to achieve any success it would be necessary for her to become aware of her anxiety, yet her whole life had been spent in avoiding this awareness. Grania was much too seriously disturbed to be able to change. And as is usual in such cases, her children and to some extent her husband had absorbed her attitude and had formed a defensive alliance to perpetuate it. The children also dealt with anxiety by producing physical symptoms themselves and had already had several operations each.

Yet another method of dealing with anxiety is to displace it onto some external object or process. This is the motivating force behind many revolutionaries, do-gooders and doomsdaymen. Many mothers who use this technique tend to displace their anxieties onto their children. Winnicott has described a case of a little boy who came to outpatients with the story 'Please doctor, my mother says I've got tummy ache.' This case is unusual only in that the boy was aware of the source of the trouble. Every family doctor is likely to have a number of such mothers and many feel plagued by them. They may induce symptoms in the child, they may worry excessively about the child's development, they may find features in the child about which they seek reassurance. 'Doctor, do you think he is tongue-tied/flat-footed/curly toed/is talking well enough for his age?' 'When he screams he makes an unusual noise. Do you think something is wrong with his throat?' 'He's a bit wheezy today. Do you think I had better keep him in bed?' Sometimes the anxiety becomes fixed on the mother's feeling about her capacity as a mother. She is then anxious about what is the right thing to do, about whether she is doing her best for her child, whether an abnormality is due to her imperfect care and so on.

We do of course live in an anxious age. This may mean no more than that during the past decades we have had tranquillizers, i.e. psychological power for doctors, and so, for the first time on a wide scale, doctors have been able to deal with problems in terms of anxiety without feeling impotent. Previously they were more likely to think of them in physical terms and most weren't even educated to recognize any but the most obvious forms of anxiety.

Each age and each culture produces its own manifestations of anxiety, and each has its forms that are especially common in women. For example, hysterical paralysis was common until the 1920s but is much rarer today except, in my personal experience, in people from the Third World. Western people now tend to express their anxiety in other ways, such as insomnia, agoraphobia, gastrointestinal disorders, alcoholism, and excessive anxiety about children.

Another form of neurotic anxiety, phobic anxiety, deserves special mention here. If I am so afraid of cats that I can't enter a house that contains one, or so afraid of ambulances that I can't go out for fear of meeting one, or if I can't go in an aeroplane or face a spider, then I suffer from phobic anxiety. As with other forms of anxiety, it is impossible to draw the line precisely between what is normal, or at least so common as to be regarded as normal, and what is abnormal. For instance, it is certainly normal to feel some anxiety about an approaching war or cholera epidemic but it is abnormal to be totally disrupted by these. Many people are conscious of a slight anxiety on entering a lift, or taking off in an aeroplane, but only a minority are unable to do these things.

Phobic anxiety, a common cause of psychological crippling, seems to develop in someone who is predisposed, usually through contact with someone who has the same phobia, or through some frightening incident. Often it is induced by the mother, sometimes father or grandmother. One patient remembered that her many phobias evolved partly as exaggerations of the lonely fears she developed because her mother, a working widow who had no phobias herself, was too busy to give her much time, and partly directly from her grandmother, who had a number of phobias. Another patient knew that she had picked up her phobia for mice from her mother and for thunder from her grandmother. I myself developed a mild phobia for heights when, aged about nine, I got stuck and frightened at the top of a tree and was rescued by my mother. I was always astonished and rather anxious when my own children showed no fear of heights, but I transmitted my phobia to at least one of them: my son was seven years old and stood with a friend on the high parapet of the roof of our six-storeyed London house looking down on the street below. I reacted to this with a mixture of anger and fear which seems to have been memorable. From that day he has shared my fear of heights. One of his brothers shares with his father a phobia for spiders, but no one knows exactly how or when this was transmitted and none of the other children shares it.

Phobic anxiety that is so severe or so widespread that it interferes with daily life seems to be fairly common among mothers. There are many 'housebound housewives' who suffer from agoraphobia, are unable to leave the house alone, and who use their children for such purposes as errands and shopping. Often one can detect an element of gain in the disability. The mother uses her phobia as a means of controlling her husband and children. Sarah, the wife of a schoolmaster, could not drive or travel on public transport because of phobia. This meant that whenever she had to go somewhere, for example to the psychiatrist, her husband either had to pay for a taxi for her or else take time off to drive her. She was unable to go shopping alone. This meant that her husband took her shopping on Saturdays. During the week, if she needed anything, she would send one of her children. She admitted that this happened more frequently when the child was playing with children whom she did not feel were compatible with her social aspirations. When something arose which appealed to her, such as an invitation to a garden party at Buckingham Palace, her phobias 'miraculously' improved and allowed her to go out to buy the necessary clothes and accessories.

Another kind of neurotic anxiety that can seriously affect relationships between mothers and their children is obsessional anxiety. This can take different forms, and some are described and discussed in the chapters on restricted and controlling mothers. Obsessional people have conflicting emotions of fear and rage which they keep secret even from themselves. The obsessional person uses thoughts to control feelings and to avoid awareness of them. In obsessional neurosis there are spells of acute indecision and brooding, bouts of ritual making, and fits of terrifying and aggressive thoughts and temptations. Thus a mother who suffers in this way might spend hours brooding on whether or not to increase the baby's feed, whether or not her child is old enough to take piano lessons, whether he should have school dinners, go out alone, go away on holiday with friends or sleep with his girlfriend. Rituals will be built round the routines of family life, which become of supreme importance. They are likely to concern food, waste, dirt and time. Aggressive thoughts, often very frightening, are likely to be directed against the nearest and dearest. Ethel developed an obsessional neurosis when her two sons were twelve and fourteen. She had always been neat, tidy, careful about cleanliness and indecisive. She also spent much time in brooding on what would be the best thing to do. Suddenly she began to get thoughts 'out of the blue' that she might be poisoning people, particularly her children. She had to keep checking all the poisonous substances in the house to make sure she had not added them to the food or drink. It became so bad that she was virtually spring-cleaning the whole house every day in an effort to control these thoughts. Her children were also becoming anxious and ritualistic. At this point she consulted her doctor. She told me that she was quite sure that her own mother had suffered from the same condition without ever admitting it. When she thought about it, Ethel could think of things her mother did and ways in which she behaved which could have no other explanation.

No one really knows how far obsessionality is inherited and how far it is induced. Probably both factors are important. Not every child or mother with an obsessional neurosis has a child or mother who suffers from the same condition. If one studies any individual sufferer we can usually understand how it arose but not why it did so. Unhappiness is often confused with anxiety and treated as such. Many mothers are disturbed by unhappiness, which also creates anxiety but is not the same as neurosis or depression.

Maria was happily married until her husband suffered a severe head injury which changed his character. From being friendly, responsible and tolerant he became bad-tempered and irresponsible. He attacked her both verbally and physically, sometimes in front of the children. She longed to escape, but since the children were small and she had no means of supporting them on her own, she felt tied. Only when they were nearly grown-up did she feel able to leave and by this time her spirit was nearly broken. Nearly, but not quite. She divorced her husband, made a life for herself, was infinitely happier and eventually remarried. She was worried about the effects that her years of unhappiness were likely to have had on her children. Many women find that unhappiness is for them an integral part of motherhood. This is true even when they are pleased and satisfied to the mothers and would not wish it any other way. Being a mother means giving up many things that may be important. For years there may be little time to read, think, use one's training, exercise talents and skills, and there may be little opportunity to visit friends, theatres or other places of stimulation and interest. Lack of suitable stimulation is unbalancing, even when one is doing what one most wants to do.

One unhappy young mother expressed her loneliness and isolation 'My husband gets so much stimulation and discussion at work that he doesn't want to talk to me when he comes home. I love my husband and children but I'm bored stiff by nearly all the things I have to do for them. At the weekends we go to the country and all he wants to do is garden and play with the children, and they love it too. But I hate it because I just transfer my normal boring activities from one place to another, organizing and washing up.'

One effect of unhappiness is withdrawal. If one is positively unhappy and aware of it, one has difficulty in keeping contact with people, even those who are close. Unhappy mothers who are aware of their unhappiness are likely to be among those mothers described in a previous chapter who are absent in spirit and whose children have to find their own compensation. Mothers whose unhappiness is hidden, especially from themselves, are likely to react in less obvious ways, perhaps by hysterical behaviour or by anxiety. Removal of the source of unhappiness leads to improvement both for them and their children.

Depression is common and widespread in western society so it is surprising that so little has been written about its profound influence on mothers and their children. One reason for this may be that the professional who treats the depressed mother and the professional who deals with the effects of her depression on her children tend to be different people in different departments or in different institutions as far apart as hospital and school. But the subject is particularly important because depression is commoner in women than in men and most women are mothers. Moreover, certain types of depression are specifically associated with childbirth and childbearing.

An authoritative book on depression opens with the words:

Depression ranks as one of the major health problems today. Millions of patients suffering from some form of this disorder crowd the psychiatric and general hospitals, the outpatient clinics, and the Offices of private practitioners. Depression may appear as a primary disorder or it may accompany a wide

variety of other psychiatric or medical disorders. Not only is
depression a prominent cause of human misery, but its bypro-
duct, suicide, is a leading cause of death in certain age groups.[1]

Most people at some time feel sad or despairing, particularly following the loss or abandoment of some loved person or a much wanted
ambition. Children as well as parents experience it. It is something
with which everyone has to learn to cope. For a time the mourner
may be overwhelmed by painful memories and thoughts. As time
passes these weaken and life returns to normal. But sometimes the
sadness and grief is prolonged, or is felt for no apparent reason.
Often the depression is converted into physical symptoms and the
person may not even recognize that he is depressed. Thousands of
sufferers visit doctors complaining of symptoms for which no
organic cause is found. Sometimes the depressed feelings are projected onto others, especially by mothers onto their children. 'Something is wrong with my child' often really means 'I am depressed. I
am not coping properly.' Sometimes the depression is masked; sufferers deny any depressed feeling but insist that the trouble is elsewhere, perhaps in their bodies, in their children or in the world
outside. They are, however, usually aware of loss of energy and
drive.

Women suffer from neurotic or reactive depression more commonly than men. It may be that men tend, and have greater opportunities, to turn their tensions and needs outwards into aggression,
whereas women turn inwards into depression. 'Men commit
actions: women commit gestures.'[2] People turn to depression when
they have lost something that is psychologically vital to them or feel
unable to escape from an impossible conflict. Depression substitutes for a 'solution' and the sufferer is trapped and gives up. Whatever the causes, the fact is that many mothers become depressed
during at least some period of their active mothering years, and this
depression, if severe or prolonged, can have a profound influence on
their mothering capacities and on their children. This is particularly
true when they are the chief or virtually the sole influence on their
children's lives. Depression in mothers is a common, and often
unrecognized, cause of psychological disturbance in children. A
woman may become depressed because she has no child. She may
see herself as barren, a failed woman. Some cannot bear the idea of
their children growing up and believe that another child would solve

their problems. Unfortunately their husbands or professional advisers sometimes agree with them and the result is often a 'disaster' child.

Sally became seriously depressed when her youngest child went to school. She persuaded her reluctant husband that another child would solve her problems. It didn't. The new baby was difficult and exhausting and Sally couldn't cope with him. Eventually she dropped him over the bannisters. The verdict was 'accidental death' but Sally admitted privately that she had done it deliberately in a moment of desperation. Claudia, always immature and unstable, had three children. At the age of 43 she again became pregnant and at five months she miscarried. She became deeply depressed, and preoccupied with the thought that she must have another child. As time passed and she failed to conceive again, she went from doctor to doctor until eventually arrangements were set in motion for her to adopt a child. Luckily before these bore fruit Claudia's depressed mental state was recognized. The real problem lay within her own personality and her difficulty in adapting to middle age. To have adopted another child would have solved nothing for Claudia and would have created considerable difficulties for the child.

Many women feel depressed and tired during the first three months of pregnancy. Some, particularly those with egocentric, hysterical personalities, are depressed, and often sick, throughout. Some resent losing their shapely figures. Others feel that their husbands or partners find them less attractive. Some have deep conflicts about producing a child and are filled with conflicting feelings. Many women of obsessional personality love being pregnant and feel better than ever before. They usually become severely depressed only if they harbour suppressed resentment against their husbands or partners.

A few days after delivery as many as 60 per cent of women suffer from an attack of 'the blues'. Much of the joy of having produced a new baby is lost and they feel miserable, gloomy and apprehensive about the future. The vast majority of women recover from these feelings in a few days but occasionally, usually one or two weeks after delivery, a mother may develop a severe depression of the 'endogenous' type and become so disturbed that she is a danger to herself and her child. She may have to be admitted to hospital. An illness of this severity may have lasting effects on the child's development.

A third type of depression, often mixed with phobic anxiety and obsessionality, sometimes develops some months after childbirth. Its roots lie in the mother's personality. Usually this happens after a first baby but sometimes the symptoms may appear after later pregnancies. In milder forms it may pass for the normal fatigue associated with looking after a young baby. It may last for months or years and seriously impair the mother's enjoyment of life, her relationship with her child and the child's own development. Matters are often made worse because the mother's depression tends to cause increasing marital friction. Her deteriorating relationship with her husband makes the depression worse and adds to the child's difficulties. For a baby or young child to pass his early years in the constant and exclusive care of his depressed mother gives him a poor start in life.

If a mother has suffered from a severe depression following the birth of a child there is a risk that the same thing will happen if she has another baby. But this is by no means invariable. A woman who has had a severe depression after the birth of her first child is likely to become depressed again, though only about one in seven to ten mothers suffer from depression of the same severity. Sometimes severe post-natal depression occurs following the birth of only one child in a family of several children.

One of the facts that has come to light in recent years has been the incidence of depression, or a depressed mood, in mothers of preschool children. This is often due to a lack of satisfaction in a life in which there is no escape from the constant presence and demands of young children, often in an environment in which no provision is made for them. Planners of modern housing have seldom made adequate provision for younger children. The subject was investigated by Hannah Gavron, a young sociologist and mother who herself suffered from depression and committed suicide shortly before her influential book, *The Captive Wife*, was published in 1966. She quotes mothers describing why their lives and those of their young children were depressing: the impersonal life of the city got them down, and they were aware that both they and their children were isolated and lonely. Boredom is not the same as depression but one often leads to the other. This comes out strongly in Gavron's book. She quotes women who wrote to the *Observer*:[3] 'Being at home all day is terribly boring, frustrating and to my mind very *inferior*.' '... measured by the values of a society like ours where the real business of life is held to be what people do during their working hours, I'm standing still. I don't exist,' and 'Bored, I'm just fed up.' Gavron also points out that this is a 'time which involves a great loss of confidence to many a young woman.' One said, 'I felt such a failure as a mother not knowing whether the baby was warm enough, or fed enough, or why it was crying. I began to doubt that I could ever do anything properly again;' and another: 'I felt I was a failure as a person too.'

But bad housing, lack of facilities for young children are by no means the only cause of depression in mothers. Some doubt whether they are really of great importance. Financial problems, marital problems and personality problems are probably more important. Neurotic women have as many children as other women and tend to act out their neurotic problems in their relationships with them. Some lavish on their children the feelings they were unable to satisfy in their own childhood, and find they are still depressed. Some are chronically depressed anyway. Depression often makes them insensitive to their children's needs and unable to satisfy them even if they detect them. In particular, they are unable to deal adequately with their children's normal aggressive behaviour and may react to it aggressively themselves. The aggression may be open or hidden.

Much is written about 'involutional depression', particularly in women. This occurs in middle age and is often thought, rather loosely, to be due to the menopause. Many people believe that it is due to hormone changes and many doctors will try to treat it with hormones, though the evidence of careful research suggests that only physical symptoms such as hot flushes and heavy or irregular bleeding are relieved by this treatment. We now know that in most cases of involutional depression the causes are no different from those of depression at other times of life. For mothers in our time middle age has become a time for decision about a 'new life ahead'. Yet many have made no provision for it. In the past women went on having babies into their forties and were unlikely to see their youngest child grow up. Even if they survived as long as this they were by now in their sixties and ready for old age. Nowadays a mother is likely to have her small family off her hands when she is in her forties. She still has half her adult life ahead of her. Yet she may never have thought about the vast difference in this respect between her life and that of her mother and grandmother and she may be totally unprepared for it. Even if she was once trained for a profession the chances are that unless she has continued to work while her children were young, she will find it difficult to find a job or will lack the confidence to do it. Large numbers of middle aged mothers now find themselves without enough to do, without purpose and without qualifications. When they were young they never thought beyond marriage and rasing a family. They are not prepared or equipped for change, choice or challenge.

Middle age is the time when difficulties and disorders of personality which were previously hidden come to light. Quite suddenly, so it seems, some mothers become depressed and hopeless. In fact often they had for years hidden their problems in their family lives and in the raising of their children. Now, when the children leave home they are faced with themselves for the first time. In these days when divorce is common many women have new husbands at this age and would like to have at least one child of the marriage. Others have been abandoned by their husbands or fear that their marriages will be damaged by this evidence of lost youth. They may recognize, yet also fear, the fact that each middle aged woman now has to make her own choice about her life. They suffer because society no longer supports them if they are unwilling to make this choice. If they are unhappy in their role of 'just housewife' they will get little sympathy. Other people tend to believe that this is no longer inevitable and that those who don't like it should do something else as well. Yet a mother faced with this may feel unable to do anything else. She may feel that she has no choice because she is incapable of even being aware of choice. This is particulrly true of women who married controlling husbands who would not allow them to work during the first years of marriage. Such women, if they stick to their husbands, have no real chance of preparing for the future. If they realize that a controlling husband jeopardizes the future the marriage may break down. If it does not break down the wife may become depressed in middle life and the depression is often triggered off by children leaving home or by the prospects of their doing so.

Depression at this age is likely to include physical symptoms. We tend to think that there is 'a pill for every ill' rather than really work out what is wrong and what to do about it. Everything seems drab and empty. Nothing seems worthwhile. There is nothing to fill the gap. There is danger that the depressed woman may try to lift her spirits with alcohol or tranquillizing drugs. Many of these mothers have adolescent children who are likely to have difficulties too. An adolescent needs a steady, reliable, optimistic mother just as much as does a small child. If she is depressed she increases his problems. Many so called 'adolescent problems' are actually due to having a depressed mother. The luckiest are those families in which mothers and their adolescent children are all preparing for their new, adult lives. The healthy adolescent prepares for the first half of his adult life. His healthy, optimistic mother looks forward with enthusiasm to the second half of hers.

Many mothers, as we have seen, go through periods of depression. Fewer can actually be described as disturbed, but their numbers seem to be rising dramatically.

Two little boys of 4 and 2 wake in the night. One of them vomits. They call for their mother but the house is empty. Their mother has taken a massive overdose of drugs and rushed out into the underground. An hour later she is found unconscious on a train at the other side of the city. She is taken to hospital. Eventually police break into the house and rescue the children. It has happened several times before.

A young mother hurls her baby across the room, screaming at her husband 'You don't love me so why should I love the baby?' The baby's skull is fractured.

A bewildered four-year-old stands at the top of the stairs in his home which is suddenly full of chaos and strange people. The furniture is thrown about and broken. His parents' clothes cover the stairs. His mother is screaming in the next room. Unknown to the child strangers have come to take her to the mental hospital and she is refusing to go. Presently an ambulance arrives and after a while the screaming stops.

In the late afternoon three children are bundled by their mother into a car. They wonder whether they are going to visit their father, who has recently left home, or one of the friends of the 'uncle' who has been visiting lately. But they simply drive around. Mother drives in a strange way, as though looking for someone, then eventually sees a police car and stops. All sorts of things happen but the family does not return home for the night. Though the children do not know it, their mother has never in her whole life spent a night without another adult in the house and is too frightened to do so. Since father left home she has managed to persuade friends or relatives to stay, or else has picked up men and brought them back for the night. Tonight she cannot find anyone and she is desperate. She cannot tell anyone the truth because she is ashamed of it but when she finally appeals to the police she makes up a story which gets them involved. She is good at telling stories. She survives another night.

A little girl demands the attention of her mother who has promised to help her with her homework. But her mother is talking to a friend. The little girl interrupts and whines. Her mother becomes angry and throws the budgerigar cage out of the window. The budgerigar is the little girl's much-loved pet. It is killed. The mother says it serves her daughter right for interrupting.

An eight-year-old boy makes breakfast for himself and goes off to school, leaving his mother sitting in an armchair and staring into space. She does not speak or acknowledge him. When he returns she is still sitting there in exactly the same way. Nothing has been done in the house. She does not greet him. He finds himself some food and goes to bed. She has been like that all the week and there isn't much food left but father is coming home at the weekend and will buy some. He may arrange for her to go away like he did before, and then she may come back better.

A mother is obsessed with dirt. All day while the children are at school she scrubs and cleans the whole house through. She installs a bath tub in the porch of the house. The minute the children return from school she makes them take off all their clothes and then she scrubs them all over before she allows them to enter the house. They are not allowed to invite friends or to go to other houses for fear of the dirt they would pick up there.

These are all true stories and come from my own psychiatric practice. We have already met many disturbed mothers earlier in this book. The ones just described are extreme but some of them had been good mothers before they were ill and became so again. Probably most mothers can be disturbed in some degree at some time.

The word 'disturbed' is vague. I use it here in the simplest way to describe feelings or behaviour likely to cause harm to self or others. In this sense 'disturbance' is by no means always extreme, dramatic, or even obvious. Its most dramatic forms are usually short-lived, though they may recur. The most damaging forms are often well concealed from the world. A mother who made her children terrified of their father held a high position as a teacher in a school. The mother who threw the birdcage out of the window was, by her own

265

assertion, 'very respectable'. The most sinister forms of disturbance may lurk behind net curtains, a well-turned out appearance, or a successful career.

I do not intend to go through the various forms of mental illness in mothers or attempt to examine the effects of each on the children. Clearly each type of illness affects the children in different ways, but often the effects are more strongly related to what actually happens. For instance, serious illnesses such as schizophrenia or manic-depression may be punctuated by acute crises, in which the mother may need to be removed to hospital and the children may have to go elsewhere, or they may involve long periods when the mother is withdrawn or depressed and, even though present, has little contact with the children. Occasionally there is a danger that a quietly disturbed mother may actually be in danger of attacking her children. A depressed mother may kill her children because she feels that there is not future for them. A schizophrenic may attack them because she believes that they are part of the devil. A grossly disturbed perception of the world is bound to have gross effects on a mother's behaviour towards her children. Yet many seriously disturbed or psychotic mothers are able to care for their children in a way that society would find acceptable. Psychopathic mothers and mothers who have immature reactions and are unable to deal with the normal stresses and strains of life, often manage to use their children to protect themselves from the world outside. Alcoholic mothers often train their children to look after them and help them to perpetuate the condition. Mothers with agoraphobia often use their children to do their shopping and help them to mask the condition.

Thus disturbance in mothers is often concealed. The concealment is frequently aided by the children themselves. For them, their mother is both their personal environment and their link with the outside world. Particularly when they are young, they do not question what she says or does. They accept it as part of life, and they may continue to do this for a long time, especially if she manages, as so many disturbed mothers do, to keep the children relatively isolated from the outside world and make it difficult for them to become attached to other adults such as teachers, or to make friends with children of their own age. Since the children know no one with whom to compare, they accept the situation without question and cannot envisage alternatives. This happens particularly frequently at the present time when it is extremely easy for mothers to isolate themselves and their children and indeed, often difficult for them not to do so.

Some people whom one might think are quite normal have areas of what one might call 'encapsulated areas of disturbance', and these may be almost totally hidden. For instance, one mother outwardly cared efficiently for her children but had a secret desire to have bits of herself removed by surgery. She read up medical textbooks and would then produce symptoms which led one surgeon after another to remove parts of her body. She therefore had periods of 'physical illness' when she retired to hospital but in between she was an efficient housewife and devoted much love and attention to her children. Sometimes these 'encapsulations' are actually connected with the children. One mother, who ran a successful business of her own, lived in a private fantasy world which she kept hidden from everybody, and no one could think why her pleasant well-brought up child behaved so badly at school. It turned out that the mother saw herself and her daughter as the 'core of the world' which nothing and no one must penetrate. Whichever teacher was at that moment prominent in the child's life, whether form teacher or housemistress, represented to the mother The Big Threat. Subtly, in the way that mothers do, she conveyed this to the child without ever putting it into words, and the child absorbed the fantasy in the way that children do. As a result the child always managed to make an enemy of the current teacher, and no matter how hard the teacher tried and however sympathetic and competent she was, matters always went from bad to worse until the child was eventually expelled or asked to leave, and went to another school, where the whole process started again.

Sometimes the 'encapsulated disturbance' is a disturbance of symbolism in the mother's mind about the child. Thus one mother who herself had a fine academic record, had no trouble with her elder daughter who was academically brilliant and took a first class degree at Cambridge. But the younger daughter was a slow-learner and expressed a desire to be a hairdresser which the mother, while professing to be tolerant, could not accept. She made every effort to insist that there was 'something wrong' with the girl. This mother was unable to project anything but bad things onto the younger girl. This case shows how close 'madness' is to normality because many apparently 'normal' people do things like that.

Hostility and antisocial fantasy are often projected onto children by disturbed mothers. We have seen some examples of these already. A mother may allow her children to wreck other people's property, often that of her own relatives. Or she may insist on her children wearing different clothes or hairstyles or eating different food from others. One mother had a boyfriend who lived alone. She sent her 14 year old daughter to visit him. The man made a serious pass at the girl who was terrified and ran home to tell her mother. The mother blamed her for 'provoking' him. Closely associated with disturbed fantasy is collusion, the process by which mothers (and not always mothers) actually encourage children's difficulties and problems while seeming to be concerned about them. Thus a mother who is anxious about being left alone may transmit this anxiety to her child who then becomes anxious about going to school. A mother whose child is clearly mentally ill may keep him at home to 'protect' him from the world, make sure that he receives no treatment or that treatment is ineffective. She uses her sick child to maintain her own mental balance or that of her marriage.

Thus children whose mothers are disturbed suffer in a variety of ways. They may suffer because the mother is incapable, either temporarily or permanently, of being motherly towards them or of making and maintaining a good relationship with them. They may suffer from the insecurity that results from inconsistency and incompetence in practical matters. They may absorb the disturbance themselves. They may be profoundly affected by an inability to grasp the real world. They may be used by the disturbed mother as part of her disturbed fantasies, or abused by her either physically or psychologically. All these things will be much worse if they have virtually no other relationships with adults.

Here the influence of fathers is important. A father who sees much of his children and who participates greatly in their lives is usually the most effective countermeasure to distortions and disturbances in the mother's personality. This is important in all families but especially when the mother is disturbed. One sometimes sees children of severely disturbed mothers who grow up normal, even if not unscathed, because the father's influence has been strong. Other adults are also important, most frequently grandmothers. Grandmothers who live close enough and have the time, inclination and ability can do a great deal for their grandchildren, and they are especially valuable if the mother is disturbed. Unfortunately it often happens that if a mother is disturbed the grandmother, particularly, the maternal grandmother, is also disturbed. Sometimes children find mother-substitutes, or partial mother-substitutes, in other adults, perhaps nieghbours or teachers. The disturbed mother whose influence actively prevents her children from making close contact with other adults is usually more damaging than the one who lets her children go free or neglects them.

CHAPTER SIXTEEN
Modern Dilemmas

Anyone who has read thus far in the book will by now be aware that in western society motherhood is in crisis and is no longer the straightforward purpose of a woman's life or her *raison d'être*. It has become a subject full of difficulty, uncertainty and paradox and surrounded by contradiction, confusion and illusion. I have investigated the nature and origins of the changes that have brought this about. In this chapter, I shall try to clarify the subject – so far as it can be clarified – for the benefit of individual people who are caught somewhere in the uncertainties and paradoxes of motherhood and its complex relationships both with parenthood and with individuality.

First, why should anyone wish to bring children into this unsatisfactory, uncertain, dangerous and overcrowded world? Before those children grow up the whole of civilization and the best part of the human race may well be destroyed by war, atom bombs, famine or economic collapse. Into what sort of world are we thinking of bringing children and what for? In any case, there are too many people and too many children in it already. Why add to them? It is doubtful whether we shall be able to give them a good life. It is also doubtful whether we shall be able to lead a good life while raising them, and this will certainly affect them adversely. Good housing is scarce and expensive. Good food is expensive. Good education is hard to find and in many places non-existent. The environment in which most of us live is unsuitable for children and if we have them we make it worse and life will become even more difficult. What expectations can we have for them in such a world? I would call this the depressive standpoint. Although it is not uncommon to hear people talk like that, I do not believe that in reality people decide not to have children for such reasons. Ruminating on these questions in this way is a reflection of how they feel about themselves and one of the reasons these questions are asked at all is that parenthood is now optional.

Partly because parenthood is now a choice it has also become more difficult. Physically it is now easy to raise children. On the whole we can expect to be able to have children when we want and we can expect those children to grow up in physical health. But financially, psychologically and socially parenthood, particularly motherhood, is difficult. As our society has become increasingly complex, children have no part in it. They have to be segregated away from much social life and from most of the world of work. Since children do not make money and do not have the vote and will not have it in twenty years time, they have no power. So politicians of all parties will pay lip service to children's needs but in practice will spend as little on them as they feel they can get away with. This usually means using parents, particularly mothers, as a means of not spending money on them. Since we are now in a period of economic recession it is unlikely that this state of affairs will change in the foreseeable future. Later on I shall discuss possible radical changes that would improve the lot of parents and their children but first of all I intend to concentrate on what individuals can and might do for themselves.

Let us start with prospective motherhood. This affects particularly young women who are today enjoying opportunities in education, training and work which are far greater than anything previously available to women, and which, more than anything else, enables them to participate in the world in a way women never could in the past, to keep up with its pace and keep pace with its changes. Women can now be independent, have jobs, and support themselves – whether they are married and with or without a partner. It is much more difficult and may be impossible with a small child. Small children need constant care. They also need continuity and a slower pace of living.

Not all young women can cope with the choice and opportunity available to them. Some genuinely feel drawn to domesticity. Many women are more fulfilled at home, however relentless the chores and however demanding the children, than they would ever be in an office or a profession or out elsewhere in the world. Many of these women possess the valuable and undervalued qualities of motherliness already discussed. They are people who deserve more respect

271

than they get and who could make much more valuable contributions to society than they are given the opportunity to make at present.

But unfortunately all too often now motherhood seems a soft option, an excuse to drop out and not to have to compete. It is still possible to cover this up by finding social pressures urging towards domesticity and motherhood. You do not have to look far to find them. Motherhood can still be used as a means of living vicariously and in a state of dependence. To some women having a baby may represent more a personal fulfilment and success, a boost to self-confidence, or a project that must be done. Many people still have the feeling that a woman has not proved herself, fulfilled herself or demonstrated her true femininity until she has a child. It is still easy to latch on to these feelings that are prevalent in society and to use them to reinforce one's own.

Some women go through their early adult lives aware that some day and somehow they would like a family. They know that for them raising children is probably the most rewarding and fulfilling thing that they will ever do. The question for them is when, with whom, and how it can be achieved without losing or giving up other aspects of life which are essential to their well-being. They know of course that they cannot raise children without giving up many things and they are prepared to forgo these – perhaps prospects of promotion or going right to the top, or travelling. But they feel they cannot give up everything they have been trained to do and all professional life, for to do so would damage them as people and would inevitably effect their children adversely. So the question for these people is how they can give of their best to their children while retaining those things in themselves that make them what they are. They want children to be part of their lives, they are prepared to give up much for a family and to invest a great deal of themselves in their children. But they are not prepared to give up everything. They know that there lies the way to disaster. This last is the new modern dilemma, the dilemma of the healthy modern young woman.

Some are uncertain. Do I really want to be a mother? What does it really entail? What will it do to me? Am I fit to do it? All new phases of life create doubts and anxiety in normal people. But if anxiety is severe and doubts are prominant, that person would probably do better to remain in the office for the time being. She has not yet suf-

272

ficiently imposed herself on her environment or gained enough self-confidence to take on so large and important an area of life. A young woman today is likely to need maturity and self-confidence before she embarks on successful motherhood. She will also need the courage and the confidence to submerge herself for a while and to emerge both intact and enriched. Yet in other ways maturity and self-confidence make it harder to be a good mother. This is another dilemma.

The question of a partner has often been settled long before the decision to embark on parenthood, but many women when they reach the stage of wishing to become mothers are still on their own, have broken marriages or relationships behind them, or are involved with men with whom they do not wish to form a partnership for parenthood. Choosing a man because one feels that one would like him to be the father of one's children is not the worst motive for choosing a partner but it is certainly not the best, particularly if it is the main motive. Having and raising children always turns out to be different in reality from anyone's expectations, so there must be much more in a relationship than this. But in contemplating a long-term partnership it would be unwise not to ask oneself whether one likes the prospect of this person being a parent to one's children. Furthermore, the type of involvement envisaged is also important. A woman who finds domestic life satisfying and who enjoys building her own little world in nursery and kitchen may be attracted by a man who shares these desires but when it comes to the reality she may find it intolerable. One example of this was Catherine. She was thirty when her marriage broke up and she had three young children. Her husband had played virtually no part in their care and she much resented this. Once he had left her and married someone else he showed no further interest in the children and proceeded to found a new family with a new wife. Catherine felt bereft. For three years she struggled on her own, lonely, unsupported and often desperate. Then she met John, whose wife had deserted him leaving him with a two-year-old son. John was everything Catherine's first husband had never been. He was loving, attentive, domesticated. They joined forces and soon married and had another child. John organized his work so that most of it was done from home. He did the shopping and the cooking, he ran the household, took the older children to school and fetched them again in the afternoon. He never minded getting up in the night for a crying child or altering his business arrangements to attend a school function and he became a real father to Catherine's children, whom he adopted. He also earned a good living for them all and was always loving, patient and generous. His energy, interest and involvement astonished Catherine and she withdrew into a dreamy state, participating less and less in the household and writing poetry and short stories, which she sometimes managed to sell. But gradually she felt invaded and disintegrated. She was used to having her own little world to organize, which revolved around her and was dependent on her. Now she felt she had nothing. She became depressed and developed many physical symptoms that she had never had before. John responded by being ever more attentive. She lost interest in having sex with him and began to daydream about having affairs with other men. She said she felt 'like a pet bird in a gilded cage', with no outlet for her frustration.

Many women with a real interest in the world outside might have welcomed marriage with a man like John. In many ways he was today's ideal husband, not simply helping with the chores but actually doing them, not simply being a weekend father but a loving day-by-day father to all the children. But Catherine was not sufficiently developed as a person to be able to cope with this, and it may well be that this was an important reason why John was attracted to her. Her dependence and inadequacy enhanced his own competence and protected him from his own feelings of insecurity.

This was an unusual relationship. It may be that in the future we shall see this kind of set-up more frequently. But much more common is the man who, however much he wishes to participate, is not willing or able to do so much for the household and children and who could not do it even if he wished because for most men such a life would be incompatible with earning the living that the family needs.

Even commoner is the man who is willing to give a hand in the evening and at weekends but who expects his wife to be basically in charge at home. If he is ambitious his work will become more arduous and he may then expect direct support such as errands run, suits pressed and, if not slippers warming by the fire, at least supper ready in the oven. This brings us to a common conflict between parents in our time. They may start equal but ambition and financial success tend to be incompatible with close involvement in rearing children. A man with an eye on worldly success is likely to require a wife who sticks to her role of supporting him, raising his children and generally servicing him, even if he was quite different when he was younger. And as things are at present, if the couple is keen on a high standard of living, this will probably be the most effective way to provide it. And if he has to move frequently or spend periods abroad, she will have to move with him if these standards are to be maintained. A woman contemplating sharing her life and her children with such a man should be aware of what it is likely to entail and understand herself well enough to know whether it will be likely to suit her.

Mary Kenny has pointed out that almost the first utterance that a successful, married lady makes on being appointed to a new job or attaining some new height of distinction is a warm tribute to her husband, 'who has Made It All Possible'.[1] Marjorie Proops, doyenne of British agony columnists, wrote in her book *Dear Marje:*

> Sometimes readers write to me, asking what special qualities a married woman needs to do a demanding job as well as run her home and keep her family happy. A good, tolerant, patient, intelligent and sensitive husband, I tell them. One who is ready to make sacrifices, share chores, share worries, give support and encouragement and recognize a woman's right to choose a career if she wants to. One who doesn't denigrate her efforts or put her down in order to bolster his own masculine ego. One who doesn't believe that a woman's career is a joke or a bit of self-indulgence or that she works for pin money. One who believes that women have quite as much to contribute to society, to industry, to the professions, as have men. One who is, in a word, an adult man, secure enough in his own masculinity never to feel threatened by a successful wife. I married just such a man at the very start of my career . . .[2]

Mary Kenny concludes:

> The ideal husband, then, is not just someone who is helpful, supportive and mature; not just someone who is not competing for the same things and at the same time as his wife; not just someone who is flexible, uses his initiative, and is ready to turn his hand to anything; not just someone who gets on with his mother and encourages his wife; not just not a selfish egotist,

275

and not just not a yes-man. It's someone who is all these things and who on top of that has an acutely tuned sensitivity to just how far he should go in encouraging her, in helping her, in sharing roles.[3]

A woman who can choose such a man and predict correctly what he will be like will have no need to struggle, to become a domestic drudge, a frustrated career woman or a superwoman.

Not many women are so clever, so perceptive or so lucky as to find a life partner like this, or to make the relationship work if they do. Male chauvinism abounds and there are strong social pressures that increase it. The feminine mystique lives on and there are economic pressures to increase it – it is, after all, an economic measure and, on the surface at least, it saves a lot of public money.

The other great problem for modern young parents and would-be parents is today's instability of the couple. It seems likely that between one third and half of today's marriages will end in divorce, and although it is easy these days to produce and raise children without being married, such partnerships are probably even more likely to break down. The possibility of becoming a single parent is high. To do this successfully requires even greater personal development, stability and maturity, and also the capacity to finance the family as well. Having to be two parents in one and perhaps work as well may be better than being one half of a bad marriage and some women even choose to be single from the start, but it is tough going, and the single mother usually needs all the help she can get. Inner city life, for all its difficulties, may be more satisfactory than suburb or country since shops and entertainment are at hand, other people are closer and, especially if there is a nearby college, babysitters are easier to come by.

Although most young children in our society probably have several older people in their lives to whom they become attached, nevertheless mothers and their young children tend to be totally exposed to each other and totally bound to each other. The official view reflecting much of public opinion is that this is desirable and to be encouraged. This situation, as we have seen, has been popular with politicians of all parties, except in wartime, ever since there has been a women's movement. During the last thirty years they have been joined by academics and by those in the so-called 'caring professions' (who are trained by the academics). The situation of isolating mothers and children is often presented as though it was a natural state of affairs which always used to exist, which was somehow ruined by industrialism and social change and must now be restored. Sometimes this is even regarded as going back to some kind of golden age, a dream of bygone days, of paradise regained. In the first part of this book we saw how untrue this is, for the situation is new and only developed during the present century. The total and exclusive exposure of mothers to their young children has never existed on a wide scale in any other society since civilization began, and it does not exist in many societies today. It arose out of the social changes of the twentieth century. The reasons why it has been presented to us as though it was time-honoured and proven are discussed elsewhere in this book.

The justification of the idea is based on theory that stems from psychoanalysis. This theory has itself influenced and increased some of the social changes which have led to the binding together of mothers and children in relative isolation. The theory is that young children need the exclusive and continuous care of their mothers and that without this they run a high risk of a permanent sense of insecurity and an inability in later life to form warm and loving relationships.

Yet in thirty years of intensive research this theory is still unproven. What has been shown is that young children need a central, permanent, person in their lives to whom they can become attached, and this is usually the mother. No one has been able to show that they need this person *all the time*. It has also been amply demonstrated in both human and animal studies that experiences in early life may have serious and lasting effects on development. Rutter, who assessed the whole subject with great clarity in his book *Maternal Deprivation Reassessed* wrote: 'We may now take for granted that the extensive evidence that many children admitted to hospital or to a residential nursery show an immediate reaction of acute distress; that many infants show developmental retardation following admission to a poor-quality institution and may exhibit intellectual impairment if they remain there for a long time; that there is an association between delinquency and broken homes; that affectionless psychopathy sometimes follows multiple separation experiences and institutional care in early childhood; and that dwarfism is particularly seen in children from rejecting and affectionless homes.'[4]

The evidence produced to support the original theory was largely based on children in institutions. It has often been pointed out that these children lacked much more than their mothers. They led totally deprived lives. What was actually being studied was not simply lack of a mother or mother-figure but the whole effect of institutionalization. No one has been able to show for instance, that the children of mothers who work develop less well or are more delinquent than children who have the constant attention of their mothers, though judges continue to make statements from the bench asserting that the cause of juvenile crime is mothers going out to work (such a statement is reported on the very day on which I am writing this and scarcely a week passes without a report of similar opinions). It has also not been demonstrated that children who have several important adults in their lives with whom they have strong mutual attachments develop less well than those who have only one. Indeed there is some evidence that young children who have several attachments and who are capable of forming new relationships suffer less if misfortune overtakes the person to whom they are most attached or if they suddenly have to be separated.

The idea that a young child should have the constant and exclusive attention of his mother (supplemented perhaps by his father during evenings and weekends) has replaced the acceptance of a much more usual and traditional situation. This is and has always been that mothers are usually the most important people in their children's lives but to some extent they share their children, right from birth, with others – not only with fathers and grandmothers but with aunts and older siblings, neighbours, workmates, servants and friends. Moreover, this tying of mother and baby together to the exclusion of all others (except possibly fathers if they are ever at home at times when the child is awake) has never before been actively encouraged, deliberately enforced, idealized, used for political purposes or made the subject of a protest.

What has been happening over the last forty years is that we (that is, society, guided by 'experts' and politicians) have been trying to condition babies to become attached to their mothers exclusively and, having done that, we (that is, academics and research workers) proceed to do research which reveals the undoubted distress caused when an infant who has been conditioned in this way is suddenly separated from his mother, perhaps because the family breaks up or because the child or mother has to go to hospital. Some heartrending films have been made on this topic to propogate this gospel to a wider audience. This research is then used by academics and politicians to 'prove' that young children should be tied even more totally and exclusively to their mothers, which leads either to further measures to induce this or to failure to take measures to assist mothers who are not able or willing to conform to it. Thus a cycle is formed which strengthens the situation.

Western society has had this pattern now for some thirty to sixty years, depending on where or how one looks. Of course it is impossible to 'prove' that it is good or bad, but a cynic might point out that the theory that emotional security and enduring loving relationships are created or enhanced by isolating mothers with their young children does not seen to have worked out well for society as a whole. Feelings of insecurity abound in both mothers and children. We have a society with large numbers of neurotic, unhappy and antisocial people and if these are not themselves mothers or children, their unhappiness often stems from their relationships with their mothers. The 'crisis of identity' is a characteristic dilemma of our age, and almost invariably the mother has had a profound influence on this. We are faced with unprecedented epidemics of, on the one hand, depression, neurosis, psychosomatic illness, anorexia nervosa and suicidal gesture, and on the other hand of delinquency, violence, vandalism and anti-social behaviour. It is impossible to assess how far these can be traced to difficulties between mothers and their children, but many individual cases can. And as for 'warm and enduring relationships' – we have a phenomenal divorce rate that climbs ever higher. In some areas as many as one in two couples get divorced. Those who remain married may be more enduring in their relationships but these are often far from warm. Either the theory is wrong, or we have failed to implement it in the right way or the tide of social change is so much against it that it would be impossible to implement it even if it were true.

Of course we cannot say that all our widespread problems of emotional disturbance and failure of relationships to endure have been caused by modern theories of maternal and child care or by the way in which our society treats mothers and their children. But what we can say is that these theories and this treatment have alarming implications which have not really been faced.

These include the implications of exclusive relationships between young children and mothers who are either toally unsuited to caring for them, mothers who have personalities which will make it difficult or impossible for those children to adjust later to the world outside, mothers who are temperamentally unsuited to the rigours of full-time mothering but who can be good mothers if they have some respite and other activity, and mothers who for economic reasons have to go out to work. The last group has been increasing enormously. I suspect the other groups have also been increasing though it is not possible to demonstrate this in figures.

It is interesting that none of these are viewed officially as having any special need, despite the fact that the idea of 'certain categories of need' are very much part of the official way of thinking. This can be seen clearly in an otherwise wise and excellent book, *The Needs of Children*, by Mia Kellmer Pringle. This book was specially commissioned by the Department of Health and Social Security. It is advertised as 'a landmark in our understanding of childhood' and can be taken as the enlightened official view. The special categories of need, children who are recorded as 'vulnerable' or 'at risk' are listed as large families with low incomes, handicapped children, children in one-parent families, children living apart from their families and children belonging to a minority group. There is nothing in the book about the personality of parents, though this, combined with a difficult environment and absence of other contacts and opportunities, is certainly frequently the cause of children eventually being categorized in the official way. The official view has long been to help only those mothers in certain categories of need, by such means as giving single mothers priority in state nurseries and otherwise to concentrate on picking up the pieces when disaster occurs. There is no apparent official awareness that ordinary mothers often cannot bring up children successfully in today's environment and that if they are to do so, special thought has to be given to their circumstances and their surroundings. Sir Keith Joseph once remarked 'We seem to have created a difficult social soil in which to grow families,' but no one has been able to do anything about it.

Some mothers are themselves aware of the dangers and are able to organize their lives in ways that are suitable both for them and for their children. Most cannot do this. Society as a whole and the institutions and experts within it have chosen to ignore the dangers and instead have tended to idealize close, compulsive ties between mothers and their children. This has even been done to the extent of spreading the idea, as though it were gospel truth, that this system is the only way to give children psychological security. On the surface, this has saved money and thought. The true and more profound effects are yet to be realized.

Another category of children who are at special risk and one which has now become well recognized by the authorities concerns those who have been 'battered' by their parents. About 700 infants die every year in England and Wales as a result of being brutally assaulted by their parents and several thousand children under the age of four years suffer 'non-accidental injuries' inflicted by their parents. Some of these are left crippled or with permanent brain damage. Battered children grow up to be battering parents. In some families it has been traced through for four or five generations. In her report Pringle writes 'Those who come to official notice may be only the tip of the iceberg.'

But what most children receive if they are isolated with unsuitable mothers is psychological battering. This is more difficult to detect than physical battering but few attempts are made to do this, and still fewer to prevent it. No one has yet categorized these children as being in special need. More important, no one has seriously tried to improve the way of life and environment of the families in which they live to lessen the extent and effects of the battering. On the contrary, everything is done, albeit unwittingly, to make it more likely to occur. For example the story of Lester Chapman, an eight-year-old boy who kept running away from home and was eventually found dead in a sludge heap, is unusual only in its abrupt and dramatic end. An enquiry team headed by a Queen's Counsel concluded that he was the victim of 'emotional deprivation', the result of parental immaturity with an inability to comprehend or to respond to the child's basic needs. The report said that little or no training on child abuse had been given to many of those involved in the case and emphasized the need for such training. But it did not lay the blame on professionals or on local authorities or the way in which society treats mothers and children. It says 'All that can usefully be done is to recognize the intractable nature of the problem and to suggest that patience and perception, firmness and diligence are the qualities which are likely to be most helpful to the social worker, the client and the community.'[5] This again is very much the tip of the iceberg. It is doubtful whether much can be done until society puts real rather than idealized value on mothers and young children and recognizes, develops and rewards qualities of motherliness.

The ideas of a society tend to be reflected and eventually enshrined in its way of life, its institutions and architecture, and its economic structure and planning. The idea of segregating mothers and children together and providing the minimum of amenities and services for them is now powerful in all these areas. One might say it has become entombed because many things that have been done would not be very difficult to undo even if public policy changed. The present system now appears to be the one which saves public money or allows it to be spent on 'more important' projects. But it also endangers what is any nation's most precious asset, its mental health, the foundation of which is laid down in the childhood of individuals. Unless things exist or happen which can improve the situation, poor mental health is passed on to the next generation. By our present system we are actually ensuring that it is handed down in this way, and probably increased in the process.

Many people are aware that something is wrong, but I have not seen it analyzed in this way. Some sensitive people who become aware of these problems are so appalled by what they see that they tend to deny the real issues involved. Politicians demand support for the family (which usually, as we have seen, means tying mothers and young children even more closely). Feminists tend to demand collective child care and abortion on demand as though these are what motherhood is all about. The ultimate horror of the way our present system is developing is described in Zöe Fairbairns' futuristic novel *Benefits*. In the year AD 2001 women are forbidden to work and state benefits are paid to 'good' mothers. Those who offend public morals or leave their husbands or do anything regarded as undesirable have their benefits withdrawn and are sent to institutions until they toe the line and once again accept a cloistered life with their children.[6]

We have built or rebuilt cities with no thought of where mothers might gather or where children might play. Since mothers and children are supposed to be tied together all the time, concrete jungles and isolated high-rise apartments were deemed to be good enough for this purpose. Too late we discovered the error, and then largely because the apartment blocks were vandalized (perhaps by the children who were at least escaping from total exposure to their mothers), because many of the mothers had nervous breakdowns from loneliness and isolation and many of the children suffered from nervous disorders, and had no idea how to get along with anyone other than their mothers. Even so, the philosophy remains. Feminist writers have detected and attacked it but have not as yet analyzed it or produced convincing alternative ideas.

Ironically, in my experience, it is often the very women we are discussing who cost the state vast sums in unnecessary investigations and operations for their psychosomatic disorders while the true cause of the trouble lies in their personalities and they are at the same time damaging their children permanently. Mothers who are sick or not at their best as people are also not at their best as mothers.

Yet the idea is prevalent in our society that mothers and children can be kept together on the cheap and with total moral justification, so there is no need for large expenditure on them. Welfare clinics (largely using cheap labour from doctors who are themselves mothers and so are unable to pursue structured careers or gain promotion) immunize against serious disease and give advice about feeding but little else is done. We are prepared to pay millions of pounds on expensive and often fruitless medical investigations or on surgical operations the usefulness of which no one has taken the trouble (or obtained the money) to survey. We pay millions of pounds to keep unhappy women quiet with tranquillizers, sedatives, sleeping pills and anti-depressants, and millions of pounds to look after children whose parents are unable to cope with them in today's conditions. But we build even our shopping centres without thought for mothers and with nowhere for young children to play. We build our public lavatories without small seats for small children and with no facilities for changing babies. Our sidewalks and subways have no slope for push chairs and buses and tubes seldom have room for them. In myriad ways our society makes unspoken statements that it is prepared to support mothers and children who have collapsed but not to pay towards their well-being. They are supposed to be together, aren't they? Well, let them get on with it. At least we can save money on *that* and keep the women quiet at the same time.

In Gavron's survey eighty-one per cent of the middle class mothers and sixty-five per cent of the working class mothers had had no experience with children. From the time their first child is born many are likely to have experience of little else, at least until the last child goes to school, and sometimes not until he leaves school. No wonder there are problems. Meanwhile, how does the mother develop as an adult, which she needs to do in our modern world? Raising children may be the most important and most satisfying thing in her whole life but it can only be an interlude of ten, perhaps even twenty years. She is likely to have another forty or fifty years ahead of her when it is over. What will she do with that? And what is she doing to prepare for it? How can she prepare under today's conditions? Of course she can if she really wants to and is aware of what is coming. But how many women are aware? The number reaching middle life with grown children who have given no thought to their future lives is staggering. And probably no one has ever mentioned it to them, certainly not enough to penetrate. Ask a mother who is totally involved in her family what she intends to do when they are grown up and you are likely to receive an uncomprehending stare. Yet the question is as important as what the children will do when *they* grow up. In a way it's the same question. What are you going to do with the next stage of your life?

Meanwhile what does the mother do for herself? She may go out to work and many do, though often not for herself but to get money for her children. If the work is satisfying it will probably lead to other and better things when the children are grown – perhaps to new qualifications, promotion, new responsibilities and openings. But a woman is lucky if these things come to her without forethought and planning. Mostly they do not drop out of the sky for good fortune mostly helps those who help themselves. Our society makes it difficult for all but the most stalwart and determined to do this. The rest are liable to be submerged unless they are lucky enough to be vocational homemakers and find total satisfaction in this role.

Mothers and children who are totally exposed and bound to each other are particularly liable to suffer not only from constriction and lack of growth and development but also from the quirks and peculiarities of each other's difficulties, moods and personalities. At best, if difficulties are small, moods are constant and personalities suitable, the suffering is only from constriction, absence of opportunity and lack of variety of experience. These can even affect babies who, once conditioned to interact with one person exclusively, may have great difficulty as they get older in making contact with others. At worst the personalities of mother and child are incompatible or the mother's personality is bizarre, abnormal or out of touch with the world outside, in which case a child who is exclusively, exposed to her and bound by her cannot develop normally. We have met a number of such mothers in this book. If there is no escape for the child in the form of physical space for exploration and the presence of other interested, caring adults, then his future is indeed black. Of course he needs a mother. He needs her continuous goodwill and her regular loving care. But if that is all he has and she lacks motherliness or is unable to present the outside world to him in a way that makes sense when he ventures into it for himself, then he may become a psychological cripple.

Much research has been done in recent years on mothering, the attachments of young children, mothers working and so on. But the personality of the mother and her qualities of motherliness are conspicuously absent from it. In an excellent review of research in this field Pilling and Pringle make only passing reference to it.[8] A few studies have indicated that 'the mother's attitude, measured before the child's birth, can affect mother-child interaction. Positive attitudes towards infants have been found to be related to maternal responsiveness to the baby's crying and to his social behaviour in the early months of life. Interest in children and adaptation to each stage of pregnancy with relatively little anxiety have been found to be related to various aspects of the mother-infant reaction in the first six months – the mother's responsiveness to her infant and her ability to relate sensitively to his capacities and individual characteristics.' Mothers 'who had been rated as highly anxious during pregnancy were evaluated ... as having a less satisfactory interaction with their babies at eight months than mothers who had been rated low in anxiety ... Maternal responsiveness to the child's signals appears to be a crucial influence in the child's development in the first two years, affecting his attachment to his mother and his cognitive development.'[9] 'It appears that a child will become most attached to those in his environment who are most responsive to his signals of distress and who themselves initiate interaction with him. Mostly, his mother will be the child's first and main attachment object, but not invariably so, even when she is the principle caretaker. Sometimes the father may be the first attachment object and sometimes the main tie is with him.'[10] 'Sensitivity of the mother in perceiving and responding promptly and appropriately to the child's signals appear to be the key determinant of a "secure attachment."'[11] 'Infants whose mothers are insensitive appear to develop attachment behaviour differing in various ways from the normative behaviour of children of similar age. They may be ambivalent in re-

285

lation to mother, some are unable to use her as a secure base for exploration of the unfamiliar, and others tend to spend much of their time in activities independent of the mother.'[12] '. . . the quality and pattern of the child's social attachments in infancy may possibly have great importance for his future development. So far there have been no longitudial studies attempting to link attachments in infancy to later behaviour.'[13] 'Current research emphasizes the importance of sensitive interaction with the child for his optimal development.'[14]

That is about all. One difficulty with this kind of research is that it often involves an enormous amount of work to demonstrate the validity of common sense. Another difficulty is that though it is more accurate than common sense, it is limited to that particular field. Most of this research has been directed at political and social questions such as whether or not it damages children to be separated from their mothers or to have mothers working. The potential damage of 'insensitive' or unsuitable mothers, or the ways in which they and their children might be helped to a better life never seems to be the direct object of enquiry. Yet doctors' surgeries, psychiatric clinics, courts of law and all institutions for criminal detention are full of people whose mothers were 'insensitive' and so could not provide for their needs as young children in a society where little else was available to them.

Earlier in this book we examined some characteristics of certain mothers who tend to have an adverse effect on their children. Here I shall describe briefly a few of the areas of life in which there is frequently difficulty between mothers and children and which, when this happens, are seldom solved in the outside world.

First is the sense of security and the ability to deal with new situations. In a fast-changing world such as ours these are essential qualities for successful survival. In a traditional world that changes little from generation to generation, the environment tends to support the individual who has grown up in it. Ours does not. A traditional world tends to support the distortions and limitations of parental influence. Ours tends to increase them. Thus an adequate early environment is particularly important in a changing world. Yet it is increasingly difficult to provide and depends more than ever before on the personality of the mother. We lead different lives from our parents and we know that our children will lead very different lives from ours. We all need to be able to deal with these differences and changes and to bring up children who have the capacity to cope with whatever comes. We cannot cope or help our children to cope if we are insufficiently developed or have developed in a distorted or unsuitable way. The environment is unlikely to help us unless we can impose ourselves upon it (in the French sense of *s'imposer*). Not only is it frequently hard, harsh, ugly and competitive but it is increasingly remote from nature and open spaces – both enormously influential in developing a sense of security and self-reliance. Although contact with nature is not essential to satisfactory integration, it makes it easier not only because of the positive things it provides but also because it eases the strain on the mother. Among the most supportive influences that can surround a mother and aid her in her efforts to bring up healthy children are a safe countryside with plenty of space to move about, a number of other caring, supportive adults to take an interest in the child and free access to children of a similar age. Access to these things has been declining for two hundred years. In 1798 Wordsworth wrote:

> For a multitude of causes unknown to former times are now acting with a combined force to blunt the discriminating powers of the mind, and unfitting it for all voluntary exertion to reduce it to a state of almost savage torpor. The most effective of these causes are the great national events which are daily taking place, and the increasing accumulation of men in cities, where the uniformity of their occupations produces a craving for extraordinary incident which the rapid communication of intelligence hourly gratifies.[15]

The loss of God which has occurred over the same period is also important. Nowadays we hear much more from theologians about God inside us than about God 'out there', and this again throws more strain on the mother. Many of the emotional aspects of Christianity that used to provide support no longer do so. Paul Tillich has written:

> The anxiety of doubt and meaningless is, as we have seen, the anxiety of our period . . .
> The decisive event which underlies the search for meaning and the despair of it in the twentieth century is the loss of God in the nineteenth century. Feuerbach explained God away in terms of the infinite desire of the human heart; Marx explained

him away in terms of an ideological attempt to rise above the given reality; Nietzsche as a weakening of the will to live. The result is the pronouncement 'God is dead', and with him the whole system of values and meanings in which one lived. This is felt both as a loss and a liberation. It drives one either to Nihilism or to the courage which takes non-being into itself.[16]

How can a mother cope with this if she is shut up with her young child in a high-rise apartment in an area made dangerous by traffic, hooliganism, crime and impersonality? Personal relationships cannot provide what is missing. Yet they are expected to do this as the foundation of mental health, and it is not surprising that personal relationships have become more vulnerable or that their development is hazardous. More than fifty years ago a survey of futurology discussed the rapidly declining ability of parents to bring up well-adjusted children.[17] The situation has become much worse since then and is most marked in large cities. The tensions and burdens of parents are transmitted to their children, affect them, and are passed on in altered form to yet another generation. Sense of security and the capacity to cope with new situations are profoundly affected by these things.

Another area of life in which difficulties arising in childhood are seldom solved in the outside world is love and sex. On the whole mothers are by far the strongest influence on their children's sex lives. Since infants' needs are usually satisfied by mothers, it is mothers who must influence the growth of the capacity to love. A marriage or love affair always tends to elicit feelings that were experienced in early life. Aberrant development of the relationship between mother and child can lead to a variety of difficulties. Infants become dependent on whatever satisfies their needs and this forms the framework of the way in which in later life they will feel and express their love. Thus loving and being loved covers a wide variety of situations, some of them far from the usual idea of love. Loving or being loved can be associated with such feelings as uneasiness and unrest; conflict, competition, rivalry; humiliation, feelings of rejection and fear of abandonment; anxiety; hating or being hated; feeling angry, resentful and not understood; being controlled, violated or beaten; controlling, violating or punishing; manipulation and playing one person off against another; feeling empty, meaningless or futile.

From this comes the way in which children find their sexual identity, the extent to which they are secure in this, and the form it takes. On it is imposed the parents' direct attitude to sexual matters. Much of the way in which a mother influences her children's sex lives depends on her own early experiences and in particular the way in which her own mother, and her father too, behaved towards her. Mothers who are unsure of their own sexual identity or sexual capacity and who lack the capacity to trust are less likely to be able to help their children than are mothers who are secure in these matters. The feelings tend to be passed from generation to generation. D. H. Lawrence in *Sex and Trust* wrote: 'If you want to have sex you've got to trust the core of your heart, the other creature.' (Trust, perhaps, more than all other qualities, is passed from mother to child).

Another part of life in which children are often fixed for life by their mothers concerns hostility and the ways in which it is expressed, for this develops only in the self and within close relationships. Only in recent years has society accepted the existence of hostility between parents and children, particularly hostility of children towards parents. Traditionally a great deal of hidden hostility of parents towards children was permitted in the guise of moral training. These have been discussed already in various parts of this book. Freud pointed out:

> Daily observations can show us how frequently the emotional relations between parents and their grown-up children fall behind the ideal set up by society, how much hostility is ready to hand and would be expressed if it were not held back by admixtures of filial piety and affectionate impulses.[18]

Since Freud's time it has been socially permissible to believe that not only is it normal for children to feel hostile towards their parents but also that all children have such feelings and that most hostility in adults stems from hostility against the parents induced in childhood. At the same time traditional methods by which parents were permitted covertly to express hostility towards their children have been exposed and have ceased to be acceptable. Parents are now expected to accept hostility from their children and to be understanding about it but they are not expected to retaliate. Part of the idealization of mothers has been the spread of attitudes which are intolerant towards individual variation in mothers, make no concession to any personal difficulties they may have, and allow them little antagonism or hostility towards their children. Only now are we beginning to be able to speak of the falsity and denial that lies under the idealization.

For example, mothers often feel physical distaste for their newborn babies. 'My baby reminds me of a skinned rabbit,' said one. Most are conscious that however much they love their young children, they are at times an almost intolerable burden or they behave in an intolerable way. The existence of 'battered babies' was not even discovered until the late 1940s and it was another two decades before the syndrome was freely discussed, even in professional circles. Even now, 'battered babies' tend to be other people's children, and most mothers' manuals and magazines assume that the baby is wanted and loved. It is no longer even permissible for mothers to unload their hostile feelings by excessive insistence on such matters as cleanliness and toilet training. Nowadays if you are unhappy with your baby or young children you are likely to encounter the attitude that you have only yourself to blame for having them at all. Society provides little support. Yet hate is part of love. So how do mothers deal with it? We have already seen how the anxiety and depression that is so common in our age develops in certain mothers against the cultural background and changes of our times. Unhappiness in mothers can manifest itself in many different ways.

The mother may show straight dislike of her child or, more frequently, of certain aspects of her child's behaviour. She may feel resentment at the way she is tied by the child and hark back to freer days with regret. She may become jealous of the child over the father's affection. She may envy the child its youth or the attention it commands. Some mothers are conscious of straightforward malicious thoughts towards their children. They may have fantasies of smothering them or of attacking them with knives. Such mothers usually feel a strong need to reassure others that they love their babies. Sometimes they acknowledge that they feel hostile but refuse to accept how strong those hostile feelings really are. Often the hostility does not come into consciousness at all. It is repressed, denied, displaced or changed into something else. The mother may idealize the child. She may project her malice onto the school or onto other people's children or onto some political cause. Sometimes the hostility may be turned into what appears to be its opposite and the mother is intensely preoccupied with her child's welfare.

Excessive solicitude contains a powerful element of malice. Others convert their hostility into some form of action either directly, in some form of attack, either physical or verbal, or indirectly. Action that is an indirect form of hostility can be helpful to both sides. If the mother retains her love the child will too, and will himself learn to express hostility without fear of losing love and approval – one of the most valuable abilities in the modern world. But psychological battering can be just as damaging and crippling as physical battering, though it is much more difficult to assess. A common form is contingent love. The child is only loved as long as he is a credit to his parents. Failure to be pretty or clever or to pass examinations or be a social success leads to withdrawal of love. Or else hostility is leaked in any number of ways. For instance a mother of a child who has failed to wash his face when asked to do so may seize him angrily and scrub his face herself, roughly and painfully. She may be unduly careless of his safety at home or outside and she may fail to educate him about dangerous situations such as cliffs, stray dogs and nasty strangers. She may make her children feel guilty if they do not dress up and look nice, or, conversely, if they do. She may ridicule them. Often hostility masquerades as genuine concern, for instance in directing a child towards an occupation in which he has no interest, or in being insistent that clothes must not be dirtied, or in refusing to let him play with other children who 'aren't good enough for my child'. Some hostile mothers try to control everything and insist on knowing what their children do every minute of the day. Some damn with faint praise and undermine confidence, or overreact, behaving as though a child's drawing was that of a genius. Some 'forget' to keep promises or find excuses for not keeping them. Some deliberately put their children into humiliating situations. One mother was deeply ashamed that her child wet the bed, yet sent him to stay with relatives without warning them, thus expressing her hostility towards both the child and towards them.

There are thousands of ways in which hostility that is not acknowledged can be leaked and when they are multiplied or repeated thousands of times, as they usually are, one can see that they can have a far-reaching influence on the child's developing personality, especially when the hostile person is the dominant influence on the child and one from whom he has no escape. One begins to see how many people can make good mothers but that the more they are totally exposed to children and totally in control, the more difficult

291

it is to be a good mother. The good mother knows her own weaknesses and, if the environment permits, makes allowances for them in the upbringing of children. But when the environment offers no alternatives, she may run into difficulties. Alternatives for mothers necessitate choice of action and opportunities for escape. These are only possible when the environment provides for many of the child's basic needs without specific effort on the part of the mother or the need for her constantly to be anxious about their supply. These basic needs include space and opportunities for play, freedom of choice and movement suitable to the child's age, companions of his own age, travelling to and from school. In good environments such things are available automatically, without special effort on the part of the mother, who then, unhurried and unharrassed, can provide the love and caring that can come only from her and also have time and freedom for herself as a person. But in our present society she so often has to provide those other needs as well so that there is no time for herself or for the tranquility that is necessary to good mothering.

Many mothers and their children have benefited enormously from the modern way of life. Many women have found that in closeness with their children for 24 hours a day they can fulfil themselves and bring up fine, healthy children. This is particularly true if housing is good and the outside environment congenial and suitable to the needs of young children. Large numbers of modern mothers have found and continue to find that this period at home with their young children is one of the most satisfying of their lives, and they would not have missed it for anything. For them, if they have enough money and good living conditions (and these are big 'ifs') the situation that prevails today is the best possible. Unless they are the wives of diplomats or of other husbands who expect them to participate in their careers, no one exerts any pressure on them to do anything but stay at home and care for their children.

But many mothers recognize that total isolation with their children day after day is bad for both sides and they know that if they are going to do their best by their children they must have some escape from them or earn money for them or both. This usually means going out to work. More and more women with children of all ages are going out to work. Some of them need the stimulation and some need the money. Often the motives are mixed.

In a society such as ours, in which a great many things have to be bought if we are to survive economically, mothers face special problems. Consumer pressures urge them constantly to buy things, advertisements suggest that by buying they are helping their children and imply that failure to do so is somehow letting their children down. In such a materially competitive society it is probably impossible for a mother not to feel a need for her children to be as advanced, as well-dressed, as well educated and generally as well provided for as other children and to feel a failure if they are not. This failure may be projected on to the father, the school or society in general, but basically it is experienced as a personal failure and is at the root of much anxiety and depression in mothers. Constant striving for material, social and psychological standards creates anxiety and also provides a focus for other anxieties.

At a time of world recession these anxieties are often increased still further. Having and rearing children has become very expensive. Prices rise constantly. Inflation is always with us. Public services are erratic. Even services concerned with life and death are no longer dependable. Standards have risen yet are increasingly difficult to achieve and maintain. Increasingly, mothers have to earn money in order to achieve or maintain what seems to them and their families a reasonable standard of living. Yet work that can be done at home is difficult to find and tends to be poorly paid. So they have to go out to work. But reliable substitute maternal care has become extremely difficult to find and pay for. Even though such care is essential if a mother is to go out to work, in some countries, including Britain, it is not even tax-deductible.

During the whole of this century more and more women have gone out to work, and, among them, more and more mothers have gone out to work. This increase is one of the notable changes that have been taking place and it has been constant in spite of great pressures from state and society (lifted only in time of war) to keep mothers at home. Little help is offered those who wish or need to work. There has been no state policy to help them and none to elevate the professions concerned in substitute mothering. Advertisers want them to stay at home to consume the goods they advertise and, doubtless, to support and service the men who earn the money (far more of it than women could ever earn). The state, unwilling to face the cost, has made virtually no effort to assist them and in many ways hinders, for example by taxing their earnings, giving them fewer allowances than men and making it, for many, not worth their while to work, and by offering no facilities to help them with their children. Official policy has tended to pick on those current psychological theories which insist that a young child needs the constant care of his mother, and to use these as a justification for not investing money in this way. Yet in spite of all this opposition, more and more mothers have gone out to work.

It is significant that the idea of a paid job outside the home is implicit in anything that is written about modern mothers working. And usually the job is low-paid without good future prospects. Even if the woman is highly qualified, perhaps a teacher or a doctor, the chances are that if she is a mother she is on the lower rungs of the career ladder and probably chooses her job because she is glad to get it or because it fits in well with her commitments at home. She may well have a part-time job or would like it to be part-time if this could be arranged. A career structure, with few exceptions, is not for her. A career involves competition, not only with women whose ties are fewer, but also with men. In most careers it is impossible to reach the top without more time and dedication than most mothers are able to give. In many careers, such as in industry or the diplomatic service, not only is it necessary to compete with those without domestic duties but those who do best usually have supportive wives who devote a great deal of their energies to their husband's careers. Since women have no wives, they are automatically at a disadvantage even if they are not actually excluded. If they have children the situation is even more difficult. Hence they mostly settle for a job of work which suits their home life and feel satisfied if it is at least interesting. But, when the interlude of mothering is over, they are then unlikely to be in a position that suits their age and capabilities. The top jobs and positions of power are not open to them for they have not put in the necessary years of climbing the ladder. This situation affects chiefly the ablest and most highly trained women in our society and it is one of the important reasons why women are attaining liberation but not power. An occasional mother may become the head of a university college, a consultant in a teaching hospital, or even prime minister, but such women are extremely rare. The number of women in the British House of Commons has fallen from 28 in 1964 to 19 in 1979. This is out of 625 Members.

Economic and consumer pressures and the need to earn money are not the only reasons why more and more mothers are seeking occupations apart from keeping house and rearing children. Another important reason is that women's horizons have widened and are widening fast. The serious education of women began more than a century ago and many women now have several generations of higher education for women behind them. Many of them find, however much they desire to be mothers, that professional training and years of professional work, a degree in mathematics or a Ph.D., are difficult to reconcile with washing, cleaning and the company and care of toddlers. This difficulty is found not only in the highly educated. Many who have worked for years in offices and perhaps reached positions of responsibility find the same difficulty.

This difficulty became serious in Europe after World War II and in America somewhat sooner. The main reason was the loss of servants. Between the two world wars was a golden age for many career mothers. True, married women were barred from some professions such as the civil service. But an educated woman whose chosen career was open to her could have the best of both worlds. There were plenty of servants available and she did not have to be rich to employ them. She could be mistress of a comfortable household, bring her children up in customary manner, run her career during the hours when other ladies of a similar station were pursuing their lives of leisure and still appear in the evening, as did their more leisurely sisters, to go out with her husband or be hostess at the dinner party which her employees had prepared. It is probably significant that in the elections to the Fellowship of the Royal College of Physicians in London, one of the highest honours that can be conferred on British doctors, during the 1930s ten per cent were women, and many of them were mothers. By the late 1960s, despite a great increase in women doctors after the World War II, only two per cent of Fellows were women. Women who had children after the war were not in a position to compete in the way their mothers and aunts had done. They had been caught up in the movement that drove them back to the home with little or no domestic help, strongly supported by government policy, using the current psychological theories that idealized motherhood.

CHAPTER SEVETEEN

Men and Children

No assessment of motherhood is adequate without reference to fathers and other men in children's lives. *Men and Children*: the very phrase sounds peculiar. *Women and Children, Men, Women and Children, Fathers and Children, Men and Boys*: all these sound apposite, have their own connotations, and evoke a multitude of acceptable situations. But *Men and Children* without the interposition of women, and without a statement of parenthood or female exclusion, sounds incongruous, unsuitable or even immoral. This fact tells us quite a lot about our society. In general, men and children, particularly children of both sexes, do not get together, and do not do things together. It is difficult to think of any activity that they have in common. This may be the first time a chapter with this title has ever been written, for what is there to write about?

Let us consider first the men whom a small child in our society is likely to know. Of course, professionally some men – far fewer than women – work with children. There are male teachers, though few for the younger children, and in the nursery school or infants' class they are rare. There are male nurses, but seldom in children's wards. Most doctors and police are men, though often it is the woman doctor to whom the children are allotted. School bus drivers are usually male. Some social workers, sweetshop proprietors and even 'lollipop ladies' are male. But in their dealings with professionals and in their social lives young children are likely to encounter few men. Children seldom have the opportunity to make friends with men other than their fathers, and perhaps grandfathers. In these days of small and scattered families they are lucky if they have uncles or older brothers and cousins who form close relationships with them. If their own fathers are absent or work long hours away from home or are in some way unsatisfactory children are likely to grow up without really knowing or making a satisfying relationship with any men at all. In our society the closest male relationship a child has is often with his mother's boyfriend. This can be satisfying on both sides for just as children are excluded from the world of men, so men are excluded from the world of children, and it can be an opportunity for both. But for many mothers' boyfriends the existence of children is a nuisance, a burden that must be borne for the sake of the relationship. Also, mothers' boy friends may come and go with a speed that is confusing to young children. Sometimes the children are a factor in the break-up of the relationship or in its failure to develop. Sometimes the relationship is prolonged because the children have become fond of or dependent on the man or because the man has developed feelings of love and responsibility towards them.

Among men a child's strongest attachment and greatest influence is usually his father. Most books on child development or child care devote a chapter to him. An increasing number of studies now include father-child relationships in their investigations. Pilling and Pringle in their comprehensive review of research in this field point out that there is a relative scarcity of research on the father's role in the development of children. Such research as exists does not really tell us which aspects of the father's behaviour and attitude affect the child or how this works. We do not know whether fathers on the whole behave in the same way towards children of both sexes or whether children are influenced differently according to their sex and according to the combination of maternal and paternal behaviour. We do not even understand the father's indirect influence through the way in which he does or does not support the mother.[1]

One of the difficulties in studying fathers has been getting hold of the fathers in order to study them. (This difficulty is in itself an indication of the father-child situation in our society.) The result is that much information for research has been obtained by asking the mother or even the child himself about the father's behaviour. This obviously produces different results from studying the father's behaviour directly. Even when it has been possible to set up experimental situations in order to study the father's behaviour, the artificiality of the situation and knowledge of being observed is likely to distort the behaviour that is being studied. However, Pilling and Pringle state firmly: 'Overall research findings using different approaches are consistent enough to justify the conclusion that the father has a direct influence – in addition to his indirect influence, as the mother's economic and emotional support – on the child's development, probably from the earliest years.'[2] It would be surprising if this had been found *not* to be true. One example of paternal influence is in verbal achievement, which is associated with close interaction with and verbal stimulation from adults in early years. Here the father is likely to be the second adult and so increases the child's experience of conversation. Another conclusion of Pilling and Pringle is particularly interesting in view of the many observations in this book about the effects on a child of being constantly exposed to his mother and to scarcely anyone else. The support of the father to a mother in childrearing has been found to give her the self-confidence to allow more autonomy in the child, and this is true of girls as much as boys. Encouragement of independence and autonomy in making decisions has been found to be beneficial.[3] Fathering has also been found to be associated with emotional and social adjustment. Affection for the father has been found to be associated with good adjustment with other children and with leadership qualities. In boys, inadequate affection from the father is associated with delinquent behaviour.[4]

Another finding which may be of considerable significance in understanding the changing position of women in our society, in the development of women's equality and liberation, and in the ability of women to deal with choice and change is: 'The girl too seems to be affected by the warmth of the father-child relationship but here there appears to be some danger that over-affection, at least in the middle-classes, will have a depressing effect on the child's independence and leadship qualities.'[5] This may turn out to be an important reason why so many women fail in our society, despite the enormous improvement in their status and the increase in choice for them. The 'overaffection' to which Pilling and Pringle refer may well turn out to be bound up with encouragement in a girl of 'traditional' virtues such as passivity, dependence and pleasing men rather than developing herself. These qualities are becoming increasingly unsuited to women in the modern world. As a result, when the girl grows up she rebels against the idea of further development or increased independence and this makes her particularly vulnerable to modern pressures and liable to depression and self-destructive activity. I have written about this in another book, *Why Women Fail*.

Current research suggests that the absence of a father in a family has relatively little effect on a child's social, emotional and intellectual development when the material deprivations of father-absence have been taken into account.[6] This is surprising and it may be that research techniques are not yet sufficiently sensitive to detect effects that may in fact be of considerable importance. 'It is an oversimplification to expect the father's influence in the intact family to be measured by differences between father-present and father-absent children in attainment or adjustment, though many investigators have adopted this view.' For instance, many fathers live with their children but scarcely ever see them and play little part in their lives. It seems that, however 'warm' the relationship between father and child, the child suffers if the father is hardly ever there.

Such adverse effects of a father's absence as have been detected tend to be associated with divorce, separation and desertion rather than with death.[7] There is no doubt that in families that are apparently intact there is often tension and conflict and an unhappy family atmosphere. The personalities of the parents have considerable influence on children's development and well-being, but these are difficult to detect and study and even more difficult to measure. Pilling and Pringle point out that the father's absence 'cannot be conceptualized as an unfilled gap in family relationships but means, actually, that there is a complex change of relationships. This involves the mother herself, and others, including relatives, neighbours and friends, and even the children themselves, taking over some aspects of the father's role.... The change in relationships that occurs when the father is absent appears to result quite often in the creation of a family situation which is relatively satisfactory for the child. Findings suggest that the mother's attitudes and her ability to cope with the situation are crucial factors in how far the loss is made up.... The findings of this review highlight the importance of the mother in the father-absent family as a determinant of the child's attainment and adjustment.'[8]

Something must be said here about hybrid families, since these are now common and in many sections of society are virtually the norm. These are families in which there are parents and children but not all the children are the offspring of both parents. As we saw, hybrid families were common in the past, when many adults died young, especially women. As health and mortality rates improved hybrid families become much less common and until recently little thought has been given to them by writers and researchers, except sometimes as 'unfortunate' or 'tragic' results of divorce or family breakdown. But now hybrid families are so common that we have to look at them with new eyes. They tend to differ from the hybrid families of past centuries in that most of the children involved have two living parents though they only live with one of them, or with only one at a time. Many of these families now consist of a chain of parents, step-parents and step-siblings, half-stiblings, temporary step-parents and step-siblings, and so on. I met one women who mothered twelve children. Five of them were her own by three husbands and the rest were the children of her various husbands and their former wives. One of the children was the offspring of one of her ex-husbands' ex-wives by yet another ex-husband, which just shows how complicated these families can become. With the high and increasing divorce rate and the acceptibility of unmarried parenthood the number of such families is increasing rapidly, and we cannot write them off as social casualties. Sometimes the relationships within them are so tenuous and shortlived that they play little or no part in the lives of the members of the family, but often they are of considerable importance, sometimes in an unusual way.

A stepmother, or even an ex-stepmother, can be life-saving to a child with a difficult or inadequate mother. Or sometimes the quality of 'motherliness' is stronger in one or more of the men. One sometimes finds men who 'mother' children who are the offspring of other men and become more important in their lives than their own parents. But of course these ill-defined and complicated relationships are also fraught with hazard. Many adults are not happy living with other people's children. The 'wicked stepmother' of old fairy tales has many counterparts today. Sometimes a couple get on well with each other's children until they have a baby of their own, and then reject the children of previous partners. Sometimes a husband is irrestistibly drawn towards his nubile stepdaughter, or she sets her cap at him as a means of manipulating or disrupting family harmony and relationships. Sometimes children are hostile to the new step-parent in an effort to drive him or her away. The permutations and possibilities are infinite and so far serious sociological or psychological research has not really gone beyond 'the children of divorce', 'one-parent families', or occasional studies of step-parents. Most writers still seem to think of the nuclear family as 'normal' and anything else as 'abnormal'. I suspect that in the near future we shall have to change our attitudes to adjust to the changing situation.

One question that arises out of this is often; who does the mothering? This brings us to an important point. 'Motherliness', which has been discussed in earlier chapters, is not a prerogative of women. It is unfortunate that the word in inextricably bound up with the female sex. This fact is itself the result of the historical processes through which our language has developed, and the restrictions and imperatives of language inevitably influence our thought and make change and objective appraisal more difficult. Although I would like to write about 'mothers' without any indication of sex, I know that it is impossible. Instead I shall tell a true story which illustrates something of what I wish to say, and also the way in which our society insists that children shall be mothered by women, however unsuitable. The story is of Mary and Paul.

Mary was the youngest by twelve years in a family of two boys and two girls. Her father had always been an ambitious, hard-working and successful businessman who had been away from home a great deal. By the time Mary was born he had realized that with his other children he had missed most of the experience of fatherhood and much regretted that he had had to work so hard. He determined to make it up with Mary. He had reached a position of such eminence that it was possible for him to spend a great deal of time at home. Mary became the main interest in his life and their 'love-affair' lasted until his sudden death when Mary was fourteen. By this time Mary was already beautiful, sophisticated and extremely attractive.

Soon after her father's death Mary went 'off the rails'. She accused her mother, a pleasant, mild, competent woman, of having killed her father. She started to have casual affairs, became pregnant and, at the age of fifteen gave birth to a baby who was adopted. During the next five years she led a wild life and seems to have been irresistibly attractive to many men. She travelled the world in luxury with a series of lovers and began to drink too much and to take drugs. At the age of twenty she set up house with an alcoholic, became pregnant deliberately and married him. The marriage was an immediate disaster and it soon became clear that Mary could neither keep house nor care for her newborn daughter Ruth. There was much violence between the couple from the beginning and soon they were both in court, not only for divorce proceedings but also for charges involving drug offences, drunken driving and behaviour likely to cause a breach of the peace. The court decided that neither parent was fit to care for Ruth and gave custody of the child to

Mary's mother, Ruth's grandmother. She herself had just acquired a new husband who was not enthusiastic about having the peace of his beautiful, antique-filled house disrupted by his new wife's three-year-old granddaughter. Mary's mother struggled hard to make her marriage work, to be a good mother to her grandchild and also to cope with Mary who was becoming increasingly extreme in her behaviour and was in and out of psychiatric clinics.

Then along came Paul, burly, gentle and with great qualities of motherliness. He fell in love with Mary, married her and set up house in which he cared for her and for the child Ruth, who became passionately attached to him. For a while Mary adored him as she had adored her father. He really became mother to both of them. Paul was a successful professional entertainer who had made a great deal of money. For two years he undertook few professional engagements and none which took him away from home. During this time Mary had her ups and downs, a few short admissions to the psychiatric hospital and several short disappearances from home. She could not be left alone with Ruth or be trusted even to fetch her from school or provide her tea. Paul employed a series of 'mother's helpers', all of whom Mary eventually drove from the house, always saying that she wished to care for her own child by herself. Eventually Paul found that his professional career was suffering and his bank balanace was becoming unhealthy. He had to work and travel more if he was to survive. When he was absent Mary became worse and was often drunk, drugged and incapable. Ruth became desperately unhappy and insecure without her stepfather. Sometimes the child had to return to her grandmother until Paul came home. Eventually Mary turned against Paul and made life increasingly difficult for him. She did her best to drive him from the house. Paul stuck it as long as he could. His chief concern was now for Ruth's welfare but the situation became impossible and he came to see that there was now no way in which he could 'mother' his wife and her child successfully. The family broke up, Ruth returned to her grandmother and Mary continued relentlessly with her self-destructive way of life. One wonders what future lies in store for Mary, still only 26, and for poor little Ruth.

In the past, even a generation or two ago, it was much easier than it is today for men and children to have social contact with each other. Before the roads were so dangerous children had much more freedom to wander and explore, both in town and country. Men were more visible and approachable while they worked. Nowadays children are lucky if there is a little corner shop with a friendly man who talks to children. Mother is more likely to keep them in because of the traffic or the dangers of 'nasty men' (who also seem to have increased in numbers). She may buy the child's sweets at the supermarket. Or the sweetshop, having suffered from juvenile thieves, has a prominent notice saying 'Not more than two children at any one time' and its keeper is more concerned with his stock than with making friends with his customers. There is no longer a milkman or baker with a horse and cart who lets the children ride with him and perhaps drive the horse. The men who do drive round are likely to be too aware of union regulations and laws against carrying passengers to offer the children amusement and education. There is no longer a cobbler working at his open door with hammer and nails and chatting with the children. He is now inside the shop operating a noisy and dangerous machine or simply collecting the shoes to be sent off to the workshop. The man who used to call to cane the chairs and sharpen the knives no longer comes.

The segregation of men from children is almost complete. It is now unlikely that a child can make friends with a man outside his own family. Even if he does, the relationship is likely to be regarded with suspicion because, in our society, we tend to see sex in everything and perhaps to put sex into everything.

Because of these changes a whole generation of men has grown up who, unless they are involved professionally, have virtually no contact with or experience of children other than their own. This cannot help them to be good fathers. It cannot be psychologically healthy for anyone. Does it, I wonder, increase the incidence of 'nasty men' about whom all parents are anxious, and with good reason? What effect does it have on people to deprive them of legitimate contact with all children unless they happen to have their own?

We cannot put the clock back but we can at least ponder about these things and wonder what we can do to overcome the problems we have produced in our 'progress'.

CHAPTER EIGHTEEN

Day Care and
the Education of Babies

In our modern world more and more mothers leave their homes regularly, and go to work either for economic or for personal reasons. Their difficulty in doing this is the basis of much of what feminists see as the oppression of women. Politicians and advertisers of consumer goods find it on the whole more convenient if mothers stay at home. There are strong pressures to keep them there and few to help them. It is not surprising that this subject is of considerable interest and concern not only to the mothers themselves but to all who work professionally with mothers, babies and small children.

'Free 24-hour nurseries' is one of the six demands which are a major unifying force in the women's liberation movement. (The others are equal pay; equal education and job opporunity; free contraception and abortion on demand; financial and legal independence; and an end to discrimination against lesbians and the right to a self-defined sexuality). One can envisage such institutions available to all well-equipped, staffed by adults of both sexes including nurses, specially trained housemothers and also by teachers trained in educationing needs of babies and young children, run with awareness of the needs of young children, with continuity of care so that the same child is always looked after by the same loving, caring, motherly person, where parents could leave their children as and when they please and which would indeed be a second home to the children and an enriching experience in their development.

It is not difficult to imagine such places and how they might be run. But it is also easy to see the impossibility of establishing them or paying for them in the foreseeable future. In the present political climate and in our current situation of economic recession the establishment of such institutions on a national scale can be only a pipe dream. Although the idea is useful as a possible ultimate standard, to campaign for the scheme now and to discuss it as though it were a practical possibiity in the near future is unrealistic and so can easily be used as an excuse to avoid looking deeply into the situation or to work for more practicable schemes.

The whole question of public day nurseries and day care centres is intimately bound up with politics at several levels. Revolutionaries see them as part of necessary radical change to liberate the oppressed. Politicians, governments and employers see them according to circumstances as a useful means of manipulating the labour market, or of saving public money, or as a minor welfare service for deprived children. They are not at present regarded as potential benefits to children or parents or as a valuable investment in the future of society. State nurseries and day care centres tend to spring up quickly in wartime when governments need the work of women and they tend to be closed once the war is over and governments wish to keep the women at home. During World War II the governments of both Britain and the United States regarded female participation in the labour force as essential to victory. Previously the employment of married women had been discouraged. Now there were no unmarried women left to draw upon, so the services of wives and mothers were assiduously sought. In the United States over 3.7 million of the 6.5 million women who entered the labour force listed themselves as former housewives. Many had children of school and pre-school age, including sixty per cent of those hired by the War Department.[1] The proportion of women who were employed jumped from slightly over twenty-five per cent to thirty-six per cent – a rise greater than that of the previous four decades.[2]

These conflicting views were reflected in the effort and lack of effort that was made to provide care for the children of the women whose work was needed. Little was done. High turnover and absenteeism became a problem among women in the war industries in both Britain and the United States. For every two women workers hired in war-production factories in the United States June, 1943, one quit. It was estimated that female turnover and absenteeism in one factory alone cost the loss of forty planes a month.[3] 'Put in simple terms', writes Chafe, 'many women workers who were full-time housewives found it impossible to do both jobs without either succumbing to exhaustion or taking time off work. . . . The lack of child-care facilities directly affected war production.'[4] Yet there was still disagreement about providing child-care facilities and argument about whether the benefits of maternal employment outweighed the costs involved. The Children's Bureau in Washington declared, '[A] mother's primary duty is to her home and children. This duty is one she cannot lay aside, no matter what the emergency.' The Women's Bureau observed that 'in this time of crisis ... mothers of young children can make no finer contribution to the strength of the nation than to assure their children the security of the home, individual care and affection.' This feeling was also present in many mothers. In 1943 George Gallup asked a cross-section of women in the U.S. whether they would take a job in a war plant if their children were cared for in a nursery free of charge. Only 29 per cent said yes while 56 per cent said no.[5] Yet the fact remained that millons of women were employed and many children were not receiving adequate care. The number of child-neglect cases increased markedly and a social worker counted forty-five infants locked in cars in a single war-plant parking lot.[6] The Roosevelt Administration compromised initially by insisting that responsibility for child care rested with the local community and President Roosevelt eventually gave the impression of national commitment to day care while actually postponing such commitment. In 1942 he allotted $40,000 to help local communities ascertain the need for child-care centres, but no funds were provided for operating existing centres or for hiring people to run the centres.

Such ambivalence in the presence of clear and widespread need is typical of the attitudes of governments and politicians towards working women and their children.

In Great Britain, wartime needs were more pressing. At the outbreak of war the fact that London and other major cities were likely to be bombed forced the government to assume direct responsibility for children and evacuate them, mostly without their mothers, to safer areas. Women were drafted ('called up' was the term used in Britain) and the government set up a wide network of day nurseries for the children of working mothers. But, predictably, as soon as the war finished, both countries set about dismantling their systems of day care. In Britain the Ministry of Health issued its circular 221/45 which stated: 'The proper place for a child under 2 is at home with his mother ... the right policy would be positively to discourage mothers of children under 2 from going to work ... and to regard day nurseries and daily guardians as supplements to meet the special needs . . . of children whose mothers are constrained by individual circumstances to go out to work or whose home conditions are in themselves unsatisfactory from the health point of view, or whose mothers are incapable for some good reason of undertaking the full care of their children.' In 1951 the Ministry published a fresh circular which recommended that cost of day-nursery provision 'should not be incurred when the question of day care *arises solely from the mother's desire to supplement the family income by going out to work.'*

As a result most day nurseries have been closed down. The rest serve only about one quarter of the wartime number and these are mostly for disadvantaged chilren. No attempt has been made to bring day nurseries into the modern world. They are staffed by nurses and have no educationalists on their roll – at a time when the profound importance of education even for the youngest age is being recognized. The political nature of the policy behind day nurseries and the lack of them is highlighted by the action of the British Department of Education which, when short of teachers, recruited mothers of under-fives who were trained teachers by giving funds to local authorities specifically to provide nursery places for their children.

In the United States political vacillation over the question of child care has been qually obvious. Early in the century a movement known as Mother's Pensions developed to provide income for widows in order to keep them out of the labour force. After World War I provision was made for the children of widows and disabled men. But gradually the children eligible for benefit became the children of unmarried or deserted women and feelings changed. These women were supposed to go to work to support their children. Therefore it was regarded as legitimate to provide day-care centres for their children so that the women were free to work. In 1969, President Nixon in a message establishing the office of Child Development said, 'So critical is the matter of early growth that we must make a national commitment to provide all American children an opportunity for healthy and stimulating development during the first five years of life'.[7]

Three years later, in December, 1971, he said in a veto message on the Comprehensive Child Development Bill: 'Neither the immediate *need* nor the desirability of the national child development programme of this character has been demonstrated. . . . For the Federal Government to plunge headlong financially into supporting child development would commit the last moral authority of the national government to the side of communal approaches to child rearing over against the family-centred approach.'[8] On both sides of the Atlantic day care centres have become very much a provision for disadvantaged mothers and their children.

A number of books have been published recently which indicate the actual function of these nurseries and centres.[9] In the United States less than two per cent of working mothers' children are enrolled in non-profit day care. In Britain day nurseries have become less and less helpful to working mothers. In England and Wales, there are about 850,000 children under five whose mothers undertake paid employment outside their homes (compared with three million whose mothers look after them full-time at home). About 172,000 of these children have mothers who work outside the home for more than thirty hours a week. There are now in the whole of England and Wales fewer than 26,000 day nursery places, and most of these go to the children of single mothers who have to work and to children from 'crisis' families. Even if all these children have working mothers, which they do not, the figure is little over three per cent of the total number of children with working mothers. Clearly the state day nursery or care centre is providing for the needs of only a tiny proportion of these children.

Without doubt, one reason for this is the cost. Group day care is the most expensive form of out-of-home care. The cost in the United States may be as high as $80 per week per child. In Britain the cost of providing a nationwide service might be as much as £500 million a year. The Jacksons have worked out that (in 1975 figures) the cost of building one day-nursery place for a child was £3,000 and rising fast. The cost of training each member of staff was around £2,000 and the annual running cost for each child was £700 or £14 per week. These figures are for 1975 so they would be at least double today.

Such day nurseries as do exist vary considerably in the quality of care that they provide and in the extent to which they serve the community. The Jacksons write that 'day nurseries (always with exceptions) are almost exclusively concerned with care and health – screening, diet, sleep, cleanliness. Indeed our impression is that the majority of the staff (whose own training and experience may be very limited) simply do not see an educational question even when they are the major actors in it; do not know when they are holding a child back – are not aware of opportunities missed; and seldom if ever operate with an educational plan for each child in mind. This is not recorded as a criticism of particular staff. How – without education and support themselves– can they be expected to have a dual professional identity as nurses and teachers? The question is how do we come to provide this institution and this profession for children, many of whom must logically be at a high educational risk? It arises, I suspect, because socially we have suffered from other people's tunnel vision. These are "other people's children".[10]

In addition to state-run day nurseries and day care centres there are those offered by employers or by private establishments. In England and Wales these give another 2,400 places while private nurseries cater for a further 22,000 children. Thus about 50,000 children under five attend collective day-care centres, about one in sixty of all children in the age group.

Nearly twice this number, over 91,000 children under five in England and Wales, are looked after by registered childminders and probably many more illegally and unregistered. The corresponding system in the United States is family day care which is 'overwhelmingly popular, accounting for approximately three out of four of the children cared for outside their homes'.[11] Norris and Miller, who have studied the system in America, point out that those in favour of family day care believe it offers 'a nurturing, homelike environment' without the drawbacks of either an institution or of isolated babysitting. Critics believe that it is no more than a child-minding service – at its worst with babies propped up in front of television sets. At its best it provides a child with a warm loving extra mother and probably other children to play with, and is an enriching experience, and more and more parents are finding it the best solution, particularly for babies.

Family day care is of particular importance to mothers today for several reasons. First, it is the most widespread system used by mothers of young children who need or wish to work outside the home. Second, it is far cheaper than state-run centres and so has the greatest possibility for improvement and growth. Third, it is a potential source of occupation, satisfaction and income to many people in our society who possess those valuable and undervalued qualities of motherliness discussed earlier. Last, the system contains a number of possibilities which, if developed, could form the foundation of profound changes of attitude in our society which could make a tremendous difference to many of the situations discussed in this book, could help to solve many of the problems of modern mothers and could be a great force for improvement of family life and for the quality of life for parents and children. It could therefore have far-reaching political significance. If incorporated into the women's liberation movement it could become immensely powerful and make that movement one for all women rather than, as at present, a movement for a small number of women. I shall leave the later questions to the last chapter of the book and deal only with the earlier ones here.

In the United States most states require that anyone caring for one or more children who are not relatives for more than ten hours a week must be licensed by the state day-care licensing agency. Yet informal estimates suggest that at least half the family day-care homes in the county are unlicensed. Many of these offer as high quality care as those that are licensed.[12] When a program is licensed, it is supervised by a public agency and those who run it may be given courses in child development, nutrition and other relevant subjects. Other forms of support may include low-cost lunches and toy-lending services.

Childminders, who look after other people's children in their own homes, care for many more children of working mothers than the state, employers' nurseries and private nurseries all put together. No one knows how many more. We know that in England and Wales 50,000 children are cared for by state, employers and private nurseries. About 92,000 children are cared for by registered child-minders. Many more are cared for unofficially. Under the 1968 Health Services and Public Health Act, anyone who looks after a child, other than a relative, for more than two hours a day, and gets paid for it, must register with the local authority. The penalty for not doing so is a £50 fine or three months in prison. The procedures of registration can take many months to complete. There are very few prosecutions for those who fail to comply (only thirteen in six years), so the authorities tend to turn a blind eye to this.[13]

In their survey the Jacksons found that the number of children looked after by childminders was 'far, far more than we had been led to expect.... More than twice as many children were with illegal minders as with registered ones.'[14] As well as a good deal of turning blind eyes on illegal childminders there is a good deal of official complacency on the subject of those who are registered. This is echoed in the feminist *Women's Directory*, which says 'If a person is registered and has experience or a modicum of training, your child will be safe and well cared for.'[15] The Jacksons comment, 'When we looked at the quality of care they were actually receiving, registration turned out to be quite irrelevant. The disturbing truth was that no more than half a dozen of these children were looked after in safe and comfortable conditions with the kind of care that might help them to develop physically and mentally. At least an equal number suffered serious neglect and harsh treatment, if not actual cruelty. And most of the rest spent their days in the typical emptiness of life with childminders who work for a pittance, without support or supervision. Day after day they sit passively on a sofa, without conversation, toys, books, visits or stimulation of any kind.'

The Jacksons uncovered plenty of scandalous stories about childminders, both registered and unregistered. Unfortunately in the few weeks between the publication of the Jacksons' report and the writing of this, their work has already been used by politicians, in the typical way in which the subject of young children tends to be used by politicians, as ammunition for further measures discouraging mothers from leaving their homes. But that was not the intention of the Jacksons' report. They point out 'Childminding is not some pocket of Victoriana preserved in old inner-city streets of Britain. It is a universal and necessry consequence of the way we live now,' and they point the way to improving it.

A universal and necessary consequence of the way we live now. State services, where they exist, do not serve working mothers and are expensive to the tax payer. Whereas the annual running cost of a state day nursery is £700 per child, on top of the cost of buildings and staff training, the annual running costs of even the most ambitious childminding schemes is £34 (and few areas at present spend more than £4 and many spend none), staff training 50p, and cost of building is zero. Childminding is flexible. It is cheap. At little cost to the community it can be enormously improved. The Jacksons proceeded to prove that this is so. They organized courses for childminders and a centre for them. They taught them about children and child development and this made their work more interesting. They arranged for the provision of toys. They organized phone-ins and features on local radio stations. They persuaded the B.B.C. to do a thrice-weekly television series for childminders with a free childminders' book. They began to give childminders professional knowledge and professional status. Childminding began to become a new profession for people (not all of them women) who had no profession and no qualifications. Above all it began to become an active occupation, advancing towards the public world, not retreating from it, in which trained people were performing the specific task of caring for and educating children, and being paid for it. The Jacksons give a number of practical and political suggestions about how the service could be extended and improved, including the appointment of a Minister for Children.

The Jacksons point out that childminding is at present a service that is on the whole provided by the poor for the poor, but as the cost of living rises more and more middle class families are turning to it. It is usually the interest and participation of the middle class that leads to improvement of a service. If childminding becomes respectable and professional it is bound to raise the general standard without excluding the participation of the uneducated. As the Jacksons show, even the most uneducated can be trained to be good at it. Lastly, we might say that the word 'childminder' is passive and unsuitable for a new, active, forward-looking profession. 'Caregiver' which is favoured in the United States is not much better. Perhaps the term 'housemother' or 'workmother' might be better, so some new word might be found with connotations suitable to its aims and true functions.

In British middle class households after World War II the traditional nanny gave way to the part-time foreign *au pair* girl, who came to learn English. Some, though fewer, of these girls also go to the United States. At best the system works well and there are now second-generation *au pairs* caring for the children of the parents to whom their mothers were once *au pairs* and so on. At worst it can be a disaster. The girls tend to change rapidly and some are not interested in small children, cannot talk to them in their own language, are incompetent in domestic affairs and interested only in boy friends. The *au pair* is unlikely to be the solution for a serious working mother, though she may be adequate to give the mother some respite or opportunity to leave home alone.

Inevitably the subject of day care raises the question of whether it is necessary for all those parents to work while their children are so young. Since it is clear that many of them do so only because they cannot survive without the money, an alternative would be a parent's wage, which pays the mother, or single father, of a small child to stay at home. This would doubtless help many parents and young children but would not make day care unnecessary. In countries where it has been tried it has been found that mothers still choose to go out to work. It is doubtful whether the state could or would pay a parent's wage as high as the money they could earn. Furthermore, many mothers, even of babies and young children, find that they need to get away from home regularly. They know that they are better mothers part-time than they could possibly be full time. For their own sakes and those of their children, they need to exercise skills other than mothering, and to have contact with the adult world. Earlier in this book we encountered many mothers who are disastrous as full time mothers and whose children would undoubtedly benefit or have benefited if they had more contact with other people. Even Bowlby, who has been attacked so often as the originator of modern policies has written that 'it is an excellent plan to accustom babies and small children to being cared for now and then by someone else.'[14] He emphasizes that particular care needs to be taken to ensure that alternative arrangements for mothering have regularity and continuity if mother goes out to work.

The way in which day care has been discussed here links it with other aspects of child care which have hitherto tended to be quite separate. These include nursery schools and nursery classes whose aim is not to free mothers who wish to go out to work but rather to help pre-school children to develop socially by stimulating their natural curiosity and bringing them into contact with adults and children outside the family circle and educationally by developing their use of language and skills and by detecting special difficulties. Government policy here has been one of stop-go-stop. In 1945 the Ministry of Health circular 221/45 stated that the right policy to pursue would be 'to make provision for children between 2 and 5 by way of nursery schools and nursery classes.' In 1960 the Ministry of Education in circular 8/60 stated that resources could not be spared for an expansion of nursery schools nor could teachers be spared who might otherwise teach children of school age. In 1967 the Plowden Committee recommended that 'part-time attendance at a nursery school is desirable for most children.' In 1968 the Urban Aid Programme was launched with an initial budget of £3 million to be spent on nursery schools and classes, day nurseries and children's homes in deprived areas. In 1972 the Conservative Government's White Paper *Education: A Framework for Expansion* announced a detailed programme for increasing the number of nursery school places with the ultimate aim of offering places to all 3 and 4 year-olds whose parents wished them to attend. In 1975 the Labour Government announced that £500 million would be cut from future spending on the under-fives and that all building projects would be stopped. Since then economic difficulties and recession have made it less and less likely that public money will be spent on pre-school children. Nursery school education is an important and enriching experience for a young child, but it seems unlikely that many will get it. Fewer than one in ten of Britain's children under 5 receive it, despite the fact that most parents want it.

Largely because of the shortage of nursery school places there are a variety of schemes to ease the isolation of mothers and their young children. The best known and most highly organized are those backed by Pre-School Playgroups Association and the Save the Children Fund. These are usually run by mothers who want to give their children a chance to play and socialize with others, and to meet other mothers. There are also one o'clock clubs, which usually consist of a play-hut, outdoor playspace and one or two paid staff. Mothers go there with their children and meet others. They do not help the mother who wishes to escape from her children but they do help to make childrearing less isolated and more interesting. There are also mother-and-toddler clubs, often run in conjunction with pre-school playgroups. Some voluntary organizations arrange groups for mothers with handicapped children. The National Childbirth Trust encourages local mothers to continue friendships formed during pregnancy. These are just a few of the schemes to help mothers and their young children through what can be one of the most difficult and also one of the most enjoyable periods of their lives.

CHAPTER NINETEEN

Future Trends

Unfortunately, the future for motherhood is not bright. Life is becoming more difficult for mothers. We may look forward to increasing improvements in the position of women and to increasing knowledge of the needs of young children but even if we do we probably feel misgivings and maybe sorrow and anger too. Looking into the future is of course hazardous, but one thing seems certain. The speed of change in our society is accelerating. The generation which grew up before World War I, many of whom are still alive, have probably seen more changes in their lifetime than any generation before them. Those who grew up after World War II will, by the time they are old, have seen far more. There will also be more of them to see it. Even a generation ago people over the age of eighty were unusual and people over ninety were rare. Nowadays, there are plenty of both and before very long many people will not die until they are between 100 and 120 years old, and a huge number will live on into their eighties. Women who today are absorbed in their young families or about to embark on producing a family would do well to remember that after their children are grown up they may live on for another fifty or sixty years in a world that is very different from our own. It is certain that, more than ever before, the active period of mothering will be a comparatively short interlude in their lives.

The immediate future is likely to be dominated by economic problems. World recession creates special problems for women and their children. Economically children are a long-term investment and in difficult times people and governments tend to think even more than usual in terms of short-term results. The idea that creating a better environment for young children and their mothers will benefit society in thirty or forty years time is not likely to have high priority in the thinking of politicians and taxpayers in the present, even though their own future probably depends on it. We can however bear in mind that there may be no other way to save civilization. This may seem dramtic but it is true.

Meanwhile the economic problems of individual mothers and their children are unlikely to improve. Life becomes increasingly expensive. The environment deteriorates. Poverty increases. The housing situation worsens. Increasingly mothers have to go out to work through economic need. There are fewer jobs and inevitably women suffer from this. It also becomes increasingly difficult for them to make arrangements for their children while they work, for public money is not allocated for this purpose. At present the situation in Britain is deteriorating for mothers and their children, and this seems likely to continue. As we have seen, the pressures to keep mothers at home are already strong but they may be reinforced still more. Mothers and children could be virtually forced to stay in increasingly unsatisfactory homes. Zoë Fairbairns' futuristic novel *Benefits* describes a situation in which this becomes government policy, strongly enforced. There would be a backlash against the increased freedom of women and against choice of their lives. In Britain the pressure to limit legal abortion, the lack of governmental interest in day care, the closure of nursery schools, and the refusal to allow the cost of child care against a working mother's tax are indications of this.

Technology may bring about many changes in the lives of mothers. For instance, one can envisage robots which clean the house, cook, serve and clear up meals and do the gardening, linked with computers which organize the necessary variations, order ingredients and supplies and so on. Technology may also bring new kinds of work into the home. The decreasing cost of communication together with the increasing cost and tedium of commuting may mean that, instead of commuting regularly to work, many people will be able to work at home with computer terminals linked to television sets, and thereby be in touch with far more people in far more places than is possible at the moment. One can envisage a mother or father running a business or practising a profession, or being an employee, perhaps executive or secretary, and working with a computer terminal at home while supervising the children at the same time. It may be that children will receive much of their schooling in the same way, through the television computer terminal at home.

Here we can envisage difficulties and conflicts for the educational authorities who will put out the programmes (thus saving themselves the cost of having the children at school). They are likely to expect mothers to supervise the programmed learning. One can imagine mother (and perhaps father too) working with her computer terminal in one room and making sure that the children, doing their 'schoolwork' in the next room, are not turning over secretly to watch a programme that they find more interesting. This system could have a profound effect on family life. It might also increase still more the segregation of many mothers and their children from the rest of the community and the dehumanization of society.

Unless and until this revolution comes about it seems likely that most forms of modern 'work', except certain forms of part-time work, will remain extremely difficult to combine with motherhood in the way that our society views motherhood at present, especially the mothering of younger children. It does not look as though governments in the foreseeable future will seriously help women to go out to work. A formal 'career' is even more difficult to combine with motherhood than a local 'job', and specialist training is almost impossible for women with young children. The idea so often put forward by feminist writers that men should take an equal share in childrearing means that, with the exception of a very few jobs, such as freelance journalism and some academic posts, the father as well as the mother is unable to follow a structured career, at least until the children are grown. This may suit some families but if all fathers participated equally with mothers in rearing children, then many careers and 'ladders of success' would be open only to nonparents. Successful nonparents would either become very much richer than everybody else or would have to be highly taxed to support the families whose energies were being put into childrearing instead of earning money. One could conceive of a society where this might work, and might be a great deal better than our own. But it will not come about easily or in the foreseeable future. One could also conceive of careers for both men and women being structured to allow for years of low productivity while doing what is actually the most important job of all for the community, raising children. But at present certain levels of career are usually linked to certain ages and it is impossible to step back onto the ladder after a decade or so at home.

One point in favour of the present system is that, at least for people with 'jobs' rather than 'careers', the length of the working week is gradually declining. This can of course make life easier for working parents and give them more time for family life.

The acceptance of nonparenthood as a respectable state is another important trend. In the past many people had children simply because it was expected of them and being childless brought a certain amount of opprobrium. Although this is still true in some sections of the community, it is much less so than formerly. Those who do not want children or who are not able or willing to commit themselves to them in the way our present society demands, are better off without them.

Single-parent families and hybrid families are increasing. The chief reason for this is the instability of the modern couple, the ease of divorce and the desire of some women to have and bring up children on their own. Being a mother in a hybrid family has its own advantages and disadvantages which of course vary according to circumstances. The commonest pattern is for a woman to live permanently with her own children together with a man who is not their father or who is not the father of them all. Some of the children may go away sometimes to visit their own fathers and the man's own children may come sometimes on a visit to their father. To discuss the workings and problems of these families in detail would require another book. So far they have usually been discussed in terms of 'problems' such as 'the children of divorce', 'children from broken homes' and so on. But they now have to be regarded more positively because they are becoming one of the norms in our society and have to be accepted as such, rather in the way that what used to be called 'living in sin' is now called 'living together', or 'stable relationships' and are widely accepted.

Mothers who are likely to have more problems than most in adapting to the future world are those from minority groups, most of whose customs and families are much more 'traditional' in type than are most Anglo-Saxon families. Many Jewish and Roman Catholic families have great difficulty in coming to terms with modern sexual permissiveness, but still more do families of Mediterranean or Asian origin. As I write this, one of my sons has invited for the weekend a Hindu girl who is studying at the same college. She was only able to come here by telling her family that she was staying with an English girl, and even then encountered disapproval and opposition. After ten years in England her mother speaks almost no

English, knows no English people and almost never leaves her apartment. The parents intend their daughter to study at university while still living at home and then to make a traditional marriage to someone of their choice. The girl intends to go to university 'as far from home and relatives as possible', have a career and choose her own husband, regardless of race, religion or colour. She knows and I know that great difficulties lie ahead for her. She is typical of many.

Anyone who has read as far as this is likely to see that the future of psychological disturbance is bad. There is likely to be more of it with fewer facilities and less tolerance in coping with it. This is as true for those who show their disturbance in the form of antisocial behaviour as for those who show it in the form of symptoms or illness. Both kinds of disturbance are increasing and it seems likely that both will continue to increase for some time.

My last book *Why Women Fail* was written because it struck me that improvements in the position of women coincided with widespread conflict, misery and self-destructiveness among those women who could not cope with this new situation. Although many women are flourishing with choice and opportunities open to them which would not have been theirs in former times, more and more women are being driven into self-destructiveness or are being encouraged by various means to bring out their latent self-destructive tendencies. The last quarter century has seen an appalling increase in 'depression' among women, often masked by psychosomatic symptoms which often lead to extensive and expensive medical investigations. For some years now there has been an epidemic, chiefly among women, of drug overdose, wrist-slashing and other self-destructive acts now labelled collectively 'suicidal gestures' (which used to be called 'attempted suicide') so that this has become the commonest cause of emergency admission to hospital. Child-battering has increased, mostly by women. Large numbers of women suffer from agoraphobia; many middle-aged women who were competent when young and brought up families are now unable to leave the house, even to go shopping or to visit the hairdresser. Many more women than men take sedatives, sleeping pills, tranquillizers and antidepressant drugs. Alcoholism and violence, both traditionally men's problems, are increasing in women. Many more women than men attend psychiatrists and more are admitted to mental hospitals. Many more women than men suffer from overt anxiety and psychosomatic complaints, or feel empty and lacking in motivation. It seems necessary to ask why these dreadful things are happening to women just when they are at last beginning to be accepted as people.

I believe these two facts are connected causally. One cause is the frequent lack of true opportunity for women in a world that pays lip service to it. But the aspect that is even more important to these problems is the inability of so many women to make use of opportunities that are open to them. It is an aspect of what Juliet Mitchell has called 'the attitude of the oppressor within the minds of the oppressed', in other words, a kind of internalized ineptitude and lack of self-esteem.

Much of this is related to motherhood in a changing world. Some women find it difficult to cope at all. Many others find that when their children are young they can create a cosy little world that supports them and they do not or dare not envisage that one day it will come to an end, their little ones will leave the nest and they will be left to make what they can of their lives. Some know that this time will come but cannot face it and so do not prepare for it. Others do not even let it enter their consciousness. When the time for separation comes the symptoms they develop are often diagnosed as being due to the menopause (anything that happens to a woman between the age of 37 and 60 is liable to be attributed to the menopause), and often treated as such. In fact the menopause itself sometimes causes menstrual irregularities, heavy bleeding and hot flushes but most other symptoms that occur at this time of life are due to other causes. They are often due to the lack of ability of a woman who has lived her adult life in the rôle of mother to adjust to the world as a person in her own right. Hormone replacement therapy is popular but seldom has more than a placebo effect in these cases.

Self-destructiveness is thought, fantasy or action that prevents or destroys development or fulfilment in personal life. In the feminine mystique women are supposed to find fulfilment in husband, children and home, and presumably after the children are gone, in husband and home. If the husband has gone too, as he so often has today either in body or in spirit, presumably she is left with home alone. The feminine mystique became 'the problem that has no name' and all over the industrialized democratic world people began to find solutions. But on the whole these solutions are for women who are sufficiently mature to recognize that there is a problem.

320

Those who are totally trapped and submerged find that the removal of obstacles and shackles actually makes their situation worse. For the solutions lie in choice and change and these are the very things with which vast numbers of women cannot cope. Their security lies in their shackles just as prisoners and inmates of institutions sometimes feel more secure in those places than in the outside world. Unfortunately these unhappy women often have husbands who support their immaturity, their anxiety and their ineptitude. It is remarkable how many agoraphobics (who suffer from fear of public places) have husbands who happily accompany them to the shops and how many psychosomatic depressives have husbands who repeatedly take time off work to take them to the doctor but somehow always manage to sabotage every attempt by the patient or her doctor to encourage them to develop their personalities or to lead a more independent life. Agoraphobia so severe that the woman is virtually housebound is extremely rare in women without supportive husbands and when it does occur it is usually much easier to treat.

Women today need to be people in their own right. People need to go on developing throughout their adult lives for only in this way can they deal with the choice and change of modern living. So women need to develop through their years of active mothering, not only as mothers but also as adult women. They need this in order to prepare their children for the modern world but they also need it for themselves. The ability of women to deal with change and choice is the true meaning of liberation.

This may seem to be a Catch 22 situation. The more developed and mature a mother is, the more difficult she may find it to devote herself to her children. The better equipped she is to be a good mother, the more difficult she may find it to put this into practice. But this is only true on the surface. Undeveloped women often find it easy to retreat into child-rearing as an escape from life. They may throw themselves into it wholeheartedly and totally, in a way that a mature woman could never do. These women often pass as 'wonderful mothers', but usually they are not. They do not use their experience of motherhood to develop themselves. They may make their children too dependent on them because they themselves are too dependent on the children. These children will have a hard time later. So will the mothers.

Women who become mothers when they are still undeveloped and immature do not necessarily make bad mothers or stop developing. If they are flexible and not trying to escape from themselves they may find that motherhood has a considerable maturing influence on them. It may help them to cope with special difficulties because motherhood is a reaffirmation of a woman's life and a reliving of her past experience. It offers opportunities to correct as well as to pass on what went wrong in her own childhood. The mother can redevelop herself and deepen and broaden her personality, understanding and imagination.

Mature women often find mothering more arduous but they are more likely to be successful in the end. For these women the experience of bearing and rearing children can be a valuable experience leading to further personal development. It can be a prolonged exercise in learning to see and respect others as separate people and a training in realism, that is, learning to foresee the likely consequences of certain events or actions and to benefit from the experience. Rearing children is also a training in responsibility, in learning how to delay satisfaction, in making realistic decisions, in resolving conflicts and in the valuable art of dealing with a number of different problems simultaneously. The mother who can do all this without losing her spontaneity, flexibility or imagination has truly benefited from the experience of rearing children and what she has gained can later be put to good use in other fields if only society will allow it.

So how can a changing society be changed for the better? Ultimately there is probably no more effective way than to improve the quality of life for infants and young children. This means improving the lives of their mothers. It means resolving the miserable conflicts that beset mothers and lead to so much unhappiness and dissatisfaction among them which are now being perpetuated through them into the next generation. If and when the combined idealization and denigration of mothers that is so characteristic of our society is replaced by realism and imagination, we shall raise better people in a better world. It would save money too. It might even solve our economic problems. No one can believe that such changes could solve all our problems but there is no doubt that if the overall quality of mothering was improved there would be a corresponding reduction in crime, vandalism, mental and physical ill-health, social inadequacy and children in the care of the authorities. All these are immensely expensive. People might even work harder too, and enjoy their work, since they would be more adequate people. Adequate people make their work enjoyable. The benefits would be enormous. I believe that even the material benefits would far outweigh the cost. Prevention of ills is nearly always cheaper and more effective in the long run than dealing with them once they have developed. The cost of protecting a population from diseases such as smallpox, diphtheria, typhoid and tuberculosis is far less than dealing with epidemics of such diseases. So even those who see the quality of life in material rather than in human terms subscribe to these measures, and may well, in the future, see that the same applies to the psychological field.

In mental health and personal welfare our civilization is still at a primitive stage. Just as cities and civilization produced ghastly infectious diseases until we learned about germs and how to clean up the water supply, so we have allowed our cities and our civilization to develop in a way that threatens the mental health and personal welfare not only of the present but of future generations. We have learned that the physical health of a nation depends largely on the physical care given to the very young. We know that similarly the mental health of a nation (and this includes crime, vandalism, children in care and so on) depends on the environment in the earliest years. But here we do not put what we know into practice. Instead we have created impossible conflicts for mothers and an environment that is unsuitable for them and their young children. In order to save public money in the present we ensure that vast numbers of people will drain public resources in the future. We have allowed a crisis to develop in the same way that epidemics of cholera and typhoid were allowed to develop: by not paying enough attention to the environment or to the future.

Only mothers and motherly people can achieve an environment of good mothering. No one else will do it for them unless they reveal the truth and insist upon it which, on the whole, they do not do and which the women's movement on the whole does not do. Why do women not see that in motherhood lies their power? It is only their weakness when they allow it to be denigrated and neglected as it is at present. Simone de Beauvoir pointed out 'It was as Mother that woman was fearsome: it is in maternity that she must be transfigured and enslaved.' That was what happened, what women allowed to happen, what mothers have accepted down the ages, and still accept. Even some of our most radical thinkers see no further than demands for beautiful childbirth or collective day care. These are important but they are details. They will follow if only mothers can use the power that is within them.

'And since woman has been subjected as Mother, she will be cherished and respected first of all as Mother,' continues Simone de Beauvour. 'Of the two ancient aspects of maternity, man today wishes to know only the smiling, attractive face.' Like man, woman is limited and like man she is endowed with mind and spirit 'but she belongs to Nature, infinite current of Life flows through her: she appears, therefore, as the mediatrix between the individual and the cosmos. When the mother has become a figure of reassurance and holiness, man naturally turns to her in love. Lost in nature, he seeks to escape; but separated from her he wishes to go back. . . . To recognize that he is the son of his mother is to recognize his mother in himself, it is to become one with femininity in so far as femininity is connected with the earth, with life, and with the past.'[1]

But women have allowed men to take over this power by the twofold method of idealizing her and at the same time denigrating her. In accepting this, mothers have no power. Yet society needs and wants children. Men want children. We all want these children to be healthy in both body and mind. Motherhood is becoming parenthood.

Women need to use their power over these early years. By becoming mothers they are performing an important service to society, perhaps the most important of all. Without adequate mothering the world becomes intolerable. We are now paying the price for idealizing and denigrating mothers in order to neglect them. This is the price for not helping them to be as good at their job as they could be, the price for thinking we can leave them to do the job alone and merely idealize them for doing it. We must stop this stupid idealization and this disastrous hidden denigration. To be a parent, to bring up a child, is a privilege and a valuable contribution to society. If we replaced idealization and denigration by realism we would surely find that such realism is powerful. The results would be so clear and obvious that people would wonder why it did not happen before. At one time no one thought of installing drains; all the rubbish and filth and sewerage was thrown into the street. The streets were disgusting and dangerous, and many people were disabled or died. We are now behaving in the same way in the psychological environment.

The first step is to be aware of these things and make others aware of them. We must think much more and much more seriously about how to help mothers to be healthy mothers and how to help bad mothers to become adequate mothers. We must think about how our environment, left to itself, is making matters worse, and about what could be done to improve it.

Young children need loving parents. They also need other people, both adults and children. Mothers need other people too. Children need open spaces, freedom to explore and stimulating experiences. Our environmental planners seldom give thought to these. Only today my newspaper reported a petition organized by children because the builders of their housing estate had left their promised playground as a heap of rubble and rubbish. The result was that the police went round to warn the children not to interfere! Thousands of housing estates are built without thought for the children or their mothers. Penelope Leach in her book *Who Cares?* makes out a brilliant case for a *Children's Community Rights Act* – yet she admits that it 'sounds like a joke'. Leach argues that what is really needed is a general recognition of the worth of mothers and small children. 'If anybody cared, there are immunerable things that could be done to make their lives easier and more fun. Many of them would cost nothing.'[2] She lists endless 'trivia' which planners simply do not think or care about, but which would make life much easier for women and children. These include not only safe places for mothers to meet and children to play but things such as gadgets to hold open elevator doors while prams and toddlers go through; kerbs, crossings and underpasses with slopes and islands in roads big enough for prams and with barriers for toddlers; courtesy from bus conductors; consideration in the shops and shop planning for small children; small lavatories and facilities for changing babies in public conveniences and consideration of the problems of mothers with small boys and fathers with small girls; places where babies can be fed and toddlers watched in safety; peepholes in hoardings round building sites and on bridges so that toddlers can watch the machines and the cranes; facilities for children to play in laundrettes and to climb round (rather than *on*) park benches; a bit of untidiness in public parks, such as branches lopped from trees and acorns left to attract squirrels, a few shallow pools, lumps and bumps and logs for small people to paddle, climb and play leapfrog; improvement in standard playground equipment, which is mostly so dangerous and unimaginative (why not a few walls for balls and rope ladders hanging from the trees?); more understanding park keepers (who are also part of the generation of men which has been segregated from children); the use of open markets with sheep pens and auction sheds for hide-and-seek.

Mothers and children need other people. There could be an extension of mother-and-toddler clubs, one o'clock clubs, pre-school playgroups and other organized meeting places. They need to be nearby and therefore there needs to be many of them. But a society that has segregated its children needs to be brought back into contact with them. Babies and children are *interesting.* Most people, including probably most mothers, do not know how interesting they are because they do not know enough about them. So the idea has spread that bringing up children is boring and restricting. Much could be done to dispel this. Penelope Leach comments. 'Women who did not set out to have children because they were *already* interested in them are given little opportunity to get interested after the event. Most people carelessly assume that interest is not necess-ary because something called "love" operates instead. . . . But in-terest and love go together, they support, create and replace each other so that when either one temporarily fails the other takes over and ensures that mother and child still get what they need.' Interest in how babies develop and react is often associated with anxiety, lest the child next door is developing more rapidly or reacting more nor-mally than one's own child. This is largely because of the way infor-mation is given. A statement like 'the average child walks at the age of 12 months' will create anxiety. A statement like 'nearly all chil-dren learn to walk between the ages of nine and twenty-two months' is more interesting and less competitive. It is interesting to learn what children can and can't do at certain ages, and knowledge of this both increases interest and helps in the actual process of child-rearing. The work of Piaget and his followers in child development is particularly interesting and helpful (if an account of it can be found that can be understood, for Piaget's writings are obscure). For instance how do children of different ages judge size, distance or family relationships? What do they actually think? How do they work out how to open a screw top jar? When are they capable of fol-lowing mother? Understanding something of these things are of great help in understanding a small child and how his mind works. It helps a mother to see things from the child's point of view and this is part of the essence of motherliness.

Encouraging motherliness and raising its status would do much to improve our society. The quality of caring about children and the capacity to plan to fulfil their needs, desires and potentials are common in our society but greatly underused and undervalued. To develop and encourage these qualities both in mothers and in others not necessarily women would be of immense benefit. In the chapter on Day Care I discussed the possibility of doing this quite simply in a professional way, to the benefit of the people concerned, not only the mothers who need or wish to leave their children for part of the day but of the children too. Leach suggests that much could be done with teenagers to encourage interest in children and that motherly women in the neighbourhood might undertake to be available to any mother who cared to come or telephone. This again might be of great benefit to both sides and help to create that climate of increased motherliness which our society so sadly lacks.

What about father? Increasingly, civilized countries are recognizing the importance of parenthood by granting paternity as well as maternity leave. The idea that parenthood is something shared by both parents is growing, though ironically this is often most obvious when the parents are divorced or separated. The more this is recognized and the more men wish to participate in childrearing, the more its importance will be recognized in the world of work, which is dominated by men; the more mothers and children will be able to participate in or at least have some experience of that world, the more men and children will come together and find that they have things in common. The idea of the 'supportive wife', in which an employer often gets two workers for the price of one, will diminish. Already there is an increase in men who are reluctant to move jobs because it will interfere with the family's established life, and often even a large increase in salary will not compensate for loss of a wife's earnings, let alone her wellbeing and convenience. It may be that as the idea spreads employers will think more about families and less about individual executives and other employees. Uprooting the family for a spell in another continent would be far more attractive to many modern families if there was interesting and well-paid work for wives and a good environment for the children.

Society could also show its increased understanding and appreciation of its youngest citizens by making life financially easier for women and their children. Some countries allow tax concessions for the expenses of child care. Others make good provision for day care in a secure and stimulating environment. Gradually, one hopes, children will be seen as people who deserve material investment, and who will repay it many times over. One day it will be realized that society needs children to develop in the best possible way, which means easing the burden of their mothers and so making childrearing more pleasurable and less of a burden.

Good environments for mothers and children do not happen spontaneously and without thought. Like good physical environments, they can exist naturally in places as yet undesecrated by modern civilization. But once industrial cities are built, they have to be made into good environments for mental health just as much as for physical health. This means careful thought, understanding and successful planning to ensure that they are suitable for the human beings who live in them and the children growing up.

CHAPTER TWENTY

Conclusion: Self-Help for Women, Men and their Children

Mothers, or at least some mothers, and young women who as yet have no children, are entering a new phase, a phase that may resolve the present crisis of women and their children. They recognize the crisis or at least are vaguely aware of it. They do not want a life of crisis for themselves and their children. They are new women, different from all women in the past. They may be conscious of the disabilities that remain. They may be appalled at both their history and the problems and choices that lie before them. But they seek solutions. Given the right questions to think about and support in thinking about them, they can help themselves. Their attitudes are freer towards work, sexuality, family relationships and individual development. They are trying to change the institutions of motherhood and parenthood in a way that is best for their children.

Many suggestions have been made for them in this book, both direct and implied, along with much information, chosen specifically to increase understanding and facilitate awareness and choice. In these last pages I propose to look directly at the ways in which these can be put into practice.

We shall start at the time when children first become aware that one day they will be grown up and will have to do something with their lives. Until recently few people thought further than that little Janet would grow up to be a Mummy like her Mummy and look after her babies and little John would grow up like Daddy and go out to work and wash the car at weekends. This will no longer do. Even small children can understand that life is long and that there are many, many things to do in it. One of these is raising children. Children can be taught that raising their own children is likely to occupy part of the life of both girl and boy, perhaps even as much as a quarter of their future lives. It is one of the most important and enjoyable things that they will ever do, but it is not the only thing they will ever do. Girls can be warned that many people will try to cheat them into thinking that having babies and raising families will be the substance of their adult lives, but that to believe them is deceptive and dangerous. Boys can be warned that people may tell them that they should settle down in marriage and that wives are there for their own convenience and raising their children. This is also a lie in the modern world. Parenthood is serious and very hard work. It should only be embarked on by those who take it seriously and who are prepared to give a great deal of themselves to it. If this puts some young people off it altogether it may be a good thing.

In adolescence these matters tend to be more serious. Forming sexual attachments becomes a reality. Contraception and possible parenthood become real issues. Here it can be emphasized, as it sometimes is, that premature parenthood is likely to be disastrous for both parents and children. It should be delayed until both parents have developed themselves as people, have imposed themselves on the environment, and are prepared, capable and willing. At this age young people know how babies are born and, one hopes, how to prevent them from being born, but few have any idea what it is like actually to have children. There is no hurry. There is no advantage in having babies so young. It is much better to gain experience of life, a means of supporting oneself and an idea of what one finds satisfying and fulfilling.

Already the young people who take this seriously may be going against what they have been taught to believe. This adjustment may, and often does, mean helping their own parents into the modern world. This may mean conflict but if they can deal with it successfully they will benefit not only themselves but also their parents, particularly their mothers, who themselves are likely to be going through a difficult phase in life if they cannot cope with choice and change.

Personal development essentially involves the development of self-respect and confidence. These come not only from early childhood experiences but also from experience in the world, doing things that succeed, that can be seen to be good, and that feel right. Success is largely a matter of how people feel about themselves. Success is not a question of worldly success. It is making good with what one has, perhaps making the best of what one has. It means being good enough in what one does or has to do and this involves subjective judgment. There also has to be appraisal that is realistic, both internally and externally, in which a person's feeling and fantasy are linked to the outside world. In the old world a woman could achieve this simply by being a 'traditional' woman. Now she needs a sense of self and the ability to cope with choice and change. For this she needs the capacity to appraise and benefit from experience rather than falsifying it for immediate personal gain. This means developing the ability to tolerate anxiety and take responsibility for herself in the unsupporting environment which is our modern society.

The next important step for the young person is to choose the right partner if s(he) wishes, as most do, to be part of a couple. Many young women sacrifice their future lives at this stage by choosing men who will balance their lack of development and prevent them from becoming people in their own right. This is still one of the major errors made by young women today, for many do not see what is happening to women in our society or are confused and frightened by what they do see. It seems safe to avoid it in the arms of a man who will 'protect'. But their protection may lead to a lifetime of emotional backwardness, hiding from life, and self-destructiveness. In many partnerships personal growth is impossible and ultimately the woman may have to choose between breaking away or being a slave, albeit a slave in a gilded cage, for life.

Before embarking on parenthood or marriage it is important to know the attitude of the other about raising a family. If the man wants to *have* children, does he also want to *raise* children, or merely to see them briefly in the evenings and at weekends? Will his work combine with this and if not, will his ambition prevent him from changing course? Is the woman prepared to change her entire life? If so, is the man prepared and able to support her?

Once the first baby is born the family is there and will be there for a long time. The next ten or twenty years is an arduous time for both parents, in many ways the most arduous in their lives. It is important to be prepared for this and it is important not to become submerged. Even if a woman wishes to devote herself totally to her family during the early years, she needs at the same time to prepare for the future. She needs to keep in touch with the outside world. One day she will not be needed by the family and a long life will stretch ahead of her. What is she going to do? Even with young children and no help it is possible to prepare. I have known women who studied and passed examinations during this period and women who started and ran successful businesses from home. With three tiny children and no domestic help Margaret Drabble wrote the first three of the novels that made her famous, 'in odd moments when the children were crawling round or in bed asleep'. Another example is Ann Jones, who is the current President of the Association for Child Psychology and Psychiatry. 'When she "retired" to have a family she became a marriage guidance counsellor, took a diploma in Sociology and began training as a Social Worker.'[1] I know another woman who used her previous art training to design and sell clothes and others who edited books, cooked at home for local restaurants and delicatessens, or became seriously involved in improving the local community life for women and their children. All these women and many more have greatly enjoyed their children and did not wish to go out to work, but they knew they had to do something else besides. It can be done. The later rewards are enormous.

When the children are of school age the organization of family life becomes extremely important. Unfortunately many women devote the extra time they now have to making the house cleaner and cleaner, doing things for other members of the family that they could perfectly well do for themselves and cooking ever more complicated and time-consuming dishes for them. Often the unconscious motive behind these activities is the desire to make them all dependent forever or to avoid personal development, or both.

Women who need or wish to go out of the house to work, either in a fixed job or in some free-lance activity, need to organize good substitute care for their children. Much has been said about this in the chapter on day care. Much needs to be done. It will only be achieved when intelligent women take an intelligent interest in the subject and refuse to allow other people to make mothers feel guilty about it. Much could be done if some of the vocational homemakers became day mothers to other people's children and if courses were organized for them along the lines suggested by the Jacksons. At present 'childminding' is largely a working class activity of low social status. Enormous advances could be made if educated women took it seriously.

The organization within the family is extremely important and each family has to work out its own. All too often it is mother who does all the organization and virtually all the work, even if father does help with the washing up and mow the lawn. This system often develops in a family in a mindless way. No one has thought it out. It is just assumed and it just happens. Too late the mother realizes her errors, or uses her powers to make the others dependent on her.

This is not good enough for the new world. Each family needs an agreement about how the family will work. Personally I think the best is one in which each member of the family is in theory responsible or potentially responsible for himself or herself and in practice receives what s(he) needs from the family and contributes to it according to capabilities. The strong needs of each individual are respected. For example, a baby needs constant loving care and cannot contribute anything except himself. A schoolchild still needs loving care, a sharing of interests and probably help with homework but he can make a contribution. Even a small child can tidy his toys, sort out clothes for washing or learn to amuse himself. An older child can help to clean, cook, lay and dispose of meals, organize the dustbin and so on, as well as being responsible for looking after his own clothes and school equipment. An eight-year-old who has to be responsible himself for remembering to take his P.E. kit to school on Tuesdays and his football boots on Fridays as well as feeding the cat and cleaning out his rabbit cage is learning to be a responsible person. He can also learn that parents may need privacy, time for studying or earning money and relief from some of the household chores.

It is difficult to define roles and usually unnecessary to do so. A good principle is that each member of the family is basically responsible for himself and does everything possible or sensible for himself but that circumstances, age of children, etc. often mean that functions and chores are divided or done communally. I am astounded at how seldom one sees this system. Many teenagers who could perfectly well wash and iron and mend their own clothes expect their mothers to do it for them – she has brought them up to believe that she should. Many husbands whose wives work just as hard as they do expect their wives to organize the household, do all the shopping, and bring supper to the table. Of course many men work long hours, are ambitious for their futures and earn a great deal of money. Such a man and his wife may choose to free him from these chores for the benefit of the family as a whole. The important thing is that it should be a *choice* and not an *assumption*. The family then understands that the reason why he does not 'pull his weight' in the house is that he contributes in other ways. It does not mean that the teenage children who have finished their homework should not iron their own jeans, clean out the fridge, and cook the family meal once a week. A successful family today is an institution for mutual support and enjoyment, not one in which a slave-mother cherishes her privileged husband and children and sacrifices or avoids her own life by taking over theirs.

When the children become independent and disperse and the woman is middle-aged her future will depend on her personal resources, her attitudes and her previous training and experience. Now is the time when she enters the second part of her adult life. If her personal resources are poor she is particularly liable to lapse into self-destructiveness, often of a manipulative kind designed to control her husband and children, attract attention from them and fill them with guilt. But it is also the age of opportunity and choice. These opportunities may be imperfect but they exist for every woman and if she takes them and makes something of them she will find new satisfactions. In many ways this is the most interesting period of women's lives, for it has never existed in the world before. 'Life begins at forty' is not a new saying and 'like forty' has long been used to express immense force and vigour. But a new life for women of forty! Our ancestors would have been astounded. But so it is.

Life does not begin at forty. By then it is probably somewhere near half-way through, perhaps less in these days of increasing longevity. Jean Anouilh wrote 'When you're forty, half of you belongs to the past.'[2] This means that the other half belongs to the future and what you have done with the first half will largely determine what you do with the second. We new women could do well to remember the words of the poet Edward Young, written about 250 years ago.

Be wise with speed;
A fool at forty is a fool indeed.

Notes and References

Preface

1. Rutter, *Maternal Deprivation Reassessed*, p. 128.

Introduction

1. Coventry Patmore, *The Angel in the House*. IV. The Queen's Room I.

PART ONE: Changing Motherhood

Chapter One *Confidence in Survival* pp. 25–43.

1. The various reasons why figures are unreliable are discussed in Hewitt, *Wives and Mothers in Victorian Industry*, Chapter Eight.
2. It is interesting to note that it was in studies such as this that the deleterious influence of a mother's employment on the life of her baby was first discussed and became the concern of philanthropists. See Hewitt: Chapter Eight.
3. Quoted by Stone, *The Family, Sex and Marriage in England 1500–1800*, p. 68.
4. Quoted by Hewitt, p. 89.
5. Quoted by Stone, p. 68.
6. Quoted in de Mause (Ed.), *The History of Childhood*, p. 325.
7. Clifford, J. L., *Hester Lynch Piozzi*, pp. 83–94.
8. Ariès, *Centuries of Childhood*, p. 39.
9. Quoted by Shorter, *The Making of the Modern Family*, p. 174.

10. Quoted by ibid., p. 174.
11. Stone, p. 409.
12. Quoted by ibid., p. 409.
13. Pinchbeck and Hewitt, *Children in English Society*, p. 7.
14. Stone, p. 101.
15. *Encyclopaedia Britannica*, 11th Edition.
16. *Chambers Encyclopaedia*, 1959 Edition.
17. Shorter, p. 9.
18. The details of Mary Wollstonecraft's confinement have been taken from Claire Tomalin, *The Life and Death of Mary Wollstonecraft*, 1974. London: Weidenfield and Nicolson.
19. This has been noticed by many doctors who have read Mrs. Gaskell. It was discussed by Philip Rhodes, a professor of obstetrics, in the Brontë Society Transactions, 1970.
20. Gaskell, *The Life of Charlotte Brontë*, vol II, p. 321–2.
21. Ibid., p. 322.
22. Gaskell, E. C., *The Life of Charlotte Brontë*. Second Edition in two volumes. 1857. Cornhill: Smith, Elder & Co. 65.
     Peters, Margaret., *Unquiet Soul. A Biography of Charlotte Brontë*. 1978. London: Hodder & Stoughton.
23. Sir Eardley Holland, *J. Obst. Gynae. Brit. Emp.* 1951. 58.905ff.
24. Stone, p. 58.
25. Quoted by Pinchbeck and Hewitt from *The Memoirs of the Verney Family*, Ed. F. P. Verney, 1892. Vol. 1, p. 52.
26. Quoted in de Mause, p. 12.
27. Haydon, B. R., *Diary*. 1808–1846. Ed. W. B. Pope, 1960 and 1963. Cambridge: Harvard University Press.
28. Banks, *Prosperity and Parenthood*.

Chapter Two   *Has Mother Love Changed?* pp. 44–53.

1. Ariès, p. 39.
2. Stone, p. 114.
3. Ibid., p. 210.
4. Ibid., p. 210.
5. Ibid., p. 211.
6. Quoted by Stone, p. 215.
7. Quoted by Walzer in de Mause.
8. Shorter, Chapter Five.

9. Ibid., p. 203.
10. Laslett, *The World We Have Lost*, p. 99.
11. de Mause, p. 1.
12. Laslett, p. 109.
13. Ibid., p. 109–10.
14. Coveney, *The Image of Childhood*.
15. Ariès, p. 9.
16. Ibid., p. 10.
17. de Mause, p. 5.
18. Laslett, p. 13.
19. Ibid., p. 22.
20. Stone, p. 6.
21. Quoted by ibid., p. 430.
22. Ibid., p. 433.
23. Ibid., p. 434.
24. Ibid., p. 479.

Chapter Three *Projection, Reversal and Attack* pp. 54–70.

1. Quoted in de Mause, p. 10.
2. Freud, *On Narcissism*, p. 4.
3. De Mause p. 15.
4. Ariès, p. 57.
5. Quoted by de Mause, p. 19.
6. Ibid., p. 19.
7. Ibid., p. 52.
8. Stone, p. 47.
9. Walzer, in de Mause, p. 352.
10. Cited by de Mause, p. 33.
11. Ibid., p. 33.
12. Augustus J. C. Hare, *The Story of My Life*. Vol. I, London, 1896, p. 51.
13. Thomas Phaire, *The Boke of Chyldren*. 1544.
14. de Mause, p. 32.
15. *Caesars*, p. 148.
16. See, for instance, Joseph Rheingold's books, *The Fear of Being a Woman: A Theory of Maternal Destructiveness*. New York, 1964; and *The Mother, Anxiety, and Death: The Catastrophic Death Complex*. Boston, 1967.
17. de Mause, p. 66.

Chapter Four *Fashions in Child Care* pp. 71–84.

1. Still, *The History of Paediatrics*, p. 1.
2. Aristotle, *On the Generation of Animals*, Vol. I.
3. Ibid., X.
4. Celsus, *De Medicina*, III.7.
5. Quoted in Still, p. 279–80.
6. Ibid., p. 382.
7. Davis, *Childhood and History in America*, p. 49.
8. Dally, *The Fantasy Factor*, p. 151.
9. Ibid., p. 151.
10. Ibid., p. 153.
11. Davis, p. 91.
12. Inglis, *Sins of the Fathers*, p. 34.
13. Quoted by Schatzman, *Soul Murder*, p. 141.
14. Schreber, *Kallipädie*, p. 32n.
15. Ibid., p. 32.
16. Ibid., p. 140.
17. Ibid., p. 281.
18. Ibid., p. 60.
19. Ibid., p. 66.
20. Ibid., p. 135, italics in original.
21. Schatzman, *Soul Murder*.
22. Schreber, p. 100.
23. Ibid., 172.
24. Ibid., p. 25.
25. Freud, *Standard Edition*, XII, p. 51.
26. Quoted by Schatzman, p. 13.
27. Singer, C., *A Short History of Medicine*, E. Ashworth Underwood, p. 655.
28. Inglis, p. 44.
29. Leila Berg in *Children's Rights*, p. 31.
30. Winnicott, *The Child and the Outside*, p. 84.

Chapter Five *Psychological Needs* pp. 85–91.

1. Bowlby, *Maternal Care and Mental Health*, p. 11.
2. Ibid., p. 12, 13.

Chapter Six *Idealization of the Mother* pp. 92–103.

1. Simon Winchester. *The Guardian*. 10 August 1974.
2. Davis, p. 40
3. Ibid., p. 50.
4. Ibid., p. 52.
5. Gathorne-Hardy, *The Rise and Fall of the British Nanny*, p. 77ff.
6. Rycroft, 'On Idealization, Illusion and Catastrophic Disillusion' in: *Imagination and Reality*, p. 29–41.
7. United Nations Economic and Social Council 1948. *Economic and Social Council. Official Records. Third Year, Seventh Session. Supplement No 8. Report of the Social Commission.* New York. pp. 28, 29.
8. Bowlby, p. 13.
9. Rutter, p. 123–4.
10. Winston Churchill, *My Early Life*, p. 12.
11. Bowlby, p. 67.
12. Adrienne Rich, *Of Woman Born*, p. 27.

Chapter Seven *The Importance of Other People* pp. 104–123.

1. Stone, p. 199.
2. Laslett, p. 1.
3. Ibid., p. 2.
4. Ariès, p. 397.
5. Quoted by Stone, p. 254.
6. *Boswell in Extremes*. 1776–1778. Ed. Weiss, C. McC. and Pottle, F. A. New York, 1970, p. 266.
7. Quoted in de Mause, p. 395.
8. Gathorne-Hardy, p. 19.
9. Bernard, *The Future of Marriage*, p. 10.

Chapter Eight *Feminism and Motherhood: Before the Vote* pp. 124–142.

1. Stone, p. 337.
2. Ibid., p. 337.
3. Ibid., p. 338.
4. Ibid., p. 338.

5. Ibid., p. 339.
6. Ibid., p. 340.
7. Poem by Lady Chudleigh.
8. Abigail Adams to John Adams. Braintree. 31 March 1776.
9. Strachey, *The Cause*, p. 12.
10. Wollstonecraft in *Feminist Papers*, p. 72.
11. Ibid., p. 70.
12. Ibid., p. 72–3.
13. Ibid., p. 73–4.
14. Stanton, quoted in *Voices from Women's Liberation*, p. 27.
15. Reproduced in ibid. p. 43–7.
16. Fuller. 1885. p. 380–1. Quoted in *Feminist Papers*, p. 157.
17. Mills, *The Subjection of Women*. 1869. Quoted in *Feminist Papers*, p. 213–14.
18. *Feminist Papers*, p. 382–3.
19. Stanton and Blatch. 1922. II 64–66. Quoted in *Feminist Papers*.
20. Quoted in *Feminist Papers*.
21. Stanton and Blatch. 1922. II. 68.
22. Gilson, 1909. 223–4. Quoted in *Feminist Papers*, p. 383–4.
23. Ibid., p. 384.
24. Quoted in *Feminist Papers*, p. 396–400.
25. Call to the Convention at Worcester, Mass. October 23–24. 1850. Quoted in *Voices from Women's Liberation*, p. 54.
26. Stanton and Anthony, *The History of Woman's Suffrage*, 1881.
27. Banks and Banks, *Feminism and Family Planning in Victorian England*.
28. Quoted by Banks, p. 11–12.
29. Davies. *The Higher Education of Women*. 1866. p. 98.
30. Ibid., p. 109.
31. Quoted in *Feminist Papers*, p. 474.
32. Ibid., p. 504.
33. Ibid., p. 515–16.
34. Ibid., p. 569.
35. Ibid., p. 575.
36. Ibid., p. 587.
37. Ibid., p. 591.
38. Ibid., p. 592–3.
39. Ibid., p. 594.
40. Ibid., p. 596–7.

41. Ibid., p. 597–8.
42. Ibid., p. 598.
43. Ibid., p.551.
44. Ibid., p. 559–60.
45. Ibid., p. 560–2.

Chapter Nine *Feminism and Motherhood: After the Vote*
pp. 143–164.

1. Chafe, *The American Woman: Her Changing Social, Economic and Political Roles 1920–1970*, p. 36.
2. Ibid., p. 102.
3. Quoted in ibid., p. 104.
4. Ibid., p. 104ff.
5. I have excluded from the figures the few women about whose subsequent lives no information is available or who died young.
6. Rowbotham, *Hidden from History*, p. 163.
7. Quoted in Chafe, p. 218.
8. Ibid., p. 219.
9. Mackie and Patullo, *Women at Work*, p. 40.
10. Ibid., p. 41–2.
11. Lundberg and Farnham, *Modern Woman: The Lost Sex*.
12. Llewelyn-Davies, *Maternity*, p. 4–5.
13. Rossi in *Feminist Papers*, p. 672.
14. de Beauvoir, *The Second Sex*, p. 202.
15. Ibid., p. 528.
16. Ibid., p. 529.
17. Ibid., p. 533.
18. Ibid., p. 536.
19. Ibid., p. 538.
20. Myrdal and Klein, *Women's Two Roles: Home and Work*, p. 2–3.
21. Ibid., p. 23.
22. Ibid., p. 117.
23. Ibid., p. 121–2.
24. Ibid., p. 126.
25. Ibid., p. 127.
26. Mead, 'Some Theoretical Considerations on the Problems of Mother/Child Separation', *American Journal of Orthopsychiatry*, Vol XXIV, No 3, July, 1954.

27. Myrdal and Klein, p. 129.
28. Ibid., p. 131.
29. Ibid., p. 132.

Chapter Ten   *Women's Liberation* pp. 165–188.

1. Quoted by Bernard, p. 217–18, in *Women, A Journal of Liberation.*
2. Chafe, p. 315.
3. Friedan, *Feminine Mystique*, p. 9.
4. Ibid., p. 311.
5. Laing, *The Politics of Experience*, p. 11.
6. Mitchell, *Woman's Estate*, p. 19.
7. Ibid., p. 11.
8. Ibid., p. 87.
9. Ibid., p. 87.
10. Firestone, *The Dialectic of Sex*, p. 12.
11. Ibid., p. 15.
12. Mitchell, p. 87.
13. Ibid., p. 100.
14. Ibid., p. 108–9.
15. Ibid., p. 119.
16. Ibid., p. 173–4.
17. Flexner, *Century of Struggle*.
18. Compiled by Margaret Anderson in 1972.
19. Greer, *The Female Eunuch*, p. 278.
20. Mitchell, p. 55.
21. 'Crisis in Childbirth' in *Conditions of Illusion*, p. 8.
22. From Vickie Pollard, 'Producing Society's Babies', in *WOMEN: A Journal of Liberation*. Feel, 1969. Reproduced in *Voices from Women's Liberation*.
23. Rich, 'The Theft of Childbirth' in *Seizing Our Bodies*, p. 161–2.
24. Ibid., p. 162.
25. From *Voices from Women's Liberation*, p. 126.
26. Ibid., p. 112.
27. Ibid., p. 287.
28. Ibid., p. 351.
29. Kenny, p. 223.
30. Ibid., p. 27.

31. de Beauvoir, p. 517.
32. Mitchell, p. 109.
33. Janeway, *Man's World: Woman's Place*, p. 157.
34. Judith Brown in *Voices from Women's Liberation*, p. 404.
35. Millett, *Sexual Politics*, p. 126.
36. Leach, *Who Cares?*, p. 40.
37. Firestone, p. 188–9.
38. Ibid., p. 193.
39. Ibid., p. 213.
40. Greer, p. 235.
41. Ibid., p. 236.
42. Lee Comer, pamphlet 'The Myth of Motherhood' in *Spokesman Pamphlet No. 21*.
43. Oakley, p. 199.
44. Mitchell, *Psychoanalysis and Feminism*, p. 231.
45. For two of the many examples of this see Deckard, *The Woman's Movement: Political, Socioeconomic, and Psychological Issues*, 1979, p. 421, and Oakley, A., *Housewife*, 1974, p. 226.
46. de Beauvior, p. 528.
47. Michelene Wandor in *Conditions of Illusion*, p. 207.

PART TWO: The Crisis of Motherhood

Chapter Eleven   *What Are Children For?* pp. 189–200.

1. Winnicott, *The Maturational Process and the Facilitating Environment*, p. 51.
2. Kitzinger, *Women as Mothers*, p. 184.
3. de Beauvoir, p. 511.

Chapter Twelve   *Conditions of Power* pp. 201–223.

1. de Beauvoir, p. 538.
2. Rich, *Of Woman Born*, p. 52.
3. Bowlby, *Separation*, p. 209–10.

Chapter Fifteen *Anxiety, Depression and Disturbance* pp. 249–269.

1. Beck, *Depression.*
2. Chesler, *Women and Madness*, p. 146.
3. Gavron, *The Captive Wife*, p. 132.

Chapter Sixteen *Modern Dilemmas* pp. 270–295.

1. Kenny, p. 84.
2. Proops, *Dear Marje*, quoted in Kenny, p. 84.
3. Kenny, p. 95.
4. Rutter, p. 121.
5. Reported in the *Evening Standard*, 16 October 1979.
6. Fairbairns, *Benefits.*
7. Gavron, p. 80.
8. Pilling and Pringle, *Controversial Issues in Child Development.*
9. Ibid., p. 37.
10. Ibid., p. 68.
11. Ibid., p. 75.
12. Ibid., p. 81.
13. Ibid., p. 153.
14. Ibid., p. 156.
15. Wordsworth, Preface to *Lyrical Ballads*, p. 249.
16. Tillich, *The Courage to Be*, p. 140, 141.
17. Discussed in *The Times*, 26, August 1974.
18. Freud, *Introductory Lectures*, p. 13.

Chapter Seventeen *Men and Children* pp. 296–303.

1. Pilling and Pringle, p. 198.
2. Ibid., p. 217.
3. Ibid., p. 217.
4. Ibid., p. 128.
5. Ibid., p. 218.
6. Ibid., p. 218.
7. Ibid., p. 218.
8. Ibid., p. 219–20.

Chapter Eighteen *Day Care and the Education of Babies*
pp. 304–314.

1. Chafe, p. 145.
2. Ibid., p. 150.
3. Ibid., p. 159.
4. Ibid., p. 60–2.
5. Quoted in Chafe, p. 164.
6. Ibid., p. 165.
7. Nixon, President's Message establishing the Office of Child Development, January, 1969.
8. Nixon, Presidential Veto Message on the Comprehensive Child Development Bill, December, 1971.
9. These include Gloria Norris and Jo Ann Miller, *The Working Mother's Complete Handbook*. 1979. New York: Dutton; Penelope Leach, *Who Cares?*. 1979. Harmondsworth: Penguin; Brian and Sonia Jackson, *Childminder*. 1979. London: Routledge & Kegan Paul.
10. Jackson and Jackson, p. 20.
11. Norris and Miller, p. 65.
12. Ibid., p. 66.
13. Jackson and Jackson, p. 30.
14. Ibid., p. 95.
15. *Women's Directory*, 1976, p. 75.
16. Bowlby, in *Can I Leave My Baby?*, pamphlet.

Chapter Nineteen *Future Trends* pp. 315–328.

1. de Beauvoir, p. 204.
2. Leach, p. 125.

Chapter Twenty *Conclusion* pp. 329–334.

1. *News*. Association for Child Psychology and Psychiatry, No. 2, Autumn, 1979.
2. Anouilh, *Time Remembered*.
3. Edward Young (1683–1765). *Love of Fame*, ii. 1. 281.

Bibliography

Abt, Isaac A. (Ed.). *Abt-Garrison History of Pediatrics*. 1965. London and Philadelphia: W. B. Saunders Co.

Ainsworth, M. D. 'The Effects of Maternal Deprivation: A Review of Findings and Controversy in the Context of Research Strategy', in *Deprivation of Maternal Care: A Reassessment of its Effects*. 1962. Geneva: W.H.O.

Ainsworth, Mary D. et al. *Deprivation of Maternal Care: A Reassessment of its Effects* (published with John Bowlby, *Maternal Care and Mental Health*). 1966. New York: Schocken Books.

Andry, R. *Delinquency and Parental Pathology: A Study in Forensic and Clinical Psychology*. 1960. London: Methuen.

Ariès, Philippe. *Centuries of Childhood*. 1962. London: Cape. Translated from the French *L'Enfant et la vie familiale sous l'ancien regime*. 1960.

Avery, Gillian. *19th Century Children*. 1965. London: Hodder & Stoughton.

Bachofen, J. J. *Myth, Religion and Mother Right*. 1967. Princeton: Princeton University Press.

Baker, A. A. *Psychiatric Disorders in Obstetrics*. 1967. Oxford: Blackwell Scientific Publications. Philadelphia: F. A. David.

Banks, J. A. *Prosperity and Parenthood*. 1954. London: Routledge & Kegan Paul.

Banks, J. A. and Banks, O. *Feminism and Family Planning in Victorian England*. 1964. London: Routledge & Kegan Paul.

Barber, Dulan. *One-Parent Families*. 1978. London: Davis-Poynter.

Bateson, Gregory. *Steps to an Ecology of Mind*. 1973. London: Paladin.

346

Beard, Mary R. *Woman as Force in History: A Study in Traditions and Realities.* 1946. New York: Macmillan.

Beck, Aaron T. *Depression: Clinical, Experimental and Theoretical Aspects.* 1967. New York: Harper & Row.

Bell, Lora. *Underprivileged Underfives.* 1976. London: Ward Lock.

Bell, Norman W., and Vogel, Ezra F. (Eds.). *A Modern Introduction to the Family.* 1960. Glencoe: The Free Press.

Bernard, Jessie. *The Future of Marriage,* 1972. New York: World Publishing.

Bettelheim, Bruno. *The Children of the Dream.* 1971. London: Paladin.

Bone, Margaret. *Day Care for Pre-School Children.* 1975. Office of Population Censuses and Surveys.

Bott, Elizabeth. *Family and Social Network.* Revised edition, 1971. London: Tavistock Publications.

Bowlby, John. *Can I Leave My Baby?* 1958. London: National Association for Mental Health.

Bowlby, John. *Child Care and the Growth of Love.* 1953. Harmondsworth: Penguin Books.

Bowlby, John. *Attachment and Loss.* 1969. Vol. I *Attachment*; 1973. Vol. II *Separation*; 1980. Vol. III *Loss.* London: Hogarth Press and Institute of Psychoanalysis.

Brehan, William. *Advice to Mothers.* 1804.

Breitbart, Vicki. *The Day Care Book.* 1974. New York: Knopf.

Bridenthal, Rendate and Koonz, Claudia (Eds.). *Becoming Visible: Women in European History.* 1977. Boston: Houghton Mifflin Co.

Bristol Women's Studies Group. *Half the Sky.* Introduction to Women's Studies. 1979. London: Virago.

Brittain, Vera. *Lady into Woman.* 1953. London: Andrew Dakers.

Brittain, Vera. *Testament of Youth.* 1979. London: Fontana Paperbacks in association with Virago Press.

Bronfenbrenner, Urie. *Two Worlds of Childhood.* 1970. London: Allen & Unwin.

Broyell, Claudie. *Women's Liberation in China.* 1977. Haverstock: Harvester Press.

Bruner, Jerome. *Under Five in Britain.* 1980. London: Grant McIntyre.

Bryant, Bridget, Harris, Miriam and Newton, Dee. *Children and Minders.* 1980. London: Grant McIntyre.

Bullough, Vern L. *The Subordinate Sex: A History of Attitudes toward Women*. 1974. New York: Penguin Books Inc.

Calhoun, Arthur W. *A Social History of the American Family from Colonial Times to the Present*. 1917. Cleveland.

Cater, Libby A. and Scott, Anne Firor. *Women and Men: Changing Roles, Relationships and Perceptions*. 1977. New York: Praeger Publishers Inc.

Census, 1961. England and Wales. London: HMSO.

Census, 1971. England and Wales. London: HMSO.

Chafe, William H. *The American Woman: Her Changing Social, Economic, and Political Roles, 1920–1970*. 1972. New York: Oxford University Press.

Chafe, William H. *Women and Equality: Changing Patterns in American Culture*. 1977. New York: Oxford University Press.

Chambers Encyclopaedia. 1959.

Chesler, Phyllis. *Women and Madness*. 1972. New York: Doubleday, London: Allen Lane.

Chodorow, Nancy. The Reproduction of Mothering. 1978. Berkeley: University of California Press.

Clifford, J. L. *Hester Lynch Piozzi*. 1968. Oxford: Oxford University Press.

Collins, A. H. and Watson, E. L. *Family Day Care*. 1976. Boston: Beacon Press.

Comer, Lee. *The Myth of Motherhood*. Spokesman Pamphlet, No. 21.

Comer, Lee. *Wedlocked Women*. 1974. Leeds: Feminist Books.

Conran, S. *Superwoman*. 1975. London: Sidgwick and Jackson.

Cooper, David. *The Death of the Family*. 1971. London: Allen Lane.

Coote, A. and Gill, T. *Women's Rights: A Practical Guide*. 1974. Harmondsworth: Penguin.

Coveney, Peter. *The Image of Childhood*. 1967. Harmondsworth: Penguin Books.

Curtis, J. *Working Mothers*. 1976. New York: Doubleday.

Dally, Ann. *The Morbid Streak*. 1978. London: Wildwood House.

Dally, Ann. *Mothers*. 1976. London: Weidenfeld & Nicolson.

Dally, Ann. *Why Women Fail*. 1979. London: Wildwood House.

Davie, Ronald, Butler, Neville and Goldstein, Harvey. *From Birth to Seven: A Report of the National Child Development Study*. 1972.

London: Longman.

Davis, Elizabeth Gould. *The First Sex*. 1975. Harmondsworth: Penguin.

de Beauvoir, Simone. *The Second Sex*. 1972. Harmondsworth: Penguin.

Deckard, Barbara Sinclair. *The Women's Movement: Political, Socioeconomic and Psychological Issues*. 2nd Ed. 1979. New York: Harper & Row.

de Mause, Lloyd (Ed.). *The History of Childhood*. 1974. London: Souvenir Press.

Department of Health and Social Security. *Report on the Committee on One Parent Families*. 1974. The Finer Report. London: HMSO.

Department of Health and Social Security. *The Family in Society: Preparation for Parenthood*. 1974. London: HMSO.

Department of Health and Social Security. *Low Cost Day Care Provision for the Under Fives*. 1976. London: HMSO.

Department of Health and Social Security. *Priorities for Health and Personal Social Services in England: A Consultative Document*. 1976. London: HMSO.

Deutsch, Helene. *Psychology of Women*. 1944. New York: Grune & Stratton.

Dicks, Henry V. *Marital Tensions*. 1967. London: Routledge & Kegan Paul.

Dinnerstein, Dorothy. *The Rocking of the Cradle: and the Ruling of the World*. 1976. London: Souvenir Press.

Dowrick, Stephanie and Grundberg, Sybil. *Why Children?* 1980. London: Women's Press.

Dreifus, Claudia (Ed.). *Seizing our Bodies. The Politics of Women's Health*. 1978. New York: Vintage Books.

Ellman, Mary. *Thinking About Women*. 1968. New York: Harcourt Brace Jovanovich.

Encyclopaedia Brittanica. 11th Edition.

Erikson, E. *Identity*. 1968. London: Faber & Faber.

Evans, E. B., Shub, B. and Weinstein, M. *Day Care*. 1971. Boston: Beacon Press.

Evans, E. B., and Sale, G. E. *Day Care for Infants*. 1973. Boston: Beacon Press.

Fairbairns, Zöe. *Benefits*. 1979. London: Virago.

Faulder, Carolyn, Jackson, Christin and Lewis, Mary. *The Women's Directory*. London: Virago.

Figes, Eva. *Patriarchal Attitudes*. 1972. London: Panther Books.

Finney, R. P. *The Story of Motherhood*. 1937. New York: Liveright.

Firestone, Shulamith. *The Dialectic of Sex*. 1972. London: Paladin Books.

Fletcher, Ronald. *The Family and Marriage*. 1962. Harmondsworth: Penguin Books.

Flexner, Eleanor. *Century of Struggle*. 1959. Cambridge: Harvard University Press.

Fogarty, Michael P., Rapoport, Rhona and Rapoport, Robert N. *Sex, Career and Family*. 1971. London: Allen & Unwin.

Fogarty, Michael P., Rapoport, Rhona and Rapoport, Robert N. *Women in Top Jobs*. 1971. London: Allen & Unwin.

Fonda, N. and Moss, P. *Mothers in Employment*. 1976. Brunel University and Thomas Coram Research Unit.

Freud, Anna and Burlingham, Dorothy. *Young Children in Wartime*. 1942. London: Allen & Unwin.

Freud, Anna and Burlingham, Dorothy. *Infants Without Families*. 1943. London: Allen & Unwin.

Freud, S. *Introductory Lectures on Psychoanalysis*. 1974. London: Pelican Books.

Freud, S. *New Introductory Lectures on Psychoanalysis*. 1973. London: Pelican Books.

Friedan, Betty. *The Feminine Mystique*. 1965. Harmondsworth: Penguin Books.

Friedan, Betty. *The Second Stage*. 1981. New York: Summit Books.

Galinsky, E. and Hooks, W. H. *The New Extended Family*. 1977. Boston: Houghton Mifflin.

Garland, Caroline and White, Stephanie. *Children and Day Nurseries*. 1980. London: Grant McIntyre.

Gathorne-Hardy, Jonathan. *The Rise and Fall of the British Nanny*. 1972. London: Hodder & Stoughton.

Gavron, Hannah. *The Captive Wife*. 1968. Harmondsworth: Penguin Books.

George, Victor and Wilding, Paul. *Motherless Families*. 1972. London: Routledge & Kegan Paul.

Gilman, Charlotte Perkins. *The Home, Its Work and Influence*. 1910. Charlton.

Gilman, Charlotte Perkins. *His Religion and Hers*. 1923. New York: Century & Co.

Gilman, Charlotte Perkins. *Women and Economics*. Carl Degler, Ed. 1966. New York: Harper and Row.

Gorer, G. *Death, Grief and Mourning*. 1965. Cresset Press.

Graveson, R. H. and Crane, F. R. (Eds.). *A Century of Family Law*. 1957. London: Sweet & Maxwell.

Greenberg, Selma. *Right from the Start: A Guide to Nonsexist Child Rearing*. 1978. Boston: Houghton Mifflin Co.

Greer, Germaine. *The Female Eunuch*. 1971. London: Paladin.

Griffin, Susan. *Woman and Nature: The Roaring Inside Her*. 1978. New York: Harper & Row.

Hare, Augustus, J. C. *The Story of my Life*. Vol 1. 1896. London.

Haydon, B. R. *Diary. 1808–1846*. Ed. W. B. Pope. 1960 & 1963. Cambridge: Harvard University Press.

Heffner, E. *Mothering*. 1978. New York: Doubleday.

Hewitt, Margaret. *Wives and Mothers in Victorian Industry*. 1958. London: Rockcliff.

Hinde, R. A. *Biological Bases of Human Social Behaviour*. 1974. New York: McGraw-Hill.

Holman, R. *Unsupported Mothers and the Care of their Children*. 1967. London: Mothers in Action.

Holt, L. Emmett. *The Care and Feeding of Children*. 1894. New York and London: D. Appleton & Co.

Howells, J. G. *Modern Perspectives in International Child Psychiatry*. 1969. Edinburgh: Oliver & Boyd.

Hoyles, Martin. (Ed.). *Changing Childhood*. 1979. London: Writers & Readers Books.

Hubback, J. *Wives Who Went to College*. 1957. London: Heinemann.

Hymowitz, C. & Weissman, M. *A History of Women in America*. 1978. New York: Bantam Books.

Illingworth, R. S. and Illingworth, C. M. *Lessons from Childhood*. 1966. Edinburgh & London: E. & S. Livingstone Ltd.

Inglis, Ruth. *Sins of the Fathers. A Study of the Physical and Emotional Abuse of Children*. 1978. London: Peter Owen.

Jackson, B. and Jackson, S. *Childminder*. 1979. London: Routledge

& Kegan Paul.

Jackson, Sonia. *The Illegal Childminders: A Report on the Growth of Unregistered Childminding and the West Indian Community.* 1972. Association of Multi-Racial Playgroups.

Janeway, Elizabeth. *Man's World: Woman's Place.* 1971. London: Michael Joseph.

Keiran, P. *How Working Mothers Manage.* 1970. Clifton Books.

Kenny, Mary. *Woman X Two.* 1978. London: Sidgwick & Jackson.

King, Sir Frederick Truby. *Feeding and Care of Baby.* 1913. London: Oxford University Press.

King, Mary. *Truby King – The Man.* 1948. London: George Allen & Unwin.

Kitzinger, Sheila. *Women as Mothers.* 1978. London: Fontana Paperbacks.

Klein, Viola. *Britain's Married Women Workers.* 1965. London: Routledge & Kegan Paul.

Klein, Viola. *Working Wives.* 1958. Institute of Personnel Management. Occasional Papers, No. 15.

Komarovsky, Mirra. *Women in the Modern World: Their Education and Dilemmas.* 1971. Boston: Little, Brown & Co.

LaFollette, Suzanne. *Concerning Women.* 1926. New York: A & C Boni.

Laing, R. D. *The Divided Self.* 1965. London: Pelican Books.

Laing, R. D. *The Politics of Experience and the Bird of Paradise.* 1967. Harmondsworth: Penguin.

Laslett, Peter. *The World We Have Lost.* 1965. London: Metheun.

Leach, Penelope. *Who Cares? A New Deal for Mothers and their Small Children.* 1979. London: Penguin Books.

Levy, David. *Maternal Overprotection.* 1943. New York: Columbia University Press.

Llewelyn Davies, Margaret. (Ed.). MATERNITY, *Letters from Working Women.* 1978. London: Virago.

Lundberg, Ferdinand and Farnham, Marynia. *Modern Women: The Lost Sex.* 1947. New York: Harper & Row.

Lynd, Robert and Helen. *Middletown.* 1929. New York: Harcourt, Brace.

Lynd, Robert and Helen. *Middletown in Transition.* 1937. New York: Harcourt, Brace.

McBride, A. *The Growth and Development of Mothers*. 1973. New York: Harper & Row.

Mackie, Lindsay and Pattullo, Polly. *Women at Work*. 1977. London: Tavistock Publications.

Maddox, Brenda. *The Half Parent: Living with other People's Children*. 1975. London: Deutsch.

Maizels, J. *Two to Five in High Flats*. 1961. Joseph Rowntree Memorial Trust.

Mead, Margaret. *Male and Female*. 1949. New York: Morrow and London: Gollancz. 1962. Harmondsworth: Penguin Books.

Mead, Margaret. 'Some Theoretical Considerations on the Problem of Mother-Child Separation' *Amer. J. Ortho-psychiatry*, XXIV, No. 3. July, 1954.

Mead, Margaret & Wolfenstein, Martha (Ed.). *Childhood in Contemporary Cultures*. 1955. Chicago: University of Chicago Press.

Mednick, M. T. S., Tangri, S. S. and Hoffman, L. W. *Women and Achievement*. 1975. New York and London: Wiley.

Miller, Jean Baker. (Ed.). *Psychoanalysis and Women*. 1973. Harmondsworth: Penguin Books.

Miller, Jean Baker. *Toward a New Psychology of Women*. 1977. Boston: Beacon Press.

Millett, Kate. *Sexual Politics*. 1971. London: Rupert Hart-Davis. 1977. London: Virago.

Miner, R. *Mother's Day*. 1978. New York: Putnams.

Ministry of Health. *Day Care Facilities for Children Under Five*. October, 1977. Circular 37/68.

Mitchell, Juliet. *Woman's Estate*. 1971. Harmondsworth: Penguin Books.

Mitchell, Juliet. *Psychoanalysis and Feminism*. 1974. London: Allen Lane.

Mitchell, Juliet & Oakley, Ann (Eds.). *The Rights and Wrongs of Women*. 1976. Harmondsworth: Penguin Books.

Morgan, Elaine. *The Descent of Woman*. 1972. London: Souvenir Press.

Myrdal, Alva and Klein, Viola. *Women's Two Roles*. 1968. New York: Humanities Press. 1970. London: Routledge & Kegan Paul.

Norris, G. and Miller, J. A. *The Working Mother's Complete Hand-*

book. New York: E. P. Dutton.

Oakley, Ann. *Becoming a Mother*. 1979. Oxford: Martin Robertson.
Oakley, Ann. *Housewife*. 1974. Harmondsworth: Penguin Books.
Oakley, Ann. *The Sociology of Housework*. 1974. Oxford: Martin Robertson.
Oakley, Ann. *Women Confined*. 1980. Oxford: Martin Robertson.
O'Faolain, Julia and Martines, Lauro (Eds.). *Not in God's Image: Women in History*. 1979. London: Virago.

Payne, G. H. *The Child in Human Progress*. 1916. New York.
Peck, Ellen and Granzig, Dr. William. *The Parent Test: How to Measure and Develop your Talent for Parenthood*. 1978. New York: G. P. Putnam's Sons.
Phaire, Thomas. *The Boke of Chyldren*. 1544. London. 1955. London: Livingstone.
Pilling, D. and Pringle, M. K. *Controversial Issues in Child Development*. 1978. London: Paul Elek.
Pinchbeck, I. *Women Workers and the Industrial Revolution*. 1930. London: George Routledge & Sons.
Pinchbeck, Ivy & Hewitt, Margaret. *Children in English Society*. Vol I. 'From Tudor Times to the Eighteenth Century'. 1969. London: Routledge & Kegan Paul. Vol II. 1973. London: Routledge & Kegan Paul.
Polybius. *The Histories*. Trans. W. R. Paton. 1927. London.
Pringle, M. L. Kellmer, *The Needs of Children*. 1974. London: Hutchinson.
Proops, Marjorie. *Dear Marje*. 1977. London: Coronet Books.

Radl, S. *Mother's Day is Over*. 1973. New York: Charterhouse.
Rapoport, R. and Rapoport, R. N. *Duel Career Families Reexamined*. 1976. London: Mark-Robertson. New York: Harper & Row.
Rapoport, R. and Rapoport, R. N. *Leisure and the Family Life-Cycle*. 1976. London: Routledge & Kegan Paul.
Rapoport, R., Rapoport, R. N. and Strelitz, A. *Fathers, Mothers and Others*. 1977. London: Routledge & Kegan Paul.
Renvoize, Jean. *Children in Danger*. 1974. London: Routledge & Kegan Paul.
Rheingold, Joseph. *The Fear of Being a Woman: A Theory of Mater-*

nal Destructiveness. 1964. New York.

Rheingold, Joseph. The Mother, Anxiety and Death: The Catastrophic Death Complex. 1967. Boston.

Ribble, Margaret. The Rights of Infants. 1943. New York: Columbia University Press.

Rich, Adrienne. Of Woman Born. 1977. London: Virago. New York: Bantam Books.

Rossi, Alice S. (Ed.). The Feminist Papers: From Adams to de Beauvoir. 1974. New York: Bantam Books.

Roth, Philip. Portnoy's Complaint. 1971. London: Corgi Books.

Rowbotham, S. Women, Resistance and Revolution. 1972. Harmondsworth: Penguin Books.

Rowbotham, S. Hidden from History. 1973. London: Pluto Press.

Rutter, Michael. Maternal Deprivation Reassessed. 1972. Harmondsworth: Penguin Books.

Rutter, M. and Madge, N. Cycles of Disadvantage. 1976. London: Heinemann.

Rycroft, Charles. A Critical Dictionary of Psychoanalysis. 1968. New York and London: Nelson.

Rycroft, Charles. Imagination and Reality. 1968. London: Hogarth Press and The Institute of Psychoanalysis.

Schaffer, Rudolph. Mothering. 1977. London: Fontana.

Schatzman, Morton. Soul Murder. Persecution in the Family. 1976. Harmondsworth: Penguin Books.

Schneir, M. (Ed.). Feminism: The Essential Historical Writings. 1972. New York: Vintage Books.

Schreiner, Olive. Woman and Labour. 1911. London: T. Fisher Unwin. 1978. London: Virago.

Seneca. Moral Essays. Trans. J. W. Basore. 1963. Cambridge, Mass: Harvard University Press.

Shorter, Edward. The Making of the Modern Family. 1977. London: Fontana Books.

Slater, E. and Woodside, M. Patterns of Marriage. 1951. London: Cassell.

Spock, Dr. Benjamin. Baby and Child Care. 1958. London: The Bodley Head.

Spring-Rice, M. Working Class Wives. 1939. Harmondsworth: Pelican Books.

Still, George F. The History of Paediatrics. 1965. London: Dawsons of Pall Mall.

Stone, Lawrence. *The Family, Sex and Marriage in England 1500–1800*. 1977. London: Weidenfeld & Nicholson.

Strachey, Ray. *The Cause. A Short History of the Women's Movement in Great Britain*. 1978. London: Virago.

Strecker, E. *Their Mother's Sons*. 1946. Philadelphia: Lippincott Co.

Sylva, Kathy, Roy, Carolyn and Painter, Marjorie. *Child Watching at Playgroup and Nursery School*. 1980. London: Grant McIntyre.

Tanner, Leslie B. (Ed.). *Voices from Women's Liberation*. 1970. New York: New American Library.

Voth, Harold. *The Castrated Family*. 1977. Kansas City: Sheed Andrews & McMeel, Inc.

Winnicott, D. W. *Collected Papers: Through Paediatrics to Psycho-Analysis*. 1958. London: Tavistock Publications.

Winnicott, D. W. *The Child, the Family and the Outside World*. 1964. Harmondsworth: Penguin Books.

Wolff, Sula. *Children under Stress*. 1969. London: Allen Lane.

Wollstonecraft, M. *Vindication of the Rights of Women* (1792). 1975. Harmondsworth: Penguin Books.

Women's Co-operative Guild. *Maternity: Letters from Working Women*. 1915. London: G. Bell & Sons.

Wordsworth, W. *The Prelude*. 1850. 1971. Harmondsworth: Penguin.

Wylie, Philip. *Generation of Vipers*. 1942. New York: Farrar & Rinehart.

Young, M. and Willmott, P. *Family and Kinship in East London*. 1957. London: Routledge & Kegan Paul. 1962. Harmondsworth: Pelican Books.

Yudkin, S. & Holme A. *Working Mothers and their Children*. 1969. London: Michael Joseph.

Index